PERSPECTIVES ON ARABIC LINGUISTICS XVII–XVIII

AMSTERDAM STUDIES IN THE THEORY AND HISTORY OF LINGUISTIC SCIENCE

General Editor

E.F. KONRAD KOERNER
(Zentrum für Allgemeine Sprachwissenschaft, Typologie und Universalienforschung, Berlin)

Series IV – CURRENT ISSUES IN LINGUISTIC THEORY

Advisory Editorial Board

Lyle Campbell (Salt Lake City); Sheila Embleton (Toronto)
Brian D. Joseph (Columbus, Ohio); John E. Joseph (Edinburgh)
Manfred Krifka (Berlin); E. Wyn Roberts (Vancouver, B.C.)
Joseph C. Salmons (Madison, Wis.); Hans-Jürgen Sasse (Köln)

Volume 267

Mohammad T. Alhawary and Elabbas Benmamoun (eds)

Perspectives on Arabic Linguistics XVII–XVIII
Papers from the Seventeenth and Eighteenth Annual Symposia on Arabic Linguistics

PERSPECTIVES ON ARABIC LINGUISTICS XVII–XVIII

PAPERS FROM THE SEVENTEENTH AND EIGHTEENTH ANNUAL SYMPOSIA ON ARABIC LINGUISTICS

Edited by

MOHAMMAD T. ALHAWARY
The University of Oklahoma

ELABBAS BENMAMOUN
University of Illinois, Urbana-Champaign

JOHN BENJAMINS PUBLISHING COMPANY
AMSTERDAM/PHILADELPHIA

The paper used in this publication meets the minimum requirements of American National Standard for Information Sciences — Permanence of Paper for Printed Library Materials, ANSI Z39.48-1984.

Mohammad T. Alhawary and Elabbas Benmamoun (eds.)
Perspectives on Arabic Linguistics XVII–XVIII. Papers from the seventeenth and eighteenth annual symposia on Arabic linguistics. Alexandria, 2003 and Norman, Oklahoma 2004.
(Amsterdam studies in the theory and history of linguistic science. Series IV, Current issues in linguistic theory, ISSN 0304-0763 ; v. 267)
ISBN 90 272 4781 1 (Hb; alk. paper)

John Benjamins Publishing Co. • P.O.Box 36224 • 1020 ME Amsterdam • The Netherlands
John Benjamins North America • P.O.Box 27519 • Philadelphia PA 19118-0519 • USA

CONTENTS

EDITORIAL NOTE

The papers in this volume were presented at the Seventeenth and Eighteenth Annual Symposia on Arabic Linguistics, held in Alexandria, Egypt in May of 2003 and at the University of Oklahoma in March of 2004, and sponsored by the University of Alexandria and the University of Oklahoma, respectively. Of the forty-one papers presented at both symposia, twelve are published here. The papers presented at the symposia were selected on the basis of an anonymous review of abstracts submitted to the program committees. The papers included in the current volume were also subject to another tier of peer review process.

The 2003 and 2004 symposia and the present volume would not have been possible without the generous collaboration of many people. We extend our thanks to all of our contributors for turning their symposia presentations into written papers. We are especially indebted to the many anonymous reviewers at the abstract and the written paper stages. Thanks also go to Rachel Muchmore from the University of Oklahoma for helping with some of the formatting.

The transcription of all Arabic materials in the body of the papers and appendices follows the International Phonetic Alphabet or standard equivalents. The Arabic emphatics are represented by a dot underneath the symbol (except in the first paper where a superscript [ˠ] symbol is used instead of the dot) and long vowels as sequences of two identical vowels or [:]. For the citation of Arabic titles in the references sections, a simplified transliteration system based on standard usage in Arabic and Middle East Studies journals has been adopted. Long vowels are marked. The symbol ' represents the *hamza* and ' represents the *'ayn*.

The preparation and printing of the final manuscript was done using facilities available at the University of Oklahoma.

INTRODUCTION

Mohammad T. Alhawary and Elabbas Benmamoun

The papers in this volume tackle a broad range of issues in current linguistic research, particularly in the areas of phonology, morphology/lexicon, sociolinguistics and first and second language acquisition. Contributions to the Perspectives series continue to be distinguished for the depth of coverage and the types of data considered.

The paper by John McCarthy addresses the long-standing problem of vowel length alternation in Arabic dialects. In various dialects, final short vowels lengthen when followed by a suffix. Within traditional analyses, there is no consensus as to which vowel form is basic and which form is derived. Both logical options have been adopted with no clear argument as to which one is more empirically adequate. McCarthy provides an alternative analysis within the Optimality Theory (OT) framework. He argues that OT provides a better account for the indeterminacy provided that one accepts the view that the base is richer than traditionally assumed. Given this assumption, together with a number of constraints, one can rely on grammar, rather than lexical stipulations governing so-called underlying representations, to filter out non-occurring forms.

Also assuming the OT framework, Abdessatar Mahfoudhi focuses attention on the related issue of the distribution of complex syllables in Arabic dialects, particularly Cairene Arabic, Makkan Arabic and Tunisian Arabic. While all Arabic dialects generally display the CV, CVC and CVV patterns, they differ with respect to the complexity of the edges of syllables. Tunisian Arabic allows complex onsets but not Cairene Arabic and Makkan Arabic. On the other hand, all three dialects allow CVVC and CVCC in the final position but only Tunisian Arabic allows the latter internally while only Cairene Arabic and Makkan Arabic allow it domain-finally. The author recapitulates arguments, mostly based on stress, that the final consonant in the CVVC and CVCC syllables in particular is not moraic, because it is not considered in the computation of weight for stress assignment. The final syllable is rather remotely licensed essentially through adjunction to the syllable. Typical of OT accounts, Mahfoudhi relies on a number of constraints that govern the distribution of syllables and their edges and 'operations' that can affect the base (faithfulness constraints) to derive the occurring patterns and the variation that Arabic dialects display.

Khaled Rifaat presents a preliminary descriptive account of the intonation of Modern Standard Arabic (MSA) on the sentence level. In particular, the study is designed to verify the widely held claim that Arabic intonation system is 'simple' and plays a minor role in the prosodic system of Arabic. Rifaat's analysis focuses on the notion of 'structural simplicity' where the notion of a 'simple' intonation system is defined as one containing few elements and rules. Rifaat relied on a corpus of approximately 15 hours of MSA recorded data from the Egyptian radio which he analyzed for tone-sequence within autosegmental metrical phonology framework. The analysis reveals that MSA has a 'simple' intonation system with a tendency of pitch accents to be accentuated, basic declined trend line tunes, association of non-final or continuation tunes with rising trend line or rising pitch accents and a limited use of pitch accents span to denote 'focus'. In addition, a small number of tune structures, pitch accent types and combinatorial properties were detected.

Hanaa Salem's paper is also descriptive in nature. The paper provides a descriptive account of phonological processes in connected speech in Colloquial Egyptian Arabic (CEA) in Alexandria together with their possible phonemic variations. The data of the study were recorded from normal, conversational speech of CEA in Alexandria on the radio. The data were analyzed for the types of processes exhibited as well as their frequency of occurrence. The analysis shows that a number of processes, such as elision, shortening, germination, and assimilation, are at play with different frequencies of occurrence.

The paper on root formation, by Lazhar Zanned, addresses the notion of polysemy in Classical Arabic lexicon. Zanned argues that the rules governing Arabic root formation generate polysemy in an unavoidable way. Assuming a root organization and generation stance divergent from those proposed in earlier models, such as the Extensionist Model, the Epenthesis Model, and the Combinatorial Model, Zanned presents the Probabilistic Model as an alternative model that can better account for the phenomenon of polysemy. Rejecting a bi-radical or any diachronic basis for Arabic root formation, Zanned argues that root formation is probabilistic and can instead be assumed to be triconsonantal, quadriconsonantal or quinqueconsonantal. Focusing on triconsonantal roots, Zanned claims that three listemes cross at any given root resulting in a polysemic form (bearing, at least, three meanings) and comprising three identical consonantal copies, each of which bears its own meaning inherited from its own listeme; hence, polysemy is unavoidable. The model is further claimed to account for the morphological phenomenon of reduplication based on the same rationale.

Amr Ibrahim engages the important, but still understudied, issue of light verbs in Arabic, with special focus on Modern Standard Arabic. The paper provides a survey of modern linguistic and traditional Arabic linguistics views on the distribution of verbal and nominal predicates, which in the latter case may involve the use of a light verb plus the nominal form of the main predicate. Ibrahim also discusses the semantic and pragmatic interpretations of constructions using light verbs and constructions that do not use them, claiming that the former are less ambiguous than the latter, which they subsume. Another important issue that arises in this context, and which the paper briefly discusses, concerns the fact that the lexical origins of light verbs vary crosslinguistically. In fact, even within the same linguistic family, such as Arabic, a light verb that has more extensive usage in Standard Arabic may have a more narrowly constructed usage in the modern dialects. This, in turn, raises its own questions related to language change and the so-called process of grammaticalization.

Mustafa Mughazy deals with lexical aspect in Egyptian Arabic, a complex topic that, with few notable exceptions, has not received the adequate attention it deserves within Arabic linguistics. He presents a number of morphological and syntactic cues to help classify Egyptian Arabic verbs along aspectual dimensions. He claims that verbs adhere to the universal classifications assumed for other languages where verbs belong to four classes of State, Activities, Achievement or Accomplishment, which are in turn based on the set of the universal primitive features [+durative], [+telic], [+dynamic]. Mughazy then argues that lexical aspect relates to event descriptions, which can vary.

Thus, the same event can be rendered by an achievement or an accomplishment predicate. Consequently, language variation has to do with how eventualities are described. This analysis allows Mughazy to account for the distribution of different classes of verbs in Egyptian Arabic and for the differences between the behavior of such verbs in Egyptian Arabic and other languages such as English and possibly other dialects of Arabic, though this potentially fruitful issue of dialectal variation as it pertains to lexical aspect still needs to be investigated.

The paper on building a computational lexicon, by Sameh Al-Ansary, discusses a corpus-based approach for building a computational lexicon of MSA. The proposed lexicon is implemented in AGFL (Affix Grammar over Finite Lattices) format to be used by any corpus analysis software designed with AGFL formalism. The lexicon contains lexical entries, a tagset for morphological, syntactic and semantic features, a text analysis interface, a database management system (to automatically examine analyzed data), an interactive component, a statistical component, and an AGFL formalism. Al-Ansary's contribution lies not so much in the discussion of the component parts and tools of the proposed lexicon, for indeed there are other attempts, as much as it lies in the specific handling of tagging corpora with the implemented set of morphological and grammatical parts of speech tags, such as categorical information, morphological patterns, suffixes, root, gender, number, aspect, etc. As the corpus gets tagged and each surface word is assigned linguistic features from the tagset, a practical lexicon does emerge from the tagging process that is adequate for a proper morphological, syntactic and semantic description of naturally occurring Arabic data and for various Arabic NLP applications. Although the lexicon in question is small (consisting of 1500 entries), it is claimed to have been sufficiently tested and proven adequate in the corpus analysis tasks for which it is intended initially, such as morphological decomposition, lemmatization, tagging, and parsing.

Naima Boussofara-Omar's paper contributes to ongoing discussions of language and power; in particular, the 'linkages' between language ideologies and speakers' language valuation and language use in institutions of power with a special focus on political speeches in diglossic and bilingual Tunisia. Boussofara-Omar analyzes the original diglossic and bilingual Tunisia. Boussofara-Omar analyzes the original text of a presidential speech/Communiqué together with the corrections brought to the original handwritten draft and attempts to explore the dialectic relation between form and ideology through an analysis of the significance of the Communiqué in terms of the socio-political conditions of its production and in terms of its linguistic forms. The main premise of Boussafara-Omar's thesis is that, following Bourdieu (1991), Spitulnik (1998) and others, language ideologies and processes of language valuation are never just about language and that language ideologies are about the construction and legitimization of power. Boussofara-Omar claims that constructs of prestige, power and authority of a linguistic code (Classical Arabic) do not "accrue" transparently and automatically to the privileged social group that uses it and that such processes may also be "costly". This is because, according to Boussofara-Omar, any incorrect or faulty use of *fuṣħaa* takes authority away from its user, especially when the text is an official presidential speech and the language of choice is being used as an attempt to legitimize the new authority. Accordingly, this accounts for the user's need to subject their linguistic texts to the scrutiny of professional and even non-professional correctors both of which seem to be in turn equally aware of 'correction' as an institution and of *fuṣħaa* as a language of authority.

In her paper on agreement alternations, Heidi Lorimor revisits the issue of subject-verb agreement in Arabic. Lorimor focuses on the issue of agreement alternations whereby the verb that usually fully agrees with a preverbal subject may agree only partially, for example, in gender but not number, or may agree with one NP only in the context of coordination. She also brings into the picture the case of singular agreement in the context of inanimate plural subjects attested in a number of dialects such as Cairene Arabic. Lorimor discusses a number of alternative options to capture the alternations. The two most prominent alternatives are whether the agreement alternations in question are semantically grounded or whether a syntactic account is better suited to the facts. The semantic account is based on findings in psycholiguistic experiments which seem to indicate that agreement morphology, whether singular or plural, depends on whether the speaker perceives the subject as notionally plural. The syntactic account relies mainly on the lexical entries of the noun phrase (the features for which it is specified) and the structural configuration it finds itself in, yielding a single output that may or may not undergo further alterations in the morpho-phonology. The question then is whether all the agreement alternations in Arabic can receive one uniform account. Lorimor provides arguments to show that, despite attempts to provide such uniform accounts, the agreement alternations in Arabic cannot all be collapsed under the same generalization. Agreement in the context of inanimate nouns lends itself readily to a semantically grounded account while first conjunct agreement is better handled by a syntactic account whereby the conjunction in question is clausal rather than phrasal.

Fatima Badry reports on a study that investigated cognitive and typological predispositions employed in the development of lexical derivational processes by Moroccan Arabic speaking children learning Arabic as an L1. The study attempted to replicate evidence from crosslinguistic studies suggesting that children's acquisition strategies are influenced both by their universal predispositions as well as by the pervasiveness and regularity of the word formation rules in their language. Based on L1 cross-sectional acquisition data, the results of the study show that 3;5 year olds are already able to derive the causative verb patterns and have begun to derive reciprocal patterns followed by the medio-passive—a sequence in line with a cross-linguistic observation attributed usually to cognitive development. More importantly, the results also showed that the pervasiveness of root-based derivations in the Arabic lexicon draws the attention of L1 Arabic children to such processes and leads them to rely on root/pattern alternations in their production of novel words to fill lexical gaps. The L1 participant children showed a tendency to rely on both vertical (root based) and horizontal (word based) derivations when dealing with sound and weak forms, respectively. By analyzing the participants' productive utterances as well as their errors in comparison with certain adult L1 Arabic speakers' errors (such as slips of the tongue, hypocoristics and aphasic errors), Badry further argues that her data support the psychological reality of the root. Hence, the paper is also a contribution to the on-going debate about the nature of the root.

Finally, Mohammad Alhawary reports on an L2 acquisition study conducted within the latest generative framework of Principles and Parameters. The study investigated the status of UG access and the nature of second language competence or ultimate attainment in adult monolingual English and French L1 speakers learning Arabic as an L2. In particular, the study examined three most recent hypotheses posited for L2 development: the Local Impairment Hypothesis, the Failed Functional Features Hypothesis and the Missing Surface Inflection Hypothesis. Based on cross-sectional acquisition data, analyzed for the feature gender and number agreement in nominal and verbal constructions, the findings indicate that L1 English participants were more likely to have problems with grammatical gender than their L1 French counterparts. The findings are argued to be in support of a modified temporary (access to UG) impairment view, especially in L2 contexts where L1 does not exhibit similar functional categories as those available in L2. The temporary status conclusion is based on the performance of (advanced) participants of both L1 backgrounds who exhibited 100% correct agreement ratios. Alhawary argues that the findings concomitantly lend further support to the role of L1 transfer in L2 acquisition.

THE LENGTH OF STEM-FINAL VOWELS IN COLLOQUIAL ARABIC*

John J. McCarthy
University of Massachusetts, Amherst

1. Introduction

In Cairene Arabic, word-final vowels are short, but the same vowels are long when followed by a suffix, as shown in (1).

(1) Cairene Arabic v̆ ~ vː alternation (Watson 2002:202)

*ʔáb**u***	"father"	*ʔab**úː**ja*	"my father"
		*ʔab**úː**k*	"your father"
*ɣátʶ**a***	"a cover"	*ɣatʶ**áː**ha*	"her cover"
*kúnt**i***	"you (f. s.) were"	*ma kunt**íː**ʃ*	"you (f. s.) were not"
*ʔúːl**u***	"tell (pl.)!"	*ʔul**úː**li*	"tell (pl.) me!"

All stem-final vowels alternate in this way. There are no stem-final vowels that remain short before a suffix (**tab**u**/tab**u**k*), nor are there any stem-final vowels that are long word-finally (**kat**uː**/kat**uː**k*).

These facts are not limited to Cairene. Nearly all varieties of colloquial Arabic have similar alternations. Because this phenomenon is so pervasive, many analysts have discussed it, and there are two schools of thought about how it should be accounted for. In the view of some, all stem-final vowels are short in underlying representation (e.g., /ʔab**u**/), and there is a process lengthening them before a suffix. Proponents of this view include Abdel-Massih et al. (1979:323), Broselow (1976:106-118),

*For their comments on an earlier version of this paper, I am grateful to Ellen Broselow, Maria Gouskova, Bruce Hayes, Shigeto Kawahara, and Jaye Padgett.

and Watson (2002:201-203) on Cairene, Bohas (1978:98) on Damascene, Abdul-Karim (1980), Brame (1971:584), and Haddad (1984) on Lebanese and Palestinian, and Hamid (1984) on Sudanese. Another group of analysts favors stem-final vowels that are underlyingly long (e.g., /ʔab**uː**/), with shortening word-finally. This approach is espoused by Abdo (1969) and Abu-Salim (1982) on Lebanese and Palestinian, Abu-Mansour (1987:134) on Mekkan, and Glover (1988) on Omani. Actual phonological differences among these dialects are not sufficient to explain this divergence of opinion. In fact, Angoujard (1978:16), discussing Tunisian Arabic, tosses up his hands, saying, "à choisir entre une règle d'abrégement et une règle d'allongement ... à vrai dire, je n'en ai pas trouvé de clairement décisifs".

It might seem, then, that the underlying length of stem-final vowels in colloquial Arabic is indeterminate. In this chapter, I will argue that Optimality Theory (Prince & Smolensky 1993) resolves this indeterminacy. Two aspects of OT are important to the argument. One is *richness of the base* (ROTB), the thesis that there are no language-particular restrictions on underlying representations. The other is the hypothesis that there is a universal constraint-set called CON. ROTB and the universality of CON together force a resolution of this indeterminacy, supplying both the linguist and, more importantly, the language learner with a fully determinate answer to the question of the underlying representation. Under ROTB, an OT grammar of Cairene Arabic must correctly dispose of inputs with stem-final short *and* long vowels, both of which are served up by the rich base. An underlying stem is correctly disposed of, if it is mapped onto a pattern of (non)alternation that is actually observed in the language. When this process of reasoning is followed through, we are led to the conclusion that the underlying form of "father" is /ʔabuː/, with a long vowel.

2. Theoretical Background

I assume familiarity with the main premises of Optimality Theory at the level of introductory works like Kager (1999), McCarthy (2002), or Tesar, Grimshaw, and Prince (1999). For present purposes, the most important thing about OT is its dichotomy between the language-particular and the universal. The set of linguistic constraints, called CON, is universal in the sense that all constraints are present in the grammars of all languages. Languages differ, however, in the ranking imposed on CON: two languages (or two dialects) will have different rankings of CON. The strongest hypothesis is that, apart from vocabulary, ranking is the ONLY difference between languages.

One consequence of this hypothesis is that all systematic, language-particular restrictions on underlying forms are eliminated. Standardly, generative phonology has relied on devices like morpheme-structure constraints, lexical redundancy rules, or underspecification as part of the analysis of many generalizations. All of these devices are now gone; in its purest form, OT says that linguistic generalizations must be entirely accounted for in the grammar without any assistance from special constraints on the lexicon.

The assumption that the lexicon is unrestricted is called 'Richness of the Base' (ROTB). For example, ROTB entails that English cannot have a morpheme structure constraint against initial stop+nasal clusters, which might appear necessary to explain the impossibility of words like **bnick*. Rather, the ill-formedness of **bnick* is the responsibility of the grammar, which says that *bn* is an impossible syllable-initial cluster. This does not mean that the word *nick* is derived, absurdly and perversely, from underlying /bnɪk/; rather, it means that, if the grammar is presented with the input /bnɪk/, the output is not **bnick* but something else. In other words, knowledge of phonotactics is encoded in the grammar's intolerance for phonotactically impermissible sequences and not by preemptively removing them from the lexicon.

ROTB imposes an obligation on the analyst to make sure that the grammar gives phonotactically permitted results even when presented with unpronounceable inputs. Care must be taken to ensure that the grammar is not being helped along by convenient, implicit restrictions on inputs. The 'base'—that is, the set of inputs to which the grammar is applied—must be 'rich' in the sense that it represents all of the diverse possibilities afforded by the world's languages.

OT is an inherently typological theory. Because it includes an explicit statement of what is universal and what is language particular, it makes strong claims about typology, the ways in which languages can and cannot differ. Typology is the acid test of any proposed constraint. Since CON is universal, any hypothesized addition to CON—that is, any newly-conceived constraint—needs to be checked out under various language-particular rankings. A specific theory of CON is therefore a theory of what are possible and impossible human languages.

3. **Analysis**

In standard generative phonology, which does not assume ROTB, the problem in Cairene can be stated like this: given a restricted set of underlying forms, how does the grammar yield the *ʔabu~ʔabu:k* alternation? In OT, which assumes ROTB, the problem is very different: given ANY input, how does the grammar derive the *ʔabu~ʔabu:k* alternation while systematically excluding other logically possible but factually non-occurring patterns of alternation, particularly *tabu~tabuk* (short throughout) and *katu:~katu:k* (long throughout)? This shift in perspective focuses attention on what does not occur as well as what does. In the standard theory, the explanation for what does not occur is distributed between the lexicon and the grammar; in OT, the explanation is entirely the responsibility of the grammar.

In keeping with ROTB, the set of underlying representations that must be considered should be diverse in all relevant respects. Therefore, we need to consider underlying stems that end in consonants, like hypothetical /batak/, stems that end in short vowels, like hypothetical /takabu/, and stems that end in long vowels, like hypothetical /kabata:/. From observation, we know that only two surface patterns actually occur, nonalternating consonant-final stems like *daras~darasha* "he learned/he learned it (f.)" and alternating vowel-final stems like *nisi~nisi:ha* "he forgot/he forgot her". The problem, then, is to explain why the grammar only allows two different patterns — surface C-final and alternating V-final—when the rich base supplies material for three different patterns—underlying C-final, short V-final, and long V-final.

A three-way underlying contrast is mapped onto a two-way surface contrast. Which underlying distinction is being neutralized? There are six logically possible ways of mapping three input items onto two output items. (For each input item, there are two choices of an output item to map it to, giving 2^3 minus 2 for the cases where all inputs have mapped to a single output). We will examine them systematically, excluding all but the correct one.

In three of the six logically possible systems, something strange happens: an underlying consonant-final stem maps onto a surface vowel-final pattern, while an underlying vowel-final stem maps onto a surface consonant-final pattern, as shown in (2).

(2)

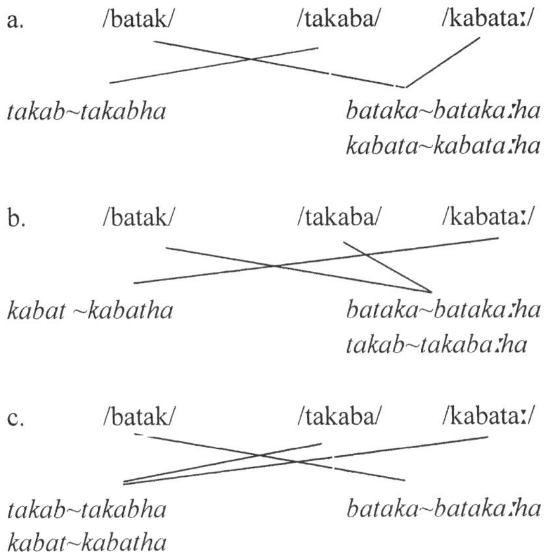

In (2a), for example, underlying /batak/ gains a short vowel when unsuffixed and a long vowel when suffixed. Meanwhile, underlying /takaba/ loses its final vowel in both the unsuffixed and suffixed forms. Similar gyrations appear in the other two systems.

Though these possibilities are supplied by considerations of logic, they are not likely to be possible human languages. What makes these patterns strange is that all of them involve circular chain shifts — that is, mappings where /A/ → *B* and /B/ → *A*. In (2a), the circular shift is /CV#/ → *C#* (i.e., /takaba/ → *takab*) and /C#/ → *CV#* (/batak/ → *bataka*). In (2b), the circular shift is /CVː+Suffix/ → *C+Suffix* and /C+Suffix/ → *CVː+Suffix*. Example (2c) combines both of these circular chain shifts.

Moreton (2003) proves that 'classic' OT grammars are incapable of producing circular chain shifts. The core of his proof is the observation that a classic OT grammar is just exactly a ranking of markedness and faithfulness constraints, so the only possible reason to be unfaithful is to become less marked. The mappings /A/ → *B* and /B/ → *A* are both unfaithful, so both must improve markedness. But that is not possible, since no single constraint ranking can provide that *B* is less marked than *A* and *A* is also less marked than *B*. Circular chain shifts are not only incompatible with OT; Moreton offers sound empirical arguments that they are impossible in human language. Since the systems in (2) all involve circular chain shifts, they can be ruled out on both theoretical and empirical grounds.

This leaves the noncircular systems in (3) for further contemplation.

(3) a. /batak/ /takaba/ /kabataː/

batak~batakha *takaba~takabaːha*
kabata~kabataːha

b. /batak/ /takaba/ /kabataː/

batak~batakha *kabata~kabataːha*
takab~takabha

c. /batak/ /takaba/ /kabataː/

batak~batakha *takaba~takabaːha*
kabat~kabatha

By first excluding the other two systems, I will show that (3b) is correct.

System (3c) requires a process that deletes stem-final long vowels—but not short vowels—when they are word-final or presuffixal. Arguably, such a process is impossible if the constraint-set CON is universal. Since the universal constraints are not known to us in advance, but must be hypothesized based on empirical investigation, this argument is necessarily somewhat indirect. The essence of the argument is that (3c) would require CON to include a constraint with implausible typological consequences. In other words, (3c) cannot be correct because it indirectly predicts unattested phenomena in other languages.

A constraint hierarchy capable of yielding (3c) must be able to produce the mappings in (4).

(4) Mappings for (3c)

Word-final	Presuffixal
/V/ → *V* (identity)	/V/ → *V:* (lengthening)
/V:/ → Ø (deletion)	/V:/ → Ø (deletion)

That is, (3c) requires that short vowels be lengthened in the same presuffixal context where long vowels are deleted. This is a type of non-circular chain shift: /CV+Suffix/ → *CV:+Suffix* and /CV:+Suffix/ → *C+Suffix*. In addition, (3c) has /CV:#/ → *C#*.

In general, an OT grammar is capable of producing a chain shift like this one, where /α/ → *β* and /β/ → Ø in the same context. (On the general theory of chain shifts in OT, see Kirchner 1996, Lubowicz 2003, Moreton & Smolensky 2002, Prince 1996). The existence of the /β/ → Ø mapping shows that some markedness constraint *β dominates the anti-deletion faithfulness constraint MAX. To get the mapping /α/ → *β*, then, it is necessary to block the effect of the ranking *β over MAX when the input is /α/. This requires that CON include a faithfulness constraint F_{CS} that militates against the fell-swoop /α/ → Ø mapping but not the /α/ → *β* and /β/ → Ø mappings. Ranked above *β, F_{CS} prevents /α/ from going all the way to Ø, thereby allowing the /α/ → *β* mapping to win.

Concretely, to analyze the /CV+Suffix/ → *CV:+Suffix* and /CV:+Suffix/ → *C+Suffix* chain shift in (3c),we must posit a faithfulness constraint F_{CS} that forbids the fell-swoop deletion mapping /CV+Suffix/ → **C+Suffix*, while still allowing the deletion mapping /CV:+Suffix/ → *C+Suffix*. Since short vowels do not delete but long vowels do, F_{CS} must be a faithfulness constraint that is violated when a short vowel deletes but not when a long vowel deletes. Therefore, (3c) can be analyzed only if CON includes a faithfulness constraint MAX(v̆) that protects short but not long vowels from deletion.

Independent typological considerations show that CON must *not* include such a constraint, from which it follows that (3c) cannot be the correct analysis. Beckman (1998) argues that there are special positional faithfulness constraints protective of *long* vowels — just the opposite of MAX(v̆). A typological argument for long-vowel faithfulness is that long vowels are often preserved in the same environments where short vowels delete or otherwise neutralize. In fact, the medial syncope processes of Cairene and other Arabic dialects show precisely this pattern of preservation of underlying long vowels in situations where short vowels are deleted, as we will see later. If CON were to supply a constraint MAX(v̆), we would expect to find languages where well-understood, uncontroversial syncope processes affect only long vowels and not short ones. No such language has been observed, so it is imperative for typological reasons that CON not contain MAX(v̆). But without MAX(v̆), there is no way to analyze the system of mappings in (3c). We can therefore eliminate it as a possible account of Cairene Arabic.

This leaves the choice to (3a) vs. (3b). In (3a), the unfaithful mappings include both word-final shortening and presuffixal lengthening, as in (5).

(5) Mappings for (3a)

Word-final	Presuffixal
/V/ → *V* (identity)	/V/ → *V:* (lengthening)
/V:/ → *V* (shortening)	/V:/ → *V:* (identity)

In (3b), the unfaithful mappings include deletion and shortening, as shown in (6).

(6) Mappings for (3b)

Word-final	Presuffixal
/V/ → Ø (deletion)	/V/ → Ø (deletion)
/V:/ → *V* (shortening)	/V:/ → *V:* (identity)

As we will see, (3b)/(6) is the right solution.

I will begin comparing these two systems by analyzing that which they share: shortening of word-final long vowels. This phenomenon has ample typological precedents. For example, in Axininca Campa, an Arawakan language of Peru, word-final vowels are shortened except in monosyllables, where they are required for reasons of foot binarity. The data are given in (7).

(7) Final shortening in Axininca Campa
(McCarthy & Prince 1993, Payne 1981, Spring 1990)

Noun	"my"+Noun		
/sampaː/	*sampa*	*nosampaːti*	"balsa"
/sawoː/	*sawo*	*nosawoːti*	"case"
/ʦʰimiː/	*ʦʰimi*	*noʦʰimiːti*	"ant"
Compare			
/miː/	*miː*	*nomiːni*	"otter"
/sima/	*sima*	*nosimani*	"fish"
/ʧokori/	*ʧokori*	*noʧokoriti*	"armadillo"

Axininca has a left-to-right iambic stress system, but words like *sáwo* are stressed trochaically.

Final shortening in Axininca is primarily a consequence of two markedness constraints. One, NONFINALITY (Prince & Smolensky 1993), prohibits word-final stressed syllables. The other, WSP (for 'weight to stress principle', from Prince 1990), is violated by unstressed heavy syllables. NONFINALITY rules out **(sawóː)* (the parentheses delimit metrical feet) and WSP rules out faithful but trochaic **(sáwoː)*. WSP and NONFINALITY dominate an appropriate faithfulness constraint, such as MAX-μ, which prohibits shortening. This constraint is defined in (8).

(8) MAX-μ
Every input mora has an output correspondent.

For an account of Axininca shortening within an analysis of the full stress system, see the appendix to McCarthy and Prince (1993).

The Axininca analysis can be easily adapted for Cairene Arabic. The well-known Cairene stress system assigns moraic trochees from left to right (Hayes 1995: 67-71; McCarthy 1979). NONFINALITY ensures that the last syllable is unstressed, even if it is underlying /CVː/ and could in principle support a bimoraic foot. The ranking argument appears in tableau (9).

(9) NONFINALITY, WSP >> MAX-μ

/kabataː/	NONFINALITY	WSP	MAX-μ
a. ☞ (kába)ta			*
b. (kàba)(táː)	*!		
c. (kába)taː		*!	

This tableau supplies two ranking arguments. Because final stress is prohibited at the expense of shortening, NONFINALITY must dominate MAX-μ. And because long vowels must bear stress or else shorten, WSP also dominates MAX-μ.

The existence of certain exceptional forms tends to confirm this analysis. Cairene has some words that have stressed final long vowels. Most involve a third masculine singular object or possessor, like *katabúː* "he wrote it", but there are also a few words like *gatóː* "cake". Significantly, these forms are doubly exceptional: they have final stress and final length. This is the expected correlation according to (9): if a final long vowel is exceptionally stressed, then it will not shorten because WSP is not in danger of being violated.

It is possible to go a step further and note that Cairene not only requires long vowels to bear stress, it actually requires them to bear *main* stress. (Other Arabic dialects are not usually so restrictive; they allow long vowels to occur in secondary-stressed syllables as well.) When suffixation draws main stress away from an underlying long vowel, it obligatorily shortens (Abdel-Massih et al. 1979:326; Broselow 1976:16-19; Mitchell 1956:111-112; Watson 2002:226-228). Examples are given in (10).

(10) Shortening without main stress

/tnaːʔiʃ-t/	*ʔitnaʔíʃt*	"I discussed"	cf. *itnáːʔiʃ* "he discussed"
/tnaːʔiʃ-na/	*ʔitnaʔíʃna*	"we discussed"	
/kitaːb-eːn/	*kitabéːn*	"two books"	cf. *kitáːb* "book"
/ʃaːfuː-h/	*ʃafúː(h)*	"they saw him"	cf. *ʃáːfu* "they saw"

Since there is considerable dispute as to whether Cairene has audible secondary stress and, if so, where it is located (de Lacy 1998; Harms 1981; Kenstowicz & Abdul-Karim 1980; Welden 1977, 1980), it is safest to formulate the observation in terms of feet: in Cairene, it is not sufficient for long vowels to be in foot-head position. They must be in the head of the head foot itself, bearing the main stress of the word. A constraint stronger than WSP, call it WMSP (for 'main stress'), should therefore replace WSP in tableau (9). The point is that shortening of non-main-stressed vowels, which is required to account for loss of vowel length word-finally, is also observed word-medially.

So much for the shared phonology of the two mapping systems (3a)/(5) and (3b)/(6). This brings us now to the points of divergence between then. In (3a)/(5), underlying short vowels lengthen before a suffix. In (3b)/(6), underlying short vowels delete finally and before a suffix, but underlying long vowels do not. Neither presuffixal lengthening nor presuffixal deletion seem particularly attractive on typological grounds. Can either of them be rationalized within a restrictive, typologically secure theory of CON?

Rationalizing (3a)/(5) seems quite hopeless. The lengthening process in (3a)/(5) requires a markedness constraint that favors long vowels before suffixes, but language typology offers little support for such a constraint. Surface contexts that are known to favor vowel length cross-linguistically are word-final position, in open syllables, under stress, and before certain segments, such as voiced obstruents. There may be other lengthening contexts, but presuffixal position does not seem to be one of them.[1]

In this light, it is striking that the majority of previous analysts nonetheless assume presuffixal lengthening (see the citations at the end of section 2). This no doubt reflects the pervasive disregard for typological considerations in standard generative phonology. Positing a traditional

---

[1]Bruce Hayes points out that Siptár and Törkenczy (2000:56-58, 170-173) describe a lengthening process in Hungarian that affects low vowels before suffixes: *alma* 'apple', *almát* 'apple (adj.)'; *epe* 'bile', *epés* 'bilious'. (The long low vowels are spelled *á* and *é* in Hungarian.) The argument that this is presuffixal lengthening rather than word-final shortening is based on words with nonalternating final long vowels, such as *burzsoá* 'bourgeois', *burzsoát* 'bourgeois (acc.)'.

There are good reasons to be skeptical of this analysis. Siptár and Törkenczy (2000:146) point out that "[w]ord-final *á* is rare and final *é* is relatively infrequent". Final *á* occurs in two suffixes and some "function words, abbreviations, and interjections", numbering altogether about 15. Only two lexical morphemes end in *á*, one of which is *burzsoá*. About 130 lexical morphemes end in *é*, but all are borrowings. Perhaps there is no final length contrast; rather, final *á* is an outright exception, and final *é* is limited to the loan-word stratum (cf. Ito and Mester 1995).

rule brought with it no typological commitments whatsoever, because rules were not seen as the basis of language universals, though rule notation was. This meant that the analyst (and the learner?) were free to posit even typologically unsupportable rules to suit the exigencies of language description.

Typological considerations are also helpful in understanding what is going on in (3b)/(6). Deletion of word-final short vowels—that is, apocope—is a common process cross-linguistically. Other languages with apocope processes, some of which are morphologized, include Hidatsa (Harris 1942), Kagoshima Japanese (Kaneko & Kawahara 2002), Lardil (Hale 1973), Latvian (Halle & Zeps 1966), Lithuanian (Lightner 1972), Middle High German (Raffelsiefen 1999), Odawa (Piggott 1975), Ponapean (Howard 1972:179-81), and Woleaian (Sohn 1975). Because the typological situation is so favorable, this aspect of (3b)/(6) presents no problem for CON.

Among the markedness constraints believed to compel apocope is FINAL-C, which is defined in (11).

(11) FINAL-C
*V/__]$_{Wd}$ 'Word-final vowels are prohibited'
= 'Every phonological word ends in a consonant.'

The typological support for this constraint comes not only from several of the apocope cases mentioned above but also from diverse phenomena like these: epenthesis in Makassarese (Aronoff et al. 1987, McCarthy & Prince 1994) adds a final *ʔ* after an epenthetic vowel (/rantas/ → *rantasaʔ* "dirty"); Semitic stem templates (McCarthy & Prince 1990) are normally consonant-final; in Yapese, all words, including the output of a truncation process, are consonant-final (Jensen 1977, Piggott 1991); and intrusive *r* in the Boston dialect creates consonant-final phonological words (McCarthy 1993). Ranked above MAX-V in Arabic, FINAL-C favors outputs with apocope over their faithful competitors, as tableau (12) shows.

(12) FINAL-C >> MAX-V

/takaba/	FINAL-C	MAX-V
a. ☞ takab		*
b. takaba	*!	

Observe that final shortening and final deletion are encouraged by different markedness constraints, WSP and NONFINALITY in the case of shortening (9) and FINAL-C in the case of deletion (12). Typological considerations show that this is correct, because final shortening and apocope can be decoupled. The Arabic dialect of San'a, Yemen is like Cairene in relevant respects except that word-final vowels are long (Watson 2002), showing that there can be apocope without shortening. As for shortening without apocope, Axininca Campa (7) is a convenient example. As expected, even in languages with both shortening and deletion, such as Southeastern Tepehuan, the conditions on them may be completely different (Gouskova 2003). If a single markedness constraint were responsible for both final shortening and final deletion, then it would not be possible to analyze these languages that have one but not the other or that have both though under different conditions.

Overly aggressive enforcement of FINAL-C presents a problem: it predicts apocope of final long vowels, which, according to (3b)/(6), shorten but do not delete. The solution has already been hinted at. Faithfulness constraints may be more protective of long vowels than their short counterparts. The typologically well supported positional faithfulness constraint MAX(Vː) dominates FINAL-C, blocking apocope of long vowels. Tableau (13) certifies this ranking argument.

(13) MAX(Vː) >> FINAL-C (>>MAX-V)

/kabataː/	MAX(Vː)	FINAL-C	MAX-V
a. ☞ kabata		*	
b. kabat	*!		*

More generally, MAX(Vː) blocks all syncope processes in Cairene and other dialects (Gouskova 2003). Though short vowels delete under various conditions, long vowels never do.

As (13) shows, MAX(Vː) protects long vowels from deletion even when they are shortened in the output. This is also true for Cairene's medial syncope process, which never affects underlying long vowels, even when they have been shortened because they do not bear main stress. Some reflection about constraint formulation shows why. MAX(Vː) references a vowel's input rather than output length. A definition for this constraint appears in (14).[2]

(14) MAX(Vː)

Let V_I be a long vowel in the input. Then there exists V_O in the output where $V_I \Re V_O$.

'Input long vowels have output correspondents.' = 'Long vowels cannot be deleted.'

Why couldn't MAX(Vː) be formulated as a constraint prohibiting deletion of output long vowels? It's just a point of logic: if a segment is deleted, it has no output correspondent, so it is neither long nor short in the output.

The other unfaithful mapping in system (3b)/(6) is deletion of short stem-final vowels before a suffix. Regarded purely as an effect of the phonology, this seems just as dubious as presuffixal lengthening, which damned the approach in (3a)/(5). But it need not be regarded as purely an effect of the phonology.

The problem, in essence, is that (3b)/(6) requires underlying stem-final short vowels to delete not only word-finally, where the deletion process is phonologically motivated apocope (12), but also presuffixally, where it is not phonologically motivated. Cairene Arabic has phonologically motivated syncope, but the conditions encouraging it have no intrinsic connection to presuffixal position (cf. Gouskova 2003). Rather, presuffixal deletion can be regarded as a kind of overapplication of word-final deletion. (The term 'overapplication' is used here in the sense of McCarthy and Prince (1995, 1999) and Benua (1997), following Wilbur (1974).) Presuffixal deletion mirrors word-final deletion, carrying the

[2]The constraint definition in (14) refers to the correspondence relation $\Re$, for which see McCarthy and Prince (1995, 1999).

effect of a phonologically-motivated process into regions of the paradigm where the phonological motivation is absent.

Phenomena like this are well-known, and they have historically been the basis for the transformational cycle (Chomsky et al. 1956), for the theory of Lexical Phonology (Kiparsky 1982, Mohanan 1986), for output-output correspondence (Benua 1997), and for stratal OT (Kiparsky 2003, and many others). Under the latter two theories and related approaches within OT, the idea is that faithfulness to the surface form *takab* (from /takaba/) is responsible for the triumph of *takab-Sfx* (from /takaba-Sfx/) over **takaba-Sfx*. Both OO correspondence and stratal OT are compatible with the data; for concreteness, I will work out the OO approach in detail.

The output-output constraint OO-DEP-V[3] dominates input-output MAX-V, favoring *takab-Sfx* over **takaba-Sfx* because the latter contains a stem-final vowel that has no OO correspondent in the unsuffixed base form *takab*. The ranking argument appears in (15).

(15) OO-DEP-V >> MAX-V

/takaba-Sfx/	OO-DEP-V (cf. *takab*)	MAX-V
a. ☞ takab-Sfx		*
b. takaba-Sfx	*!	

Apocope overapplies because high-ranking OO-DEP-V forbids zero/vowel alternations within morphologically related forms. In effect, it transmits the consequences of FINAL-C thoughout the paradigm.[4]

In summary, it has proven possible to construct a typologically responsible analysis of the system of input→output mappings described in (3b) and schematized in (6). The relevant constraints and their rankings are given in (16).

---

[3]DEP constraints are the opposite of MAX constraints. Whereas MAX constraints prohibit deletion, DEP constraints prohibit epenthesis. OO-DEP does more: it prohibits any vowel in a derived form that is not also present in the simple form.

[4]Since Cairene Arabic has vowel epenthesis, OO-DEP-V must be crucially dominated. Epenthesis relieves clusters that are phonotactically impossible, as in /katab-t-l-uh/ → *katabtilu(h)* "I wrote to him" or /katab-t-l-ha/ → *katabtilha* "I wrote to her". This shows that OO-DEP-V is ranked below the undominated constraints on syllable structure that compel epenthesis.

(16) Ranking for Cairene

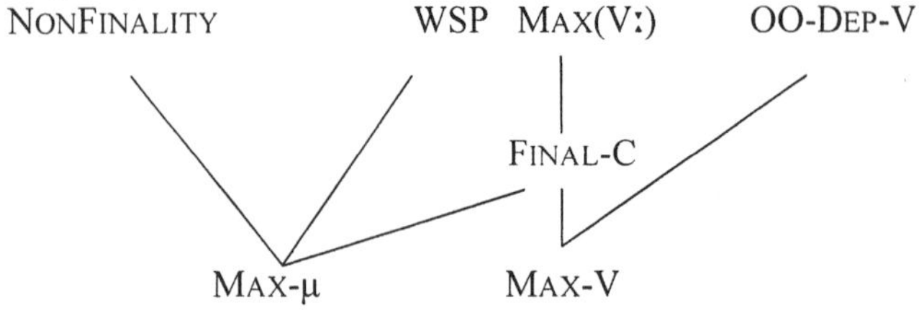

The constraints on the left account for the shortening of word-final long vowels: long vowels shorten finally because the alternative is a final stressed syllable or an unstressed heavy syllable that can be relieved by vowel shortening. On the right, FINAL-C and OO-DEP-V work together to ensure that stem-final short vowels never make it to the surface. When stem-final short vowels are also word-final, they apocopate, and even when they are not word-final, they delete in order to maintain resemblance with the apocopated forms. Since apocope deletes a vowel and its mora together, FINAL-C must dominate both MAX-V and MAX-μ. MAX(Vː) is ranked above FINAL-C, thereby preventing apocope of long vowels. The result is a chain-shift mapping final: /Vː/ → *V* and /V/ → Ø. This is, of course, the same chain shift that occurred in the history of colloquial Arabic, though it is important to note that diachronic considerations played no role in justifying the analysis presented here.

Tableaux (17)-(20) show how these constraints interact to produce the mappings in (3b) (excluding consonant-final /batak/, which is unremarkable).

(17) /takaba/ → takab

/takaba/	NONFIN	WSP	MAX(Vː)	OO-DEP-V	FIN-C	MAX-μ	MAX-V
a. ☞ takab						*	*
b. takaba					*!		

(18) /takaba-Sfx/ → takab-Sfx

/takaba-Sfx/	NonFin	WSP	Max(Vː)	OO-Dep-V	Fin-C	Max-μ	Max-V
a. ☞ takab-Sfx						*	*
b. takaba-Sfx				*!			

(19) /kabataː/ → kabata

/ kabataː/	NonFin	WSP	Max(Vː)	OO-Dep-V	Fin-C	Max-μ	Max-V
a. ☞ (kába)ta					*	*	
b. kaba(táː)	*!				*		
c. (kába)taː		*!			*		
d. (kábat)			*!			**	*

(20) /kabataː-Sfx/ → kabataː-Sfx

/ kaba(táː)-Sfx/	NonFin	WSP	Max(Vː)	OO-Dep-V	Fin-C	Max-μ	Max-V
☞ kaba(táː)-Sfx							

In (17), Final-C causes apocope of the final short vowel. In (18), the effect of apocope is carried over to the suffixed forms by the agency of OO-Dep-V, which requires that the suffixed stem not contain vowels that are absent from the unsuffixed stem. In (19), a wider range of candidates must be considered. The rejected options include final stress (19b) and an unstressed long vowel (19c). Deletion of a long vowel (19d), though it leads to better satisfaction of Final-C, is rejected because of Max(Vː)'s dominance. Finally, in (20) the winner violates none of the constraints under discussion, so it has no serious competitors.

This analysis of stem-final vowels applies with equal force to the vowels of the pronominal suffixes and other clitic-like elements. For example, /ma ʕallimuː-niː-ʃ/ "they didn't teach me" has an underlying stem-final long vowel /uː/ and a suffix-final long vowel /iː/. The surface form is *ma ʕallimuníːʃ*—underlying long vowels are not syncopated, but they are shortened when they do not bear main stress. Without the negation, this word is *ʕallimúːni*—the stressless final long vowel is shortened, as expected. Suffixes ending in underlying short vowels, though a logical possibility under ROTB, would lose those vowels throughout the paradigm and would therefore be indistinguishable from suffixes ending in consonants. This is just like the short-vowel-final stems in (17,18).

To sum up, ROTB and the universality of CON lead to the conclusion that the alternating stem-final vowel of Cairene Arabic *ʔabu~ʔabuːk* is underlyingly long. Although this result emerges from theoretical considerations, it also turns out to have solid empirical support in the language. Three additional arguments can be developed.

First, Cairene has phrasal syncope of unstressed high vowels in a two-sided open syllable context, as in (21).

(21) Cairene syncope (Broselow 1976:3)

/mudarris/	huwwa m_darris	"he is a teacher"
/ʃirib/	ana ʃ_ribt ilʔahwa	"I drank the coffee"
	ʃir_b ilʔahwa	"he drank the coffee"

However, word-final vowels never delete even when all other requirements are met, as shown in (22).

(22) No word-final syncope (Broselow 1976:112)

/katab-uː/	katab**u** gawaːb	"they wrote a letter"
	*katab gawaːb	
/ti-ktib-iː/	tiktib**i** gawaːb	"you (f. s.) write a letter"
	*tiktib gawaːb	

If stem-final vowels are underlying long, then their failure to syncopate even though short is entirely expected under the analysis proposed here. (Broselow (1976:110) notes this point, but finds that implementing it leads to an ordering paradox in her rule-based account. In parallel OT, ordering paradoxes are of course not a problem.) Undominated MAX(Vː) blocks deletion of all underlying long vowels, not only stem-finally but also medially. Because vowels are shortened when they do not bear main stress, there are medial short vowels derived from underlying long vowels that do not syncopate either: /ji-ʃiːl-uː-naː/ → *jiʃilúːna* "they take us". This is another example of MAX(Vː)'s protective effect.

If stem-final vowels are underlying short, however, special measures must be taken to prevent them from deleting in examples like (22).

Broselow (1976:20) formulates the context of phrasal syncope so as to exclude word-final vowels while allowing deletion in initial and final syllables: /V(#)C__C(#)V. This rule-specific stipulation, though certainly possible at the time (but see Pyle 1972), does not seem like the right move. One problem is that word-final vowels are also preserved in Arabic dialects with syncope rules that are otherwise very different from Cairene's, an improbable coincidence if non-deletion is stipulated in the rule itself. Furthermore, subsequent developments in prosodic domains theory (e.g., Nespor & Vogel 1986, Selkirk 1978) have made it impossible to reproduce this effect of judicious placement of '(#)'.

A second empirical argument in support of underlying long stem-final vowels comes from the behavior of epenthetic vowels. Imagine if we were to assume underlying short stem-final vowels and adopt, contrary to the typological evidence, a markedness constraint favoring long vowels presuffixally, such as the one in (23).

(23) Vː-SFX (straw man)
*v̆ / __Suffix

Appropriately ranked, this constraint would be responsible for unfaithful mappings like /nisi-na/ → *nisiːna*.

Quite apart from the absence of typological support for it, there is a Cairene-internal objection to the constraint Vː-SFX. Although stem-final vowels are long presuffixally, epenthetic vowels are short. In fact, there are minimal pairs like /katabtiː-luː/ → *katabtíːlu* "you (f. sg.) wrote to him" versus /katabt-luː/ → *katabtílu* "I wrote to him". Under the analysis proposed here, this is expected, since there is no lengthening process and therefore no reason to render an epenthetic vowel as long. But the proponent of presuffixal lengthening must explain why Vː-SFX does not affect epenthetic vowels, wrongly yielding **katabtíːlu* for "I wrote to him". Although the *katabtíːlu*/*katabtílu* minimal pair might encourage the belief that avoidance of homophony somehow blocks lengthening in *katabtílu* (cf. Alderete 1998, 2001; Broselow 1976:112; Crosswhite 1997; Kenstowicz 2002), epenthetic vowels also fail to lengthen in nouns and prepositions where no ambiguity is possible: /ʕand-naː/ → *ʕandína*, * *ʕandíːna* "with us (we possess)".

A third point in support of an analysis with underlying stem-final long vowels is the existence in Cairene of a derived contrast between tense and lax short high vowels (Mitchell 1956:10-11, 112). Long *iː* and *uː* are pronounced as the tense vowels [iː] and [uː], while their short counterparts *i* and *u* are pronounced as the lax vowels [ɪ] and [ʊ]. But when a surface short vowel is derived from an underlying long vowel, it is pronounced as tense. For instance, *ʃilíːh* "take (fem.) it (masc.) away!" is pronounced as [ʃilíːh] and not *[ʃɪlíːh]. That is because the vowel of the first syllable is underlying long and has been shortened in an unstressed syllable, as shown by forms like *ʃiːl* "take away (masc.)!". The same goes for [síbha] "leave it (fem.)!" where /iː/ has been shortened in a closed syllable.

According to Mitchell, final short *i* and *u* are also pronounced as tense: [ʃíːli] and not *[ʃíːlɪ] for "take away (fem.)!". Though the possibility of a final tensing process cannot be entirely discounted (because, e.g., English has one), this observation suggests that final vowels are tense because they are underlyingly long. A weakness of this argument is that it involves a kind of opacity, since tenseness is assigned to vowels that are underlying long, even if they are short at the surface. It therefore brings in the whole issue of the proper treatment of opacity in OT, an issue that goes well beyond the scope of this paper (see McCarthy 2002:163-6, 184-5 for relevant discussion and references).

4. **Discussion**

By forcing consideration of diverse inputs, ROTB requires greater attention to the mappings that a grammar can perform (see also Lubowicz 2003 on the importance of this point). In Cairene, underlying stems ending in consonants, short vowels, and long vowels are all within the responsibility of the grammar, and so each must map to something that is permissible in the language. Because only two surface patterns actually occur—stem-final consonants and stem-final vowels that alternate between short and long—mappings with neutralization are the ones to look at. The viable options were summarized in (3), and each was judged according to a basic criterion of OT: can this mapping system be described by a grammar based on a typologically responsible theory of CON? Only one option survived this test, (3b), and the grammar for it is given in (16).

According to this grammar, an Arabic word like *nisi/nisiːna* "he forgot/he forgot us" is derived from a stem with an underlying long vowel, /nisiː/. When it occurs word-finally, this long vowel shortens for prosodic reasons (9), and otherwise it is preserved intact. Hypothetical underlying stems that end in short vowels, like /takaba/, lose their final vowels throughout the paradigm, neutralizing with the consonant-final stems: *takab, takabna.* Language learners, who seek to infer underlying representations from observed output forms, will never be moved to set up actual lexical items that differ in the presence vs. absence of a final short vowel, since this potential underlying distinction is neutralized by the grammar. (This is a case of "paradigm occultation" (McCarthy 1998), generalizing Prince and Smolensky's (1993) notion of "Stampean occultation" (cf. Stampe 1973a:32-33; 1973b:50-51). See also Tesar and Smolensky (2000:77ff.).) Presumably, in accordance with the principle of Lexicon Optimization (Prince and Smolensky 1993), learners make the obvious move of setting up consonant-final underlying forms when they encounter surface consonant-final stems.

As we saw in section 1, standard phonological accounts of colloquial Arabic have engendered considerable controversy over the correct underlying form for alternating words like *nisi/nisiːna.* Within OT, there are no grounds for controversy: the underlying form must be /nisiː/. There are two reasons for this difference in results. First, the standard accounts proceed from a limited base that contains /nisi/ or /nisiː/, but not both. This means that the grammar is not required to deal with both kinds of inputs, and so its adequacy over both kinds of inputs is never checked. Second, standard accounts do not require typological verifiability, so they are free to include, say, a typologically unsupportable rule of presuffixal lengthening.

Two general properties of OT, ROTB and the universality of CON, have led to a specific conclusion about the phonology of Cairene Arabic: any surface word-final vowel is long in underlying representation, though short at the surface. There is no presuffixal lengthening process, contrary to the majority opinion of previous analysts. There is final shortening, however, a process that in Arabic, as in many other languages, is linked with resistance to final stress.

5. **Conclusion**

This paper has argued that richness of the base, when combined with OT's inherent commitment to typology, leads to an improved understanding of problems of indeterminacy in underlying representations. The controversy over the length of Arabic final vowels, a controversy to which many analysts have contributed without a final resolution, disappears once the phenomena are examined from the perspective of ROTB and a typologically responsible CON. It has been suggested (Hale & Reiss 1998:660) that "the notion of richness of the base [is] a computational curiosity of OT grammars that may be quite irrelevant to human language". This analysis of Arabic shows, on the contrary, that ROTB is fundamental to the theory and inextricably linked with the results that OT can achieve.

REFERENCES

Abdel-Massih, Ernest T., Zaki N. Abdel-Malek & El-Said M. Badawi. 1979. *A Comprehensive Study of Egyptian Arabic, Volume Three (A Preliminary Edition): A reference grammar of Egyptian Arabic*. Ann Arbor, MI: Center for Near Eastern and North African Studies, University of Michigan.

Abdo, Daud A. 1969. *On Stress and Arabic Phonology: A generative approach*. Beirut: Khayats.

Abdul-Karim, Kamal. 1980. *Aspects of the Phonology of Lebanese Arabic*. Ph.D. dissertation, University of Illinois,Urbana.

Abu-Mansour, Mahasen Hasan. 1987. *A Nonlinear Analysis of Arabic Syllabic Phonology, With Special Reference to Makkan*. Ph.D. dissertation, University of Florida, Gainesville.

Abu-Salim, I. M. 1982. *A Reanalysis of Some Aspects of Arabic Phonology: A metrical approach*. Ph.D. dissertation, University of Illinois, Urbana.

Alderete, John. 2001. "Dominance Effects as Transderivational Anti-faithfulness". *Phonology* 18.201-253.

_____. 1998. *Morphologically-Governed Accent in Optimality Theory*. Ph.D. dissertation, University of Massachusetts, Amherst.

Angoujard, Jean-Pierre. 1978. "Le Cycle en Phonologie? L'accentuation en Arabe Tunisien". *Analyses, Théorie* 3.1-39.

Aronoff, Mark, Azhar Arsyad, Hassan Basri & Ellen Broselow. 1987. "Tier Configuration in Makassarese Reduplication". *Parasession on Autosegmental and Metrical Phonology* ed. by A. Bosch, E. Schiller & B. Need, 1-15. (= CLS 23.) Chicago: Chicago Linguistic Society.

Beckman, Jill. 1998. *Positional Faithfulness*. Ph.D. dissertation, University of Massachusetts, Amherst. [Available on Rutgers Optimality Archive, ROA-234. Excerpted in *Optimality Theory in Phonology: A reader* ed. by John J. McCarthy, Malden, MA and Oxford: Blackwell (2004).]

Benua, Laura. 1997. *Transderivational Identity: Phonological relations between words*. Ph.D. dissertation, University of Massachusetts, Amherst. [Available on Rutgers Optimality Archive, ROA-259. Published (2000) as *Phonological Relations Between Words*, New York: Garland. Excerpted in *Optimality Theory in Phonology: A Reader* ed. by John J. McCarthy, Malden, MA and Oxford: Blackwell (2004).]

Bohas, Georges. 1978. "Quelques Processus Phonologiques dans l'Arabe de Damas". *Analyses, Théorie* 1.87-152.

Brame, Michael. 1971. "Stress in Arabic and Generative Phonology [Review article]". *Foundations of Language* 7.556-591.

Broselow, Ellen. 1976. *The Phonology of Egyptian Arabic*. Ph.D. dissertation, University of Massachusetts, Amherst.

Chomsky, Noam, Morris Halle & Fred Lukoff. 1956. "On Accent and Juncture in English". *For Roman Jakobson: Essays on the occasion of his sixtieth birthday, 11 October, 1956* ed. by Morris Halle, Horace Lunt & H. Maclean, 65-80. The Hague: Mouton.

Crosswhite, Katherine. 1997. "Intra-paradigmatic Homophony Avoidance in Two Dialects of Slavic". Unpublished manuscript, Los Angeles, CA.

de Lacy, Paul. 1998. "Sympathetic Stress". Unpublished manuscript, Amherst, MA. [Available on Rutgers Optimality Archive.]

Glover, Bonnie Carol. 1988. *The Morphophonology of Muscat Arabic*. Ph.D. dissertation, UCLA.

Gouskova, Maria. 2003. *Deriving Economy: Syncope in Optimality Theory*. Ph.D. dissertation, University of Massachusetts, Amherst. [Available on Rutgers Optimality Archive, ROA-610.]

Haddad, Ghassan. 1984. *Problems and Issues in the Phonology of Lebanese Arabic*. Ph.D. dissertation, University of Illinois, Urbana.

Hale, Kenneth. 1973. "Deep-surface Canonical Disparities in Relation to Analysis and Change: An Australian example". *Current Trends in Linguistics* ed. by Thomas Sebeok, 401-458. The Hague: Mouton.

Hale, Mark & Charles Reiss. 1998. "Formal and Empirical Arguments Concerning Phonological Acquisition". *Linguistic Inquiry* 29.656-683. [Available on Rutgers Optimality Archive.]

Halle, Morris & Valdis Zeps. 1966. "A Survey of Latvian Morphophonemics". *Quarterly Progress Report of the Research Laboratory of Electronics* 83.104-113.

Hamid, Abdel Halim M. 1984. *A Descriptive Analysis of Sudanese Colloquial Arabic Phonology*. Ph.D. dissertation, University of Illinois, Urbana.

Harms, Robert T. 1981. "A Backwards Metrical Approach to Cairo Arabic Stress". *Linguistic Analysis* 7.429-450.

Harris, Zellig. 1942. "Morpheme Alternants in Linguistic Analysis". *Language* 18.169-180.
Hayes, Bruce. 1995. *Metrical Stress Theory: Principles and case studies*. Chicago: The University of Chicago Press.
Howard, Irwin. 1972. *A Directional Theory of Rule Application in Phonology*. Ph.D. dissertation, MIT.
Ito, Junko & Armin Mester. 1995. "Japanese Phonology". *Handbook of Phonological Theory* ed. by John Goldsmith, 817-838. Cambridge, MA: Blackwell.
Jensen, J. T. 1977. *Yapese Reference Grammar*. Honolulu: University Press of Hawaii.
Kager, René. 1999. *Optimality Theory*. Cambridge: Cambridge University Press.
Kaneko, Ikuyo & Shigeto Kawahara. 2002. "Positional Faithfulness Theory and the Emergence of the Unmarked: The case of Kagoshima Japanese". *ICU English Studies* 5.18-36.
Kenstowicz, Michael. 2002. "Paradigmatic Uniformity and Contrast". *MIT Working Papers in Linguistics* 42.141-163. [Available (23 May 2003) at http://web.mit.edu/linguistics/www/kenstowicz/paradigm_contrast.doc.]
_____ & Kamal Abdul-Karim. 1980. "Cyclic Stress in Levantine Arabic". *Studies in the Linguistic Sciences* 10:2.55-76.
Kiparsky, Paul. 2003. "Syllables and Moras in Arabic". *The Syllable in Optimality Theory* ed. by Caroline Féry & Ruben van de Vijver, 147-182. Cambridge: Cambridge University Press.
_____. 1982. "Lexical Phonology and Morphology". *Linguistics in the Morning Calm* ed. by I. S. Yang, 3-91. Seoul: Hanshin.
Kirchner, Robert. 1996. "Synchronic Chain Shifts in Optimality Theory". *Linguistic Inquiry* 27.341-350. [Available on Rutgers Optimality Archive, ROA-66.]
Lightner, Theodore. 1972. *Problems in the Theory of Phonology*. Edmonton: Linguistic Research, Inc.
Lubowicz, Anna. 2003. *Contrast Preservation in Phonological Mappings*. Ph.D. dissertation, University of Massachusetts, Amherst. [Available on Rutgers Optimality Archive, ROA-554.]
McCarthy, John J. 2002. *A Thematic Guide to Optimality Theory*. Cambridge: Cambridge University Press.
_____. 1998. "Morpheme Structure Constraints and Paradigm Occultation". *CLS 32, Part 2: The Panels* ed. by M. Catherine Gruber, Derrick Higgins, Kenneth Olson & Tamra Wysocki, 123-150. Chicago, IL: Chicago Linguistic Society
_____. 1993. "A Case of Surface Constraint Violation". *Canadian Journal of Linguistics* 38.169-195.
_____. 1979. "On Stress and Syllabification". *Linguistic Inquiry* 10.443-466.
_____ & Alan Prince. 1999. "Faithfulness and Identity in Prosodic Morphology". *The Prosody-Morphology Interface* ed. by René Kager, Harry van der Hulst & Wim Zonneveld, 218-309. Cambridge: Cambridge University Press. [Excerpted in *Optimality Theory in Phonology: A reader*, ed. by John J. McCarthy, Malden, MA and Oxford, Blackwell (2004).]

_____. 1995. "Faithfulness and Reduplicative Identity". *University of Massachusetts Occasional Papers in Linguistics 18* ed. by Jill Beckman, Laura Walsh Dickey & Suzanne Urbanczyk, 249-384. Amherst, MA: GLSA Publications.[Available on Rutgers Optimality Archive, ROA-103.]

_____. 1994. "The Emergence of the Unmarked: Optimality in prosodic morphology". *Proceedings of the North East Linguistic Society 24* ed. by Mercè Gonzàlez, 333-379. Amherst, MA: GLSA Publications. [Available on the Rutgers Optimality Archive, ROA-13. Excerpted in *Optimality Theory in Phonology: A reader* ed. by John J. McCarthy, Malden, MA and Oxford: Blackwell (2004).]

_____. 1993. *Prosodic Morphology: Constraint interaction and satisfaction.* New Brunswick, NJ: Rutgers University Center for Cognitive Science. [Available on Rutgers Optimality Archive, ROA-482.]

_____. 1990. "Prosodic Morphology and Templatic Morphology". *Perspectives on Arabic Linguistics II* ed. by Mushira Eid & John J. McCarthy, 1-54. Amsterdam: John Benjamins.

Mitchell, T. F. 1956. *An Introduction to Egyptian Colloquial Arabic.* Oxford: Oxford University Press.

Mohanan, K. P. 1986. *The Theory of Lexical Phonology.* Dordrecht: Reidel.

Moreton, Elliott. 2003. "Non-computable Functions in Optimality Theory". *Optimality Theory in Phonology: A reader* ed. by John J. McCarthy, 141-163. Malden, MA and Oxford: Blackwell.[Available on Rutgers Optimality Archive, ROA-364.]

Moreton, Elliott & Paul Smolensky. 2002. "Typological Consequences of Local Constraint Conjunction". *Proceedings of the 21st West Coast Conference on Formal Linguistics* ed. by Line Mikkelsen & Christopher Potts, 306-319. Cambridge, MA: Cascadilla Press. [Available on Rutgers Optimality Archive, ROA-525.]

Nespor, Marina & Irene Vogel. 1986. *Prosodic Phonology.* Dordrecht: Foris.

Payne, David L. 1981. *The Phonology and Morphology of Axininca Campa.* Arlington, TX: The Summer Institute of Linguistics and University of Texas at Arlington.

Piggott, G. L. 1991. "Apocope and the Licensing of Empty-headed Syllables". *The Linguistic Review* 8.287-318.

_____. 1975. "More on the Application of Phonological Rules". *Montreal Working Papers in Lingustics* 5.113-150.

Prince, Alan. 1996. "Aspects of Mapping under OT". Handout from Colloquium, University of California, Santa Cruz.

_____. 1990. "Quantitative Consequences of Rhythmic Organization". *Parasession on the Syllable in Phonetics and Phonology* ed. by M. Ziolkowski, M. Noske & K. Deaton, 355-398. Chicago: Chicago Linguistic Society.

_____ & Paul Smolensky. 1993. *Optimality Theory: Constraint interaction in generative grammar.* New Brunswick, NJ: Rutgers University Center for Cognitive Science. [Excerpts appear in *Optimality Theory in Phonology: A reader* ed. by John J. McCarthy, Malden, MA and Oxford: Blackwell (2004). Available on Rutgers Optimality Archive, ROA-537.]

Pyle, Charles. 1972. "On Eliminating BMs". *Proceedings of CLS 8* ed. by Paul Peranteau, Judith Levi & Gloria Phares, 516-532. Chicago: Chicago Linguistic Society.

Raffelsiefen, Renate. 1999. "Constraints on Schwa Apocope in Middle High German". *Analogy, Leveling, Markedness* ed. by Aditi Lahiri, 125-170. Berlin and New York: Mouton de Gruyter.

Selkirk, Elisabeth. 1978. "On Prosodic Structure and Its Relation to Syntactic Structure". *Nordic Prosody* ed. by T. Fretheim, 111-140. Trondheim: TAPIR.

Siptár, Péter & Miklós Törkenczy. 2000. *The Phonology of Hungarian*. Oxford: Oxford University Press.

Sohn, Ho-min. 1975. *Woleaian Reference Grammar*. Honolulu: University of Hawaii Press.

Spring, Cari. 1990. *Implications of Axininca Campa for Prosodic Morphology and Reduplication*. Ph.D. dissertation, University of Arizona.

Stampe, David. 1973a. *A Dissertation on Natural Phonology*. Ph.D. dissertation, University of Chicago. [Published by Garland, New York, 1979.]

_____. 1973b. "On Chapter Nine". *Issues in Phonological Theory* ed. by Michael J. Kenstowicz & Charles W. Kisseberth, 44-52. The Hague: Mouton

Tesar, Bruce & Paul Smolensky. 2000. *Learnability in Optimality Theory*. Cambridge, MA: MIT Press.

Tesar, Bruce, Jane Grimshaw & Alan Prince. 1999. "Linguistic and Cognitive Explanation in Optimality Theory". *What Is Cognitive Science?* ed. by Ernest Lepore & Zenon Pylyshyn, 295-326. Oxford: Blackwell.

Watson, Janet C. E. 2002. *The Phonology and Morphology of Arabic*. Oxford: Oxford University Press.

Welden, Elizabeth Ann. 1980. "Stress in Cairo Arabic". *Studies in the Linguistic Sciences* 10:2.99-120.

_____. 1977. *Prosodic Aspects of Cairo Arabic Phonology*. Ph.D. dissertation, University of Texas, Austin.

Wilbur, Ronnie. 1974. *The Phonology of Reduplication*. Ph.D. dissertation, University of Illinois.

MORAIC SYLLABLE STRUCTURE AND EDGE EFFECTS IN ARABIC[*]

Abdessatar Mahfoudhi
University of Ottawa

1. Introduction

This paper studies (moraic) syllable structure variation, with a focus on edge-related syllables, in three varieties of Arabic (Cairene Arabic (CA), Makkan Arabic (MA), and Tunisian Arabic (TA))[1] within the framework of Optimality Theory (e.g., Prince & Smolensky 1993, McCarthy & Prince 1995) and licensing theory (e.g., Piggott 1999). The three varieties share the following basic syllables: CV, CVV and CVC but differ in relation to CVVC and CVCC syllables. CVVC-syllables are allowed both domain-internally and domain-finally in MA and TA but allowed only domain-finally in CA. CVCC syllables are allowed domain-internally only in TA and restricted to final position in the other varieties. Domain-initial syllables with complex onsets are permitted only in TA.

---

[*]This research was supported by a grant from the Tunisian Ministry of Higher Education. A much larger version of this work was originally presented to the Department of Linguistics at the University of Ottawa to fulfill the requirements of a comprehensive paper, under the very helpful supervision of Dr. M-H. Côté. Other versions of this paper were presented at the MOT Phonology Workshop, Toronto, February 7-9, 2003, and the Canadian Linguistic Association Annual Conference, June 1-4, 2003, Halifax, Nova Scotia. I thank the audiences at both meetings as well as the audience at the Eighteenth Annual Symposium on Arabic Linguistics. I also benefited from discussions with J. T. Jensen and comments from J. McCarthy and an anonymous reviewer. Any infelicities of any kind are, of course, my own.

[1]The colloquial varieties studied here (i.e., CA, MA, or TA) are spoken in big cities in Egypt, Saudi Arabia, and Tunisia (Cairo, Makka, and Tunis, respectively).

Whether domain-finally or domain-internally, syllable structure interacts with phonological processes. Inside the phonological phrase (i.e., the syllabification domain), syllable well-formedness in the three varieties partly conditions epenthesis, syncope and closed syllable shortening. Internal CVVC syllables are avoided in CA by closed syllable shortening. Internal CVCC and initial syllables with complex onsets in MA and CA as well as internal syllables with complex onsets in TA are avoided by epenthesis.

Right-edge-specific syllables (i.e., CVCC and CVVC) were previously accounted for by treating the last consonant as an extraprosodic/extrasyllabic consonant (e.g., Watson 1999, Broselow 1992, Abu-Mansour 1987, Kenstowicz 1986); an onset of a degenerate syllable (Selkirk 1981), or a result of the interaction of Markedness, Faithfulness and Alignment constraints (Wiltshire 1994, 1998, 2003 for CA; and Rosenthall & van der Hulst 1999 for Palestinian Arabic).

These studies did not deal with the change in the moraic structure of final syllables. Evidence from stress (e.g., Welden 1980, Kenstowicz 1983, Watson 1999, Bakalla 1979) shows that all final consonants in final syllables, including CVC syllables, in most Arabic varieties are non-moraic. Adopting Piggott's (1999) notion of R-Licensing and incorporating it in Optimality Theory, the paper proposes that while parsed within their syllables, all domain-final consonants in the Arabic varieties examined here are licensed by a higher prosodic category, being maximally the phonological phrase. Within each variety, internal variation depends mainly on the context, i.e., domain-internal position or domain-final position. Across-dialect[2] variation, by contrast, is determined by (i) the context-dependent syllable well-formedness (e.g., CA allows CVVC and CVCC domain-finally but not domain-internally) and (ii) the well-formedness-related processes of epenthesis and syncope. The analysis not only avoids an arsenal of alignment constraints that are independently motivated but also provides an explanation for the context-dependent variation of moraic syllable structure as well as the domain-initial specific syllables, two issues that were not satisfactorily tackled in previous research.

The paper is laid out as follows. Section 1 surveys the different

[2]I use the terms 'variety' and 'dialect' interchangeably and both are meant to be neutral.

syllable patterns and their distribution, with a focus on the asymmetry between domain-internal and domain-final syllables. Section 2 reviews previous analyses that dealt with the asymmetry in the distribution of CVVC and CVCC syllables. Section 3 makes the case that all final consonants in the varieties examined here are non-moraic and that all syllables are maximally bi-moraic. The notion of R-Licensing, which will be used to account for the major difference between domain-internal and domain-final syllables, is introduced in section 4. The constraints used to account for the data are presented in section 5. Section 6 contains a detailed analysis, couched in constraint ranking, of syllable distribution and the change in moraic structure and its interaction with phonological processes. The last section gives a summary of the ranking of constraints across the three varieties examined in this paper.

2. Syllable Patterns and Their Distribution in the Three Varieties

The three varieties examined here (MA, CA and TA) have CV, CVV and CVC syllables in all positions. They, however, differ in relation to the existence and distribution of the following syllables: CVCC, CVVC and CCV(C)/(VC)/(CC). Only TA has syllables with complex onsets, which are restricted to the left edge of the syllabification domain. The three varieties also differ in whether they allow CVCC and CVVC syllables both domain-internally and domain-finally or only domain-finally. The distribution of syllables in these varieties interacts with phonological processes. In fact, certain syllable types are avoided by resorting to either epenthesis or deletion. This internal and inter-dialectal variation is illustrated in the following subsection.

The data discussed in this paper come from the following sources: CA: (Gary & Gamal-Eldin 1982, Welden 1980, Wiltshire 1994); MA: (Abu-Mansour 1987, Bakalla 1979); and TA: (Maamouri 1967, Chekili 1982, and a native speaker).

2.1. *CVCC right-edge specific (CA, MA)*

In CA and MA (data in (1) and (2)), CVCC syllables are allowed only at the end of the word or the phonological phrase, which is taken to be the maximal syllabification domain in the three varieties.

CA

	Input	Output	Gloss
(1)	a. bard	bard	"cold (n.)"
	b. ʔalb	ʔalb	"heart"

MA

(2)	a. galb	galb	"heart"
	b. mahr	mahr	"dowry"

Domain-internally, these syllables are avoided by resorting to epenthesis (3-4).

CA

(3) katab-t-l-ha ka.tab.t**i**l.ha "I wrote to her"

MA

(4) kalb-ha kal.b**a**.ha "her dog"

2.2 *CVVC right-edge specific (CA)*

CVVC syllables exist both domain-internally and domain-finally in the other two varieties, but they are restricted to the right edge position in CA, as shown in (5).

CA

(5) ki.taab "a book"
gab.baar "mighty"

Domain-internally, these syllables are shortened (closed syllable shortening CSS) to CVC syllables, after undergoing the process of high vowel deletion (HVD), as illustrated in (6).

	Input	HVD	CSS/Output	Gloss
(6)	saaħiba	saaħ.ba	saħ.ba	"friend (f.sg.)"
	taaxudi	taax.di	tax.di	"you take (f.sg.)"

2.3 *Left-edge specific CCV(C) /(VC)/(CC) (TA)*

Syllables with complex onsets exist only in TA and are restricted to domain-initial position/left edge:

TA

(7)	a. CCV	sbi.ṭaar	"hospital"
	b. CCVC	sṭal.ha	"her bucket"
	c. CCVCC	kraht.ha	"I/you hated it/her"

d. CCVV ktii.ba "(hand) writing (fem.)"
e. CCVVC sbaaћ.kum "your morning"

Syllables with initial clusters are not permitted domain-internally and are avoided by epenthesis:

(8) bint#blaad bin.tib.laad. "a compatriot (fem.)/hometown girl"

We have, so far, seen that syllables with the patterns CVCC, CVVC and CCV(C) /(VC)/(CC) are permitted only at the edge of domains in some varieties. The distribution of these syllable types in the three varieties is summarized in Table 1 below.

Table 1

		CA	MA	TA
CVVC	final/internal	yes/no	yes/yes	yes/yes
CVCC	final/internal	yes/no	yes/no	yes/yes
CCV	initial	no	no	yes

The main purpose of this paper is to account for this variation between domain-internal and domain-final syllables. We will first survey previous accounts of the issue.

3. Previous Analyses

The previous accounts of the variation between domain-internal and domain-final syllables in Arabic dealt with right-edge specific syllables, namely CVCC and CVVC syllables. These accounts are summarized below:

(i) Final consonants in these syllables are extra-prosodic segments that are attached to the final syllable at the end of the derivation (e.g., Kenstowicz 1983, 1986; Broselow 1992; Watson 1999).
(ii) Domain-final consonants are extra-prosodic segments that are attached to the prosodic word as an appendix (Wiltshire 1994, 1998, 2003; Rosenthall & van der Hulst 1999) and are accounted for in terms of the interaction of alignment and markedness constraints.
(iii) Domain-final consonants form degenerate syllables (e.g., Selkirk 1981).

While internally consistent, these analyses did not account for the fact that the final consonant in all final syllables including CVC syllables, which exist in all environments in all varieties, is non-moraic. The evidence for the non-moraicity of final consonants comes from stress (e.g., Welden 1980, Kenstowicz 1983, Watson 1999). The following section discusses in detail the moraic structure of Arabic syllables.

4. **Moraic Syllable Structure in Arabic**

In this section, I support two assumptions made in the literature in relation to the moraic syllable structure in Arabic. The first is that all domain-final consonants in the three varieties under study are non-moraic and the second is that all syllables are maximally bi-moraic.

4.1 *Non-moraicity of final consonants in all final syllables*

As mentioned above, studies that examined stress in Arabic agree on the non-moraicity of the last consonant in domain-final syllables in most Arabic varieties (see Watson 1999 for CA and San‘aani Arabic, Kenstowicz 1980 for CA, McCarthy & Prince 1990 for Classical Arabic). In this section, I will provide more evidence from stress in the three varieties under study.

The stress rules in MA were outlined by Bakalla (1979:27) and can be summarized as follows. Stress falls on the ultimate heavy syllable (as in (9a-b), and if there is not such a syllable then the penultimate heavy syllable is stressed (as in (9c-d), and if neither exists then stress falls on the antepenultimate regardless of its weight (as in (9e-f)). Heavy syllables[3] refer to domain-internal CVC syllables and domain-internal and domain-final CVV, CVVC and CVCC syllables. Final CVC does not attract stress, suggesting that the last C does not count in weight.

(9)	a. ki.'taab[4]	"a book"
	b. wat.ti.'quu	"seize (2p. sg.) him"
	c. ʔab.'raq.ta	"you (sg.) sent a telegram"
	d. baa.'rak.tu	"I blessed"
	e. 'baa.ra.kat	"she blessed"

[3]Bakalla (1979) calls these "long syllables".
[4]Stress is indicated by an apostrophe at the beginning of the stressed syllable.

f. ʔat.'wa.la.dat "she was born"

As in MA, stress in CA is weight-sensitive and the final C does not count in stress assignment. This is clear in the case of the CVC syllable, which counts as heavy domain-internally but as light domain-finally. The following is a description of stress rules in CA based on Welden (1980).

Stress falls on the ultimate (10a-b) or the penult (10c-d) heavy syllable. Note that final CVC in (10c and e) does not count as heavy.

(10) a. ki.'taab "a book"
b. ma.ka.'litš "she didn't eat"
c. 'sim. ʕit "she heard"
d. ʔa.'lam.ha "her pencil"

If there is no heavy ultimate syllable, stress falls on the penultimate (10d-h) and does not regress to the antepenultimate syllable even if it is heavy, as in (10g-h).

(10) e. 'ka.tab "he wrote"
f. 'ba.na "he built"
g. mad.'ra.sa "a school"
h. ʔis.taʕ.'mi.lit "she used"

Only in words with three successive light syllables, does stress regress to the penult[5] (10i-j).

(10) i. 'ka.ta.bit "she wrote"
j. ʔin.'ba.sa.ṭu "they were pleased"

As in MA and CA, stress in TA falls on the last heavy syllable (11a-c), except if it is CVC (11d-g).

(11) a. sir.'waal "trousers"
b. qaṭ.'ṭaʕt "I/you tore"

---

[5]Kenstowicz (1980:39) cites Langendoen's generalization (1968) to explain the fact that stress does not regress in (10g-h) but it does in (10i-j). The generalization says: "stress the penult or the antepenult, whichever is separated by an even number of light syllables from a preceding heavy syllable, or, if there is no such heavy syllable, then from the left word boundary".

c. mist. ʕad.'diin "ready (pl.)"

If the last syllable is not heavy, stress falls on the penultimate heavy syllable (11d-i)

(11) d. 'fil.fil	"pepper"
e. 'mnaa.gil	"watches"
f. mis.'taḥ.mir	"reddish"
g. nikt.'buul.kum	"we write to you (pl.)"
h. 'kraht.na	"you (sg.) hated us"
i. nikt.bu.'huul.kum	"we write it to/for you (pl.)"

Note that CVC, CVV, CVVC and CVCC all behave similarly domain internally, suggesting that the last C in CVVC and CVCC does not count in stress (see discussion in the following section on bi-moraicity). If the ultimate and the penultimate are not heavy, stress falls on the antepenultimate (11j).

(11) j. 'maq.ru.na

We cannot, however, know for sure whether the stress regresses to the antepenultimate because it is heavy or that it does so even if it is light like the two final syllables, because there are no words with three consecutive light syllables in TA.

We have, therefore, seen that in the three varieties, the last consonant in CVC syllables is not included in weight and can be considered non-moraic. This can be said also about the final syllable in domain final CVVC and CVCC syllables. The final consonant in these syllables serves as onset in juncture position as in the following examples.[6]

CA

(12) katabt gawaab [ka.tab.**ti**. ga.waab]
"you wrote a letter"

TA

(13) ktibt žwaab [ktib.**tiž**.waab]
"you wrote a letter"

[6]See McCarthy and Prince (1990) for other evidence for the non-moraicity of the final consonant in final CVC, CVVC and CVCC syllables in Classical and Cairene Arabic.

MA

(14) kitaab hum [ki.taa.b**a**.hum]
"their book"

Furthermore, because CVCC and CVVC are restricted to final position in CA and MA and they are stressed domain-internally in the same way as CVC syllables in TA, we argue that these syllables are bi-moraic and therefore their last C is non-moraic either domain-internally or domain-finally. Further evidence, both phonological and phonetic, for the bi-moraicity of CVVC and CVCC syllables is provided in the following section.

4.2 *Syllables are maximally bi-moraic*

From a phonological perspective, there is evidence that the so-called super-heavy syllables are restricted to domain-final position. In fact, CVCC syllables are often found only in domain-final position in most varieties of Arabic (e.g., Broselow et al. 1995, Broselow et al. 1997, Abu-Salim & Abd-el-Jawad 1988). Evidence from our discussion of stress above also shows that domain-final CVVC and CVCC syllables pattern like CVC and CVV syllables (see also Kenstowicz 1983, Watson 1999). On the basis of laboratory-phonetic tests, Broselow et al (1995, 1997), argue that in domain-internal CVVC syllables the last consonant shares the second mora with the long vowel. Unlike in CVC syllables, the long vowel in CVVC syllables is shortened and the final consonant is shorter than its counterpart in CVC syllables.

The two claims made in this section, namely that all final consonants are non-moraic and that all syllables are maximally bi-moraic, seem to lead to contradictory conclusions. The conclusions that domain-internal and domain-final CVC syllables are *different* and domain-internal and domain-final CVVC and CVCC syllables are both bi-moraic and therefore *similar* seem contradictory. The explanation provided here is that all domain-final syllables with final consonants are different from their domain-internal counterparts.

In line with Hayes's (1989) moraic theory, I assume that vowels in Arabic are assigned a mora in the underlying representation and the postvocalic consonant in CVC syllables is assigned a mora by the weight-by-position rule. Final consonants in domain-internal CVVC and CVCC syllables are attached to the mora dominating the preceding vowel or consonant. The final consonants are claimed to be attached directly to the syllable. Though parsed in their dominating syllables, final consonants are R(emotely)-Licensed (Piggot 1999).

5. **R-Licensing**

The notion of (Direct) Licensing refers to the fact that a unit in the prosodic hierarchy is licensed by the immediate super-ordinate category in which it is parsed. Pigott (1999) extends the notion of licensing on the basis of the fact that in some languages an element is licensed outside the immediate super-ordinate unit where it is also parsed (syllabified). An onset, for instance, can license the place feature of the coda of the preceding syllable. Thus, parsing and licensing have to be distinct. Heads of categories (e.g., vowels in syllables), however, have to be licensed by the category where they are parsed (Head Licensing Constraint). Besides, if a coda is moraic it has to be licensed by its parsing-domain, i.e., the syllable.

To account for the cases where the licenser is not the immediate dominating category, Pigott (1999) proposes a distinction between D(irect) and R(emote) licensing. As mentioned above, D-Licensing (D-L) refers to the traditional licensing where an element is licensed by the immediate dominating category where it is parsed. R-Licensing (R-L) refers to the exceptional licensing by non-immediate dominating categories of final elements. Pigott's proposal concerns only final segments, particularly consonants since vowels, being heads of syllables, have to be licensed in their dominating category. Thus, while domain-internal consonants and final consonants in languages where R-licensing is not active are (D)irectly licensed by syllables, final *non-moraic* consonants are (R)emotely licensed by the word. While D-licensed consonants must be codas, attached to the syllable, R-licensed consonants could be either a coda or an onset in a degenerate syllable, depending on the well-formedness conditions in their respective language. The sole evidence for the distinction between coda and degenerate syllable consonants is based on Palestinian Arabic (PA), discussed below.

While D-License is the only principle licensing non-edge elements, it is the unmarked option in the case of final elements competing with the marked parameter R-License (Pigott 1999:181). Languages that choose the D-L parameter may allow either a vowel or a vowel and a coda in final position. For languages with R-L, there are two options: either R-L/Cons (final consonants are R-Licensed, e.g., PA) or R-L/seg (every final segment is R-licensed). In the former option, words have to end in either a vowel or a consonant; in the latter by contrast, words have to end in consonants because the licensing of vowels is in conflict with the inviolable constraint of Head Licensing, mentioned above.

The evidence for the parameter R-L/Cons is based on stress in PA. Like other varieties of Arabic discussed in this paper, final consonants in CVC, CVCC, or CVVC are non-moraic in PA. Pigott adopts Hayes's (1995) analysis of stress in this variety by assigning trochaic feet to words and leaving the final foot extra-prosodic, thus observing the NonFinal constraint (the head foot must be non-final, Prince & Smolensky 1993). In words with final CVC, this syllable is considered a part of an extraprosodic foot and therefore the last C is parsed as a coda. In words with CVVC or CVCC, however, the stress falls on the last syllable. To resolve this asymmetry and to observe NonFinal, Pigott, like Hayes, proposes that the final syllable is actually the degenerate syllable formed by the last consonant.

The existence in all varieties of edge-related CVC syllables with final non-moraic consonants is evidence that all Arabic varieties examined here have R-licensing[7] (see Pigott 1999:167). One change to Pigott's theory is related to the licensing category, which he takes to be the word for all languages. In Arabic, the (maximal) syllabification domain, at which edge appear the 'exceptional' syllables/clusters, is the phonological phrase and therefore the clusters are a phenomenon related to the right edge of phonological phrases in the colloquial varieties and not to words, as previous studies claimed (e.g., Wiltshire 1994, 1998, 2003; Hung 1995; Pigott 1999).

Instead of dividing the R-licensed right-edge consonants into codas and onsets of degenerate syllables, as proposed in Pigott, I treat all right-edge consonants as 'appendix-like' codas that are attached directly to the syllable where they are parsed. The distinction between 'coda-like' and 'onset-like' consonants is not maintained first because of the problematic nature of the degenerate syllable. The degenerate

[7]I propose that R-licensing is active in Arabic even in the varieties where there are domain-internal CVCC and CVVC, because there is evidence that domain-final syllables are distinct from domain-internal ones, namely in relation to the non-moraicity of final C in domain-final CVC.

syllable is not very well motivated both empirically and theoretically. The syllable in most languages must have a vowel as a head to license the segments it dominates (e.g., Hayes 1989). Besides, such a proposal will not prevent the creation of domain-internal degenerate syllables, as in the Arabic domain-internal CVCC syllables whose final consonants are believed to share a mora with the preceding segment (see discussion above).

Left-edge effects in Arabic have been studied very little, partly because they are not common and partly because they have no moraic effect. Watson (1999), however, proposes that in San'aani Arabic certain clusters that result from syncope maintain their moras, either both moras (CVC) when the first consonant is more sonorous than the second or only the second when sonority sequencing is respected. While it may be valid for San'aani Arabic, there is no reason, neither syncope nor native speaker judgment, that encourages maintaining this analysis for TA, the only variety among the three studied here that has initial clusters. I, instead, propose that the two-consonant cluster is attached directly to the syllable node, following the convention of representing prevocalic consonants.

On the basis of the modified version of R-licensing and the discussed hypotheses related to the bimoraicity of Arabic syllables and its implication for domain-internal CVVC and CVCC syllables as well as the non-moraicity of domain-final consonants, the structure of Arabic syllables of the varieties examined here should be as displayed in Table 2 below

Table 2 does not include CV syllables because they are common in all varieties and show no variability. In fact, they are not subject to R-licensing, which concerns only edge-related consonants. I also ignore the syllables preceding or following edge-related syllables. It is, however, possible to have a minimal word of one bi-moraic syllable; hence the optionality of preceding/following syllables in CVVC and CVCC syllables indicated by the parenthesized three dots. The element that is R-licensed is indicated by a subscript $_R$ index.[8]

---

[8]The second onset consonant is licensed by the syllable, as is the case in most languages. It is attached directly to the syllable, in violation of Strict Layering, because it has no moraic value (e.g., Hayes 1989).

Table 2: The internal (moraic) structure of the syllable in Arabic

Domain-internally	*Domain-finally*	*Domain-initially*
CVC (all varieties) 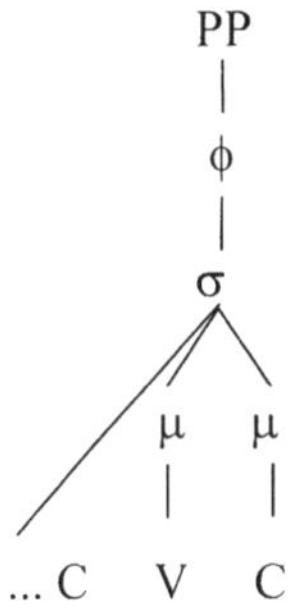	**CVC** (all varieties) 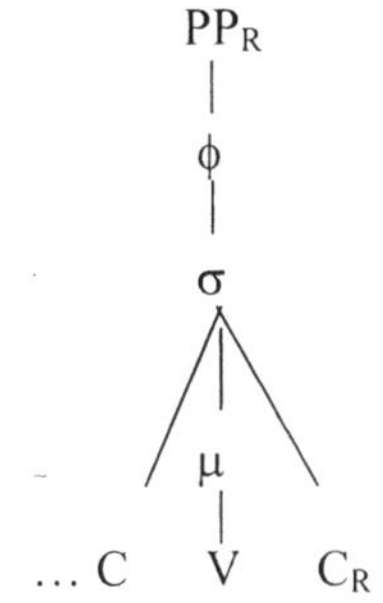	**CCV** (TA) 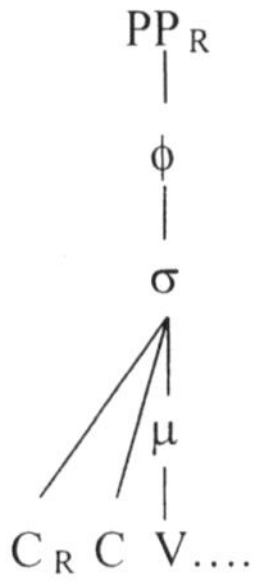
CVVC (TA and MA) 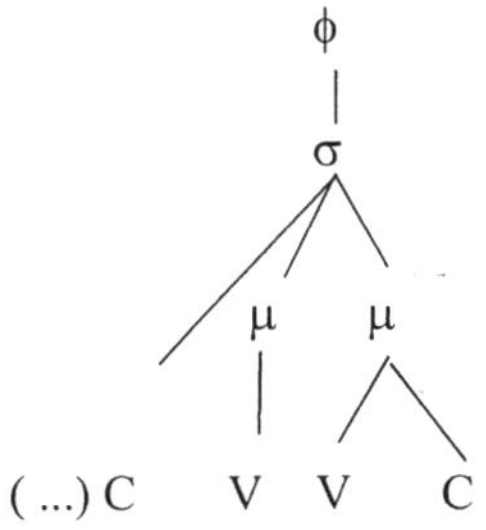	**CVVC** (all varieties) 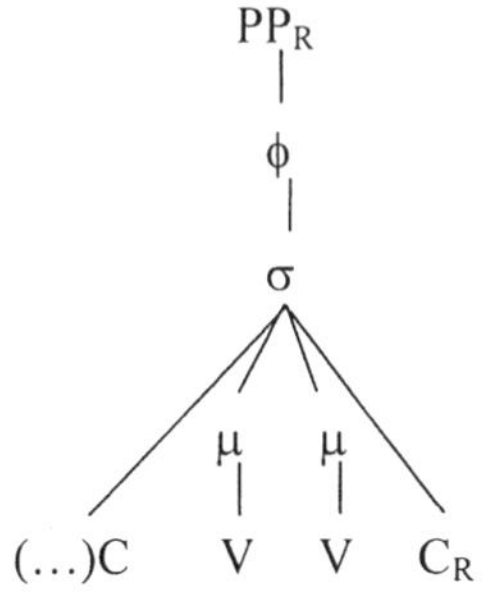	**CCVV/C** (TA) 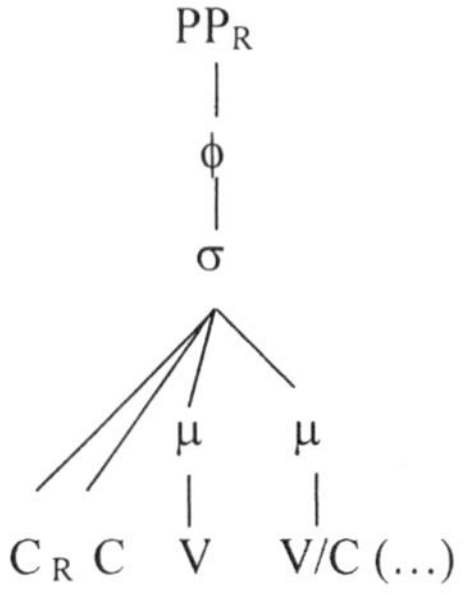
CVCC (TA) 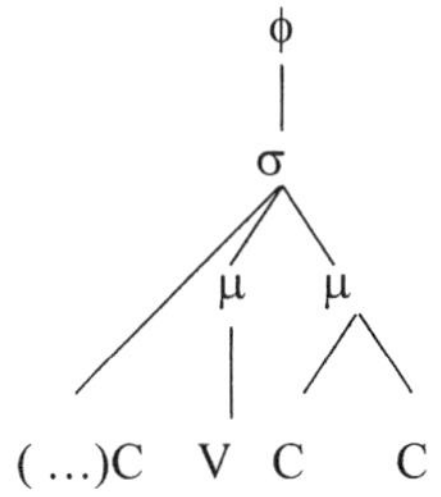	**CVCC** (all varieties) 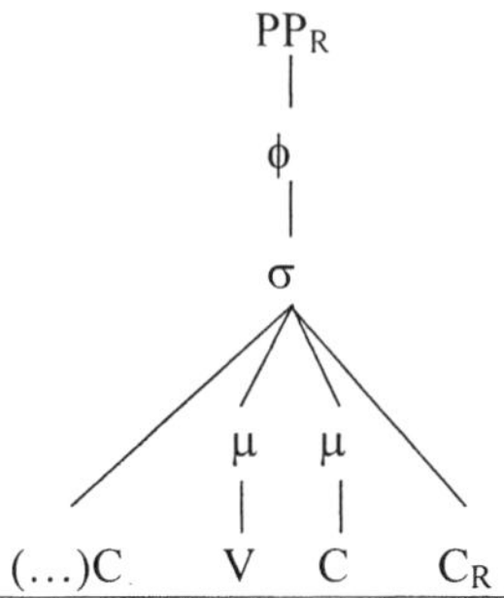	**CCVVC/CC** (TA) 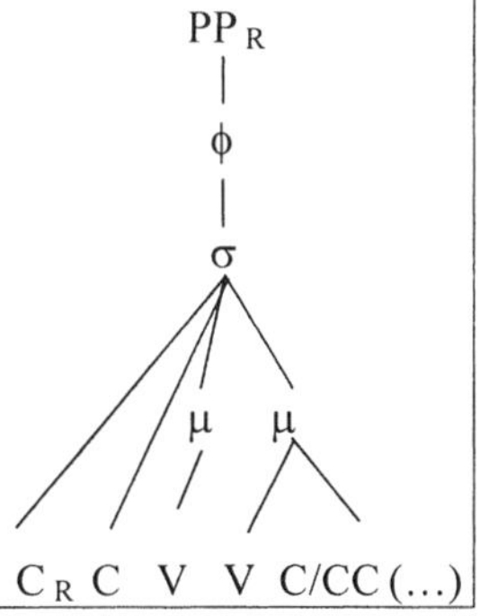

6. **Relevant Constraints**

The variation in the distribution of syllables and their interaction with phonological processes in the three varieties can be accounted for by a few markedness and faithfulness constraints.

6.1 *Markedness constraints*

The first two constraints, Onset and *Complex Onset (Prince & Smolensky 1993), are universal constraints. Both are inviolable in all varieties.

-Onset: Syllables must have an Onset (Prince & Smolensky 1993).
-*Complex Onset: Syllables must have no more than one consonant associated with the onset node (Prince & Smolensky 1993).

The next three constraints are also common in quantity-sensitive languages. In relation to NosharedMora, I distinguish NoSharedMora (CC) and NoSharedMora (VC) to account for syllables with a mora shared by two consonants and those with a mora shared by a vowel and a consonant. These two types of syllables seem to differ as only one of them is permitted domain-internally in some varieties. Noappendix militates against the annexation to syllables of a non-moraic segment. This constraint is relatively highly ranked in all varieties. It is violated only by R-License C/R to derive domain-final syllables with final non-moraic consonants.

-NoSharedMora: "Moras should be linked to single segments" (Broselow et al. 1997).
-Noappendix: "No non-moraic syllable appendix" (Rosenthall & van der Hulst 1999).
-R-License C [9] (L(eft)/R(ight)): "Edge consonants are remotely licensed" (Piggott 1999).

Both Noappendix and R-License C are used to derive syllables with final consonants. While Noappendix does not tolerate non-moraic syllable-final consonants, R-License does. The following constraint is not very common in many languages. It is used to account for the process of deleting high vowels in open stressed syllables in many

[9] Instead of R-License C, I use R-License for short.

colloquial Arabic varieties.

-*[v, +hi]$: No unstressed high vowel in an open syllable (Abu-Mansour 1995).

6.2 *Faithfulness constraints*

The following three Faithfulness constraints are very common. The first prohibits the insertion of any additional material to the input and the second militates against any deletion from the input. The third constraint prohibits the change in the moraic structure of syllables.

-DEP-IO(V/C): No epenthesis (McCarthy & Prince 1995).
-MAX-IO (V/C/Morph): No deletion (McCarthy & Prince 1995).
-MoraFaith: The number of segments associated with an input mora should be equal to the number of associations at the output level (Broselow et al. 1997).

7. **Analysis: Constraint Interaction**

The analysis consists of examining the domain-related variation of syllables and how they are derived in the three varieties through the interaction of the constraints discussed above. The analysis will proceed in the following order: CVC syllables (section 6.1), CVVC syllables (section 6.2), CVCC syllables (section 6.3), and syllables with one of the following patterns: CCV(C)/(VC)/(CC) (section 6.4).

7.1 *Domain-internal and domain-final CVC syllables (all varieties)*

CVC Syllables are permitted domain-internally and domain-finally in all varieties, but their last consonant becomes non-moraic at the right edge of domains.

Domain-internally, R-L/ C(R)[10] is not operative in either of the varieties and the coda has to be moraic. There are, therefore, no constraint violations of any sort. *Domain-finally*, however, R-L/(R) forces the parsing of the final non-moraic consonant, which is attached to the syllable as an appendix in all varieties, thus violating Noappendix. This is illustrated by the word [yaa.bis] "hard", which is the same in MA and TA. A similar word in CA would be [gaa.mid]

[10]Non-moraic (R-licensed) segments are preceded by a dash to distinguish them from moraic consonants.

"strong", "hard".

(15) R-L/C(R) >> Noappendix
/yaabis/ [yaa.bis] "hard"

Candidates	R-L/C(R)	Noappendix
a. yaa.bis	*!	
b. √ yaa.bi-s		*

7.2 *Domain-internal and domain-final CVVC syllables (all varieties)*
7.2.1 *Domain-internal and domain-final CVVC syllables in MA and TA*

Inside words/phrases, MA and TA permit CVVC syllables. The shared mora between a vowel and a consonant is allowed by the high ranking of Noappendix over NosharedMora(VC):

(16) Noappendix >> NosharedMora (VC)
/xaalna / [xaal.na] "our maternal uncle" (the same word in MA and TA)

Candidates	Noappendix	NosharedMora(VC)
a. xaa-l.na	*!	
b. √ xaal.na		*

Domain-finally, CVVC syllables in MA and TA (as well as CA), like CVC syllables (see 15) result from the ranking of R-L/(R) over Noappendix and MAX(Morph):

(17) R-L/C(R) >>Noappendix
/miftaaħ/ [mif.taaħ] PP "a key" (the same word in the three varieties)

Candidates	R-L/(R)	Noappendix
a. mif.taaħ]PP	*!	
b. √ mif.taa-ħ]PP		*

Moraic syllable structure, therefore, varies depending on the context (i.e., whether the syllables are in domain-internal or domain-final) and it is clear that a treatment of the final syllables in terms of alignment (e.g., Wiltshire 1998, 2003; Rosenthall & van der Hulst

1999) misses a fundamental characteristic of the internal structure of Arabic syllables.

7.2.2 *Domain-final vs. domain-internal CVVC syllables in CA*

While CA shares with MA and TA the ranking to derive domain-final CVVC syllables (as shown in 17 above), it relies on a different constraint interaction for domain-internal CVVC syllables. In fact, CA does not allow CVVC syllables inside domains and avoids them by the conspiracy of two processes: high vowel deletion and closed syllable shortening. The first process obeys the highly ranked constraint *[v, +hi]$ and the second process violates the FaithMora constraint. To derive the optimal candidate in (18b), Noshared Mora and *[v, +hi]$ (VC) have to outrank Max(V) and MoraFaith:

(18) NosharedMora(VC), *[v, +hi]$>> MAX(V), MoraFaith
/ṣaaħiba/ [ṣaħ.ba] "a friend (f.)"

Candidates	NosharedMora(VC)	*[v, +hi]$	MAX(V)	MoraFaith
a. ṣaaħ.ba	*!			
b. √ ṣaħ.ba			*	*
c. ṣaa.ħi.ba		*!		
d. ṣa.ħi.ba		*!		*

7.2.3 *HVD and CSS in MA and TA*

While *[v, +hi] is also highly ranked in MA and TA, these varieties do not shorten CVVC syllables, thus observing MoraFaith at the expense of Noshared Mora (VC):

(19) MoraFaith, *[v, +hi]$>> NosharedMora (VC), MAX(V).
/naažiħa/ [naaž.ħa] "successful (f.)"

Candidates	MoraFaith	*[v, +hi]$	NosharedMora(VC)	MAX(V)
a. nаž.ħa	*!			*
b. naa. ži.ħa		*!		
c. √ naaž.ħa			*	*
d. na. ži.ħa	*!	*		*

7.3 *Domain-internal vs. domain-final CVCC syllables (all varieties)*

Domain-internal CVCC syllables are rare in Arabic varieties; among the four varieties examined here only TA permits them. The other varieties disrupt them (the consonant cluster in particular) by epenthesis. Domain-finally, however, the three varieties rely on the same constraint ranking.

7.3.1 *Domain-final CVCC syllables in the three varieties*

As is the case with final CVC syllables, the three colloquial varieties share the same constraint ranking, reproduced in (20), to derive domain-final CVCC syllables.

(20) R-L/C(R) >>Noappendix
/dars/ [...dars] "a lesson" (the same word in the three varieties)

Candidates	R-L/C(R)	Noappendix
a. ... dars.]PP	*!	
b. √ dar-s]PP		*

7.3.2 *Domain-internal CVCC syllables in CA and MA*

Phrase-internally, CVCC syllables are avoided by epenthesis in CA and MA, (as shown in (21)). Candidate (a) is excluded because it violates the highly ranked NosharedMora(CC) constraint. Candidate (c) could not pass, because appendices are not allowed domain-internally in any variety. Candidate (b), therefore, wins by observing NosharedMora(CC) and Noappendix and violating DEP(V). The phrase in (21) is from CA; a similar example in MA is, for instance, /katabat-l-ha/ [ka.tab.t**a**l.ha] "I wrote to her".

(21) NosharedMora(CC), Noappendix>> DEP(V)
Input: #katabt#gawaab# [ka.tab.t**i**.ga.waab] PP "you wrote a letter"

Candidates	NosharedMora(CC)	Noappendix	DEP(V)
a.[[ka.tabt.]$_W$[ga.waa-b.]$_W$]$_{PP}$	*!		
b. √ [[ka.tab.t] $_W$ **i**.[ga.waa-b] $_W$] $_{PP}$			*
c. [[ka.tab-t.]$_W$[ga.waa-b.]$_W$]$_{PP}$		*!	

7.3.3 *Domain-internal CVCC syllables in TA*

In contrast with the other colloquial varieties, TA tolerates domain-internal CVCC syllables and does not resort to epenthesis in cases like (22). It therefore ranks DEP(V) over NosharedMora(CC) to derive the winning candidate in (22b).

(22) DEP(V), Noappendix>>NosharedMora(CC)
/ktubt xuuja/ [[ktubt][.xuu.ja]]PP "my brother's books"

Candidates	DEP(V)	Noappendix	NosharedMora(CC)
a. $[[\text{ktub.t}]_w$ **i**$[\text{.xuu.ja}]_w]_{PP}$	*!		
b. √ $[[\text{ktubt}]_w[\text{.xuu.ja}]_w]_{PP}$			*
c. $[[\text{ktub-t}]_w[\text{.xuu.ja}]_w]_{PP}$		*!	

7.4 *Domain-initial and domain-internal syllables with onset consonant clusters (TA)*

TA is also the only variety that allows *domain-initial syllables with onset consonant clusters*. The syllables with complex onsets that are allowed only domain-initially are the following: CCV, CCVV, CCVC, CCVCC, and CCVVC. The cluster is allowed by the high ranking of R-L/C(L) over *Complex Onset and DEP(V).

(23) R-L/C(L) >> DEP(V)>> *Complex Onset
/qlam/ [qlam] "a pen"

Candidates	R-L/C(L)	DEP(V)	*Complex Onset
a. q**i**lam		*!	
b. √-q-lam			*
c. qlam	*!		*

7.4.1 *Domain-internal syllables with onset clusters*

In a phrase domain juncture, a vowel is inserted to avoid internal syllables with complex onsets. Thus, to derive the optimal candidate in (24c), the *Complex Onset must dominate DEP (V). Thus, *Complex Onset and DEP(V) are freely ranked in relation to each other in TA.

(24) Onset>>*Complex Onset>> DEP (V)
#saʕaat# #l-xidma#[[sa. ʕaa.t]**i**[l.xid.ma]] "the working hours"

Candidates	Onset	*Complex Onset	DEP (V)
a. [[sa. ʕaat.][lxid.ma]]		*!	
b. [[sa. ʕaat.]**i**[l.xid.ma]]	*!		*
c. √ [[sa. ʕaa.t]**i**[l.xid.ma]]			*

8. **Conclusion**

In what follows I summarize the ranking relations in the three varieties.

Summary of ranking relations

CA

-R-L/C>>Noappendix

- NoSharedMora(VC), *[v, +hi]$>> MAX(V), MoraFaith

-NoSharedMora(CC), Noappendix>> DEP(V)

MA

-R-L/C>>Noappendix

-Noappendix>> NoSharedMora(VC)

-MoraFaith, *[v, +hi]$>> NoSharedMora(VC), MAX(V)

-NoSharedMora(CC), Noappendix>> DEP(V)

TA

-R-L/C>>Noappendix

-Noappendix>> NoSharedMora(VC)

-MoraFaith, *[v, +hi]$>> NoSharedMora(VC), MAX-IO(V)

-DEP(V), Noappendix>> NoSharedMora(CC)

-R-L/C>> *Complex Onset; DEP(V)

The analysis has shown that accounting for edge effects is necessary for any comprehensive analysis of syllable structure in Arabic and that an account of such phenomena in terms of Alignment is insufficient. The adoption in the present study of a version of R-Licensing (Pigott 1999) has proven useful for that purpose. This slightly modified notion of R-licensing, which permits the direct attachment to the syllable of all edge-related consonants in Arabic, allows us to dispense with an array of alignment constraints as well as avoid serious violations of the Strict Layer Hypothesis (e.g., Wiltshire 1998, 2003; Hung 1995; Rosenthall & van der Hulst 1999). The analysis has also shown that within-variety variation depends mainly on the context (domain-internal or domain-final). Across-variety variation, by contrast, is due to the context-dependent syllable well-formedness (e.g., domain-internal and domain-final CVCC) and the (well-formedness-related) processes of epenthesis and syncope.

REFERENCES

Abu-Mansour, Mahasan. 1995. "Optimality and Conspiracy in the Syllable Structure of Arabic". Beckman et al. 1995. 1-20.

_____. 1987. *A Nonlinear Analysis of Arabic Syllabic Phonology, with Special Reference to Makkan.* Ph.D. dissertation, University of Florida, Gainesville.

Abu-Salim, Issam & Hasan Abd-el-Jawad. 1988. "Syllable Patterns in Levantine Arabic". *Studies in the Linguistic Sciences* 18:2.1-22.

Bakalla, Mohamed. 1979. *The Morphological and the Phonological Components of the Arabic Verb: Meccan Arabic.* London and Beirut: Longman & Librairie du Liban.

Beckman, Jill, Laura Walsh Dickey & Suzanne Urbanczyk. 1995. *Papers in Optimality Theory* (*=University of Massachusetts Occasional Papers 18*). Amherst, MA: University of Massachusetts, Department of Linguistics.

Broselow, Ellen. 1992. "Parametric Variation in Arabic Dialect Phonology". *Perspectives on Arabic Linguistics IV* ed. by Ellen Broselow, Mushira Eid & John McCarthy, 7-45. Amsterdam & Philadelphia: John Benjamins.

_____, Su Chen & Marie Huffman. 1997. "Syllable Weight: Convergence of phonology and phonetics". *Phonology* 14.47-82.

_____, Marie Huffman, Su Chen & Ruohmei Hsieh. 1995. "The Timing Structure of CVVC Syllables". *Perspectives on Arabic Linguistics VII* ed. by Mushira Eid, 119-138. Amsterdam & Philadelphia: John Benjamins.

Chekili, Ferid. 1982. *The Morphology of the Arabic Dialect of Tunis.* Ph.D. dissertation, University College of London.

Gary, Judith Olmsted & Saad Gamal-Eldin. 1982. *Cairene Egyptian Colloquial Arabic* (*= Lingua Descriptive Studies, Vol. 6*). Amsterdam: North- Holland.

Hayes, Bruce. 1989. "Compensatory Lengthening in Moraic Phonology". *Linguistic Inquiry* 20.253-306.

Hung, Henrietta. 1995. *The Rythmic and Prosodic Organization of Edge Constituents: An optimality-theoretic account.* Bloomington, IN: Indiana University Linguistics Club.

Kenstowicz, Michael. 1986. "Notes on Syllable Structure in Three Arabic Dialects". *Revue Québécoise de Linguistique* 16 :1.101-128.

_____. 1983. "Parametric Variation and Accent in the Arabic Dialects". *Chicago Linguistic Society* 19.205-213.

_____. 1980. "Notes on Cairene Arabic Syncope". *Studies in the Linguistic Sciences* 10:2.39-53.

Langendoen, D. Terence. 1968. *The London School of Linguistics: A study of the linguistic theories of B. Maltinowski and J. R. Firth.* Cambridge, MA: MIT Press.

Maamouri, Mohamed. 1967. *The Phonology of Tunisian Arabic.* Ph.D. dissertation, Cornell University.

McCarthy, John & Alan Prince. 1995. "Faithfulness and Reduplicative Identity". Beckman et al. 1995. 249-384.

_____. 1990. "Prosodic Morphology and Templatic Morphology". *Perspectives on Arabic Linguistics II* ed. by Mushira Eid & John McCarthy, 1-54. Amsterdam & Philadelphia: John Benjamins.

Piggott, Glyne. 1999. "At the Right Edge of Words". *The Linguistic Review* 16:2. 143-185.

Prince, Alan & Prince Smolensky. 1993. *Optimality Theory: Constraint interaction*

in Generative Grammar. New Brunswick, NJ: Rutgers University Center for Cognitive Science Technical Report 2.
Rosenthall, Sam & Harry van der Hulst. 1999. "Weight-by-position by Position". *Natural Language and Linguistic Theory* 17.499-540.
Selkirk, Elizabeth. 1981. "Epenthesis and Degenerate Syllables in CA". *Theoretical Issues in the Grammar of Semitic Languages* ed. by Hagit Borer & Youssef Aoun, 209-232. Cambridge, MA: MIT Working Papers in Linguistics.
Watson, Janet. 1999. "The Syllable and Syllabification in Modern Spoken Arabic (San'aanii and Cairene)". *The Syllable: Views and facts* ed. by Harry van der Hulst & Nancy Ritter, 501-525. Berlin: Mouton de Gruyter.
Welden, Ann. 1980. "Stress in Cairo Arabic". *Studies in the Linguistic Sciences* 10:2.99-120.
Wiltshire, Caroline. 2003. "Beyond Codas: Word and phrase final alignment". *The Syllable in Optimality Theory* ed. by Caroline Fery & Ruben van de Vijver, 254-270. Cambridge: Cambridge University Press.
_____. 1998. "Extending ALIGN Constraints to New Domains". *Linguistics* 36:3. 423- 467.
_____. 1994. "Alignment in Cairene Arabic". *Proceedings of the 13th West Coast Conference on Formal Linguistics*, 138-153. Stanford, CA: Stanford Linguistics Association.

THE STRUCTURE OF ARABIC INTONATION
A PRELIMINARY INVESTIGATION

Khaled Rifaat
University of Alexandria, Egypt

1. Introduction

Studies on Arabic intonation have always been an echo of theories and models of intonation dominating at the time of conducting these studies. Although using similar frameworks of analyses is useful from the typological point of view, direct adoption of theories and models set up for languages different from Arabic, mostly European, has obscured the distinctiveness of Arabic intonation.

The literature on intonation does not reveal any implicit reason for assuming the universality of such, Eurocentric, theories and models. In addition, no one of the developers of such theories explicitly claims the universality of his work.

While the 'Universalist' view of intonation, which believes that universal features of intonation outweigh language-specific differences and has been widely accepted for many years, it has been shown lately that the development of 'intonational phonology', among other things, enabled the detection of subtle differences between languages (Ladd 1996). These differences show themselves not only as variations within a similar framework of analysis, but also as formal differences in models and theories.

We expect from a description of Arabic intonation to show its subtle characteristics and hypothesize on a 'theory' of Arabic intonation, a huge target that we hope to partially fulfill in this study.

1.1 *Assumptions about Arabic intonation*

To pick up the thread, we have examined the available literature for any general implicit or explicit hypotheses about the characteristics of Arabic intonation. We have concluded that Arabic intonation system is very 'simple' and plays a minor role in the prosodic system of Arabic. This is perhaps why there is no trace of intonation, and other prosodic phenomena such as stress, in the monumental work of old Arab grammarians (El-Dalee 1999). It is very unlikely that prosodic features have gone unnoticed by old Arab grammarians. The reason for this neglect is implied in Birkeland's (1952) conclusion that Classical Arabic prosodic system depends entirely on the syllabic oppositions.

Recently, El-Dalee (1999) has provided another reason for the irrelevance of intonation to the prosody of Arabic. Given the fact that particles have the function of intonation in some languages, he argued that Arabic, being a particle language, has given much of the meanings conveyed by intonation to particles.

Although there are not enough comparative intonation studies which permit a somewhat formal definition of what a 'simple' intonation system is, it seems plausible to characterize such a system as the one in which intonation is less variable with different meaningful aspects of utterances including constituent structure, discourse status, and attitudes and emotions (we shall call it functional simplicity). More importantly, an intonation system is said to be simple when it contains few elements and rules (we shall call it structural simplicity). This study is concerned only with the latter type of simplicity.

1.2 *Aim*

This study aims at presenting a preliminary description of the intonation of Modern Standard Arabic (MSA). This description should be, hopefully, capable of showing the core characteristics of MSA intonation and verifying claims about its structural simplicity. We limit our investigation to the description of the basic elements and rules of the complete 'intonational sentence' (henceforth Tune, see below for a definition). Textual aspects of intonation are also beyond the scope of this study.

2. Framework of Analysis

Our investigation is based on tone-sequence (TS) analysis (Ladd 1983a) working under the tenet of autosegmental-metrical (AM) phonology of which Pirrehumbert's is the most influential (Ladd 1996). However, some changes are presented with regard to notation, tone types, and tune structure.

In TS analysis, the tune is composed of major F0 events (targets) called pitch accents. The pitch accent is described as a sequence of two tones H (high) and L (low). There are several advantages for using these tones:

- It simplifies description of complex configurations by delimiting distinctive levels to two.
- It resolves or rather 'neutralizes' one of the prominent debates in intonation research, i.e., levels vs. configurations debate (see Ladd (1983b) for a review of this issue). However, this debate is still going in the perception realm and more perceptual studies are needed to specify how listeners hear tone sequences.
- It helps in building a theoretical analysis with different levels of abstraction, which was generally lacking in intonation research.
- Given their alignment with text, tone specifications help in specifying more accurately the surface representation of tunes.

Tone features are not used in this study as underlying phonological representations but rather as surface phonological representations (Hirst et al. 2000). These representations are analogous to a very broad segmental phonetic transcription in which basic allophones are used. Our study is too preliminary to assume abstract intonation features for Arabic.

We start our analysis assuming that structure and rules of "stress group" specification are set up and that the "metrical strength" of stress group nodes in Arabic is delineated (Angoujard 1990).

Declination or "downstepping" is left out of feature specification and treated as an independent variable. There are gathering evidence that declination of tunes is a global feature that has a "grouping" function and not a contextual trait of tonal features (Ladd 1984, 1996).

2.1 *Notation*

We substitute the original notation of TS analysis exemplified by Pierrehumbert (1980) with another notation, which we think is simpler and closer to the standard phonological notational conventions. Notational symbols are as follows:

- [']: Preceding the tone for tones associated with stressed syllables instead of [*] following the tone.
- [#]: For tune initial and final boundary tones instead of [%].
- [+]: Is used for internal boundary (phrase boundary). Bi-tonal accents are simply represented as combinations, e.g., HL.
- Downstepped tones (e.g., !H) are removed because of the abovementioned viewing of declination as an independent global variable.
- Floating tones are omitted altogether. Our preliminary observations, together with what has been reported by Rifaat (1991), suggest that bi-tonal accents in Arabic are uniform and their tone association with text can be predicted with a high degree of precision.

3. **Material**

A large corpus (approximately 15 hours) of MSA was recorded from the Egyptian radio, one of the main media in which MSA is spoken. MSA composes what is known as the formal variety of Arabic. We are aware of the doubts raised against the feasibility of obtaining a homogeneous corpus representing the formal style of Arabic (Schultz 1981). We believe that these reservations do not apply to our corpus since they were based mainly on simple segmental and grammatical variables, e.g., the use of /q/ sound, vocabulary, and grammatical endings. In addition, the original model of the levels of Arabic (Badawii 1973) was based on general segmental and grammatical features, which we think needs revising if suprasegmental features are considered. As far as intonation is concerned, we suppose that our corpus is homogenous with regard to the formality of spoken Arabic.

MSA as used in the Egyptian radio broadcast contains several styles. The dominant style is the reading or narrative monologue. This style appears basically in news broadcasts and less frequently in some cultural programs. Beside this dominant style, there are also spontaneous or quasi-spontaneous monologues and dialogues found basically in religious and cultural programs.

The corpus of this study contained all of the above styles. The dramatic style, and speeches made at Friday prayers, in parliament and other occasions are excluded. These styles are quite distinct and depart from the rest of the styles as far as intonation is concerned.

The corpus was recorded from two radio stations: the General Program, and the Quran station. The bulk of the corpus was taken from the Quran station for two reasons: first, because MSA is used extensively in it, and second, because announcers and speakers performing in this station are quite aware of the need to stick as much as possible to the formal style of speech, which would maximize the validity and homogeneity of the corpus.

The corpus was digitized and analyzed using 'PRAAT' version 4.49 by Paul Boresma and David Weenink of Institute of Phonetic Sciences, University of Amsterdam.

4. Results and Discussion

4.1 *Tune and phrase*

An intonational sentence 'tune' is said to be 'complete' when it conveys a complete intonational meaning. Finality and continuation are the most basic and important of the intonational meanings. The tune can be 'simple' or 'complex' containing more than one phrase.

There are several intonation correlates, which permit a rather formal definition of tune and phrase:

- [HL] pitch accent always denotes a final Tune boundary.
- [LH] pitch accent denotes either a final Tune boundary or a final phrase boundary.
- [H] pitch accent never occurs Tune finally, but may occur phrase finally.
- A Tune is embraced by a uniform trend line (see below). This trend line is, basically, a declined one. Any resetting or a change in direction of the trend line suggests a new Tune or phrase, respectively.

4.2 *Basic pitch accents*

['H]: This is the most frequently occurring accent (see Figure 1 (Appendix I) for an idealized contour of this accent). It occurs in all positions except tune finally. The range of this accent, and all other accents, is a function of the degree of focus given to it. Quantification of the minimum range required to identify the accent as [H] is yet to be investigated. This accent is always associated with stressed syllables. The peak is aligned with the end of the nucleus of the stressed syllable (Figure 2, Appendix I). Peak alignment is an important feature of Arabic intonation, see Rifaat (1991). Phonetic implementation rules of peak alignment of MSA intonation provided by him apply precisely to our material. Although Rifaat (1991) considered the stressed syllable as the referent point of peak alignment, our preliminary observations suggest that the whole stress group could serve as a more general domain for peak alignment. Taking into consideration that the phonetic model of this issue is still to be investigated how the speaker accomplishes the compromise between his accurate alignment of peaks with both stressed syllables and stress groups, we shall consider the domain of the idealized contour of a pitch accent as the whole stress group.

['HL#] occurs only tune finally in either poly-stress group (Figure 3a, Appendix I) or mono-stress group Tunes (Figure 3b, Appendix I). It is analogous to the British-style falling tone (see Figure 4 (Appendix I) for an idealized contour of this accent). [H] tone of this accent is always aligned with the beginning of the stressed syllable. Accent range and peak projection is also a function of the degree of focus.

4.3 *Marginal pitch accents*

[LH#] is a rise that occurs either tune medially at phrase boundary (Figure 5a, Appendix I) or tune finally (Figure 5b, Appendix I). It occurs less frequently and is associated with 'continuation' tunes for either non-finality, tune medially at phrase boundary, or much less frequently with yes-no questions, tune finally. Figure 6 (Appendix I) shows an idealized contour of this accent.

['L] is a very infrequent accent. Total de-accentuation or flattening of stress groups is an uncommon phenomenon in MSA. However, it can be predicted from stress or accentuation pattern of the stress group. First, it always occurs before or after an over-accentuated, i.e., highly focused, ['H] (Figure 7, Appendix I). Second, there are indications in our data that grouping words into stress-groups is predictable in terms of syntactic or morphological paradigms. For example, particles are usually unstressed and appended to a following noun to form one stress group (see also Figure 7, Appendix I).

4.4 *Pitch accents as peak features*

Pitch accent types can be simply described in terms of peak features. See Figure 8 (Appendix I) for a schematic diagram of pitch accents represented as peak features. Assuming a 'default' or an 'unmarked' accent [H], which has a projected peak aligned with the middle of the stress group, the shift on horizontal or vertical axes would account for all other accent types. Thus, a shift leftward on the horizontal axis results in an early peak or [HL] accent or rightward on the same axis yields a late peak or [LH] accent. A movement downward on the vertical axis generates [L] accent. Since focus is correlated with accent range, it seems that movement on the vertical scale does not result in qualitative change of accent type but a quantitative one. This entails that [H] is perceived as an elevated level tone since [L] is certainly perceived as a level tone. Our preliminary informal experiments in synthesizing Arabic intonation suggest that the previous analysis is perceptually motivated. However, formal experiments are needed to verify that.

4.5 *Boundary tones*

Boundary tones, besides pitch accents, are major elements in the AM description of intonation. They are introduced to account for contours described in the British-style as rising-falling rising. In this contour, we see a change of direction from the major pitch accent. Given that this rise is associated with unstressed syllables and with boundaries, it was thought that there is a different phonological entity called boundary tone. For theoretical consistency, the boundary tone was applied to all boundaries even if the contour direction was not altered such as the simple falling or rising accents.

Our data suggest that there is no need for boundary tones as independent phonological entities in the MSA intonation system. This is based on the following observations:

- In poly-stress group Tunes; initial pitch accents are always [H]. Thus, initial boundary tones are redundant [L] (Figure 2, Appendix I).
- Final pitch accents in poly-stress group tunes, are either simple [HL] or [LH] accents with no major change in direction. Accordingly, boundary tones are redundantly [L] or [H] (Figures 2 and 3a, Appendix I).

- Mono-stress group tunes are always [HL] (Figure 3b, Appendix I) or, hypothetically, [LH], though we have not found the latter type in our data. As such, boundary tones are predictable in terms of the pitch accents.

To sum up, boundary tones in MSA intonation are redundant. They are predictable from the flanking pitch accents and thus are not presented in the underlying representation.

4.6 *Intermediate phrase*

One of the controversial elements of AM description is the existence of phrase boundary and its implications on dividing tunes into major smaller units, i.e., phrases, and on the tone structure of pitch accents. In this analysis, phrase boundary exists if it has a qualitative effect on the preceding pitch accent or on the pitch trend line of the whole Tune. Our data provide evidence for both effects. Figure 9a (Appendix I) shows a phrase boundary correlated with a preceding [H] accent or [LH] accent which replace the basic terminal [HL] accent to denote incompleteness of the Tune. Figure 9b (Appendix I) presents a phrase boundary signaled by a change of the trend line of the Tune from a rising to declining.

4.7 *Pitch range*

Pitch range involves two parameters: global and local. Global range includes choice of a certain 'register' out of the speaker's voice range and direction of Tune trend line. Register is used for paralinguistic purposes and is excluded from the analysis. Local range of pitch accents is responsible for departure of some accents from the trend line depending on the degree of focus exerted on them. Ladd (1996) proposed 'level' and 'span' variables to account for both trend line and focus. Although these two variables seem to overlap in actual Tunes, they are theoretically useful variables and have some empirical evidence. They have been introduced in several models under different terms and conceptions.

4.7.1 *Span*

The increase in the degree of focus is directly proportional to the increase of span of pitch accents. This applies to all types of pitch accents. MSA has a dominant pattern of accentuating the first pitch accent in one-phrase tunes (Figure 10a, Appendix I) or the initial phrase in multi-phrase Tunes (Figure 10b, Appendix I). Besides this dominant pattern, any pitch accent regardless of its position in the Tune can be accentuated and depart from the decreasing span overall pattern.

Together with increase in span, focus in MSA is sometimes denoted by lengthening of stressed syllables (Figure 11, Appendix I). This phenomenon sheds light on the functionality of intonation 'focus' in Arabic on the one hand and its relevance to stress analysis rather than intonation analysis on the other; issues that require further investigation.

4.7.2 *Trend line*

MSA Tunes show the seemingly universal pattern of 'declination', i.e., gradual decrease of accents level and span or both along the time axis. Our data suggest that declination is one of the major tools to indicate completeness of the tunes.

We did not find any evidence for considering declination as a function of accent context. For example, a sequence of [H] accents can be declined or not depending on variables other than accent structure.

Declination trend line can hold small tunes or larger text to compose long multi-phrase tunes. Declination is basically global. However, it can be compensated for by final accent lowering (Figure 12a, Appendix I).

Declination is very dominant in MSA tunes but is infrequently suspended when continuation is intended. Suspension of declination is achieved either globally or locally by raising phrase accent (Figure 12b, Appendix I).

4.8 *Intonation and style*

Structurally, there are no differences between the intonation of spontaneous and non-spontaneous speech of MSA. The only difference between the two is that spontaneous speech makes a more frequent use of the feature of de-accentuation of pitch accents.

5. **Conclusions**

MSA has a simple intonation system, a system that is seemingly confined to the basic aspects of intonation: tendency of pitch accents to be accentuated, a basic declined trend line tunes, association of non-final or continuation tunes with rising trend line or rising pitch accents and a limited use of pitch accents span to denote 'focus'. In addition, this simplicity unveils in the relatively small number of pitch accent types and tune structures and in the relatively small number of rules governing pitch accents distribution and combinations. A major reason of this alleged simplicity might be the styles of discourse to which MSA is restricted. Complete spontaneous style of speech with rich and divergent styles is clearly lacking in MSA. Reaching such an elegant generalization about the simplicity of Arabic intonation is very tempting. However, it seems that much work has to be done to exhaust different styles of Arabic to verify this claim.

Appendix I

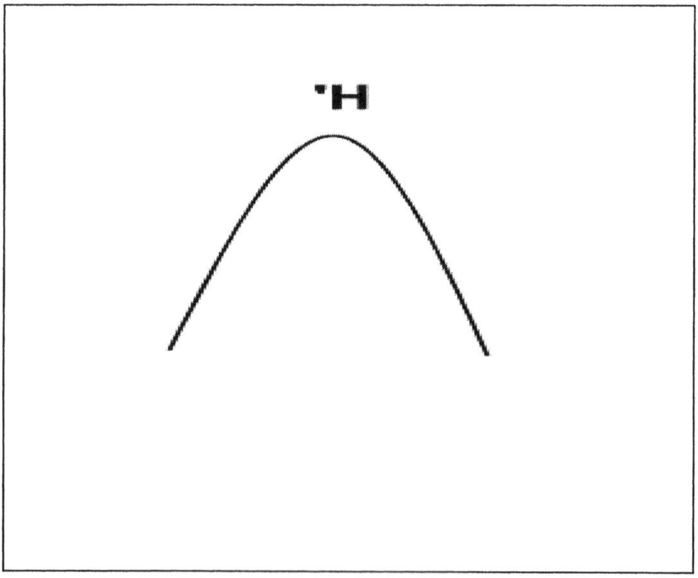

Figure 1
Idealized contour of [H] accent

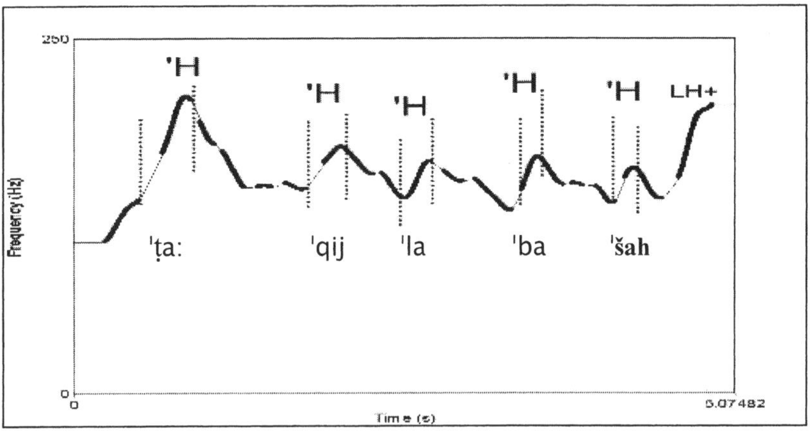

Figure 2

إن الطاقة الحقيقية التي تنبعث في شهر الصوم +
/ʔinna ʔal'ṭa:qata ʔalħaqi:'qijjata ʔal'lati tan'baʕiθu fi 'šahri ʔal'ṣawm+/
"The real energy that is revived in the fasting month,"
Note. The vertical dotted lines delimit stressed syllables. Stressed syllables are transcribed below parallel to their places in the Tune.

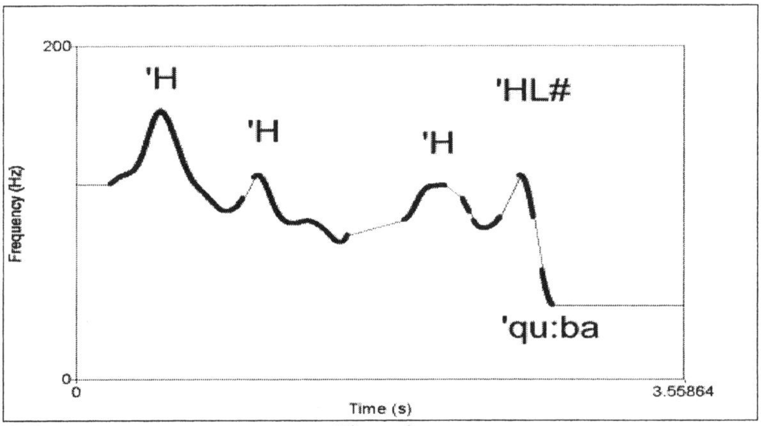

Figure 3a

النوم لأهل الغفلة عقوبة #
/ʔal 'nawmu li'ʔahali ʔal'ʁaflati ʕu'qu:ba #/
"Sleeping for the inadvertent is a punishment"

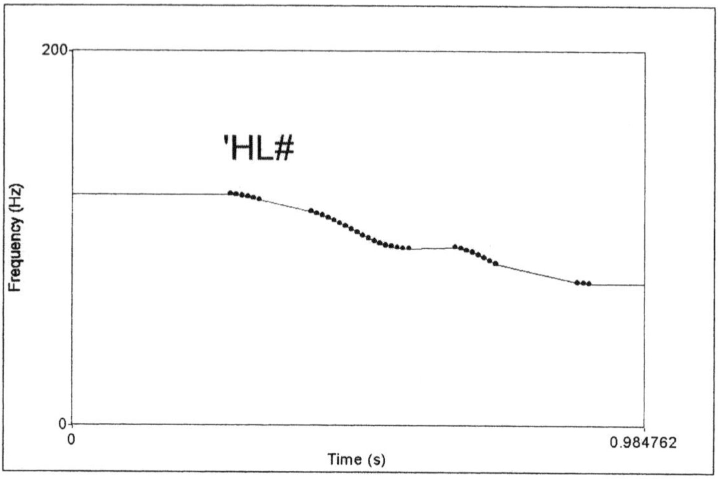

Figure 3b

أهلا وسهلا #

/'ʔahlan wa'sahlan #/
"Hello"

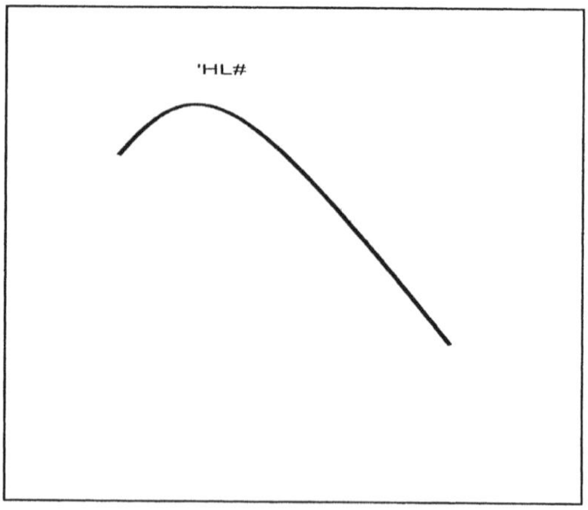

Figure 4
Idealized contour of [HL] accent

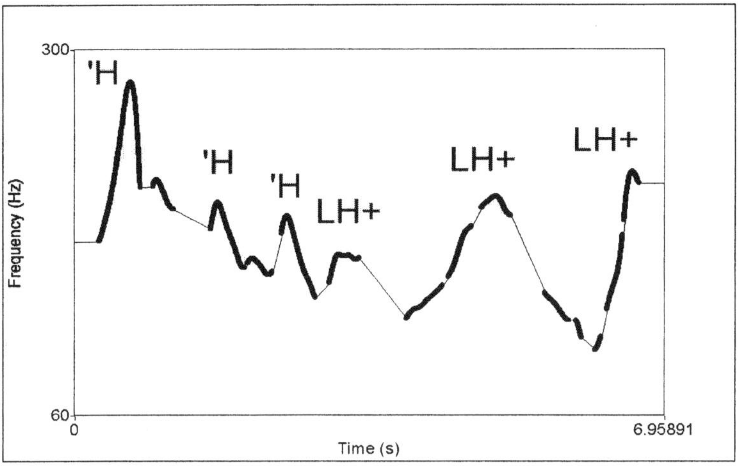

Figure 5a

المنادى إما أن يكون مفردا+ أو مضافا+ أو مشبها به +

/ʔal mu'na:da 'ʔimma ʔan ja'ku:na muf'radan +ʔaw mu'ḍa:fan+ ʔaw muša'bbahn bih +/

"The vocative is singular, adjunct, or quasi prefixed"

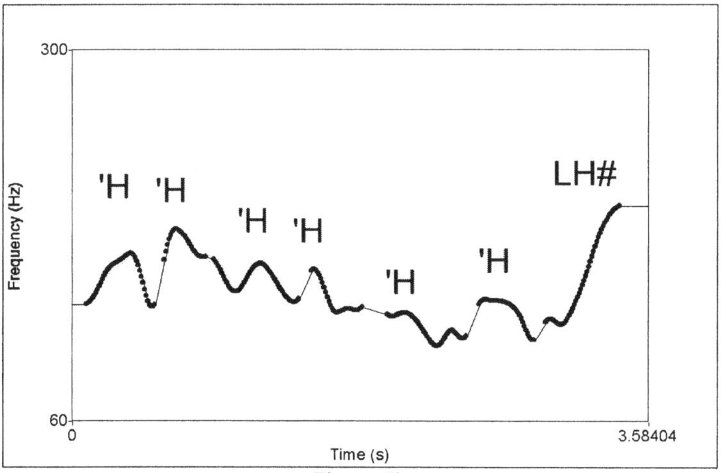

Figure 5b

أليس فينا كلنا حب الحياة و التعلق بها؟ #

/ʔa'lajsa 'fi:na 'kulluna 'ħubbu ʔalħa'ja:ti wa ʔal'taʕalluqi 'biha #/

"Do not we all love life and cling to it?"

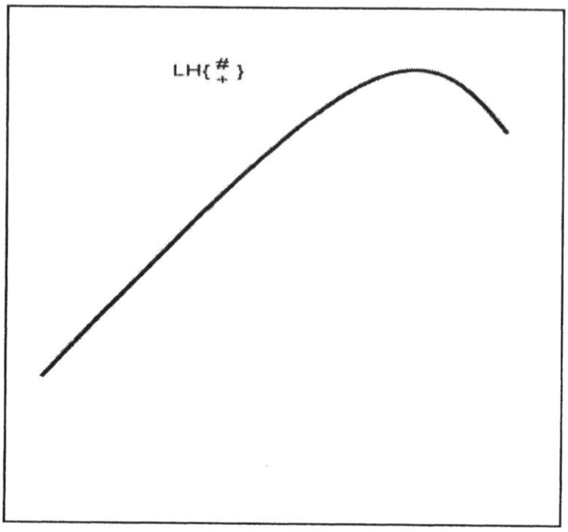

Figure 6
Idealized contour of [LH] accent.

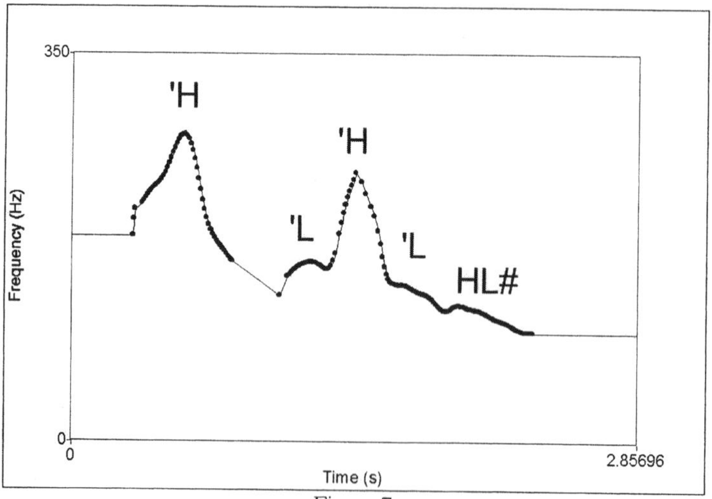

Figure 7

و ماذا لو جاء ولد عاق #

/wa ʻmaːða ʻlaw ʻɟaːʔa ʻwaladun ʻʕaːq #/

"What if a disobedient son comes?"

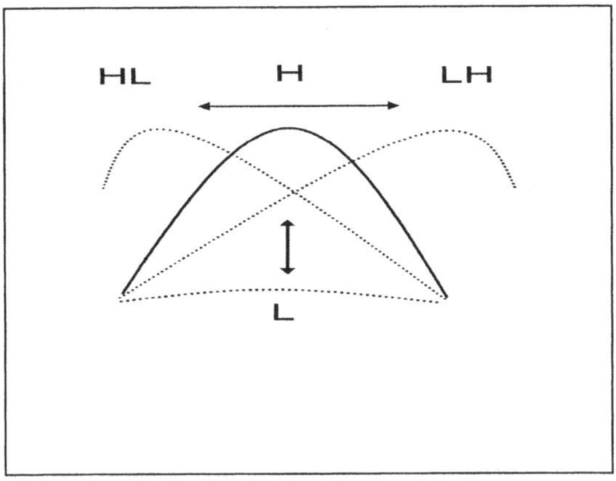

Figure 8
Schematic diagram of pitch accents represented as peak features.

Note. The arrows represent the horizontal and vertical axes. The movement of the peak on the horizontal axis changes the basic accent [H] into either [HL] or [LH], while movement on the vertical axis changes the basic accent into [L]. The basic accent [H] is represented with solid lines and the other accents with dotted lines.

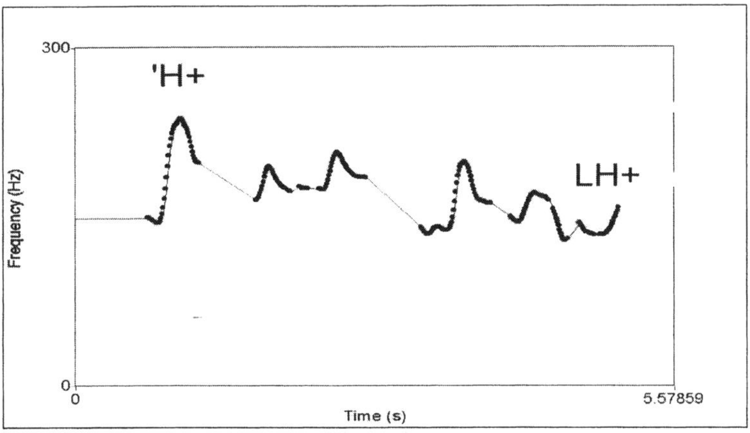

Figure 9a

أولا + إن الإسلام يجيز الثناء على الأموات +

/ʔaw'walan + 'ʔinna ʔalʔis'la:ma ju'gi:zu ʔalθa'na:ʔa ʕala ʔalʔm'wa:t+/

"First, Islam permits praising the dead"

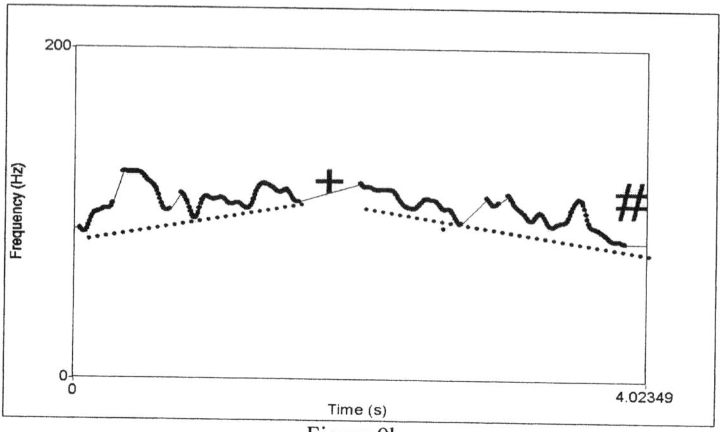

Figure 9b

إذا كان في غير ذلك + كان هذا الطفل هادئا #

/ʔiða 'ka:na fi 'ʁajri 'ðalika + 'ka:na 'ha:ða ʔal'ṭiflu 'ha:diʔan #/
"In another situation, the baby would have been calm."

Note. The dotted trend lines show the change of the level of Tune from rising to declining.

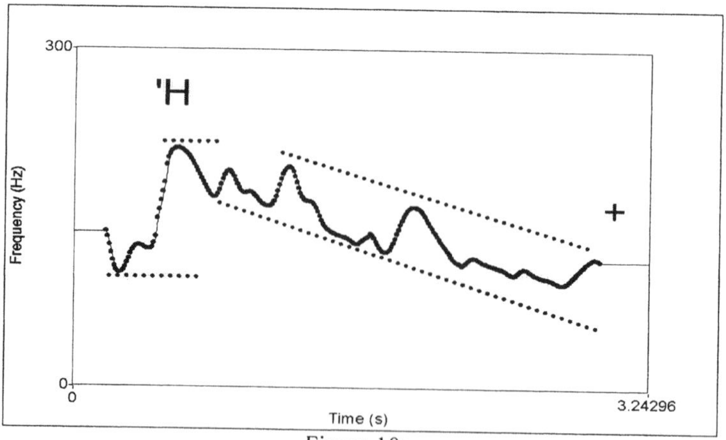

Figure 10a

الإنسان الذي يريد أن يتعالى على غيره +

/ʔal ʔin'sa:nu ʔal'laði ju'ri:du ʔan jata'ʕa:la ʕala 'ʁajrih +/
"The man who looks down upon others,"

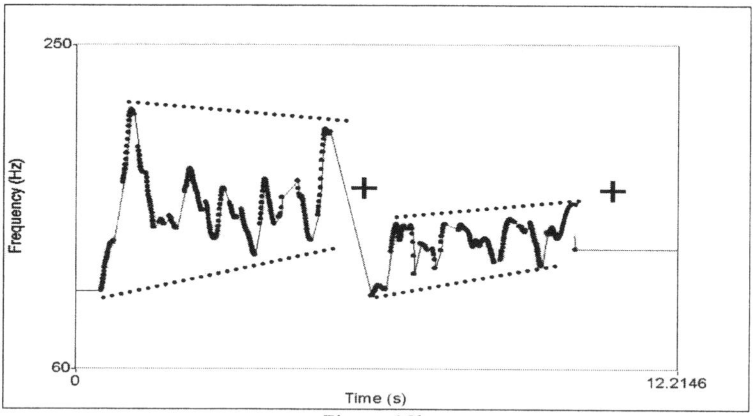

Figure 10b

إن الطاقة الحقيقية التي تنبعث في شهر الصوم ينبغي أن تؤدي إلى طاقة تعليمية +

/ʔinna ʔal'ṭa:qata ʔalħa'qi:qijjata ʔal'lati tan'baʕiðu fi' šahri ʔal'ṣawm +

jan'baʁi ʔantu'ʔaddi ʔila 'ṭa:qatin taʕ'li:mijja +/

"The real energy that is revived in the fasting month should lead to a learning energy"

Note. The dotted trend lines in both figures show the interactive characteristics of level and span of pitch accents.

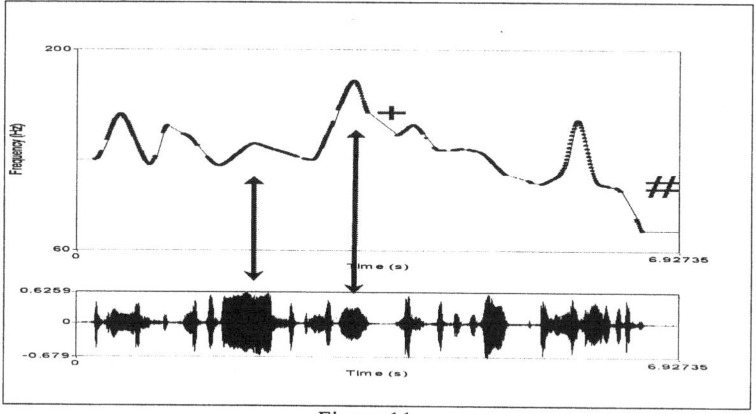

Figure 11

فإن الحكمة ضالة المؤمن + يلتقطها أينما وجدها #

/fa'ʔinna ʔal'ħikmata 'ḍa:llatu ʔal'muʔmin +

jal'taqiṭuha ʔaj'nama waga'daha #/

"Wisdom is the target of the believer; he gets it wherever he finds it."

Note. The arrows align the pitch accents with their places in the waveform; the figure shows lengthening and increase of span as phonetic correlates of focus.

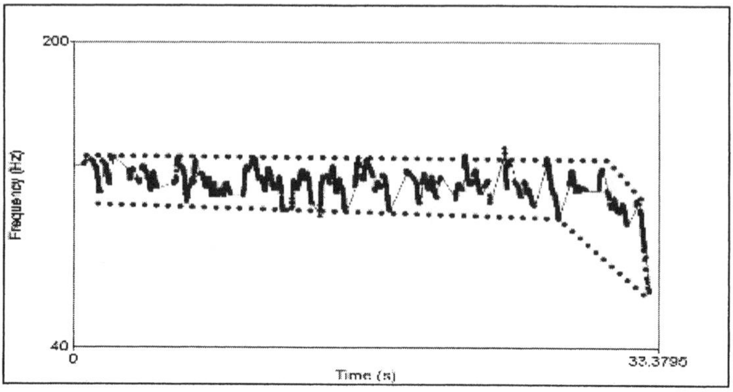

Figure 12a

البرنامج بيقدم شكره للأستاذ الشاعر الكبير محمد إبراهيم
أبو سنه وألف شكر لحضرتك يافندم و سعدنا بلقائك النهارده #

/ʔilbir'na:mig bij'ʔaddim 'šukruh lilʔus'ta:z ʔiš'ša:ʕir ʔilka'bi:r mu'ħammad ʔib'ra:him ʔabu 'sinna wi 'ʔalf 'šukr li'ħadritak ja'fandim wi sa'ʕidna bili'qa: ʔak ʔinna'harda #/

"The program thanks the great poet Mohammad Ibrahim Abo Sinna, thanks to you sir and we were happy to have you today."

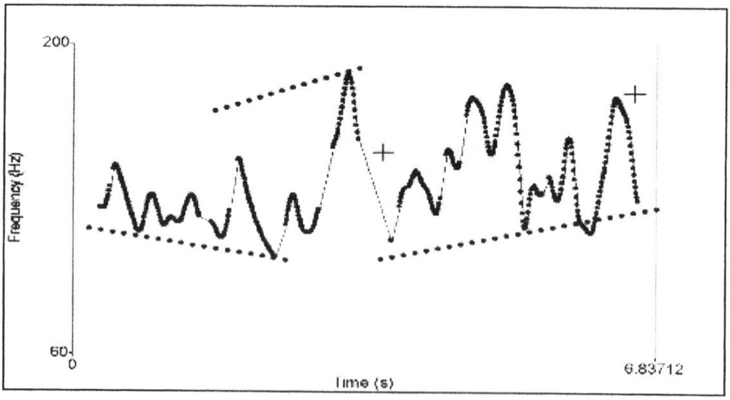

Figure 12b

لكن زوجي ما أن سمع هذا الاقتراح +
عن طبيبي المعالج +

/la'kinna 'zawgi ma'ʔan 'samiʕa 'ha:ða ʔalʔiqti'raħ + ʕan 'ṭabi:bi ʔalmu'ʕa:lig + /

"As soon as my husband heard that suggestion about my doctor,"

Note. The dotted trend lines in both figures show the interactive characteristics of level and span of pitch accents.

REFERENCES

Angoujard, Jean-Pierre. 1990. *Metrical Structure of Arabic*. Dordrecht: Foris.

Badawii, Alsa'iid. 1973. *Mustawayaat al'Arabiyya Al-Mu'aaṣira fii Miṣr: Baħth fii 'alaaqat al-lugha bi-al-ħaḍaara*. Cairo: Daar al-Ma'aarif.

Birkeland, Harris. 1952. *Growth and Structure of the Egyptian Arabic Dialects*. Oslo: Dybwad.

El-Dalee, Mohammad 1999. "Fundamental Problems of Intonation in Arabic". *Arab Journal for the Humanities* 67.9-32.

Hirst, Daniel, Albert Di Cristo & Rober Espesser. 2000. "Levels of Representation and Levels of Analysis for the Description of Intonation Systems". *Prosody: Theory and experiment--studies presented to Gosta Bruce* ed. by Merle Horne, 37-88. Dordrecht: Kluwer.

Ladd, Robert. 1996. *Intonational Phonology*. Cambridge: Cambridge University Press.

_____. 1984. "Declination: A review and some hypotheses". *Phonology Yearbook* 1.53-74.

_____. 1983a. "Phonological Features of Intonation Peaks". *Language* 59.721-759.

_____. 1983b. "Levels versus Configurations Revisited". *Essays in Honor of Charles F. Hockett* ed. by F. B. Agard, G. B. Kelley, A. Makkai & V. B. Makkai, 93-131. Leiden: Brill.

Pierrehumbert, Janet. 1980. *The Phonology and Phonetics of English Intonation*. Ph.D. dissertation, MIT.

Rifaat, Khaled. 1991. *The Intonation of Arabic: An experimental study*. Ph.D. dissertation, University of Alexandria.

Schultz, David. 1981. *Diglossia and Variation in Formal Spoken Arabic in Egypt*. Ph.D. dissertation, The University of Wisconsin, Madison.

PHONOLOGICAL PROCESSES IN CONNECTED SPEECH IN COLLOQUIAL EGYPTIAN ARABIC

Hanaa Salem
Alexandria University, Egypt

1. **Introduction**

Speech is organized in a hierarchical fashion. Individual sounds are organized into syllables, syllables are grouped into words, words into sentences and sentences into utterances (an utterance is a unit of conversation bounded in either side by a relatively long pause) (Cummins 1998). Language in every day use is not conducted in terms of isolated, separate units; it is performed in connected sequences of larger units, in sentences and longer utterances (Hawkins 1992). The spaces between words in writing are used to aid the eye, but they have nothing corresponding to them in phonetic fact (Gairdner 1925). There is a difference between the way words are pronounced in isolation and in the context of connected speech (Roack 1997). Words pronounced in isolation are called citation forms. In citation forms, phonemes are hyper-articulated, meaning that the articulators fully achieve the ideal articulatory position for each phoneme in the word. In connected speech, phonemes are hypo-articulated, meaning that the articulators do not fully achieve the ideal articulatory position for each phoneme in the word (Small 1999).

Phonological processes which occur across word boundaries in connected speech are called between word processes, external sandhi[1]

[1]*Sandhi* is the Sanskrit grammarians' term for the phonological alternations that one segment may cause in another (*san* "together" *dhi* "put"). Kaisse (1985) restricted the term to refer to the syntactically conditioned phonological rules.

(Stemberger 1988) or post-lexical rules (Katamba 1989). Adult phonologies generally involve both within-word and between–word processes (Stemberger 1988). Connected speech processes are changes in the pronunciation of words in a given sentence. Each type of change has a different name such as assimilation and elision (Knight 2003).

This paper focuses on the description of between-word processes in Colloquial Egyptian Arabic (CEA). This study is concerned with the phonemic variations which occur in connected speech at word boundaries.

The extent of variation in connected speech depends on the type of speech (casual conversational speech or formal careful speech) and the rate of speech (rapid or slow speech). The variation appears more in casual conversational, rapid speech (Cruttenden 2001).

1.1 *Previous studies*

In previous works on Arabic, at least four studies were conducted on connected speech. Gairdner (1925) was based on Classical and Colloquial Arabic. Selim (1967) focused on contrasting Classical with Colloquial Arabic. Mitchell (1978) examined elision in CEA. Gaber (1986) analyzed Cairene Arabic.

The present study examines phonological processes in connected speech in CEA in Alexandria. Tables 1-2 show the consonants and vowels of CEA according to Selim (1967).

Table 1. The Consonant Phonemes of CEA according to Selim (1967)

Manner of Articulation	Voicing	Point of articulation								
		Bilabial	Labiodental	Dental	Alveolar	Palatal	Velar	Uvular	Pharyngeal	Laryngeal
Stops	voiced	b		d	ḍ		g			
Stops	voiceless			t	ṭ		k	q		ʔ
Fricatives	voiced			z	ẓ		θ		ʕ	
Fricatives	voiceless		f	s	ṣ	š	x		ħ	h
Trills	voiced				r					
Laterals	voiced			l						
Nasals	voiced	m			n					
semivowels	voiced	w				Y				

Table 2. The Short and Long Vowels of CEA according to Selim (1967)

	Short			Long		
	Front	Central	Back	Front	Central	Back
High	i		u	ii		uu
Mid				ee		oo
Low		a	A		aa	AA

2. Purpose and Importance

The aim of this paper is to study the phonological processes in connected speech of Colloquial Egyptian Arabic: the changes which occur at word boundaries in connected speech (i.e., between–word processes) such as elision and addition of a segment.

This study is important in speech synthesis. In mechanical speech, scientists must feed the machines with the changes which occur in connected speech in normal conversational speech. It will help in teaching Arabic to foreigners and in speech recognition.

3. Method

The data of this study was recorded from acts of normal conversational speech on radio which represents CEA in Alexandria. The recorded data were transcribed phonemically. Appendix 1 shows a sample of the transcribed data. The changes which occurred across word boundaries were noted and classified. This was carried out by comparing the words pronounced in connected speech for the recorded data and the same words pronounced in isolation by the author as a native speaker of CEA in Alexandria.

The phonological processes which occurred in connected speech are described. The frequency of occurrence and the calculation of the percentage of each process are shown in Figure 1, Section 4 below. A comparison was made between the results of this study and previous works on Arabic.

4. Results and Discussion

The frequencies of occurrence and the percentages of phonological processes in connected speech occurring at word boundaries in the data of this study are illustrated in Figure 1.

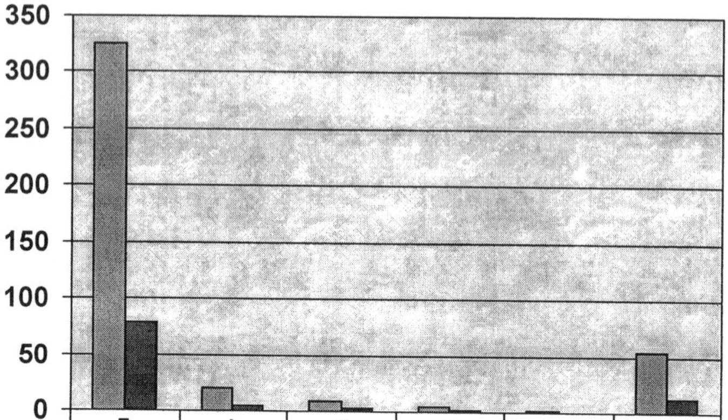

	E	A	Æ	Ç	As	Vs
NO	326	20	10	4	2	54
%	78.37	4.8	2.4	0.96	0.48	12.98

Figure1. The frequencies of occurrence and the percentages of phonological processes in connected speech in CEA.[2]

Figure 1 shows that elision is the most frequent process, then vowel shortening. The order of the other phonological processes are addition, then addition and elision at the same sequence across word boundaries and, finally, gemination and assimilation

4.1 *Elision*

Elision means the disappearance of one or more sounds in connected speech which would be present in a word pronounced in isolation (Neel 2002). Elision occurs more in fast casual speech (Knight 2003). The results indicated that elision is the most frequent process in connected speech. This result support the previous works on other languages, i.e., elision is very common in every language in connected speech.

[2]Note: E = Elision; A = Addition; Æ = Addition & Elision; Vs = Vowel shortening; G = Gemination; As = Assimilation.

4.1.1 *Consonant elision*

4.1.1.1 *Elision of /ʔ/*

The results reveal that the non-radical initial glottal stop /ʔ/ is elided either alone or together with a following vowel, when it preceded by another word. This finding is supported by Gairdner's and (1925) and Gaber's (1986) studies. The data of the present study confirmed Gairdner (1925) who reported that the glottal stop that replaces Classical / q / is never elided (e.g., *wala ʔa:dir* "and not able").

The data show that the glottal stop in the definite article {-ʔil} is always deleted as illustrated in example (1) below.[3]

(1)

Isolated words	Connected speech
تدخل # المينا	تدخل المينا
"enter" # "the port"	"enter the port"
/'titxul/ /**ʔ**il'mina/	/titxu**lil**'mina/
'CVC.CVC CVC.'CV.CV	CVC.CV.**CVC**.'CV.CV

Thus, the structure of the syllables of words in connected speech is changed than that in isolated words.

4.1.1.2 *Elision of /ʔi/*

The word initial glottal stop with a following close vowel /i/ is deleted as shown in example (2).

(2)

Isolated words	Connected speech
ده # أنت	ده أنت
"that" # "you"	"that is you"
/da/ /'**ʔ**inta/	/'danta/
CV 'CVC.CV	'CVC.CV

Elision of /ʔi/ caused a re-syllabication by reducing the number of syllables from three to two syllables. The structure and number of

[3]C = consonant; V = Vowel; . = syllable boundary; # = Word boundaries; ' = Stress; / / = Phonemic transcription.

syllables of words in connected speech is changed than is the case in isolated words.

4.1.1.3 *Elision of /ʔa/*

The word initial glottal stop with a following open vowel /a/ is deleted as shown in example (3).

(3)

Isolated words	Connected speech
أنا # أخدته	أنا أخدته
"I" # "took it"	"I took it"
/ˈʔana/ /**ʔa**ˈxattu/	/ʔanaˈxattu/
ˈCV.CV CV.ˈCVC.CV	CV.CV.ˈCVC.CV

The elision of the initial syllable /ʔa/ reduced the number of syllables in connected speech.

4.1.1.4 *Elision of /h/*

The results showed that word final position /h/ is elided across word boundaries. This finding is supported by Mielke (2003) who reported that /h/ is deleted word-finally in casual speech in Arabic.

Most of the previous work in English described /h/ as an example of the most obvious deletion of consonant (Hawkin 1992, Murad 2003). Mielki (2003) introduced a good explanation for the elision of /h/ in the study of /h/ perceptibility in Turkish, Arabic, English and French. He indicated that /h/ is a perceptually weak sound, vulnerable both to misperception and to deletion. Traditional Arab grammarians (Al-khalil, Sibawayhi, and Ibn Jinni) described /h/ as a weak and hidden sound. An example of word final elision /h/ is given in (4) below.

(4)

Isolated words	Connected speech
نفرح # بيه # باه	نفرح بيه باه
"We will be happy" # "with him"	"We will be happy with him"
/ˈnifraħ/ /ˈbi:**h**/ /ˈbaʔa/	/nifraħbiˈbaʔa/
ˈCVC.CVC ˈCVV**C** ˈCV.CV	CVC.CVC.CV.ˈCV.CV

The syllable structure of the word containing the elision of /h/ in connected speech is changed than that in isolated words.

The data showed that two or more phonological processes could occur across word boundaries as discussed below.

4.1.1.5 *Elision of /hʔi/*

Word final position /h/ and word initial position /ʔi/ of the definite article /ʔil/ are elided across word boundaries as in (5).

(5)

Isolated words	Connected speech
إيه # العبارة	إيه العبارة
"what" # "the story"	"what the story"
/ˈʔe:**h**/ /**ʔi**lʕɪˈbɑ:rɑ/	/ʔe:lʕɪˈbɑ:rɑ/
ˈCVVC CVC.CV.ˈCVV.CV	CVVC.CV.ˈCVV.CV

The number of syllables in connected speech is reduced than that in the isolated words.

4.1.1.6 *Elision of /wwaʔi/*

Word final position /wwa/ is elided together with initial syllable /ʔi/ of the following word as in (6).

(6)

Isolated words	Connected speech
ما هو # إحنا كده	ما هو إحنا كده
"This is" # "the way we are"	"This is the way we are"
/ma/ /ˈhu**wwa**/ /ˈ**ʔi**ħna/ /ˈkida/	/mahuħnaˈkida/
CV ˈCVC.CV ˈCVC.CV ˈCV.CV	CV.CVC.CV.ˈCV.CV

The number of syllables is reduced from seven syllables to five syllables in connected speech.

4.1.1.7 *Elision of /nʔi/*

The coda of the preposition /min/ "from" is elided with the initial syllable /ʔi/ of a following noun which begins with a definite article as in example (7).

(7)

Isolated words	Connected speech
من # المركب "from" # "the boat" /mi**n**/ /**ʔi**l'markib/ CVC CVC.'CVC.CVC	من المركب "from the boat" /mil'markib/ CVC.'CVC.CVC

The number of syllables in connected speech is reduced than that in the isolated words

4.1.1.8 *Elision of /laʔi/*

The second syllable of the preposition /ʕala/ "on" is elided with the initial syllable /ʔi/ of a following noun which begins with a definite article as in (8).

(8)

Isolated words	Connected speech
على # المركب "on" # "the boat" /'ʕa**la**/ /**ʔi**l'markib/ 'CV.**CV** **CVC**.'CVC.CVC	على المركب "on the boat" /ʕal'markib/ CVC.'CVC.CVC

The number of syllables is reduced from five syllables in the isolated words to three syllables in connected speech.

The results indicate that elision in the preposition /min/ or /ʕala/ occurred only before the definite article; elsewhere they are not. The data showed prevention of elision as in *min kull* "from all" and *ʕala ku'm* "on hill". This is supported by Selim (1967) who considers it an optional process.

4.1.2 *Vowel elision*

The findings showed that the closed vowel /i/ or /u/ is elided when it occurs in an unstressed syllable CV in word initial position and preceded by a word ending with an open short syllable CV. This is supported by findings in Gairdner (1925), Selim (1967) and Mitchell (1978).

4.1.2.1 *Elision of /i/*

The first vowel /i/ of the second word is elided when it occurs in an unstressed open short syllable CV and preceded by an open short syllable CV as illustrated in (9).

(9)

Isolated words	Connected speech
ده # كتير	ده كتير
"too" # "much"	"too much"
/da/ /**ki**ˈti:r/	/dakˈti:r/
CV CV.ˈCVVC	CVC.ˈCVVC

The structure and number of syllables of words in connected speech is changed than that in the isolated words.

4.1.2.2 *Elision of /u/*

The first vowel /u/ of the second word is elided when it occurs in an unstressed open short syllable CV and preceded by an open short syllable CV as in (10).

(10)

Isolated words	Connected speech
دي # دموع	دي دموع
"these are" # "tears"	"These are tears"
/di/ /**du**ˈmu:ʕ/	/didˈmu:ʕ/
CV CV. ˈCVVC	CVC. ˈCVVC

The structure and number of syllables of words in connected speech is changed than that in the isolated words.

4.2 *Addition*

Addition is the appearance of a vowel or a consonant in connected speech which was absent in words when pronounced in isolation (Gaber 1986). This process takes place because in a certain context a phonetic sequence is either difficult to pronounce or it violates the phonotactic rules of the language and therefore a vowel is introduced to break up the unacceptable consonant clusters (Baciu & Avram 2003).

4.2.1 *Consonant addition of /t/*

The consonant /t/ is added after a feminine noun (generally ending in an /a/ vowel) precedes another noun forming a noun-noun construct and the vowel /a/ is replaced by /i/ as shown in (11) below.

(11)

Isolated words	Connected speech
كوباية # شاي "cup" # "tea" /kub'ba:ja/ /' ša:j/ CVC. 'CVV.CV 'CVVC	كوباية شاي "cup of tea" /kubba:jit' ša:j/ CVC.CVV.CVC. 'CVVC

The structure and number of syllables of words in connected speech is changed than that in the isolated words. This finding is supported by Gaber (1986).

4.2.2 *Vowel addition of /i/*

A short vowel is added after the word ending in two consonant clusters, followed by another word beginning with a consonant. This rule is applied because Arabic does not allow a sequence of three consonants as illustrated in (12).

(12)

Isolated words	Connected speech
تحت # رجليك "under" # "your legs" /'taħt/ /rig'le:k/ 'CVCC CVC. 'CVVC	تحت رجليك "under your legs" /taħtɪrig'le:k/ CVC.CV.CVC.'CVVC

The structure and number of syllables of words in connected speech is changed than that in the isolated words. This result confirms Gairdner's (1925), Selim's (1967) and Gaber's (1986) findings.

4.3 *Addition and elision*

4.3.1 *Addition of /i/ and elision of /i/*

The vowel which is added at word boundaries to avoid the sequence of three consonants may cause a deletion of the first vowel in a following word (due to vowel elision process discussed in 4.1.2). This result is supported by Gairdner (1925). Example (13) illustrates this phenomenon.

(13)

Isolated words	Connected speech
ما تخش # تمدد	ما تخش تمدد
"go to" # "sleep"	"Go to sleep!"
/matˈxušš/ /t**i**ˈmaddid/	/matxuššɪtˈmaddid/
CVC.ˈCVCC CV.ˈCVC.CVC	CVC.CVC.CVC.ˈCVC.CVC

The structure and number of syllables of words in connected speech is changed than that in the isolated words.

4.3.2 *Addition of /t/ and elision of /ʔ/*

Three phonological processes occur at word boundaries comprising the addition of /t/ to the feminine noun, the vowel /a/ is replaced by /i/ and the deletion of the onset /ʔ/ in a following word. This phenomenon is illustrated in (14) below.

(14)

Isolated words	Connected speech
قمة # السعادة	قمة السعادة
"top" # "happiness"	"top of happiness"
/ˈqimm**a**/ /**ʔ**issaˈʕa:da/	/qimm**it**issaˈʕa:da/
ˈCVC.CV CVC.CV.ˈCVV.CV	CVC.CV.CVC.CV.ˈCVV.CV

4.4 *Vowel Shortening*

The results of this study indicated that vowel shortening in CEA is the second frequent process.

4.4.1 *Shortening of /ii/*

The long vowel /ii/ of the preposition /fii/ is shortened in connected speech as in (15) below.

(15)

Isolated words	Connected speech
في # وسط	في وسط
"in" # "middle"	"in a middle"
/fii/ /ˈwisṭ /	/fiˈwisṭ/
CVV ˈCVCC	CV.ˈCVCC

4.4.2 *Shortening of /aa/*

The long vowel /aa/ of the interjection /jaa/ is shortened in connected speech as illustrated in example (16).

(16)

Isolated words	Connected speech
يا # بنتي	يا بنتي
"O" # "my daughter"	"O my daughter!"
/jaa/ /ˈbinti/	/jaˈbinti/
CVV ˈCVC.CV	CV.ˈCVC.CV

This result lends support to Gairdner's (1925) argument who reported that long vowels lose their length when the syllable occurs in unstressed syllable.

4.4.3 *Vowel shortening and vowel elision*

Two phonological processes occurred at word boundaries: vowel shortening of the particle and elision of the first vowel /i/ in the syllable CV as in (17) and (18), respectively.

(17)

Isolated words	Connected speech
يا # سليم	يا سليم
"O !" # Seleem	"O ! Seleem"
/jaa/ /siˈliːm/	/jasˈliːm/
CVV CV.CVVC	CVC.ˈCVVC

(18)

Isolated words	Connected speech
في # صباعي	في صباعي
"in" # "my finger"	"in my finger"
/f**ii**/ /ṣ**u**'baːʕi/	/fiṣb'aːʕi/
CVV CV.'CVV.CV	CVC.'CVV.CV

In (17) the long vowel /aa/ of the interjection /jaa/ is shortened and the first vowel in the syllable CV of a following word is elided in connected speech. In (18) the long vowel /ii/ of the interjection /fii/ is shortened and the first vowel /u/ in the syllable CV of a following word is elided in connected speech.

4.4.4 *Vowel shortening and elision of /ʔi/*

Two phonological processes occurred at word boundaries: vowel shortening and elision of the first syllable /ʔi/ of a following word as illustrated in (19) below.

(19)

Isolated words	Connected speech
فى # الكلام	فى الكلام
"in" # "the speech"	"in the speech"
/f**ii**/ /**ʔi**kka'laam/	/fikka'laam/
CVV **CVC**.CV.'CVVC	CVC.CV.'CVVC

4.5 *Gemination*

The data showed germination occurring at word boundaries in connected speech. When the coda of a word and the onset of the following word were identical consonants, they formed a germination as illustrated in (20) and (21).

(20)

Isolated words	Connected speech
تلعب # بعرايسها	تلعب بعرايسها
"she plays" # "with her dolls"	"She plays with her dolls"
/'tilʕab/ /biʕara'jisha/	/tilʕabbiʕara'jisha/
CVC.CV**C** **C**V.CV.CV.'CVC.CV	CVC.CV**C**.CV.CV.CV.'CVC.CV

(21)

Isolated words	Connected speech
أوراقك # كلها	أوراقك كلها
"all" # "your papers"	"all your papers"
/aw'raaʔak/ /kul'laha/	/aw'raaʔakkul'laha/
CV.'CVV.CVC CVC.'CV.CV	CV.'CVV.CVC.CVC.'CV.CV

The study conducted by Maneva (1999) on consonant germination in Bulgarian indicated that the two identical consonants at the phonological level are almost always produced as one consonant with longer duration. This result confirms that there is no gaps between words in connected speech.

4.6 *Assimilation*

Assimilation is the process or result of two sounds becoming identical or similar, due to the influence of one upon the other (Hartmann & Stork 1973). In connected speech, assimilation occurred when sounds that belonged to one word caused changes in sounds belonging to other words (Knight 2003). This assimilation phenomenon is illustrated in (22).

(22)

Isolated words	Connected speech
سعادة # البيه	سعاة البيه
"highness" # "Bek"	"Highness Bek"
/sa'ʕaadit/ /ʔil'beeh/	/saʕat'tilbe/
CV.'CVV.CVC CVC.'CVVC	CV.CVC.'CVC.CV

The vowel /i/ in syllable final position of the first word and word initial /ʔ/ of a following word are elided and /d/ changed to /t/ before /t/ forming a regressive complete assimilation. The assimilated consonants occurred at word boundaries.

5. **Conclusion**

The analyzed data of the present study led to the following conclusions:

1. Elision is the most frequent connected speech process in CEA.

2. CEA tends to shorten the vowel
3. Elision, vowel shortening and assimilation produce speech economy. In connected speech, these processes make sound sequences easier to pronounce
4. Two or more phonological processes could occur across word boundaries
5. Elision and addition across word boundaries cause a resyllabification of words in connected speech.

Appendix:
Sample data of connected speech in CEA in Alexandria

الحمد لله يا بنى إن ربنا مد فى عمري لحد ما شفتك دكتور ملو هدومك يا شهاب

/ʔilħamduˈlilla ˈyabni ʔinnirɑbˈbina maddif ʕumrilħadˈdima šuftak dukˈtoor malwihˈduumak yašˈhaab/

إيه لزمتها الدموع دي لوقتي

/ʔelazmithadduˈmuuʕ dilˈwaʔti/

سيبه سيبه ما هو إحنا كده يا دكتور نفرحوا نعيط نزعلوا نعيط

/ˈsiibu ˈsiibu maˈhuħna kida yadukˈtoor nifrɑħunˈʕayyɑṭnizʕalunˈʕayyɑṭ/

دي دموع الفرح يا بني

/didˈmuuʕilfaraħ yabni/

الود ودي آخد بعضى وأروح أعد فى المينا جنب البضاعة لغاية ما تخرج من الجمرك و تتباع

/ʔilwiddiwiddaxud baʕḍi waˈruuħaʕud filˈmina gambil biˈḍɑɑʕɑl ˈɣaayit maˈtuxrug migˈgumruk wititˈbaaʕ/

يبقى فى الحالات دي توحش الست دينا بقى.

/yibʔa filħaˈlaat di tiwˈħašissittiˈdina ˈbaʔa /

أصل الإجراءات دي طويلة قوى ، و حتاخد لها أسبوع على الأقل.

/ʔɑṣlilʔigrɑˈʔɑat diṭɑˈwiilɑ ˈʔawi wiħaˈtaxud ˈlaha ʔizˈbuuʕ ʕalʔɑˈʔɑll/

البضاعة دي أنا حاطط فيها تلات تربع راس مالي ياقنديل.

/ʔilbiˈḍɑɑʕɑ dinaˈħɑɑṭiṭ ˈfiiha talat ˈtirbaʕ ˈrɑɑs ˈmaali ya ʔanˈdiil /

REFERENCES

Baciu, Ileana & Andrei A. Avram. 2003. "English Phonetic and Phonological Theories: 20th Century approaches".[http://www.unibuc.ro/ebooks/filologie/mateescu/pdf/67.pdf]

Cruttenden, Alan. 2001. *Gimson's Pronunciation of English*. London: Arnold.

Cummins, Fred. 1998. "Sound Patterns in Human Language: Syllables". [http://www.ling.nwu.edu/~fcummins/teach/B07/syllables.html]

Gaber, A. 1986. *Sounds of Arabic*. Giza, Egypt: New Offset Printing Shop.

Gairdner, W. H. 1925. *The Phonetics of Arabic*. London: Oxford University Press.

Hartmann, R. R. K. & F. C. Stork. 1973. *Dictionary of Language and Linguistics*. London: Applied Sciences Publishers.

Hawkins, Peter. 1992. *Introducing Phonology*. London: Routledge.

Kaisse, Ellen M. 1985. *Connected Speech: The interaction of syntax and phonology*. London: Academic Press.

Katamba, Frances.1989. *An Introduction to Phonology*. London: Longman.

Knight, Rachael-Anne. 2003. "Understanding English Variation". University of Surrey. [http://www.rachaelanne.co.uk/teaching/uev/uev4.doc]

Maneva, Blagovesta. 1999. "A Temporal Model of Consonant Gemination in Bulgarian". [http://wwwrdesc.pu.acad.bg/fassbl3/ Blagovesta_Maneva.htm]

Mielki, Jeff. 2003. "Interplay between Perceptual and Contrast: /h/ perceptibility in Turkish, Arabic, English and French". Paper presented at the Second International Conference on Contrast in Phonology, Toronto, Canada. [http://www.ling.ohiostate.edu/~mielki/papers/MielkiContrast.pdf]

Mitchell, T. F. 1978. *An Introduction to Colloquial Egyptian Arabic*. Oxford: Oxford University Press.

Murad, Tareq. 2003. "Phonology: Phonological processes". [http://www.sakhnin.macam. ac.il/english1/phonology.htm]

Neel, Amy T. 2002. "Connected Speech and Coarticulation". University of Mexico. [http//www personal rdg ac uk/~llsroah/phon2/assoareli-into htm]

Roack, Peter. 1997. *English Phonetics and Phonology*. Cambridge: Cambridge: University Press.

Selim, George Dimitri. 1967. "Some Contrasts between Classical and Egyptian Arabic". *Linguistic Studies in Memory of Richard Slade Harrell* ed. by Don Graham Stuart, 133-152. Washington, DC: Georgetown University Press.

Small, Larry H. 1999. *Fundamentals of Phonetics*. Boston: Allyn & Bacon.

Stemberger, Joseph Paul 1988. "Between-word Processes in Child Phonology". *Journal of Child Language* 15.39-61.

ROOT FORMATION AND POLYSEMIC ORGANIZATION IN ARABIC LEXICON
A PROBABILISTIC MODEL

Lazhar Zanned
University of Manouba, Tunisia

1. Introduction

Describing the organization of the lexicon in natural languages is one of the most challenging tasks in linguistic theory. It is the core of the system where the minimal links are established between sound and meaning. The lexicon is one of the basic components of the grammar in different linguistic theories. Many issues related to the lexicon are dealt with from different theoretical frameworks in linguistics and from many different disciplines in human sciences.

The Arabic lexicon has many peculiarities related to the nature of nonconcatenative morphology in Arabic, in particular, and in Semitic languages in general. Many theoretical claims are proposed in an attempt to describe its phonological and semantic organization. Traditional Arab grammarians and lexicographers established the basic issues within a classical framework. In modern times, there are two main directions in dealing with the lexicon in Arabic and Semitic languages. One is a reconstruction of the paths that the roots in Semitic languages took through their evolution where it is assumed that the root was biconsonantal and became triconsonantal (Ehret 1989, 1995; Bohas 1991, 1993; Bohas et al. 1993; Bohas et al. 1994). The other is a combinatory account based on the semiotic values of the binary sequences that make the word in Arabic (Barbot 1997, 1998). The prosodic account proposed by McCarthy (1979, 1981) in nonlinear phonology (Leben 1973, Goldsmith 1976, etc.,) is a convenient framework to handle many aspects of the organization of the lexicon in Arabic.

In this paper, we deal with polysemy in the Arabic lexicon and we argue that the rules governing root formation generate polysemy in an unavoidable way. The first part will focus on a brief review of the most important models dealing with the organization of roots in the Arabic lexicon. In the second part, the probabilistic model will be presented (the principles and rules generating roots in the Arabic lexicon) with a special focus on polysemy, morphology, and the different devices working to minimize the phenomenon of polysemy.

2. Root Formation in Arabic Lexicon

2.1 *The historical perpective*

2.1.1 *The Extensionnist Model*

Ehret (1989) deals with the origin of the third consonant in Semitic roots through an internal reconstruction applied to Arabic. The main claim is that triliterals in Semitic languages are extended forms of once-simpler roots (biliterals). This assumption is built on comparative evidence between Semitic and the other branches of Afroasiatic. The strategy in dealing with the phenomenon in Arabic consists of taking sets of triliteral roots which share similar or related meanings and have in common the first and the second consonants but differ in the third consonant. Then the roots that have the same consonant at the third position are grouped and compared to sort out the possible semantic variation related to the presence of that consonant in them. Ehret claims that third consonants probably originated in pre-Protosemitic as verbal extension suffixes expressing some kind of grammatical meanings. He concluded that all or nearly all of the consonants of Protoafroasiatic had developed the capacity to act as verb extensions, modifying the meaning of simple biconsonantal roots in regularly definable ways. This strategy is based on the fact that verbal morphology requires a triliteral surface that made the biconsonantal roots convert formally into triconsonantals by extension or by gemination of the second consonant. Gemination is a formal operation motivated by triliteral verbal morphology rather than semantics.

Ehret deals with polysemy and observes that it is a common phenomenon in Semitic at both levels: triconsonantal roots and the underlying reconstructed biconsonantal roots. Polysemy in Semitic roots is the result of many once-distinct Afroasiatic roots falling together in pre-Proto- and Proto-Semitic. The collapsing of many root-shapes into one occurred at both vocalic and consonantal levels.

The Extensionist Model elaborated by Ehret fails to explain many phenomena related to polysemy in Arabic roots. Although we agree that there is a kind of collapsing at the origin of polysemy, we can not admit easily that the single consonant at the level of the root may have some kind of grammatical meaning modifying the meaning of the biconsontal root that it extends. All the semantic values attributed to single consonants at the extension position are withdrawn from the semantic features proper to the lexical meaning expressed by the root. Since every third consonant in the root is supposed to bear a grammatical meaning, Ehret's model is challenged when this consonant is geminated because gemination is considered a formal operation. So there may be roots where this consonant has a meaning and has none in others. This fact remains unexplained in the Extensionnist framework:

qaram	<to retain, hold>	*m fortative	
qardam	<to take all>	*m fortative	*d durative
našam	<to be covered with black and white spots or dots>	*m fortative	
hmm	< to melt fat >	none	

The Extensionist Model can not handle polysemy conceived as having many different unrelated meanings. The data presented in Ehret (1989) include many roots, each of which may have different meanings and figures in different subsets. Regardless of the problem of the number of consonants and the reconstructed meaning for the extension consonant, a root like *nšr* (where *r is diffusive) has the following list of meanings as presented in Ehret (1989:194-195):

nšr	
našar	- to blow
našar	- to spread out, unfold or unroll, exhibit, spread about, make publicly known, communicate, propagate, separate, disperse, be scattered.

našar	- to put forth leaves, grass, to sprout forth, raise the dead, revive, be revived, rise from the dead.
našar	- to cut or carve wood, saw,
našar	- to have the mange.

The main aim is to explain how these different meanings are grouped together at the triconsonantal root *nšr* in Arabic or at the level of the biconsonantal reconstructed root corresponding to each subset elaborated by Ehret. The samples given above figure in different subsets having one biconsonantal reconstructed root:

*nš to overflow,
to imbibe, absorb, take in liquid, etc.
to send away, take away,
to rise,
to make a low sound,
to cut.

Assuming that the reconstructed root with its different unrelated meanings belongs to an early ancient period of Semitic (called pre-Proto-Semitic or Proto-Afroasiatic, etc) goes against the minimal requirements of communication: words must be distinct in phonetic form to insure the distinction between meanings.

2.1.2 *The Epenthesis Model*

Brockelmann claimed that there is a tendency in Arabic to make the correspondence between a group of defined consonants in Arabic roots and a certain semantic value or notion. There are many roots composed of a velar and a dental consonant which are specialized in the meaning of 'cutting'. Following Brockelmann, Bohas (1993) considers that the Arabic lexicon is organized in three levels:

1. The matrix: the combination of two articulatory places: (dental, labial), (velar, dental), etc.
2. The etymon: the combination of two consonants, each belonging to one place of articulation. The order of the two consonants is reversible.
3. The root: the consonantal shape that the etymon takes in morphological forms (triconsonantal or other). This realization may be achieved by spreading (diffusion), epenthesis and reduplication. These operations take

place when the biconsonantal etymon is mapped to a triconsonantal template.

The etymon *bx* <subside>, for example, when mapped onto a triconsonantal template, takes four consonantal shapes: the third c-slot is filled by spreading one of the two consonants or by epenthesis of the glides w/y in the median or the final position. If it is mapped onto a quadriliteral template, it will go through reduplication of both consonants as follows:

/bx/			
Spreading	(bxx)	baxxa	<subside after anger>
Epenthesis			
Middle	(bwx)	baaxa	<subside>
final	(bxw)	baxaa	<subside>
Reduplication	(bxbx)	tabaxbaxa	<subside>

The epenthesis operation works on glides (w, y), other sonorants (ħ, ʕ, ʔ, h), following Diakonoff, 1988 and Petracek, 1987 and l, r, m, and n. A biconsonantal root may take the following realizations:

CCi	
Reduplication:	
CCiCi	reduplication of the second consonant
CCCi	reduplication of the first consonant
CCiCCi	total reduplication
Epenthesis of a glide or a sonorant (S):	
SCCi	initial epenthesis
CSCi	median epenthesis
CCiS	final epenthesis

The model proposed by Bohas, though based on statistical evidence from Arabic data and other Semitic languages, leaves many questions unanswered, because it is trapped in the idea of biliterality and root expansion by sonorants. In fact, if the basic principle of biliterality is accepted and the semantic relation is established between the different roots related to different *etymons* and matrices, there are too many aspects which can not be handled by this model.

Looking for a biliteral hypothetical stage which evolved to a triliteral or quadriliteral one is problematic. The principles (articulatory, phonological, semantic, etc.,) governing the formation of matrices and *etymons* are not clear.

There are many matrices sharing one common semantic field. This fact is unexplained and the idea of specialized Matrices in semantic values is not strong enough to explain this phenomenon:

dental, labial:	bt	btt	batta	< to cut>
dental, velar :	qt	qtt	qatta	< to cut>
labial, velar :	jb	jbb	jabba	< to cut>

Following the realizations of any etymon, there are roots related to that etymon and bear a different meaning which has no relation to the meaning shared by the other roots belonging to that etymon. The epenthesis model can not explain the polysemy in the Arabic lexicon and how a single root may have many different unrelated meanings.

The epenthesis model claims that basically the sonorants are the unique elements that occur in *etymons* expansion. That is true in part, but if we take any etymon, there are many roots related to that etymon where the third element is neither a glide nor a sonorant and they bear the same semantic value. The matrix (velar, dental) comprise many *etymons*, one of which is the etymon /qṭ/ and /ṭq/ when reversed. It has many roots related to it that are expanded by consonants and has the same meaning as those expanded by sonorants:

/qṭ /	qṭb	qaṭaba	<cut, divide by cutting>
	qṭf	qaṭafa	<cull-pluck-gather>

The epenthesis model predicts that every etymon is realized by reduplication or epenthesis. The epenthesized segment is always a single sonorant at one of the three positions in the root. However there are many quadriliteral roots which are related to the triliteral ones by sharing a common semantic value: /qṭ/ → *qʕṭ*, *qʕṭb*, *qʕṭr*, *qʕṭl* "throw someone to the ground".

This situation can not be handled by the epenthesis model. It is not clear, for example, whether epenthesis occurs by two sonorants (ʕ and r in *qʕṭr*, or ʕ and l in *qʕṭl*), or by a sonorant and a consonant (ʕ and b in *qʕṭb*). The status of sonorants is not clear. They are conceived as being expansion elements which fill in the third C-slot required by the template. There are many roots with two sonorants (e.g., *hdm* "destroy") and three sonorants (e.g., *mlħ* "salt", *ħlm* "dream", *lmʕ* "shine", etc.,).

2.2 *The semiotic perspective: The Combinatory Model*

Barbot (1998) refutes the concept of the root, the different ways of root formation (extension, epenthesis, metathesis, etc.,), the concept of root and template as the basic components of the word. Barbot instead argues that lexical items are organized in a network based on the phonetic and semiotic interconnections called *naħt akbar*. The lexicon is divided into two levels: deep structure and surface structure. At the deep structure, the combinatory system between minimal sequences each corresponding to a minimal isoseme is working to generate the different minimal units that combine freely to form elements making together a semiotic network. At the surface, these combinations are mapped onto the rigid morphological templates and take the shape of a numbered consonantal root (bi-, tri-, quadri-, and quinqueliteral). The root shape is not determined at the combinatory level: combinations are not ordered. Barbot considers the linear representation not valid to show the semiotic and phonetic connections sequence-isoseme and suggests graphs based on a multidirectional and simultaneous representation of the correlations between elements making a semantic field.

Although the semiotic approach is tempting and the concept of network is strong enough to handle the organization of any system, the model of *naħt akbar* fails to answer many questions related to the organization of Arabic lexicon in general and to polysemy, in particular. Connections would explain how different elements are grouped together in a unifying common aspect but can not explain how different elements are grouped together with no common aspect at all. Different roots or words may be grouped together regarding their common meanings but the fact that different meanings are grouped together in one single root or word has to be explained.

Root formation can not be conceived as an independent operation, of any kind, cut away from the morphological shape in which it is licensed. Surface-deep structure dichotomy, as drawn by Barbot, can not be the key to understand polysemy since the distinction between those two levels can be accepted neither in a generativist conception nor in the common linguistic sense.

3. The Probabilistic Model

In Zanned (1998) we tried to describe the organization of Arabic lexicon: the phonological and semantic aspects of root formation related to morphology and syntax. The main focus of this paper is to deal with polysemy as a general phenomenon governing the majority of lexical entries in the Arabic lexicon.

3.1 *Basic principles*

All rules and principles discussed in this section are based on data analysis. Our concern is not to determine the origin of things or their evolution. Our conclusions may agree with some facts suggested in some of the models reviewed above and may disagree with some of them. In both cases, they are based on the description of the data.

We assume that roots in Arabic are triconsonanatal, quadriconsonantal and quinqueconsonantal. Roots are structures of ordered consonantal positions. The number of the positions determines the number of the consonantal segments in the root. The order of the consonants determines the identity of the root in both the aspects of phonological shape and semantic aspect.

Consonants are elements of the articulatory space framed between labials and laryngeals. The articulatory space is a continuum of domains and places of articulation. Places of articulation are established in a diffusive way through history in an attempt to explore all the articulatory possibilities required by the distinction between meanings expressed by language. There are 28 consonantal articulatory places in Arabic. Roots are formed by combination of consonants from different articulatory places. Combination of consonants is a chaotic combination between places of articulation within the limits of the articulatory space.

The positional structure of the root is governed by phonological rules such as features, places and so forth. Root formation in Arabic is governed by the law of the variable and the fixed. This law yields listemes of twenty-eight roots. The fixed element (F) is the consonant which is common to the elements of the same listeme. The variable element (V) is the consonant in which all the elements of the listeme differ. The value of F and V is one of the 28 consonants in Arabic. It is determined in many ways discussed below.

Assuming that the root is triconsonantal, the combination of F and V allows three kinds of structures regarding the number of the Fs and Vs in each one. Fs and Vs are ordered in the root positional structure as follows:

a. structure operating with three Fs.
b. structure operating with three Vs.
c. structure operating with both Fs and Vs.

Structure (a) generates a series of unlimited copies of the same root in language use by different speakers in different times. The values of Fs are determined once in language and make the phonetic shape (identity) of the root as a lexical entry. Suppose that Fs have the values in a root F1=k , F2=t, F3= b, then ktb is the only root generated by this structure:

F1F2F3
k t b <write>
k t b
k t b
...

Structure (b) generates all the triliteral roots in Arabic Lexicon. This structure includes all the roots, since it is the most abstract one. It is the absolute triconsonantal root structure:

V1V2V3
k t b <write>
r q d <sleep>
q r ʔ <read>
...

Structure (c), which operates with Fs and Vs, is of two kinds:

c. 1) structure operating with two Vs and one F.
2) structure operating with two Fs and one V.

Each one of c-1 and c-2 yields three schemes regarding the position of F in c-1 and V in c-2 at the level of the triconsonantal root shape: initial, median, and final.

Each one of the three schemes of c-1 generates listemes of roots with a common consonant corresponding to the F position. Structure c-1 affords the phonetic link between different roots without any obligatory semantic relation between them. The structure c-1 (below) is a source of the consonantal phonetic network providing any kind of arbitrary use or arrangement of the roots in the Arabic lexicon: rhymes in poetry and prose, lexical entries in dictionaries, language games, cross words, scrabbles, etc.

c.1 (V1,V2,F)

V1V2F		V1FV2		FV1V2	
k t b	<write>	r q d	<sleep>	ħ f ẓ	<learn>
r k b	<ride>	y q n	<be sure>	ħ r q	<burn>
- - b		- q -		ħ - -	

The schemes of c-2 are productive in root formation in Arabic on the basis of the correspondence between phonetic and semantic forms. The two Fs, regardless of their positions, are the elements common to the listeme and make its phonetic identity and semantic unity: lexical field. The members of each listeme differ in the V element which insures the distinction (opposition) at the phonological aspect corresponding to a semantic distinction between the different roots included in the same listeme. The schemes of c-2 are responsible for the polysemic organization of roots in the Arabic lexicon as we will demonstrate below.

Triliteral root formation in the Arabic lexicon, based on the law of F and V, is governed by the following structures:

C1C2C3	a.	V1V2V3	triconsonantal root
	b.	F1F2F3	root : lexical entry
	c.1.	V1V2F	
		V1FV2	phonetic network: resemblance
		FV1V2	at the F element
	c.2.	F1F2V	
		F1VF2	root listemes : phonetic and
		VF1F2	semantic correspondences

3.2 *Root formation*: *(F1, F2, V)*

The schemes of c-2, above, work to generate triliteral roots. Then any consonant in this kind of root may be at the position of Fs or Vs. In this way, any root, in theory, is generated by the three schemes of c-2, being the point where they cross or intersect. We call the three copies of the same root which are common to the three listemes, each generated by one scheme, the archiroot. The archiroot is polysemic.

Every listeme is governed by two principles which unite its members in both cases: phonological and semantic. The phonological principle is based on the articulatory continuum at the position of the V element, so the listeme will have 28 roots, in theory, where Vs are consonants from the different articulatory places situated between the labials and the laryngeals. The semantic principle is based on the semantic continuum: the different roots in the listeme bear common semantic features since they belong to one semantic field and may differ in particular semantic features. The semantic distinction corresponds to the phonological distinction.

Consider, for example, the Archiroot *hjr*. The structure which generates *hjr* is c-2 with its three schemes. Every consonant of the root *hjr* may be the value of V or F in the different listemes generated by the schemes. For every scheme, the values of Fs are given, and the value of V is one of the 28 consonants in Arabic. Listemes are given below following the places in the articulatory space:

F1F2V	F1VF2	VF1F2
h j -	h - r	- j r
h j b	h b r	b j r
h j m	h m r	m j r
h j w	h w r	w j r
h j f	h f r	f j r
h j θ	h θ r	θ j r
h j ð	h ð r	ð j r
h j ẓ	h ẓ r	ẓ j r
h j t	h t r	t j r
h j d	h d r	d j r
h j ṭ	h ṭ r	ṭ j r
h j n	h n r	n j r
h j s	h s r	s j r
h j z	h z r	z j r
h j ṣ	h ṣ r	ṣ j r
h j ḍ	h ḍ r	ḍ j r
h j l	h l r	l j r
h j r1	h r r	r j r

h j š	h š r	š j r
h j j	**<u>h j r2</u>**	j j r
h j y	h y r	y j r
h j k	h k r	k j r
h j q	h q r	q j r
h j x	h x r	x j r
h j γ	h γ r	γ j r
h j ʕ	h ʕ r	ʕ j r
h j ħ	h ħ r	ħ j r
h j h	h h r	**<u>h j r 3</u>**
h j ʔ	h ʔ r	ʔ j r

The three listemes have the form *hjr* in common. Every occurrence of *hjr* is a copy of the archiroot, having its meaning through the listeme in which it is included. Since every listeme is a semantic field, then each copy of *hjr* bears a meaning related to the listeme in which it is included, following the semantic principle governing the formation of the listemes. Then, at least, three different unrelated meanings, are grouped together and coincide in one single root: the archiroot. This fact makes of every archiroot a polysemic lexical entry.

Root formation in Arabic is probabilistic. Polysemy is the result of the crossing of many listemes in a common phonetic form (Archiroot). The Archiroot *hjr*, for example, is a hybrid element in both phonetic and semantic aspects.

Lexicographers put all the lexical items related to the phonetic form *hjr* in one lexical entry in the dictionary, grouping together the different meanings and sorting out polysemy. Some of them tried to explain polysemy by establishing some kinds of logical relations between the different meanings in an attempt to handle the variety of uses. Others related polysemy to the variety of uses in the different eras and places in the history of Arabic. These explanations fail to handle polysemy, because there is no relation between the different meanings related to one singular root. The root *hjr*, for example, is many lexical entries in the mental Lexicon of Arabic speakers, since they make easily the difference between its different uses and meanings.

3.2.1 *The archiroot: the stratified polysemy*

The meanings related to the entry *hjr* are usually presented in the dictionary following the morphological forms. Any verbal or nominal form may have different meanings. This kind of presentation is not convenient for our issue in this paper. The different meanings will be presented in sets of common semantic features. The sets will be divided into main or principle meanings and secondary meanings. This distinction is based on the frequency of the bearing forms and the ability of the meaning to fit in one set or not.

In this section, we deal with the main meanings in the framework of the Probabilistic Model. For the secondary meanings, see section 3.2.3. Consider the main meanings of *hjr* below:

hjr (main meanings):

a) to break with, leave, forsake, renounce, emigrate, flee
b) to be delirious, to dote, talk at random, idle obscene talk, custom, manner, habit, mockery.
c) to travel in the heat of midday, hottest time of the day, hot midday, bitter dry plant.

The archiroot *hjr* is formed by the crossing of the three listemes generated by the schemes of c-2. Our model predicts that each copy of the root *hjr* in each listeme bears a meaning which fits easily in the semantic field or general notion related to the attested roots in the listeme.

Consider the first scheme of c-2 (F1F2V) where the values are as follows: F1=h, F2=j, V= any C of 28. The general notion common to the listeme is <leave, break> including many related notions like separation, ceasing (activity, state), cutting relations, leaving a place, discordance, etc. Thirteen out of fifteen attested roots bear this general notion. This gives one source of the meanings related to *hjr*:

F1F2V = hj- <leave, break>
hjb -urge, beat, hasten, thrust.
hjm -overthrow, pull down, drive away, expel.
hjw -direct a satire against, lampoon, biting speech, mokery.
hjf -be thrown into disorder (country).
hjn -deem or call one mean, damage one's honor or character.
hjs -repel-prevent, desist, murmur to one's self.
hjz -make a secret communication to.
hjl -let the camels go at large, *haajil*: who travels often.
hjr1 a)-break with, leave, forsake, renounce, emigrate, flee.

hjš -drive slowly, bring about mischief, discord.
hjj -leave one's country, emigrate.
hjʕ -sleep, subside, cease, appease one's hunger.
hjʔ -subside, cease, start doing something and interrupt it.

The second scheme of c-2 (F1VF2) where the values are: F1=h, F2=r,V= any C of 28, generates a listeme of roots having in common the general notion of <talk> including many related notions: organs of talk, ways of talk, contents of talk, frequency of talk, etc. Fourteen out of fifteen attested roots bear this general notion:

F1VF2= h-r <talk, dote, insult>
hbr -habr: a sudden pause made at the beginning of Koranic verse considered a very bad reading, to mangle (with the teeth).
hmr -*hammaar*: talkative, garrulous -*hamrat*: growling, snarling.
hwr -surmise-suspect of.
hðr -talk nonsense, foolishly, get delirious, dote, be talkative.
htr -idle frivolous talk, insult, call names, confusion of mind, get delirious from old age.
hdr -roar, give utterance, bray, shout.
hţr -humility of a beggar.
hzr -thrash, ill treat, slander badly.
hrr -whine, yelp, detest, abhor, twang, *haarr*, weak from old age, decrepit, be of a bad character.
hšr -pertness, haughtiness, ingratitude.
hjr2 b) –get delirious, dote, talk at random, idle obscene talk, custom, manner, habit, mockery.
hyr -*yahyarr*: dispute, quarrel/*hayyir* (who engages inconsiderately in...)
hkr -admiration, astonishment.
hʕr -*hayʕarat*: a woman who always shouts and quarrels.

The third scheme of c-2 (VF1F2), where F1=j, F2=r, V= any C of 28, generates a listeme of roots sharing the notions of thirst, liquid (water, wine, blood, etc.,) and heat (natural or man-made). Fourteen out of nineteen attested roots bear this general notion:

VF1F2 = -jr < heat, thirst, liquid>
bjr -be full of water or milk without being satiated.
mjr -be thirsty, have the stomach full of water without being satiated, instill milk into someone's mouth.
wjr -instil medecine into a child's mouth.

fjr -drain water by breaking the rock, open a passage, a channel for water, blood, etc., to flow forth.
θjr -mix anything with the fermenting juice of a fruit-VIII: break forth (water, blood) flow over copiously.
djr -be confused in one's speech, drunk, *dayjuur*: dry herbage.
njr -be seized with violent thirst, to boil water or milk with a hot stone, heat, hot time of the day.
sjr -heat the stove, start a fire.
šjr -to lay clothes on the *mišjar-mišjar*: a tripod made of three pieces of wood used to lay clothes on.
xjr -*xaajir*: the noise that water makes at the bottom of a mountain.
ʕjr -to become dry on the teeth and stuck (saliva)-V: to cover oneself with *miʕjar*, *ʕijaar*: veil for women, hat (men).
ħjr -stove of a pipe, brazier of a hookah.
hjr3 c)- travel in the heat of midday, hottest time of the day, hot midday, bitter dry plant.
ʔjr -bake bricks by the heat of fire.

The main meanings related to the Archiroot *hjr* may be represented as three layers anchored to one consonantal shape at which three listemes cross, each from a different departure depending on the values of Fs and Vs. Thus, *hjr* is three lexical entries in one as shown in Table1.

Table 1. ARCHIROOT *hjr*

Schemes	F1F2V	F1VF2	VF1F2
Values	h j -	h - r	- j r
Roots	h j r 1	h j r 2	h j r 3
Meanings	break	talk	heat
Listeme notions	break, leave, separate	talk, dote, insult	heat, thirst, liquid

3.2.2 *The Archiroot: the network of stratified polysemy*

The Probabilistic Model predicts that any root in Arabic lexicon is the crossing point of three listemes, each one generated by one of the schemes in c-2. Any root is an Archiroot. This phenomenon generates a network of relations between different listemes and roots: any listeme crosses with two other listemes in any root. Every root is common to three listemes since it is the point where they cross. Any root, when taken outside the network, is polysemic but it is monosemic when anchored in a determined listeme.

To test this hypothesis, we will follow the network starting at *njr* included in the listeme containing *hjr3* with the common notion <heat, thirst, liquid>. Another path which consists of the root *hwr* will be examined later. The main attested meanings of *njr* are the following:

a) be seized with violent thirst, be seized with violent thirst from eating bitter seeds or drinking sour milk; heat, hot time of the day; to boil water or milk with a hot stone.
b) cut or plane wood, hew, carve wood.
c) hasten, beat to make moving fast.

The scheme F1F2V, where F1=n,F2=j, V= any C of 28, generates a listeme of roots with a common general notion related to the <speed, velocity> in movement (any activity, walk, travel, etc.,). Fifteen out of eighteen attested roots bear this general notion:

F1F2V = nj- < speed, velocity>
njb -to flee, escape, *najiib*: fleet camel.
njm -to appear suddenly.
njw -run and pass by rapidly (horse, man, etc.,), hurry, hasten, flight, speed.
njf -II: to start taking away (wind blowing the dunes).
njθ -to make a scream of distress, shout for help.
njd -start running, *minjadat*: small stick used to hasten the horse, swift and strong, to sweat, prespire.
njz -complete speedily and successfully.
njl -walk fast, throw away, fling, kick .
njr1 c)- hasten, beat to make moving fast.
njš -hunt up the game, excite, initiate, hasten.
njj -hasten, hurry, *najuuj*: swift, agile.
njx -rapid torrent which digs in the ground, carry off parts of a precipice (torrent, water).
njʕ -go after good food, water, good pasture.
njħ -*naajiħ, najiiħ*: fast walk.
njh -come suddenly upon, I,V: drive away, expel someone with insults.

The scheme F1VF2, where F1=n, F2=r, V= any C of 28, generates a listeme of roots with a common general notion related to <piercing, spreading, carving>. Twenty out of twenty-three attested roots bear this general notion:

F1VF2 = n-r < piercing-spreading-carving>
nbr -pierce through and draw the lance quickly back, cattle, fly.
nmr -*namirat*: crooked piece of sharp metal in which a piece of meat is hanged to catch wild animals.
nwr -brand an animal with a piece of iron heated in fire-tattoo.
nfr -flee and disperse.
nθr -scatter, spread, wound so as to make the blood run.
nðr -doom to death, place in front in a combat, amulet for wounds.
ntr -pierce, tear with hands or teeth.
ndr -be isolated, cut into something so as to drop the cut piece.
nṭr -II: tear off (Tunisian Arabic).
nsr -tear off-tear with the beak-wound, II divide into small parts.
nṣr -water abundantly, conduct water into a river, *naaṣir*: canal, channel, gutter.
nšr -spread, cut or carve wood.
njr2 b)-cut or plane wood, hew, carve wood.
nkr -blood, pus etc issuing from the body.
nqr -pierce through, excavate, carve or engrave in stone, pierce with the beak.
nxr -be carious, putrid.
nγr -make the blood run out abundantly.
nʕr -making the blood to spurt out with a noise.
nħr -slaughter a camel, wound at the collar bone.
nhr -dig until one meets with water, enlarge the bed of a river.

The scheme VF1F2 generates *njr3* with F1=j, F2=r and V=any C of 28. *njr3* fits in the listeme containing *hjr3* presented above. The Archiroot *njr* is presented Table 2.

Table 2. ARCHIROOT *njr*

Scheme	F1F2V	F1VF2	VF1F2
Values	n j -	n - r	- j r
Roots	n j r 1	n j r 2	n j r 3
Meanings	hasten	carve	heat
Listeme notions	speed, velocity	piercing, spreading, carving	heat, thirst, liquid

The other sample is the Archiroot *hwr*. The attested main meanings of *hwr* are the following:

a) -cause, incite, rush heading into (danger etc).
b) -suspect of, surmise.
c) -turn from, make to roll down.
d) -be demolished, fall, destroy, pull down, fall from on high.

The scheme F1F2V, where F1=h, F2=w, V=any C of 28 generates the following listeme of roots that share the notion of <rush, incite, excite>. Fifteen out of nineteen attested roots bear this general notion:

F1F2V = hw- < rush, incite, excite>
hwb -cry to, call to, bid, invite.
hwm -mad love, crazed.
hwf -*huufun*: stupid, idle good for nothing fellow.
hwð -*hawðal*: be swift, shaken, swing to and fro, trotter.
hwt -cry out, call to.
hwd -make someone drunk (a drink), abate.
hws -II: excite a keen desire, give one pleasure, *hawas*: folly, passionate desire.
hwl -frighten, inspire with terror.
hwr1 a)-cause, incite, rush heading into (danger etc).
hwš -be excited, agitated, II: confuse, agitate, set dogs against one another, III: quarrel, VI: be set against.
hwj -*hawija*: be foolish, thoughtless and precipitate, blow violently, precipitation.
hwy -IV: rush against with something, X: madden with love.
hwk -*hawika*: be half mad / V: *tahawwaka*: rush into danger.
hwʕ -be easily excited, be about to attack one another, *hawaʕun*: disorderly desire.
hwʔ -*hawaʔ*: purpose, intend.

The scheme F1VF2 where F1=h, F2=r, V=any C of 28 generates *hwr2* in the listeme including *hjr2* with the notion of <talk-dote-insult>:

F1VF2 = h-r < talk, dote, insult>
...
hwr2 b)- suspect of, surmise, suspicion.
...
hjr2 b)- to be delirious, dote, talk at random, idle obscene talk.

The scheme VF1F2 where F1=w, F2=r, V=any C of 28 generates a listeme of roots sharing notions related to the circular movement <turn-

roll> with its ramifications: the direction of the movement, the place, the nature of activity, the object and any aspect which suggests a circular movement. All the attested roots bear this notion:

VF1F2 = -wr < turn-roll>
bwr -*baaʔir*: hole in the ground to make fire in.
mwr -oscillate, swing from side to side, roam, rove-, IV: raise dust.
fwr -boil, babble, throw out foam and froth.
θwr -stir and rise-rise and spread.
ðwr -frighten, *ðuurat*: earth, dust.
twr -flow, roam about, *taarat*: turn, time.
dwr -move in a circle, revolve, walk around.
ṭwr -go around anything, *ṭawr*: turn, time.
nwr -avoid something, walk around respecting a certain distance.
swr -get into one's head, II surround a place with walls.
zwr -IX: deviate, go astray, swerve aside.
ṣwr -bend, incline to one side, turn the face towards.
ḍwr -V: writhe, roar from hunger.
šwr -exhibit, show (a horse, a slave).
jwr -astray from, IV: to cause one to turn aside from.
kwr -wind in a spiral form, roll along, dig in the ground, fall down.
qwr -surround the pray, make a circular cut or a round hole in any thing.
xwr -IV: turn, twist, bend.
γwr -make a foray, a raid on a tribe.
ʕwr -take away, to cause one to turn aside from.
ħwr -return, come back, *ħaaʔir*: confused, perplexed.
hwr3 c)-turn from, make to roll down.
ʔwr -flee and disperse, be in violent anger, have a sexual intercourse with a woman, motion of clouds, north-wind.

The Archiroot *hwr* is generated as in Table 3.

Table 3. Archiroot *hwr*

Scheme	F1F2V	F1VF2	VF1F2
Values	h w -	h - r	-w r
Roots	hwr1	hwr2	hwr3
Meanings	incite-rush	suspect	turn-roll
Listeme notion	rush, incite, excite	talk, dote, insult	turn, roll

We can imagine a wide operation, following the different archiroots and their consonantal interconnections with their corresponding semantic interconnections, to go through the nebula of Arabic Lexicon. Any root taken for itself has no value. It acquires its value(s) from the network in which it is involved. Any root should be considered at two levels: as a member of a listeme (a root) and as a crossing point between three listemes (archiroot).

The network of the crossing listemes in the different roots studied above shows the way polysemy in Arabic Lexicon works. This network may take the representation illustrated in Table 4:

Table 4. Lexicon

	... ARCHIROOT			ARCHIROOT		ARCHIROOT ...	
Scheme	F1F2V	F1VF2	VF1F2	F1F2V	F1VF2	F1F2V	VF1F2
Values	n j -	n - r	- j r	h j -	h - r	h w -	-w r
	---	---	---	---	---	---	---
	---	---	---	---	hwr2	hwr1	hwr3
	---	---	---	---	---	---	---
Roots	---	---	hjr3	hjr1	hjr2	---	---
	---	---	---	---	---	---	---
	njr1	njr2	njr3	---	---	---	---
	---	---	---	---	---	---	---
Meanings	hasten	carve	heat	break	suspect	incite	roll

3.2.3 *The archiroot: the stratified polysemy in the network of crossing listemes*

The Archiroot is the product of crossing listemes: each listeme charges the root copy with a semantic value making polysemy a current phenomenon. Meanings are assumed to be organized in strata in the Archiroot. The strata are of two kinds, depending on the level of crossing: the main crossing level would give the main meanings to the Archiroot; the secondary crossing level gives secondary meanings.

In this section, secondary meanings of the Archiroot *hjr* are examined. They are considered secondary, because they do not occur in frequent morphological forms related to *hjr*. They are the result of another layer of stratified polysemy related to the crossing between listemes. The Archiroot gets one main meaning from each listeme in which it fits following the scheme that generates it. This meaning is related to the most frequent notion in the listemes. However, being member of the three listemes at the same time enables the Archiroot to bear some other meanings, proper to one or many roots in one listeme or more. The secondary meaning in an Archiroot like *hjr* may be one of the main meanings of the Archiroot which is the source of that meaning, since every root is an Archiroot. Explaining the presence of these secondary meanings at the Archiroot, using the same general principles elaborated above insures the explanatory adequacy of the Probabilistic Model.

The different secondary meanings of *hjr* are presented with the forms bearing them and their lexical category (Verb, N=Noun, A=Adjective), followed by their possible sources in the different listemes generated by the schemes:

a) -rope used to tie up the foot of the camel-bridle, halter-chain:[hajar (Verb), hijaar(N), hajr(N)]
F1F2V = h j -
hjj -hujj: yoke.
VF1F2 = - j r
mjr -*mijaar*: a rope used to tie the last articulation of the foot of a camel to its higher part, so that the camel stands only on three feet and can not move.
bjr -*ʔabjar* (pl. *bujr*): cable, thick rope (of a ship).
sjr -*saajuur*: a piece of wood tied to the neck of a dog.
šjr -*šijaar*: a piece of wood put into the mouth of a small goat to prevent it from milking its mother.

b) -good, excellent, noble, handsome, beautiful-first rate: [*hajar*(Verb), *hajr*(A), *hijr*(A), *haajir*(A), *haajiriyy*(A)]
F1F2V = h j -
hjn -*hijaan*: be from a noble family and well-considered (man, woman), white camel(s) from an excellent race.
VF1F2 = - j r
njr -najr : root- origin, be well-considered, esteemed.
ħjr -*ʔaħjaaru-l-xayl*: horses of pure race chosen to propagate the race.

c) -large cistern, watering-trough, large cup used to drink: [*hajiir* (N)]
F1F2V = hj -
hjm -*hajm*/*hajam*: large cup used to drink.
VF1F2 = -jr
mjr -*maajuur*: pottery vase.
ʔjr -maajuur : red pottery vase -earthen pot- flower vase.

d) -slight meal, lunch taken at midday:[*hajuuriyy* (N)]
VF1F2 = -jr

njr -IV: give to someone the food called *najiirat*: milk mixed with butter and flour.

e) -diadem: [hijaar(N)]
VF1F2 = -jr
ʕjr -*ʕijaar*: veil worn over the face or head.
miʕjar: veil for women, turban.

f) -chain put at the neck as an ornament:[hijaar(N)]
VF1F2 = -jr
sjr -*saajuur*: chain at the neck (leather, metal).

g) -curdeled milk (coagulated):[*hajiir*(A)]
F1F2V = hj-
hjm -*hajiimatun*: milk put in a new goat skin intended to be drunk.
hjs -*haajisatun*: turned milk in a goat skin.
hjn -*hajiin*: milk that is no longer colostrum but is not yet totally pure.
F1VF2 = h-r
hdr -*haadir*: milk when it starts to curdle by being thicker at the surface and thin below the surface.
VF1F2 = -jr
njr -najiirat: milk mixed with flour.

h) -numerous, very great number: [*muhjir*(A)]
F1F2V = hj-
hjm -*hajmat*: herd of camels from forty to one hundred.
hjš -haajišat:great number of men which is just formed -new band of men.
F1VF2 = h-r
hwr -*hawr* : considerable great herd of sheep.
hrr -*hurr*: big quantity of water or milk.
hyr -*yahyarr*: great quantity of water.
VF1F2 = -jr
mjr -*majr*: big quantity, numerous army.
fjr -*fajar*: considerable quantity of wealth.
θjr -*θujrat*: a band of men separated from the others.

i) -to be (very) old :[*hajrat*(A)], an old stallion which has no force to cover females: [*hajiir*(A)], who walks heavily, slowly:[*hajir*(A)]
F1F2V = hj-
hjf -hijaff : old ostrich.
hjl -hawjal : someone who is heavy and walks slowly.
F1VF2 = h-r
hmr -*hamiirat*, *haymarat*: old woman.
hwr -*haar*: weak from old age (man).
hyr -*hayyaar*: weak (man).
hʕr -*hayʕarat*: old woman.

j) -architect :[haajiriyy (N)]
VF1F2 = -jr

ħjr -*ħajjaar*: stone builder, sculptor.

ʔjr -*ʔaajurr*: bricks.

k) -year, some time [*hajrat*(N), *hajr* (N)]; applying the notion of emigration to time periods (year, some time) may be related to the Islamic calendar based on the Prophet Muhammad's emigration from Mecca to Medina which was the starting year of the *hijriy* calendar.

l) -citizen, inhabitant of a town: [*haajiriyy* (A)]; this meaning is related to the main meaning of *hjr1*: <*hijrat*: removal from the desert to a town>.

3.3 *Archiroot-morphology interface: polysemy and triliteral verb templates*

In theory, every linguistic unit should be monosemic. However, the formation of the root in Arabic Lexicon makes polysemy unavoidable with the different layers of meanings grouped together at the phonetic shape of the Archiroot within the network of crossing listemes. Nevertheless, there exists in Arabic Morphology a systematic tendency to reduce polysemy. The existence of different verbal forms or nominal forms with a single meaning is limited in Arabic. If that fact is attested, even in a limited amount, then it supports many of our claims. Morphology and consonantal roots interaction needs to be investigated deeply in the framework of the Probabilistic Model. So far we noticed that the same root, *ħsb*, for example, takes three verbal forms with different vocalic segments expressing three different lexical meanings:

C1aC2aC3	ħasab	aa	(past)	<count, calculate>
C1aC2iC3	ħasib	ai	(past)	<opine, surmise, think, consider>
C1aC2uC3	ħasub	au	(past)	<be esteemed, of a noble family>

The traditional account of this fact bears on the nature of the vocalic segments. Each verbal template corresponds to a kind of lexical meaning (action, thought, process, etc.,). Therefore, the distinction between the three meanings is related to the verbal template and the root bears all of them. However, we may posit the problem in an opposite way: how can a single root take three different verbal forms?

We assume that *ħsb* is an Archiroot made of three copies of *ħsb*, each one being generated separately by the schemes of c-2. *ħsb* is the crossing point between three listemes where each copy is a member of a listeme of roots having one unifying semantic field. In verbal derivation the root will take the corresponding form to its meaning. The distinction is at the heart of the system and does not occur after the root generation.

The scheme F1F2V where F1=H, F2=s, V=any C of 28, generates a listeme of roots sharing the notions of <cut, select, separate>. Calculation has to be conceived in its primitive aspect related to the early stages of human evolution: counting with one's fingers is a kind of separation, selection and accumulation. The perfective-active verbal form corresponding to the notions <cut, select, separate> is C1aC2aC3 giving *ħasab* from *ħsb1*. This verbal form denotes transitivity. Ten out of eleven attested roots bear this general notion:

F1F2V = ħs-<cut-select-separate>
ħsb1 -*ħasab*: count, calculate, suffice.
ħsm -cut, cut off, substract, deduct, *ħaasim*: destructive.
ħsw -to drink a little at a time.
ħsf -shave off the moustache, select, mow, reap.
ħsd -envy, grudge, punish (God).
ħss -burn, make vanish, kill, VII: be extracted, fall out, decay (teeth).
ħsl -select and separate the worst part
ħsr -peel the skin of the tree, pare, shell, destroy with a forceful movement.
ħsy -dig for water in saturated ground, to drink a little at a time.
ħsk -*ħskl*: slaughter a young camel.

The scheme F1VF2 where F1=H,F2=b,V=any C of 28, generates a listeme of roots sharing the notion of <think, feel, attitude>. The perfective verbal form corresponding to the notions <think, feel, attitude> is C1aC2iC3 giving *ħasib* from *ħsb2*. Ten out of fourteen attested roots bear this general notion:

F1VF2 = ħ-b < think, feel, attitude>
ħbb -love, desire, wish.
ħwb -sin, transgress,V-be sorrowful, grieved, *ħawb*:love of a mother.
ħdb -be devoted, benevolent, kind, compassionate.
ħṭb -help, calumniate, *ʔaħṭabu*: miserable.
ħnb -feel pity for someone.
ħsb2 *ħasib*: opine, surmise, think, consider.
ħzb -cause anxiety, *ħaazib*: difficult, grave, serious.
ħrb -be ceased with anger, have a fit of rage.
ħšb -be ceased with anger, irritate.
ħjb -*ħijaab*: modesty.

The scheme VF1F2 where F1=s,F2=b,V=any C of 28, generates a listeme of roots sharing the notions related to a well- considered social position or personal moral qualities inherited or acquired: <family-esteem-nobleness>.The perfective verbal form corresponding to the notions <family-esteem-nobleness> is C1aC2uC3 giving *ħasub* from ħsb3. Seven out of seven attested roots bear this notion:

VF1F2 = -sb < family, esteem, nobleness>
nsb -origin, genealogy, pedigree, family, *ħasab wa nasab*:descent and personal merit.
lsb -bite, wip.
rsb -*raasib*: gentle, mild, meek, fit in.
ksb -gather riches, knowledge, *kaasib*: executor.
qsb -be hard.
ʕsb -cover (stallion), *ʕasuub*: chief of a tribe, descendant.
ħsb3 -ħasub: be esteemed, be of a noble family.

The Archiroot *ħsb* is represented in the following Table 5 below.

Table 5. *ħsb* Archiroot

Scheme	F1F2V	F1VF2	VF1F2
Values	ħ s -	ħ - b	- s b
Roots	ħsb1	ħsb2	ħsb3
Meanings	count	opine	be noble
Listeme notions	cut, select	think, feel	family, esteem
Verbal forms	C1aC2aC3	C1aC2iC3	C1aC2uC3
Action/state	transitive	temporary	permanent

3.4 *Reduplication in the Probabilistic framework*

Reduplication (gemination) in Arabic roots is of two kinds: partial and total. Partial reduplication applies to the second C of the triliteral root. Total reduplication applies to two consonantal roots giving quadriconsonantal ones. Bohas assumes reduplication as a particular way of root realization. His argument is based on the semantic relation (strong or weak) between different roots having in common the two consonants of the etymon. The argument is sound but reduplication itself is not founded. It is conceived as a phenomenon apart, unrelated to other rules of the root formation. Ehret (1989) considers reduplication a formal operation applying to biliteral roots to meet the triconsonantal shape required by the verbal form.

In the Probabilistic Model, not only polysemy is taken into account, but also the root formation rules, including reduplication, are established considering semantic and phonological articulatory aspects. Reduplication is part of the principles governing root formation. A reduplicated root is part of the listeme generated by the different schemes of the structure c-2: F1F2V, F1VF2, and VF1F2.

Starting from the canonical schemes, reduplication occurs when the value of V is the same as the immediate preceding or following F. This device generates the following forms of reduplication:

F1F2V	where F2=V	C1C2C2	(productive)
F1VF2	where F1=V	*C1C1C2	(non productive)
VF1F2	where V=F1	*C1C1C2	(non productive)

Forms (b) and (c) are ruled out by a general principle governing root formation in Arabic Lexicon which stipulates that C1 and C2 of the triliteral roots must be distinct. However exceptions are attested but they are very limited (*bbr*: *babr* "tiger"). Form (a) where C2 is identical to C3 is productive. The listemes generated by the schemes of C-2 including the Archiroot *hjr* are presented briefly showing how reduplication works while ruling out the unattested roots:

Schemes	F1F2V	F1VF2	VF1F2
Values of F	h j -	h - r	- j r
Root listemes	......	.....	......
	h j r1	h r r	*r j r
	......	.....	......
	h j j	h j r2	*j j r
	......	......	......
	*h j h	*h h r	h j r3
	......	....	....

Some pairs of corresponding roots (the non-reduplicated and the reduplicated) are presented (from the data analyzed above) as follows:

F1F2V = hj-
hjr1 -break with, leave, forsake, renounce, emigrate, flee.
hjj -leave one's country, emigrate.

F1VF2 = h-r
hjr2 -get delirious, dote, talk at random, idle obscene talk, custom, manner, habit, mockery.
hrr -whine, yelp, detest, abhor, twang, decrepit, be of a bad character.
F1F2V = nj-
njr1 -hasten, beat to make moving fast.
njj -hasten, hurry, *najuuj*: swift, agile.
F1F2V = ћs-
ћsb1 -*ћasab*: count, calculate, suffice.
ћss -burn, make vanish, kill, VII, be extracted, fall out, decay (teeth).
F1VF2 = ћ-b
ћsb2 -*ћasib*: opine, surmise, think, consider.
ћbb -love, desire, wish.

The phenomena of reduplication represents an entry to a huge network between archiroots in Arabic Lexicon. Following the principles established in the Probabilistic framework, *hjj* is an Archiroot and therefore polysemic, since it includes three copies (roots) each generated separately by one scheme of the structure c-2 as follows:

F1F2V where F1=h, F2=j, V=any C of 28 → hjj1
F1VF2 where F1=h, F2=j, V=any C of 28 → hjj2
VF1F2 where F1=j, F2=j, V=any C of 28 → hjj3

The archiroot *hjj* has the following principle meanings:

hjj:
a) leave one's country, emigrate.
b) X: stimulate, hasten (e.g., voyagers so they walk fast), *hajaaj*: fast walk.
c) pull down, be deep set or sunk (eye).
hajiij: deep valley-long beach through which voyagers always go to their destinations, to descend into a valley.

The scheme F1F2V with the values hj- generates a listeme dominated by the notion of < break> (as we have seen above) as follows:

F1F2V = hj- <leave, break>
....

hjr1 - break with, leave, forsake, renounce, emigrate, flee.
....
hjj1 a)-leave one's country-emigrate.
....

The other scheme F1VF2 where the values are h-j generates a listeme dominated by the notion of <agitation-rapid move> including some related meanings like violence in speech or behavior, confusion, excitement, etc. Ten out of ten attested roots share this notion:

F1VF2 = h-j <agitation, rapid move>
hbj -beat repeatedly, *habjat*: blow .
hmj -dispatch (well or badly), IV: strain the nerves in running, *haamij*: violent.
hwj -blow violently, be foolish, thoughtless and precipitate, tempest, hurricane.
hdj -walk with a tremble, trotter, V: tremble.
hnj -V- come to life and move (fetus).
hzj -quiver (tremble, to shake tremulously).
hlj -*hulj*: confused dreams.
hrj -excitement, agitation, tumult, great confusion.
hjj2 -X: stimulate, excite, hasten (voyagers so they walk fast), *hajaaj*: fast walk.
hyj -be agitated, be moved with a violent passion, rush against and attack.

The third scheme VF1F2 with the values -jj generates a listeme of roots sharing the notions of <deep, sunk, liquid>. The relation may not be obvious. It has to be built through the elementary features making the image of an eye (shape, color, brightness, physiological liquid (tears) etc., being deep or sunk (far in the distance) into the head with both salient brows. This image fits into the general notion shared by the roots in the listeme that is built up by the depth (pull down, cut, the movement of the liquid (bleed, flow, drink, water, blood, etc.), the movement in the liquid (sink, plunge) and the extraction of the liquid. Sixteen out of nineteen attested roots bear this general notion as follows:

VF1F2 = -jj <deep, sunk, liquid>
bjj -prick open (a tumour), pierce.
mjj -spit out.
fjj -cut in two, split into several pieces, open wide, interval, an opening between two mountains, a wide road between two moutains, *ʔifjiij*: narrow and deep valley.

sjj -drink, be just returning from a journey.
θjj -flow abundantly, *θajj*: blood pouring out from a victim.
ẓjj -call for assistance in a battle.
njj -bleed, suppurate.
zjj -pierce with the point of a lance.
ḍjj -drop, drip (rain, tent), to be armed to the teeth.
ljj -be deep, deeply furrowed, plunge to the deep, *lujj*: enormous quantity, immense mass of water.
šjj -plough the sea, mix the wine with water, cleave or break the head, be wounded or scarred, *šujjat*: broken skull, wound in the head.
xjj -to descend into the valley, *xajxaj*: hide his feeling deep in the heart.
ʕjj -to descend into the valley.
ħjj -to probe, to sound (a wound), extraction of sequestrum, incision (of a wound, a head wound), *ħijjat*: hole (in the ear lobe).
hjj3 -be deep set or sunk (eye), *hajiij*: far-stretching deep valley, far, stretching beach through which voyagers are always going to their destinations.
ʔjj -*ʔajaaj*: bitter, salt.

3.5 *The Continuum: phonology-semantic interface*

One of the basic principles of root formation established in the Probabilistic Model consists of the correspondence between the phonological and semantic aspects. The listeme generated by the schemes of c-2 is supposed to be governed by the articulatory continuum which corresponds to a semantic continuum. The two Fs are common to the whole members of the listeme and make its phonetic identity. All the roots sharing the same Fs bear a common general notion which makes the semantic unity of the listeme.

The consonants representing the values of Vs are the distinctive segments between roots in the same listeme. This distinction corresponds to a semantic distinction between different meanings proper to any root from the listeme. This distinction is not systematic because of the synonymy relation between roots in the listeme due to use or to lexicographer's definitions.

The correspondence is established between phonological features and semantic features. It may be of three levels as follows:

a) The two Fs in the listeme bear the semantic field.
b) The phonological features which are common to a group of Vs in the listeme correspond to semantic features common to a subfield of the general semantic field.

c) The particular phonological feature of a variable consonant corresponds to a particular semantic feature born by the particular root in the listeme.

Table 6. Representation of a listeme generated by the scheme F1VF2 = n-r <piercing, spreading, carving>

Action	Agent	Object	Manner	Place	Instrument	Goal
nbr pierce	human	flesh	quickly	into+out	lance	kill and withdraw
nmr pierce	-	mouth	0	-	metal	catch _
nwr burn	-	skin	heated	surface	-	mark__
nfr disperse	0	0	all directions	surface	0	flee
nθr spread	0	0	circular	surface	0	0
wound	0	flesh	through	into	0	run blood
nðr stand	human	0	0	front	0	combat
amulet	-	wound	0	0	0	heel__
ndr cut	-	0	drop	into	0	0
ntr tear	-	0	0	0	hands-teeth	0
nṭr tear	-	0	off	surface	0	0_
nsr tear	bird	flesh	0	into	beak	0
divide	0	0	small parts	0	0	0__
nşr dig	human	earth	long	into	0	conduct water_
nšr spread	human	0	all directions	0	0	0
cut	-	wood	0	into	0	0
carve	-	-	0	surface	0	polish-design
njr2 cut	-	-	0	into	0	0
carve	-	-	0	surface	0	polish-design
nqr carve	-	stone	0	- / into	0	0
pierce	0/bird	0	0	through	0/beak	0
nxr carious	0	bone	round	inside	0	0__
nkr run	liquid	body	0	out	0	0
nγr run	blood	vein	abundance	-	0	0
nʕr spurt	blood	vein	noise	-	0	0
nħr wound	human	vein	0	collar bone	0	for food_
nhr dig	-	earth	deep	into	0	for water

To demonstrate the continuity in root formation based on the principles established in the Probabilistic Model, the listeme generated by the scheme (F1VF2=n-r) is represented in Table 6. The two Fs < n> and <r> make the phonetic identity of the listeme to which corresponds the semantic field (general notion) of <piercing, spreading, carving>. The segments corresponding to Vs in the listeme summarize the phonological features. The following semantic features (thematic roles) are entries to the classification of the different meanings related to each root in the listeme: Action, Agent, Object, Manner, Place, Instrument, and Goal. The space between lines glossing the meanings indicates the distribution of roots corresponding to the semantic differences between subsets of the semantic field (__) or differences between peculiar meanings in the same subset (_).

4. Conclusion

In this paper we tried to present an account of the organization of the lexicon in Classical Arabic in both phonological and semantic aspects. Three main issues were discussed: the root formation, the relation between the root component and Morphology and the phenomena of gemination. We argued that the formation of the roots is probabilistic, governed by schemes working with two kinds of elements: fixed and variable. Each scheme generates a listeme of roots having a general notion in common. It happens that three schemes, thus three listemes, cross at one particular root and the result is a polysemic form bearing, at least three meanings. We called this form Archiroot which comprises at least three identical consonantal copies, each one bearing its own meaning inherited from its own listeme. This fact makes polysemy unavoidable. Morphology works to minimize polysemy by establishing some kind of correspondence between the lexical meaning related to one particular copy in a particular archiroot and a particular morphological verbal or nominal template. These correspondences make each copy in an archiroot have its own derivational network. This aspect needs to be dealt with further. This will be the focus of the next step in elaborating the probabilistic model in future work. We also demonstrated that gemination is not a formal arbitrary device. Instead it is an integral part of the probabilistic functioning of root formation in Arabic lexicon. Any geminated root is an archiroot like any other regular root.

REFERENCES

Barbot, Michel. 1997. "La Voie Droite (SiraaT) de l'Islam ou le Sens au bout du Chemin". *Images et Représentations en Terre d'Islam* ed. by Hossein Beikbaghban, 143-179. Strasbourg: Université des Sciences Humaines.

Barbot, Michel & Kenza Bourja. 1998. "Le Système Lexical de l'Arabe Classique". *Luqmaan* 14:1.67-116.

Bohas, Georges. 1993. "Le PCO et la Structure des Racines". *Développements Récents en Linguistique Arabe et Sémitique* ed. by Georges Bohas, 9-44. Damascus, Syria: Publications de l'Institut Français de Damas.

_____. 1991. "Le PCO, la Composition des Racines et les Conventions d'Association". *Bulletin des Etudes Orientales* XLIII.119-137.

Bohas, Georges & Abdullah Chekayri. 1993. "Les Réalisations des Racines Bilitères en Arabe". *Semitica, Serta Philologica Constantino Tsereteli Dicata* ed. by Contini Rossini, F.A. Pennachietti & M. Tosco, 1-13. Torino, Italy: Silvio Zamorani.

Bohas, Georges & Noureddine Darfouf. 1994. "Contribution à la Réorganisation du Lexique de l'Arabe, les Etymons non-ordonnés". *Linguistica Communicatio* 5:1 et 2.55-103.

Diakonoff, M. 1988. *Afrasian Languages*. Moscow: Nauka Publishers, Central Department of Oriental Literature.

Ehret, Christopher. 1995. *Reconstructing Proto-Afroasiatic (Prot-Afrasian) Vowels, Tone, Consonants and Vocabulary*. Berkley and Los Angeles, California: University of California Press.

_____. 1989. "The Origin of Third Root Consonants in Semitic Roots: An internal reconstruction (Applied to Arabic)". *Journal of Afroasiatic Languages*. 2:2.109-202.

Goldsmith, John.1976. "An Overview of Autosegmental Phonology". *Linguistic Analysis* 2:1.23-68.

Leben, William. 1973. *Suprasegmental Phonology*. Ph.D. dissertation, MIT.

McCarthy, John. 1981. "A Prosodic Theory of Nonconcatenative Morphology". *Linguistic Inquiry* 12.373-418.

_____. 1979. *Formal Problems in Semitic Phonology and Morphology*. Ph.D. dissertation, MIT.

Zanned, Lazhar. 1998. *Lexicon in Arabic: Its formation and its relation with syntax*. Ph.D. dissertation, University of Tunis.

LIGHT VERBS IN STANDARD AND EGYPTIAN ARABIC

Amr Helmy Ibrahim
Université de Franche-Comté

1. Actualizing Nouns: A Quick Survey

One of the main issues in modern linguistics, regardless of the theoretical framework, is to explain how a language achieves its predication, that is its *ʔisnaad* إسناد or *ʔixbaar* إخبار. Since the work done for over a century in the various fields of typology, has become widely known, and at least in its broad outlines recognized, it is admitted that the main tool of predication ranges from the verb, a category common to almost all languages and for some the only one noticed by the grammatical tradition of Indo-European languages, to almost any grammatical category as it has been shown by Michel Launay (1992, 1994, 2003, and in press) for what he called "omnipredicative languages" like Classical Nahuatl.[1]

However, the precise way in which new information, a predicative association, a genuine *ʔixbaar* or *ʔisnaad* is brought to discourse, even with the verb being the main category to do so, has often been and still is, a controversial issue. As noted by W. Wright:

> "Every sentence which begins with the subject (substantive or pronoun) is called by the Arab grammarians جُملة إسْمِيَّة a nominal sentence. Wether the following predicate be a noun, or a preposition and the word it governs جار ومَجرور or a verb is a matter of indifference... What characterizes a nominal

[1]The Uto-Aztecan language of the Nahuatl people in Southern Mexico and Central America.

sentence, according to them, is the absence of a logical copula expressed by or contained in a finite verb." (1874:Vol. II, 251)

Therefore, the differences between the way predication works when centered on a verb and the way it works when centered on a noun has never, as long as we know, been studied except for a discussion about the status of the copula, and more generally, what has been called *defective verbs* الأفعال الناقصَة *ʔal-ʔafʕaal ʔal-naaqiṣa*.[2]

As a matter of fact, copulas and light verbs have sometimes been mixed up, probably because in almost all languages where both can be found, light verbs have at least two properties in common with copulas. First, they are much more of a link or a support for predication than a genuine predication. Second, they do not constitute a lexically independent category. One can say about them what Ide (1975) wrote in his grammar about copulas:

هذا وجَميع أفعال هذا الباب الثلاثةِ عَشَر تُستَعْمَل ناقِصة وتامة ما عدا ثلاثة أفعال هى ليسَ - زالَ - فَتِىء فلا تُستَعْمَل إلا ناقصَة فَقَط.

"All of the thirteen verbs of this section are used both as defective or complete verbs except three of them: *laysa*, *zaala* and *fatiʔa* which can only be defective." (Ide 1975:251)

The question could have been raised within the broader discussion around two problems: the first is the nature and the number of items that can be attached to a predicate be it verbal or nominal; the second is the nature and the effects of the opposition between *intransitivity* and *transitivity* اللازم والمُتَعَدي. It seems it would very quickly be dealt with under the assumption that *transitivity* could hold for the مَصدَر *maṣdar,* called sometimes إسم حَدَث *ʔism ħadaθ* "event nominals," in almost all cases and with the same effects that it does for the verb, and that therefore the same item that could be attached to the predicative noun could also be attached to the verb.

Nevertheless, a Tunisian researcher (Achour 1999:464) pointed out that المُبَرِّد *Al-Mubarrad* (or *Al-Mubarrid*), while arguing in his المُقتَضَب *Al-Muqtaḍab* why an intransitive verb still, from the point of view of the agent, describes a transitive process, writes:

[2]For instance, see Cohen (1985).

قَولُكَ **قامَ زَيدٌ** بِمَنزِلَةِ قَولِكَ **أحْدَثَ قِياماً** وتَعْلَم أنّ ذلكَ فيما مَضى من الدَهر وأنَّ لِلحَدَثِ مَكاناً وأنَّه على هَيْئة.

"When you say Zayd stood up it is as if you said made a standing up. You know that this occurred in the past, that it took place somewhere and had a shape." (Al-Mubarrad, Vol. 3:187-190).

Unfortunately, *Al Mubarrad* (826-900) did not elaborate. Actually, by paraphrasing the intransitive verb *yaquumu* with the complex or composite predicate *yuħdithu qiyaman* he was putting his finger on a phenomenon described for the first time in English by Poutsma (1914-26), that is more than 1,000 years later, when he wrote:

> "There is a marked tendency in Modern English to express a verbal idea by means of a combination consisting of a verb with a vague meaning and a noun of action. (...) [to give or to make an answer or reply; to pay or to give attention ; to pay, to give or to make a call; to give, to raise, to set up or to utter a cry; to drop or to make a curtsy; to make or to give a promise; to make or to pay a visit.] (...) The latter is then the real significant part of the predicate, while the former mainly serves the purpose of a connective (...) The grammatical function of the nouns in these connections is mostly that of an effective object...but owing to the connective verb having only a vague meaning, the whole combination may, from a semantic point of view, be regarded as an intransitive verb-group." (Poutsma 1914:394-6)

Poutsma's expressions "verb with a vague meaning" and "combination" will become the "light verb" and "complex predicate" of modern English Linguistics, the "verbe support" and "prédication nominale" of modern French Linguistics and the "Funktionsverb-gefüge" of modern German Linguistics. We will call them respectively in Arabic رَكيزة فعليَة *rakiiza fiʕliya* or دعامَة فعْليَة *diʕaama fiʕliyya* and إسناد إسمى *ʔisnaad ʔismii*.[3]

As far as we know, we can say of most if not all languages what was pointed out by Ray Cattell (1984) about English when he wrote:

> "It is extraordinary how little attention was given to the 'light' verbs in English by grammarians of the past. Krusinga (1932, Vol. 3:96) makes the following statement 'The absence of almost all formal distinctions in present-

[3]Light verb is also called *ʔal-fiʕl ʔal-ʕimaad* by Kchaou (2003).

day English between the parts of speech makes it easy for a word to be used in different functions. Thus, although dig is generally a verb, we can say to give a person a dig in the ribs. In the latter expression dig is used as a noun, so that the verb dig has been converted into a noun. The speaker of Modern English, however, still feels that the word is 'properly' a verb'. Apart from providing a few examples a little later, he appears to say little else about the phenomenon in a three-volume work running to some 1500 pages." (Cattell 1984:20)

2. First Analysis and Basic Properties

In English, the term light verb was first coined by Otto Jespersen (1965, Vol. 6:11):

> "The most usual meaning of sbs [substantives] derived from and identical in form with a vb [verb] is the action of an isolated instance of the action. This is particularly frequent in such everyday combinations as those illustrated in the following paragraphs after have and similar 'light' verbs. They are in accordance with the general tendency of Mod E [Modern English] to place an insignificant verb, to which the marks of person and tense are attached, before the really important idea. [**have a** care, look (peep) at, chat, wash, shave, swim, drink, smoke, ... **make a** bolt, plunge, ... **give a** sigh, groan, laugh, shout]."

However, as pointed by Cattell (1984:20), there was "no further characterization or analysis of the 'light' verbs."

The first in-depth and extensive analyses of the phenomenon, following Cattell's doctoral thesis (1969) on *give,* took place in French in the seventies within the *argument/operator transformational* framework of Harris (1968, 1970, 1988) and the *lexique-grammaire* framework of Gross (1976, 1981, 1996). A now classical reference paper of the latter (1976) became the starting point for an intensive lexical and syntactic investigation of the phenomenon that achieved an impressive coverage, first of French and Romance languages, then of a number of languages of other language families.[4]

Gross's paper points to a property of light verbs unnoticed before: the possibility of a *double analysis* of their complements, which

[4]For an extensive bibliography of works done within the framework of the Lexique-grammaire and, partly, within that of the Lexical Functional Grammar, see Ibrahim (1996, 2002) and Butt (1995).

distributional verbs,[5] in corresponding structures, do not allow. Furthermore, this property ranges over a certain number of transformations, the main one being the passive as shown, for English, in the examples below:

(1) The coalition launched an attack on a group of civilians.
(2) The coalition monitored an attack on a group of civilians.
(1a) **An attack on a group of civilians** was launched by the coalition.
(1b) **An attack** was launched by the coalition **on a group of civilians.**
(2a) **An attack on a group of civilians** was monitored by the coalition.
(2b) ***An attack** was monitored by the coalition **on a group of civilians**.

The same phenomenon, which we shall call التَحليل المُزدَوَج *ʔal-taħliil ʔal-muzdawaj*, can be stated in Arabic in (3)-(4b) below (corresponding to the English equivalents of (1)-(2b) above) in spite of the differences between English (or French) and Arabic regarding the passive:

(3) شَنَّ التَحالُفُ هُجوماً وَحْشيّا على مَجْموعَة من المَدَنيين.
šanna ʔal-taħaalufu hujuuman waħšiyyan ʕalaa
launched the-coalition attack-idef savage against
majmuuʕatin min ʔal-madaniyyiin
group-indef of the-civilians

(4) تابَعَ التَحالُفُ هُجوماً وَحْشيّا على مَجْموعَة من المَدَنيين.
taabaʕa ʔal-taħaalufu hujuuman waħšiyyan ʕalaa
monitored the-coalition attack-idef savage against
majmuuʕatin min ʔal-madaniyyiin
group-indef of the-civilians

(3a) شُنَّ هُجومٌ وَحْشيٌ على مَجْموعَة من المَدَنيين.
šunna hujuumun waħšiyyun ʕalaa majmuuʕatin
was-launched attack-idef savage against group-indef
min ʔal-madaniyyiin
of the-civilians

[5]That is, verbs that are fully predicative have a plain meaning, suffice to build an autonomus utterance and are always the core of the argument structure of an utterance. For a thorough distinction between distributional, operator, auxiliary, light or support, set and pro-verbs, see Ibrahim (2000).

(3b) وَحْشِيٌّ (حَقاً) (ذَلِكَ) الهُجومُ الذى شُنَّ على مَجْموعَة من المَدَنيين.
waħšiyyun (ħaqqan) (ðaalika) ʔal-hujuumu ʔallaðii šunna ʕalaa
savage indeed that the-atack which was-launched against
majmuuʕatin min ʔal-madaniyyiin
group-indef of the-civilians

(4a) توبِعَ هُجومٌ وَحْشِيٌّ على مَجْموعَة من المَدَنيين.
tuubiʕa hujuumun waħšiyyun ʕalaa majmuuʕatin
was-monitored attack-idef savage against group-indef
min ʔal-madaniyyiin
of the-civilians

(4b) *وَحْشِيٌّ (حَقاً) (ذَلِكَ) الهُجومُ الذى توبِعَ على مَجْموعَة من المَدَنيين.
waħšiyyun (ħaqqan) (ðaalika) ʔal-hujuumu ʔallaðii tuubiʕa ʕalaa
savage indeed that the-atack which was-monitored against
majmuuʕatin min ʔal-madaniyyiin
group-indef of the-civilians

The light verb *yašunnu* "launch" allows a double analysis of the complements *hujuumun waħšiyyun* "a savage attack" and *ʕala majmuʕatin min ʔal-madaniyin* "on a group of civilians" since (3a) and (3b) are equally grammatical while the distributional verb *yutabiʕu* "follow" does not, since (4b) is not grammatical.

This property leads to another, perhaps even more obvious, when considering Arabic than it is when we limit our scope to Indo-European languages. It is that of the very strong appropriateness تَجانُس *tajaanus* between the light verb and its object which makes the latter look semantically as a *cognate object*, that is a مَفعول مُطْلَق *mafʕuul mutlaq*: شَنَّ هُجوماً وَحْشِيّاً *šanna hujuuman waħšiyyan* is a synonym of هَجَمَ هُجوماً وَحْشِيّاً. *hajama hujuuman waħšiyyan.* This equivalence entails another syntactic property: the necessary coreference between the agent of the light verb and the agent of the process expressed by the noun. With a distributional verb one can say:

(5) The coalition monitored an attack by a militia on a group of civilians
(5) تابَعَ التَحالُفُ هُجوماً وَحْشِيّاً لقوات غَير نظاميّة على مَجْموعَة من المَدَنيين.
taabaʕa ʔal-taħaalufu hujuuman waħšiyyan li-qwwaatin
monitored the-coalition attack-indef savage for-forces
ɣayri niẓaamiyyatin ʕalaa majmuuʕatin min ʔal-madaniyyiin
not regular against group-indef of the-civilians

where it is clear that the agent of the monitoring and that of the attack in both languages are different (in English "the coalition" and in Arabic التحالف *ʔal-taħaaluf* for the *monitoring* and in English "a militia" and in Arabic قوات غير نظاميّة *quwwaatin γayra niẓaamiyyatin* for the "attack"). But it cannot be said with a light verb. Examples (6) and (7) are not grammatical:

(6) * شَنَّ التَحالُفُ هُجوماً وَحْشيّاً لقوات غَير نظاميّة على مَجْموعَة من المَدَنيين.
šanna ʔal-taħaalufu hujuuman waħšiyyan li-qwwaatin
launched the-coalition attack-indef savage for-forces
γayri niẓaamiyyatin ʕalaa majmuuʕatin min ʔal-madaniyyiin
not regular against group-indef of the-civilians
"The coalition launched an attack by a militia on a group of civilians."

(7) * هَجَمَ التَحالُفُ هُجوماً وَحْشيّاً لِقواتٍ غَير نِظاميّة على مَجْموعَةٍ مِن المَدَنيين.
hajama ʔal-taħaalufu hujuuman waħšiyyan li-qwwaatin
attacked the-coalition attack-indef savage for-forces
γayri niẓaamiyyatin ʕalaa majmuuʕatin min ʔal-madaniyyiin
not regular against group-indef of the-civilians
"The coalition launched an attack by a militia on a group of civilians."

We find that the same constraint holds between a verb and its cognate object.

3. Light Verbs Constructions as a Source for Other Equivalent Utterances

This equivalence is one of the most striking features of Arabic light verbs but it could also be the reason for which traditional Arabic grammarians did not notice or pay much attention to the light verbs phenomenon. Instead of explaining قام *qaama* by أحْدَثَ قياماً *ʔaħdaθa qiyaaman* Al Mubarrad could have said قامَ قياماً *qaama qiyaaman.* The difference lies only in that the light verb more precisely shapes its object from a semantic and aspectual point of view, and that was indeed what Al Mubarrad wanted to show. Thus, compare examples (8) and (8a):

(8) طالَما نَصَحْتُهُ.
ṭaalamaa naṣaħ-tu-hu
often advised-I-him
"I advised him often."

(8a) طالَما أَسْدَيْتُ لَهُ النُصح.

ṭaalamaa ʔasday-tu la-hu ʔal-nuṣħ
often gave-I to-him advise
"I often gave him advice."

where *yusdii* has a light verb function, and try to investigate the semantic difference, however small it could be, between (8) and (8a).[6] Ibn Manẓuur's *Lisaan ʔal-ʕarab* elaborates:

سدا، السَدو مَدُّ اليَد نَحو الشيء كما تَسْدو الصبيان إذا لَعبوا بالجوز فَرَموا به في الحُفَيرَة (...) سَدَت الناقَة تَسدو وهو تَذَرُّعِها في المَشي وإتِّساعَ خَطوِها، السَدو إتِّساعُ خَطَوَ الناقَة وقدَ يَكون ذَلكَ مَع رِفقٍ أو مَعَ لين.

> "*sadaa*, *yasduu* to stretch one's hand towards something as children do when playing with walnuts and throwing them into a little hole (...) the she-camel *tasduu* that is slows its pace and widens her steps. *ʔal-sadw* is the widening of the steps of the she-camel possibly with some sort of kindness and smoothness." (Vol. 3:1977-78)

Ibn Manẓuur tries to describe here the details of a very specific kind of movement. When you give advice to somebody you do not really *give* him something, but you act as if you did. When used with a predicative noun, *yusdii* loses most of its original lexical meaning but keeps, as a memory of this plain meaning, the general kinetic shaping of the process.

Actually, in most, if not all, light verbs we do find this kind of persistent meaning as a residue of an original plain lexical meaning, since it seems most of these verbs have undergone a grammaticalization process. If you return to *yusdii* and try to put together some of its different meanings, their origins and evolution, we find, for instance, that it is linked to another verb نَسَجَ *nasaja* "to weave" which also acts as a light verb in the context of other noun predicates. One of the meanings noted for *yusdii* by المعجَم الوَسيط the dictionary of the Egyptian *Arabic Language Academy* is:

[6] These analysis can be generalized to most speech acts. For instance, يُحَذر *yuħaððir* "to warn" or يُهَدِدُ *yuhaddidu* "to threaten" يُوَجهُ تَحذيراً / تَهديداً *yuwajjihu taħðiiran/ tahdiidan* "to give a warning/ a threat" with the light verb *yuwajjihu* instead of *yusdii*. For an open list of Arabic light verbs, see Ibrahim (2002).

سَدى الثَوبَ – سدى سَدياً: مَدَّ سَداه والسَدى من الثَوب خُيوطُ نَسيجَهُ التى تُمَدُّ طولاً
sadaa the garment - *sadaa sadyan*: he stretched its *sadaa* - the *sadaa* of a garment are the threads of the tissue that can be stretched in length. (Part 1:440)

In other words, *sadaa* and *nasaja* can both mean "to weave" via the word and notion of أطراف *ʔaṭraaf* "fringes" we find in the expression تَجاذُب أطراف الحديث *tajaaðub ʔaṭraaf ʔal-ħadiiθ* "to pull together the fringes of conversation." Actually both words are linked and their evolution explained in another place in *Lisaan ʔal-ʕarab*:

وإذا نَسَجَ إنسانٌ كَلاماً أو أمراً بينَ قَوْم قيلَ :سَدى بَيْنَهُم والحائكُ يُسْدي الثَوْبَ ويَتَسَدى لنَفْسه
وأما التَسْدِيَة فهي لَهُ و لغَيْره – وأسْدَى بَينَهُم حديثاً :نَسَجَهُ .و فى الحَديث مَن أسدى إَليكُمَ
مَعروفاً فكَافئوه أسْدى وأولَى بمَعنى أَعْطى.
"If a human weaves words or facts between people we say *sadaa* between them. The tailor *yusdii* the garment and *yatasadda* to himself. Regarding *ʔal-tasdiya* it can be for him or for somebody else. *ʔasdaa* between them a conversation means he weaved it. Within the sayings of the Prophet we find 'the one who *ʔasdaa* to you that which is good reward him'–*ʔasdaa* means "give." (Ibn Manẓuur, Vol. 3:1978)

Thus, between two fairly equivalent sentences, the one that includes a light verb will always be less ambiguous and more accurate descriptively than the other. Furthermore, we can say that the sentence containing the light verb subsumes the one without it. For instance, if we compare the following:

(9) "اللهُمَّ إنى أعوذ بك من نَفْسٍ لا تَشْبَع" (مُسلم - ذكر ٧٢)
"Oh my God, do protect me from a nature never satisfied"

(10) "يا رَسولَ الله إنّا نأكُل ولا نَشْبَع" (النَوَوى - رياضُ الصالحين - الأطعِمَة)
"Messenger of God! We eat but are not sated"

(11) بَعَثَ مُقَوْقَسُ مصرَ بهَديَّة إلى رَسولِ الله صلى الله عليه و سَلَّم كان فيها مارية القَبْطِيَّة
وطَبيبِ .قبل صَلي الله عَليّه و سَلَّم كُلِّ عناصرَ الهَدية عدا الطَبيب وقالَ لَهُ :"إرجَعَ إلى أهْلكَ
نَحْنُ قَوْمٌ لَا نأكل حتى نَجوع وإذا أكَلنا لا نَشْبَع" (كتاب رَسولِ الله صلى الله عليه و سَلَّم إلى
المُقَوقس عَظيم القِبط سنة ٧ هـــ - عن محمد رَسولِ الله صلى الله عليه و سَلَّم لمحمد رضا)
"The governor of Egypt sent a present to the Prophet consisting of Coptic Mary and a doctor. The Prophet accepted all the elements of the present except the doctor to whom he told "Go back to your people we are from those who do not eat unless they are hungry and when they eat they do not get sated."

In (9) *laa tašbaʕ* and in (10) *laa našbaʕ* mean *laa yaʔtiihaa/ laa yaʔtiinaa –l šabaʕ* "satiety does not come to it/to us/ not fulfilled with satiety" or *laa tašʕuru / laa našʕuru bil šabaʕ* "it does/ we do not feel satiated" while in (11) it means something completely different: *laa nantaẓiru ħatta našʕuru bi ʔal-šabaʕ* "we do not wait until we feel satiated." The semantic difference between (9) and (10) on one hand and (11) on the other is entirely accounted for by the difference between *yaʔtii* or *yašʕuru* on one hand and *yantaẓiru ħatta yaʔtii* or *yantaẓiru ħatta yašʕuru* on the other.

The light verb can therefore be deleted, because it is subsumed under the predicative noun. The light verb is so subsumed that its presence in some contexts may be felt as redundant. This may not be the case when this context allows an overt kind of ambiguity or calls for a definition, a legal statement or an emotional description. In all cases, it is one of the main tracks for the building of meaning. You cannot speak of or understand what you hear about *satiety* if you do not take into account that it is something that 'comes' or that you 'feel gradually' and at the same time something that could be desired and 'awaited'.

This is the reason why deletion and realization of light verbs and how their meaning can be recovered from the noun is crucial to dealing with the properties and the usefulness of this phenomenon. Moreover, it seems there are no two languages for which deletion and recoverabilty follow exactly the same tracks:

(12E) [BE][7]

Form a queue if you want to be served! ↔Queue up if..! ↔(In) the queue!
Stand in the queue if.......!

[AE]

(Stand in + Get in + Form) a line if..... ....! ∅ ↔ (In) the line!
[BE / AE] Join the queue if .... !

(12F) [F]

Faites (la +une) queue si vous voulez être servis ! ∅ ↔ (Dans) la queue!
Mettez-vous dans la queue si vous voulez... ∅

[7]BE = British English; AE = American English; EA = Egyptian Arabic; F = French; MSA = Modern Standard Arabic.

(13M) [MSA]

برَجاء الوقوف صفّاً واحداً إصطفّوا صَفّاً واحِداً ↔ (في) الصف!
برَجاء الإنتظام صَفّاً واحَدا
إنْتَظِموا فى الصَفّ

(13E) [EA]

من فَضلَك أُءَف فل طَبور ∅ ↔ (فِ) إل طَبور!
من فَضْلُكو أُءَفو صَفّ واحِد
إعْملوا طَبور لو عَوْزين الكُشك يشْتَغَل
أُءَفو طَبور لو عَوْزين الكُشك يِشْتَغَل

In British English, according to the situation, more or less disorder in front of a counter or a ticket office, the light verb is *to form*–if there is no queue or *to stand*–if there is already one but not fully respected. In both cases, the utterance is a regular nominalization of the corresponding verbal sentence. This configuration is unique among the languages observed, including American English. In MSA, the closest configuration to BE, we find an analogous *to stand* in an analogous light verb construction with *yaqifu* but it has, contrary to English and other observed languages, a corresponding derived verbal cognate object construction إصطفّوا صَفّاً *ʔiṣṭaffu ṣaffan* * "rank a rank" which is likewise unique among the languages observed including EA.

Some differences appear quite striking when looking at the distribution of light verbs in this construction among the languages observed. For instance, EA has in common with French, where *faire* "to make" or "to do" is the most common light verb, the use of an equivalent of *to make* or *to do* although *yaʕmal* or *yafʕal* can never have this function in MSA. We can also notice that a kind of light verb allowed in some language may not be allowed in another as it is the case for *to stand* which is not possible in French, or *yantaẓimu* which seems exclusive to MSA.

Another interesting phenomenon is the difference between the degrees of grammaticalization. In our examples, the most advanced is undoubtedly what we find in EA with *get in* and what we could call a *light* name: "line". In EA أُءَف *ʔuʔaf* "stand" could be considered a causative verb as in (13E). Yet, it is not, since it can be deleted and reduced to the preposition فِ *fe* while a causative verb cannot. Deletion or reduction through a process that does not change the meaning of the utterance is one ot the three main properties defining a light or support verb, the two others being appropriatness – to form a queue or a line you need to be standing – and partial loss of plain lexical meaning.

Actually, although nearly every language has a dominant or perhaps a more 'generic' light verb--for instance *faire* in French, *ḍaraba* in Classical Arabic, *daar* [8] in Libyan Arabic, *ʕamal* in Egyptian Arabic-- there are no two languages or even two varieties of a same language that use exactly the same range and the same number of light verbs,[9] thus showing that light verbs are extremely sensitive to the specific properties of the language and its usage. At the same time we notice that many differences between languages arise from the difference of the material that can be deleted or not realized overtly in a particular language. This is indeed a crucial point not only for understanding the nature of the light verbs phenomenon but, in a much wider perspective, for working out a coherent explanation of much of the grammatical differences between languages, since light verbs play a role in introducing and realizing in discourse, one of the most important basic categories in language: nouns.

4. The Specific Features of the Actualizing Process in Arabic

These were the differences within the common ground. What is much more specific to MSA can be summed up in the following points:

1. Light verbs constructions compete with cognate object constructions as seen above.
2. An actualization equivalent to a light verb can hide in the *wazn* "pattern" or "template" under which occurs the predicative noun like in CA أنا ظَمآن *ʔanaa ẓamʔaan* or EA أنا عَطشان *ʔanaa ʕaṭšaan* "I am thirsty" (Ibrahim 2002:339-341) or have itself the schema of a *masdar* like in إسداء النُّصح *ʔisdaaʔ ʔal-nuṣḥ* "the giving of an advice."

---

[8]See *Les verbes supports en arabe classique, arabe moderne et arabe libyen*, Ph.D. thesis under way by Adel Ahnaïba (under my supervision at Université de Franche-Comté).

[9]The first attempt for a precise survey on formal grounds in French (Daladier 1978) counted 14 verbs. The number has increased and is now around 100. Our own attempts on the same grounds for CA, MSA and EA counted about 40 verbs (Ibrahim 2002). Further investigations and the theses under way of Adel Ahnaïba (on CA, MSA and Libyan arabic) and Fayez Naifar (on CA, MSA and Tunisian Arabic) put the figure around 60.

3. The most genereric light verb, in CA and MSA is *ḍaraba*. This seems very specific to CA and MSA may be with the exception of modern spoken Chinese. This point is of some interest in the study of the evolution of the different varieties of Arabic, since it seems that none of the Arabic dialects kept this verb in this function. As described in Ibrahim (2002:328-336) *ḍaraba* is in CA and MSA the light verb that has the widest scope of constructions (sixteen) as well as the widest range of synonymy with other nominal predicate actualizers. This verb did not disapear in other dialects but its scope became narrower while the scope of other verbs arose to the status of a generic actualizer as it is the case with عَمَل *ʕamal* in EA, سَوّى *sawwa* in Levantine Arabic as well in other dialects of the Arabic Peninsula, دار *daar* in Libyan Arabic, etc... The study of the evolution of actualization through all the categories of *support items*, due to its strong linkage with grammaticalization, is key to understanding the differentiation of Arabic dialects. Since support items, although different in each dialect all have a living source in CA and MSA, it is possible to analyze and understand the phenomenon by simple comparison.
4. It is frequent that the introduction of the preposition before a noun under the scope of a verb in a direct object construction or the changing of an existing preposition in this position into *be* shifts the given construction to a light verb construction (Ibrahim 2002:341-3). For instance, دَخَل الغُرفة *daxala ʔal-ɣurfa* or دَخَل على فاطمة في الغُرفة *daxala ʕalaa Faaṭima fil ɣurfa* compared to دَخَل بفاطمة *daxala be Faaṭima* and in EA خَرَج زَىّ عَدتُه من الموضوع *xarag zay ᶜadtu min el maudʼuuᶜ* compared to خَرَج زَىّ عَدتُه بمَوضوع جديد *xarag zay ʕadtu be mawḍuuʕ gedeed.*

5. Conclusion

The light verbs issue and more precisely the actualization of nouns issue, because of its status between grammar and lexicon, is important to understanding contrasts between contemporary varieties of Arabic. A thorough account of the function of the lexically weak items that shape the likelihood of occurrence of lexically plain items in discourse can help, if we take into account the variety of attested usages and locate the connection between the classical language and the modern dialects.

A the same time, its key role in monitoring the thread language follows to achieve, through appropriate deletion and recovery of items, its predication, leads us to locate, with a relatively precise tool, one of the main sources of differentiation and evolution of languages.

REFERENCES

Achour, Al-Moncef. 1999. *Ẓaahirat Al-'ism fii Al-tafkiir Al-naħwii: Baħth fii maquulat al-'ismiyya bayna al-tamaam wa al-nuqṣaan*. Tunis: Publications de la Faculté des Lettres de la Manouba.

Al-Mubarrad. 826-900. [1963.] *Al-Muqtaḍab* Vol. 4 [ed. by Muhammad A. A. Adima]. Beirute: 'Aalam Al-Kutub.

Al-Nawawii. 1233-1277. [1983]. *Riyaaḍ Al-Ṣaaliħiin*. Beirute: Mu'assasat Al-Risaala.

Butt, Miriam. 1995. *The Structure of Complex Predicates in Urdu*. Stanford, CA: Center for the Study of Language and Information Publications.

Cattell, Ray. 1984. *Composite Predicates in English - Syntax and Semantics* Vol. 17. New York: Academic Press.

Cohen, David. 1985. *La Phrase nominale et l'évolution du Système verbal en Sémitique - Études de syntaxe historique*. Tome LXXIII de la Collection Linguistique de la Société de Linguistique de Paris. Réimprimé en 2003. Leuven-Paris: Peeters.

Daladier, Anne. 1978. *Quelques problèmes d'analyse d'un type de nominalisation et de certains groupes nominaux Français*. Thèse de 3e cycle, Universite Paris 7.

Gross, Maurice. 1996, "Les verbes supports d'adjectifs et le passif". *Langages* 121, *Les Supports* ed. by Amr Helmy Ibrahim, 8-18. Paris: Larousse.

_____. 1981. "Les bases empiriques de la notion de prédicat sémantique". *Langages* 63, *Formes syntaxiques et prédicats sémantiques* Sept.:7-53. Paris: Larousse.

_____. 1976. "Sur quelques groupes nominaux complexes". *Méthodes en grammaire française*. [Textes présentés par Jean-Claude CHEVALIER & Maurice GROSS] Paris: Klincksieck

Harris, Zellig Sabbetai. 1988. *Language and Information*. New York: Columbia University Press.

_____. 1969. "The Two Systems of Grammar: Report and paraphrase". *Papers in Structural and Transformational Linguistics*, 612-692. [1970.] Dordrecht: Reidel.

_____. 1968. *Mathematical Structures of Language*. New York: Wiley.

Ibn Manẓuur. 1290. [1981]. *Lisaan al-'Arab*. Cairo: Daar Al-Ma'aarif.

Ibrahim, Amr Helmy. 2002. "Les verbes supports en arabe". *Bulletin de la Société de Linguistique de Paris* XCVII, fasc.1.315-352. [Louvain: Peeters.]

_____. 2000. "Une classification des verbes en 6 classes asymétriques hiérarchisées". *Syntaxe et Sémantique* 2, *Sémantique du Lexique Verbal* ed. by

Françoise Cordier, Jacques François & Bernard Victorri, 81-98. Caen, France: Presses Universitaires de Caen.
_____. 1996. "Les supports: le terme, la notion et les approches" / "La forme d'une théorie du langage axée sur les termes supports". *Langages* 121 ed. by Amr Helmy Ibrahim, 3-8. / *Les Supports*, Mars:99-120.
Ide, Mohammad. 1975. *Al-Naħw Al-Muṣaffaa*. Cairo: Maktabat Al-Shabaab
Jespersen, Otto. 1965. *A Modern English Grammar on Historical Principles*. London: Allen & Unwin.
Kchaou, Salah. 2003. "Al-Jumal Al-'awwaliyya fii 'ibaaraat Al-'azaa' wa Al-'anħaa' Al-Maħalliyya". *Al-Ma'naa wa Tashakkuluh* ed. by Al-Moncef Achour, 737-752. Tunis: Publications de la Faculté des Lettres de la Manouba.
Launey, Michel. In press. "The Features of Omnipredicativity in Classical Nahuatl". Sprachtypologie Universitat Forschung.
_____. 2003. "Le type omniprédicatif et la morphosyntaxe du nahuatl". *Faits de langue* 21 vol. 2, *Méso-Amérique, Caraïbes, Amazonie*, 9-24. Paris: Ophrys.
_____. 1994. *Une grammaire omniprédicative*. Paris : Editions du Centre National de la Recherche Scientifique
_____. 1992. "La logique omniprédicative dans la syntaxe nahuatl". *Lalies* 10. 215-234.
Muslim Ibn Al-ħajjaaj Al-Naysabuurii. [1956]. *Al-Ṣaħiiħ* [ed. by Muhammad Abd Al-Baaqii]. Cairo: Daar Iħyaa' Al-Kutub Al-'arabiyya.
Poutsma, H. 1914-1926. *A Grammar of Late Modern English*. Groningen Holland: Noordhoff.
Reḍaa, Mohammad. [1986]. *Muħammad Rasuul Al-laah*. Beirute: Daar Al-Kutub Al-'ilmiyyah.
Wright, W. 1874. [1896]. *A Grammar of the Arabic Language*. Cambridge: Cambridge University Press.

RETHINKING LEXICAL ASPECT IN EGYPTIAN ARABIC

Mustafa Mughazy
Western Michigan University

1. **Introduction**

Lexical aspect is a semantic classification of verbs according to the structural and temporal properties of the eventuality descriptions in their denotations. Aspectual distinctive features, such as [+telic], [+durative] and [+dynamic], provide the basis for the perception of eventualities, and therefore, they affect the ways in which verbs can be used and interpreted. For example, only verbs that are marked for the feature [+durative] occur in the progressive, and active participles can be derived only from verbs that are marked for the features [+dynamic] and [+telic]. However, there is little agreement in the literature regarding the number of aspectual classes in Egyptian Arabic, as various language-specific classes, such as 'translocatives', 'agentive statives', 'inceptives' and 'pseudo-inchoatives', have been proposed. The motivation for positing these ad hoc language-specific classes is that adverbial diagnostics are quite often inconsistent. For example, many achievement verbs that describe changes of mental and emotional states do not allow *in X time* adverbials. Moreover, several morphological diagnostics are inconsistent, as some stative verbs do not occur in the *bi-* imperfect or the perfect forms. Another difficulty with determining the lexical aspect of Egyptian Arabic verbs is that many of them correspond to English verbs of other aspectual classes. For example, the achievement verbs *ṭaar* and *saaʔ*, are often translated as *fly* and *drive*, both of which are activities. In this paper I argue that lexical aspect concerns a universal classification of verbs and predicates rather than events or situations, i.e., there are only four classes of verbs in Egyptian Arabic: statives, achievements, activities, and accomplishments. Moreover, I present a series of morphological and syntactic diagnostics that definitively specify the aspectual nature of any given verb.

2. Lexical Aspect as a Classification of Verbs

Lexical aspect is often viewed as an ontological classification of discrete eventualities or situations in the real world rather than a classification of verbs or predicates (Parsons 1990, Fleischman 1990, Bache 1995, Smith 1997, Sanz 2000, Bertinetto & Delfitto 2000). These analyses are motivated by the observation that verbs can be used to describe eventualities with different internal structures (Verkuyl 1972, Carlson 1977, Dowty 1979). For example, what Vendler (1967) classifies as activity verbs denoting durative atelic events such as *run* and *scrub*, as in (1a) and (2a), can be used to describe durative telic situations if they have direct objects, as in (1b), or if they are used in resultative constructions, as in (2b).

(1) a. Adam ran for hours.
b. Adam ran a mile.
(2) a. Cinderella scrubbed the floor.
b. Cinderella scrubbed the floor clean.

Accomplishment and achievement verbs that describe telic situations in Vendler's scheme can be used to describe atelic situations if one of their arguments is a bare plural. For example, the predicate *spot* in (3a) describes an instantaneous change of state, as indicated by the punctual adverbial *at six o'clock*. In (3b) the same verb with a bare plural direct object describes an atelic situation, as indicated by the durative adverbial *for hours*. Mass noun arguments have the same effect of inducing atelic interpretations. For example, the accomplishment predicate *cook* in (4a) describes a telic event, but when the direct object is a mass noun, as in (4b), the same predicate has an atelic interpretation.

(3) a. The bird watcher spotted a canary at six o'clock.
b. The bird watcher spotted canaries for hours.
(4) a. Chef Ramsey cooked a chicken in half an hour.
b. Chef Ramsey cooked chicken for three hours.

Despite the above observations regarding the type-shifting of aspectual classes, I adopt the view that lexical aspect concerns a classification of predicates according to the descriptions of events in their denotations relative to a context (Ryle 1949, Kenny 1963, Krifka 1998, Rothstein 2004). Speakers choose to profile situations in ways that best suit their communicative purposes. For example, if Mona is taking the elevator to the fifth floor, she can be described as standing still (stative) relative to the context of the elevator or as going up to the fifth floor (accomplishment) relative to the building.

There are two main arguments in support of the position that lexical aspect is a property of event descriptions, not situations or events. First, situations in the real world are not discrete entities. Rather, events and states can be individuated and classified only under particular descriptions (Davidson 1969, Parsons 1990, Steward 1997, Landman 2000, Rothstein 2004). The philosophical literature on event identity and the individuation of events is too vast to cover here, but the following scenario illustrates the point. Chef Ramsey decides to prepare a healthy dinner, so he immerses one raw chicken in boiling water for thirty minutes and then serves it without doing anything else to it. Did Chef Ramsey do one thing or two different things, namely cooking the chicken and boiling it? I believe that Chef Ramsey did only one thing, i.e., the cooking and the boiling are identical. In this scenario there is only one event, which took thirty minutes and had Chef Ramsey as its agent and the chicken as the patient. This event, however, can be described either as a cooking of the chicken by Chef Ramsey or as a boiling of the chicken by Chef Ramsey, as in (5a)-(5b).

(5) a. Chef Ramsey cooked the chicken in thirty minutes. (accomplishment)
b. Chef Ramsey boiled the chicken for thirty minutes. (activity)

Assuming that events can have multiple descriptions, it is possible to use predicates with different aspectual properties to describe them. For example, if a soccer player kicks the ball from the center of the field into the goal, there are at least two ways to relate that event, as in (6a) and (6b). Even though the player's kicking the ball from the center of the field into the goal, which is a durative description, is identical with his scoring, which is instantaneous, both are valid descriptions of the same situation.

(6) a. The player scored. (achievement)
b. The player kicked the ball into the goal. (accomplishment)

The previous examples demonstrate that an event can be described using an achievement or an accomplishment predicate. The sentences in (7a) and (7b) below describe the same situation even though the first involves an activity predicate while the other involves a stative one.

(7) a. The train is moving. (activity)
b. The train is in motion. (stative)

Another argument in support of analyzing lexical aspect as properties of predicates according to the event descriptions in their denotations is that cross-linguistically the same situations are described by predicates belonging to different aspectual classes. For example, the English verbs *fly*, *drive* and *run* (=engine) are all activity predicates whereas their Egyptian Arabic corresponding verbs *ṭaar*, *saaʔ*, and *ʔištaɣal* are achievements. Moreover, the English verb *wait* is a stative predicate whereas its Egyptian counterpart *yestanna* is a dynamic predicate. The remainder of this paper elaborates on this argument.

The fact that the same situation can be described by predicates belonging to different aspectual classes and that languages differ with regard to how corresponding predicates describe eventulaties provide strong support for viewing lexical aspect as a property of predicates. However, the observations regarding aspetucal type-shifting mentioned earlier require an explanation. Olsen (1997) argues that aspectual properties are lexically specified semantic privative features as represented in (8).

(8)

Aspectual class	**Telic**	**Dynamic**	**Durative**
Statives			+
Stage-level statives	+		+
Activities		+	+
Achievements	+	+	
Accomplishments	+	+	+

Each verb is specified in the lexicon for one or more of the privative features [+dynamic], [+durative] and [+telic]. These features do not exclusively specify the possible aspectual interpretations of a predicate. Rather, they constrain these interpretations, as some features may not be specified, in which case aspectual interpretations are dependent on the pragmatic context.

Predicates that are specified as [+telic], e.g., accomplishments and achievements, denote event descriptions with inherent end points, and these events cannot be described as atelic (Verkuyl 1993, Olsen 1997). Therefore, the predicate in *John built a house* describes a situation with an inherent end, viz. the coming into existence of a house, and no other interpretation is available. Bare plural and mass arguments induce descriptions of iterative accomplishments or achievements, not atelic interpretations. Predicates that are not marked for [+telic] allow both telic and atelic interpretations via conversational implicature. For example, the sentence *John ran* can describe a telic situation if it is part of the speakers' shared background knowledge that John runs a mile every morning. The same pattern is attested with stative predicates, as the sentence *The Royal Guards are standing at attention* can describe a telic situation if the speakers know that the guards stand still only for the duration of their on duty shifts.

The feature [+dynamic] distinguishes predicates that describe events (accomplishments, achievements and activities) from those that describe states (statives). A predicate describes a dynamic eventuality if, and only if, that description involves change, which constitutes a transition in some object from a state of having a property P to a state of not having that property, or vice versa (Lombard 1986, Steward 1997). For example, an event of falling asleep is a change from a state of not having fallen asleep to a state of being asleep and an event of running a mile is a change from a state of not having run a mile to a state of having run a mile. The idea that every event or sub-event, whether instantaneous or durative, is bounded by states is also proposed by Davidson (1969), Dowty (1977) and Binnick (1991). Therefore, activity, accomplishment and achievement predicates that are marked for the feature [+dynamic] cannot describe states. Stative verbs, which are not marked for the feature [+dynamic], allow dynamic interpretations only via conversational implicature relative to a particular pragmatic context. For example, in (9a) and (9b) the verbs *believe* and *be* are used in the progressive only to implicate change of degree in the same attribute or to implicate agency.

(9) a. Mary is believing in God more and more. (Binnick 1991:282)
b. John is being obnoxious.

The feature that distinguishes achievements from other types of eventuality descriptions is [+durative] (Olsen 1997). Predicates marked for this feature, namely statives, activities, and accomplishments describe eventualities as durative even if these eventualities last for only a moment. Predicates that are not marked for the feature [+durative], namely achievements, describe events that culminate the instant they begin, such as noticing a mistake, or they can be used to trigger the implicature that the eventualities they describe include preceding durative sub-events as in *The old man is dying*. Support for the claim that sentences with progressive achievement predicates do not entail preceding processes is that such implicatures can be cancelled, as in *The old man died suddenly*, which does not entail that the old man was dying.

The aspectual classification of Egyptian Arabic verbs proposed in this paper provides strong evidence for the view that there are only four universal aspectual classes: statives, accomplishments, achievements and activities, with statives including two sub-classes, namely individual-level and stage-level statives. This classification is based on three privative features: [+dynamic], [+telic] and [+durative], which constrain the syntactic and morphological behavior of all verbs. Finally, these features are assumed to constitute universal properties that are the basis of event perception. However, verbs in individual languages differ in the ways they describe eventualities depending on their parametric feature valuations that are lexically specified.

3. The Active Participle and Lexical Aspect

Most of the work that has been done on lexical aspect in Egyptian Arabic draws a connection between aspectual classes and the alleged varied temporal interpretations of verbless sentences with active participle predicates such as those in (10a)-(10f).

(10) a. ʔana šaayif mona dilwaʔti (present simple)
I see$_{(AP)}$ Mona now
"I see Mona now."

b. naadir maaši hinaak ʔaho (present progressive)
Nadir walk$_{(AP)}$ there right now
"Nadir is walking over there right now."

c. mona lissa mixallaṣa el-waagib (present perfect)
Mona just finish$_{(AP)}$ the-homework
"Mona has just finished the homework."

d. ʔana saayiʔ baʔaa-l-i noṣ saaʕa (present perfect progressive)
I drive$_{(AP)}$ remain-for-me half hour
"I have been driving for half an hour."

e. xaalid kaatib eg-gawaab imbaareħ (past simple)
Khaled write$_{(AP)}$ the-letter yesterday
"Khaled wrote the letter yesterday."

f. ʔiħna rayħ-iin es-senima bukra (future)
we go$_{(AP)}$-p. the-movie theater tomorrow
"We are going to the movie theater tomorrow."

The main premise of this approach is that the aspectual properties of a given verb determine the temporal interpretations of the active participle derived from it. For example, El-Bakry (1990), Michell and El-Hassan (1994), and Eisele (1988, 1999) agree that sentences with active participles derived from stative and inchoative verbs have present simple interpretations, whereas those with participles derived from non-inchoative accomplishment and achievement verbs, so-called 'resultatives', have present perfect or past simple interpretations. El-Bakry (1990) notes that active participles derived from a lexically specified sub-set of activity verbs such as *taabeʕ* "follow" and *ʔištaɣal* "run (for an engine)", have present progressive interpretations. These verbs are classified as a language-specific class that Eisele (1999) calls "pseudo-inchoatives". Finally, there seems to be a consensus that sentences with active participle predicates derived from the assumed language-specific aspectual class of "verbs of motion" or "translocatives" have future or futurate interpretations (Wild 1964, Woidich 1975, Michell 1978, Jelinek 1981, El-Tonsi 1982, El-Bakry 1990, Michell & El-Hassan 1994, Eisele 1999, Brustad 2000). These generalizations are often used as diagnostics to determine the aspectual properties of verbs.

Despite the intuitive appeal of this approach, it suffers from a major drawback: sentences with active participle predicates have only present tense semantics, just like all other types of verbless sentences. In other words, these sentences do not have VARIED temporal interpretations even though they license temporal adverbials belonging to different time frames. Moreover, verbless sentences with active participle predicates allow past, present, and future adverbials regardless of the aspectual nature of the verbs the participial predicates are derived from. If these two claims are true, then the patterns of temporal adverbials in verbless sentences with active participle predicates cannot be used to determine the lexical aspect of verbs.

I have argued earlier (Mughazy 2004) that deverbal active participles are adjectival predicates, i.e., they are not nouns as argued by Qafisheh (1968), Wise (1975), Jelinek (1983, 2002) and Gadalla (2000) or members of a VERBAL category, as argued by Cowell (1964), Cantarino (1975), Wager (1984), El-Bakry (1990), and Brustad (2000). Deverbal active participles are not verbs because they do not mark person, formal aspect or tense, and because they allow only continuous truth-functional negation (Mughazy 2003). Support for the claim that deverbal active participles are not nouns that refer to the agents of events comes from the observations that they do not allow determiners,[1] quantifiers, or adjectival modifiers, as indicated by the ungrammaticality of (11a)-(11d).

(11) a. *el-waaṣil rann garas el-baab
the-arrive$_{(AP)}$ rang bell the-door
"The one who arrived rang the doorbell."

b. *koll kaatib gawaab baʕat-oh
every write$_{(AP)}$ letter sent-it
"Every one who wrote a letter sent it."

c. *fiih kaatib gawaab
∃ write$_{(AP)}$ letter
"There is someone who wrote a letter."

d. *nadya katba gawaab šaṭra
Nadia write$_{(AP)}$ letter clever
"Nadia is a clever letter writer."

Support for the claim that deverbal active participles are adjectives comes from the observation that they are used only as indefinite

[1]Devebral active participles are sometimes prefixed with *el-*, an observation that motivates the analyses that treat participles as nouns. However, this is not the definite article, but a relative pronoun that is used only when no nominal antecedent is available (see Mughazy 2004).

predicates, and that they cannot be used in argument positions, as in (12a) and (12b). The most significant argument that active participles are adjectives comes from the observation that they allow comparative and superlative forms in Standard Arabic as well as in spoken Egyptian Arabic, as in (13a) and (13b). Comparative and superlative forms are rarely used with active participles because the kinds of states they denote describe uniform rather than scalar attributes.

(12) a. *daafiʕ el-ʔigaar ʔaxad waṣl
pay$_{(AP)}$ the-rent took receipt
"The one who paid the rent took a receipt."
b. *ʔana šuft maaši fi wiṣt eš-šaariʕ
I saw walk$_{(AP)}$ in middle the-street
"I saw someone walking in the middle of the street."
c. ʔal-kinaaya-t-u ʔastar-u li-l-ʕayb
the-metaphor-f.-nom. conceal$_{(AP)}$.comp-nom for-the-uncomely
"Metaphors are better at concealing what is uncomely."
(Al-Tawħiidii 1985:1)
d. ʔiħna ʔaʔdar minn-ak ʕala ħal el-muškila di
we become able to$_{(AP)}$.comp from-you on solving the-problem this
"We are better able to solve this problem than you." (Ratib 1975:22)

Verbless sentences including those with active participle predicates have only present tense semantics and their predicates denote states that hold of the subjects at speech time or longer intervals that include speech time regardless of the aspectual properties of the verbs the predicates are derived from, as in (14a) and (14b). These examples demonstrate that the claim that only sentences with active participle predicates derived from stative and inchoative verbs have present simple interpretations is unwarranted.

(14) a. ʔana ʔaari kitabeen liħad dilwaʔti
I read$_{(AP)}$ two books until now
"I am in a state of having read two books up until now."
"I have read two books up till now."
b. mona lissa misafr-a
Mona still set off to travel$_{(AP)}$-f.
"Mona is still in a state of having set off to travel."
"Mona is still traveling."

Sentences with active participle predicates grammatically license past adverbials regardless of the aspectual properties of the verbs the participles are derived from, as in (15a)-(15c). In these sentences the past adverbials do not locate the states denoted by the predicates in time. Rather, they specify the event time of the onsets: "an event is an onset of a state if, and only if, the change that constitutes the event is completed at some moment *t* such that the state begins to obtain at *t*" (Mughazy 2004:185).

(15) a. ʔana šaayif er-raagil da ʔabl keda
I see$_{(AP)}$ the-man this before this
"I am in a state of having seen that man before."
"I saw that man before."
b. ʔana ʔaari ek-kitaab da men zamaan
I read$_{(AP)}$ the-book this from past time
"I am in a state of having read this book a long time ago."
"I read this book a long time ago."
c. ʔana naayim mitʔaxxar imbaareħ
I fall asleep$_{(AP)}$ late yesterday
"I am in a state of having fallen asleep late last night."
"I fell asleep late last night."

The adverbial *imbaareħ* "yesterday" in (15c) locates the onset inchoative event of falling asleep in the past while the state of having fallen asleep holds of the speaker at speech time. Note that the state of having fallen asleep is different from the state of being asleep even though they have the same theme and both start to hold the moment the speaker falls asleep. The difference is that the state of having fallen asleep holds of the speaker indefinitely, while the state of being asleep ends when he/she wakes up. This explains why the sentence in (15c) is acceptable despite the fact that the speaker is not asleep at speech time, and why the sentence in (15d) is not a contradiction, i.e., the participles *naayim* and *ṣaaħi* cannot be translated as "asleep" and "awake".

(15) d. ʔana naayim mitʔaxxar we-ṣaaħi badri
I fall asleep$_{(AP)}$ late and-get up early
"I am in a state of having fallen asleep late and gotten up early."
"I fell asleep late and got up early."

Deverbal active participles differ from other adjectival forms in that they are complex predicates that denote current states and entail preceding events. Therefore, a sentence with an active participle predicate entails a past tense sentence describing the onset event that brings about the state denoted by the participle. For example, the sentence in (16a), where Mona is described as the theme of a state of having written the letter, entails the sentence in (16b), which asserts that Mona wrote the letter. The relation between these two sentences is not that of conversational implicature, as conjoining (16a) with a sentence that denies (16b) results in logical contradiction, as in (16c). Moreover, the onset entailed by the active participle must be a complete telic event (or more accurately a telic event description). If the entailed event is not complete, the sentence is also a contradiction, as (16d).

(16) a. mona katba eg-gawaab
Mona write$_{(AP)}$ the-letter
"Mona is in a state of having written the letter."
"Mona has written the letter."
b. mona katabet eg-gawaab
Mona wrote the-letter
"Mona wrote the letter."
c. #mona katba eg-gawaab bass ma-katabet-h-uuš
Mona write$_{(AP)}$ the-letter but NEG-wrote-it-NEG
"Mona is in a state of having written the letter but she did not write it."
#"Mona has written the letter, but she did not write it."
d. #mona katba eg-gawaab bass ma-xallṣet-h-uuš
Mona write$_{(AP)}$ the-letter but NEG-finished-it-NEG
"Mona is in a state of having written the letter but she did not finish it."
#"Mona has written the letter, but she did not finish it."

Since deverbal active participle predicates assert a state and entail a preceding event, the truth conditions of a verbless sentence with an active participle predicate, such as that in (17a), involve quantification over state and event variables, as represented in (17b).

(17) a. ʕali kaatib eg-gawaab men ʔisbuuʕ
Ali write$_{(AP)}$ the-letter from week
"Ali is now in a state of having written the letter a week ago."

b.∃s∃e [Writing(e) & Agent(e, Ali) & Patient(e, the letter) & A week ago(e) & Having written the letter(s) & Theme(s, Ali) & Now(s) & ONSET(e, s)]

This logical form reads as follows: there is an event of writing such that it is a writing of the letter by Ali, and this event took place a week before speech time. Moreover, there is a state such that it is a state of Ali's having written the letter, and this state holds of Ali at speech time and it came about at the point in time when the event of Ali's writing the letter was completed. More specifically, the event of Ali's writing the letter occurs over an open interval t_1-t_2 and the target state of him having written the letter begins to hold over an interval that is closed at its beginning (viz. t_2) and it holds indefinitely (see Mughazy 2004 for the motivation of this analysis).

Assuming that adjunct temporal adverbials are semantically licensed as predicates of eventuality variables (Davidson 1967; Higginbotham 1985, 2000; Parsons 1990, 2000), there are two eventuality candidates for adverbial modification in sentences with participial predicates: the state denoted by the active participle and the onset event that brings it about. Since the states denoted by active participles are required to hold at speech time, or longer intervals that include speech time, only present adverbials can be predicated of the states. Moreover, since the onset events are required to precede the states denoted by active participles, only past adverbials can be predicated of the event viriables. Therefore, a sentence with an active participle predicate can license a present adverbial, as in (18a), a past adverbial, as in (18b), or both, as in (18c).

(18) a. naadir dilwaʔti waaxid kart aṣfar
Nadir now take$_{(AP)}$ card yellow
"Nadir is now in a state of having received a yellow card."
"Nadir has received a yellow card."

b. naadir waaxid kart aṣfar fi eš-šooṭ el-ʔawwal
Nadir take$_{(AP)}$ card yellow in the-half time the-first
"Nadir in a state of having received a yellow card in 1st half time."
"Nadir received a yellow card during the first half time."

c. naadir dilwaʔti waaxid kart aṣfar fi eš-šooṭ el-ʔawwal
Nadir now take$_{(AP)}$ card yellow in the-half time the-first
"Nadir is now in a state of having received a yellow card in the 1st half time."

Verbless sentences allow future adverbials on futurate readings if the speaker has the ability to control future states, as in (19a), uttered by a soccer team coach, if the future state can be planned, as in (19b), or predicted with a high degree of certainty, as in (19c).

(19) a. ʔenta eg-goon fi maṭš en-nahaaʔi bukra
you the-goal keeper in match the-final tomorrow
"You are the goal keeper in the final match tomorrow."
b. ʔana f-el-maktab bukra ṭool en-nahaar
I in-the-office tomorrow throughout the-day
"I am in the office tomorrow all day."
c. eg-gaw bukra ħarr ʔawi
the-weather tomorrow hot very
"The weather is very hot tomorrow."

Since sentences with active participle predicates have present tense semantics, they license future adverbials on futurate readings, as attested by the grammaticality of the sentences in (20a) and (20b). It is important to note here that the verbs the participles in these sentences are derived from are not 'translocative' verbs, in that they do not describe change of location.

(20) a. ʔana mistannii-k bukra es-saaʕa setta
I $\text{wait}_{(AP)}$-you tomorrow the-hour six
"I am waiting for you tomorrow at six."
b. el-maktaba ʔafla bukra
the-library $\text{close}_{(AP)}$ tomorrow
"The library is closed tomorrow."

If sentences with active participle predicates allow past, present, and future adverbials regardless of the aspectual nature of the verbs they are derived from, the temporal adverbials used in these sentences cannot be used as diagnostics to determine the lexical aspect of verbs.

Even though temporal adverbials in sentences with active participle predicates cannot be used to determine the aspectual properties of verbs, the grammaticality of deriving participles plays a crucial role in determining the aspectual properties of verbs. The truth conditions of a sentence with an active participle predicate require there to be an event that brings about the state denoted by the participle. Therefore, no active participles can be derived from stative verbs, as these verbs denote states rather than changes of state, and states cannot be onsets of any other eventualities. Sentences with active participle predicates derived from stative verbs have no truth values because of presupposition failure, as there are no event descriptions in the universe of discourse that satisfy the value assignment of the onset variable, as in (21a). Since sentences with active participle predicates are grammatical only if the onset events are complete telic changes of states, participles derived from activity verbs are also ruled out, as in (21b).

(21) a. *ʔaadam šaabih ʕomar ešširiif
Adam resemble$_{(AP)}$ Omar Sheriff
"Adam is in a state of having resembled Omar Sheriff."
b. *ʕali gaari
Ali run$_{(AP)}$
"Ali is in a state of having run."

The grammaticality of deriving active participles, rather than their temporal interpretations, is the most crucial diagnostic that determines the aspectual properties of verbs. The availability of grammatical participles distinguishes verbs denoting states from verbs denoting events, and verbs that denote telic events from those denoting atelic events.

4. Individual-level and Stage-level Statives

English stative verbs such as *belong, own, depend,* and *matter* denote states (or more specifically sets of descriptions of states), which are typically durative, atelic and non-dynamic (Ryle 1949, Vendler 1967, Kenny 1963, Dowty 1979, Binnick 1991, Smith 1997). Events are defined in terms of change from one state to another (Lombard 1986, Sterawd 1997), but states do not involve change at all. For example, if John owns a house for three years, it is true at any time during those three years that he owns the house and he continues to own it until some event occurs resulting in his moving into a state of not owning that house. Since states are homogeneous, i.e., they do not have internal structure or stages, stative verbs are generally ungrammatical if marked for the progressive aspect, as in (22a). Moreover, states are typically non-agentive; therefore, they are excluded from pseudo-cleft constructions, as in (22b), imperatives, as in (22c), as complements of *force* and *persuade*, as in (22d), and they do not allow agent oriented adverbials such as *deliberately* and *willingly* as in (22e).

(22) a. *John is owning a house.
b. *What Mona did was love Adam.
c. *Know the answer!
d. *I forced/persuaded John to miss his mother.
e. *Bill dislikes Mary willingly/deliberately.

Eisele (1999) proposes three types of diagnostics to determine whether an Egyptian Arabic verb is stative or not: morphology tests, adverbial tests, and agentivity tests. The first morphological test is based on the observation that the *bi-* imperfect forms of stative verbs have both true-present and habitual, but no progressive readings. The second test is that, according to his analysis, active participles derived from stative verbs either denote current states or no active participles can be grammatically derived from them. The third morphological test is that the perfect forms of these verbs denote states rather than changes of state.

Although these tests are based on the fundamental properties of states, namely that they are non-dynamic eventualities with no internal stage structure, these tests are not without complications. First, some stative verbs in Egyptian Arabic do not occur in the imperfect *bi-* form, i.e., they are used only as bare imperfects, as in (23a) and (23b). Moreover, disjunctive tests, such as the claim that some statives have corresponding active participles whereas others do not, cannot be used as diagnostics because verbs with the same semantic properties are expected to pattern uniformly. As discussed earlier, deverbal active participles cannot be grammatically derived from stative verbs because these verbs denote states rather than changes of state, as indicated by the ungrammaticality of the sentences in (23c).

(23) a. el-ʕarabi (*bi-yefreʔ) yefreʔ ʕan el-ʔingiliizi kitiir
the-Arabic prog./hab.-differ differ.imperf from the-English a lot
"Arabic differs from English a lot."
b. ʕali (*bi-yešbeh) yešbeh ʕomar eš-širiif
Ali prog./hab.-resemble resemble.imperf Omar Sheriff
"Ali resembles Omar Sheriff."

c. *elqaahira baʕda ʕan ʔiskindiriyya 250 kilo
Cairo be $far_{(AP)}$ from Alexandria 250 kilometers
"Cairo is in a state of having been 250 kilometers far from Alexandria."
"Cairo has been 250 kilometers away from Alexandria."

Finally, the third morphological test, namely that the perfect forms of stative verbs denote past states, is not consistent. The verbs that have *bi-* imperfect forms denote states in the perfect, while those that occur only in the bare imperfect are not allowed in the perfect, as in (24a) and (24b). The pattern that emerges from applying the diagnostics related to the *bi-* imperfect and perfect forms indicates that there is an asymmetry within stative verbs.

(24) a. el-fustaan da (*bi-ygannen) yigannen
the-dress this (hab.prog.bedazzle) bedazzle.imperf.
"This dress bedazzles/is impressive."
b. *el-fustaan da gannen
the-dress this bedazzled
"This dress bedazzled/was impressive."

The adverbial tests for stativity that Eisele (1999) proposes include the claim that the adverbial *lissa*, which is ambiguous between a *still* sense and a *just* sense can only mean *still* when used with active participles derived from statives. Moreover, the aspectual verb *raaħ* "went" cannot be used with active participles derived from stative verbs to profile the onset event as happening suddenly. A third test is that the perfect forms of stative verbs do not co-occur with *in X time* adverbials. The first two of these tests are not compatible with an analysis that assumes that sentences with active participle predicates derived from stative verbs are ruled out because of presupposition failure. The diagnostic regarding the unacceptability of *in X time* adverbials with statives is a valid test, yet it is not sufficient because some statives do not occur in the perfect form as mentioned above.

Since states are typically non-agentive eventualities, stative verbs are excluded from constructions that presuppose agency. Both Eisele (1999) and El-Bakry (1990) note that pseudo-cleft constructions disallow stative verbs as in (25a). Moreover, agent oriented adverbials such as *bimazaagi* "willingly" and *ʕan ʔaṣd* "on purpose" are unacceptable with stative verbs, as in (25b).

(25) a. *koll elli ʕamalt-oh huwwa ʔenni šabaht ʕomar ešširiif
all that did.1st.s.-it he that-I resembled Omar Sheriff
"All I did was resemble Omar Sheriff."
b. #ʔana ʔastaahil el-mukafʔa ʕan ʔaṣd
I deserve the-reward on purpose
"I deserve the reward on purpose."

The diagnostics for stativity reviewed above fail to distinguish stative verbs from others, particularly because stative verbs do not pattern in the same way. Even the diagnostics based on agentivity are not sufficient because there are non-stative verbs that describe happenings, which are non-agentive non-stative changes of state. For example, bleeding, passing out, and waking up are not volitional events, hence (26a) and (26b) are unacceptable. Moreover, non-human subjects of change can only metaphorically be interpreted as agents, as indicated by the unacceptability of (27a) and (27b) on literal readings. Even though agentivity frames do not allow stative verbs, they also disallow non-action verbs that describe happenings. Therefore, these diagnostics cannot be used to definitively distinguish states from events.

(26) a. #What John did was pass out.
b. #John woke up deliberately/willingly.
c. #What the tornado did was destroy the town.
d. #The tree fell on my car deliberately/willingly.

Although the above mentioned diagnostics cannot be used to clearly distinguish statives from non-statives, an important pattern emerges. There are two groups of stative verbs: statives that do not have *bi*-imperfect or perfect forms and those that do. The first type describes inherent states, which hold of their subjects without there being inchoative events that bring them about. For example, the sentence in (28a) describes a state that starts to hold the moment the speaker or his uncle enters existence. Since such states start to hold as their themes enter existence and persist until speech time, they cannot be described using perfect forms, as in (28b). That is because perfect forms presuppose that the eventualities they describe end before speech time. Finally, these states do not recur, which explains the unacceptability of the habitual *bi-* imperfect, as in (28c).

(28) a. ṣaaliħ yeʔrab l-i xaal-i
Salih be related to-me uncle-my
"Salih is my uncle."
b. ṣaaliħ ʔarab l-i xaal-i
Salih was related to-me uncle-my
#"Salih used to be my uncle."
c. *ṣaaliħ bi-yeʔrab l-i xaal-i
Salih prog./hab.-be related to-me uncle-my
#"Salih is (habitually) my uncle."
*"Salih is being my uncle."

The other group of statives includes verbs that denote descriptions of potentially recurrent states. These are states that come about because of preceding changes, hold of their subjects for a while (over an open interval), and if they cease, they may start to hold again. For example, if Ali is jealous over his fiancée, this state does not start to hold when either of them is born. Rather, there are certain kinds of stimuli that cause Ali to experience the feelings of jealousy. These feelings do not persist indefinitely until one of them dies, or during every moment he is awake, but they emerge for a while and then cease to hold, until they emerge again. However, if Ali is experiencing feelings of jealousy between ten o'clock and noon on Monday and then again on Tuesday, these are not the same state. Rather, they are two individual states that have different causes and onsets, and hold over different time intervals, but both states are members of the set of states of jealousy denoted by the predicate. The fact that these states have onsets and can recur accounts for the observation that the verbs denoting them require the use of the *bi-* imperfect forms on habitual readings, as in (29).

(29) ʕali (*yiɣiir) bi-yɣiir ʕala xaṭibt-oh
Ali be (jealous.imperf.) hab.-be jealous on fiancée-his
"Ali is (habitually) jealous over his fiancée."

The *bi-* imperfect forms of verbs that describe recurrent states have habitual, but no progressive readings, which accounts for the observation that these verbs are not acceptable in embedded circumstantial clauses. Only verbs that describe durative and dynamic eventualities are allowed in these constructions, where the eventuality described in the main clause is profiled as taking place over an interval that is a sub-interval of that described in the embedded clause.

Therefore, it is grammatical to use predicates such as *bi-yegri* "run" in circumstantial clauses, as in (30a), but not verbs that describe recurrent states such as *yi-γiir* "be jealous", as in (30b).

(30) a. šoft mona w-heyya bi-tegri
saw.1st.s. Mona and-she prog.-run
"I saw Mona while she was running."
b. *ʕali kallem-ni w-huwwa bi-yγiir ʕala xaṭebt-oh
Ali talked-me and-he prog.-be jealous on fiancée-his
"Ali talked to me while being jealous over his fiancée."

The diagnostics proposed above are sufficient to distinguish statives from all other types of verbs. Verbs that describe inherent states are the only ones that do not have *bi-* imperfect forms in indicative independent clauses, whether on progressive or habitual readings. Moreover, they are not used in the perfect. The *bi-* imperfect forms of verbs that describe recurrent states have habitual but no progressive readings, and therefore they are excluded from embedded circumstantial clauses. This frame distinguishes statives from verbs that describe dynamic and durative events, but achievements are also excluded from embedded circumstantial clauses because they describe dynamic yet non-durative events. The test that distinguishes statives from achievements is that deverbal active participles can be grammatically derived from achievements, but not from statives. Examples of verbs that describe inherent states include those in (31a), and recurrent statives are exemplified in (31b):

(31) a.	yešbeh	resemble	yeʔrab	be related
	yefreʔ	differ	yeħeʔ	be lawful
	yesaħ	be right	yebʕed	be far
	yesaaʕ	be wide	yehem	matter
	yegannen	bedazzle	yestaahil	deserve
	yewzen	weigh (int.)		
b.	yeʕaani	suffer	yeγiir	be jealous
	yeʕezz	endear	yeħenn	yearn

The difference between the two groups of stative verbs is one of telicity, which is a privative aspectual property. The term 'inherent' is not accurate because some of the verbs that do not have *bi-* imperfect forms describe states that do not start to hold at the moment the subject enters existence. For example, the state described by the verb *yestaahil* "deserve" is not truly inherent. If Ali deserves an award today, he did not start to deserve it when he was born or when the award was created. Therefore, it is not inherentness that distinguishes the two groups of statives. The difference is that the verbs that have *bi-* imperfect forms, such as *yeʕaani* "suffer", describe states with inherent end points. If Ali is suffering, this state holds only as long as the cause of his suffering is in effect. The moment the cause is eliminated, his suffering ends. In other words, the state of suffering has an inherent end, i.e., the state is telic. The fact that these states are telic is what allows these verbs to have habitual interpretations.

5. Diagnostics for Achievement Verbs

Achievements are verbs that denote descriptions of instantaneous complete changes, i.e., they have the features [+telic] and [+dynamic], but they are not specified for [+durative] (Olsen 1997). The events described by achievement verbs such as *arrive, realize,* and *lose* are instantaneous, as they end the moment they start. For example, the moment John arrives home, he moves from a state of not being at home to a state of being at home; his arriving has no internal structure or stages. Therefore, these verbs do not typically occur in the progressive, as in (32a), license durative adverbials, as in (32b), or occur as complements of *finish*, as in (32c).

(32) a. *John is arriving.
b. *John realized that he had no money for an hour.
c. *John finished losing his book.

These tests apply directly to Egyptian Arabic, where the *bi-* imperfect forms of achievement verbs have habitual, but no progressive readings, as indicated by the unacceptability of punctual adverbials in (33a), and the use in embedded circumstantial clause in (33b). Moreover, achievements do not allow durative adverbials such as *limoddet noṣ saaʕa* "for half an hour" unless they are interpreted on an iterative reading. That does not apply in the case of (33c) because dying is not the kind of event that can be repeated.

(33) a. ek-kahraba bi-te ʔaṭaʕ men waʔt le-t-taani (*dilwaʔti)
the-power hab.-cut off from time to-the-other (now)
"The power goes off from time to time (*now)."
b. *samaʕt el-ʕarabiyya w-heyya bi-te-xbaṭ ʕamuud en-nuur
heard.1st.s. the-car and-she prog.-hit post the-light
"I heard the car while it was hitting the light post."
c. *er-raagil maat li-moddet noṣ saaʕa
the-man died for-period half hour
"The man died for half an hour."

Although the diagnostics for achievements seem straightforward, there is considerable disagreement regarding the membership of this class in Egyptian Arabic. Several sub-classes of achievements such as 'agentive statives', 'stative/inchoatives', 'momentaneous inchoatives', and 'psuedo-inchoatives' have been proposed (El-Tonsi 1982, El-Bakry 1990, Michell & Hassan 1994, Eisele 1999). This controversy stems from four basic observations: (a) some verbs in Egyptian Arabic are ambiguous between a stative and an achievement sense, (b) non-agentive achievements pass the tests for stativity, (c) the perfect forms of inchoative achievements allow durative adverbials, and (d) active participles derived from inchoative achievement display inconsistent patterns of licensing adverbials. I demonstrate below that there is no motivation for positing such language-specific sub-classes of achievements because agentivity and inchoativity are not privative aspectual features, and they cannot be used to distinguish aspectual classes.

The tests for stativity discussed earlier are based on two assumptions regarding states: (a) states are non-agentive, and (b) they have no internal structure. Because states are non-agentive, stative verbs do not occur in imperative or pseudo-cleft constructions, they cannot be used as complements of *ʔaqnaʕ* "persuade" and *ʔagbar* "force", and they cannot be modified by agent oriented adverbials. The fact that states do not have internal stage structure accounts for the observations that the *bi-* imperfect forms of statives do not have progressive readings, and they do not occur in embedded circumstantial clauses. Achievements also have no internal structure since they are punctual. Therefore, the *bi-* imperfect forms of achievements do not have progressive readings and they do not occur in embedded circumstantial clauses. Moreover, many achievements are non-agentive changes in mental and emotional states such as losing conscience and remembering a name. These observations demonstrate that non-agentive achievements pass the tests for stativity, hence the need for other diagnostics.

It is important to note here that not all achievements in Egyptian Arabic are non-agentive as asserted by El-Bakry (1990). Predicates such as *šaaṭ* "kick", *laʔaṭ* "catch" and *waṣṣal ek-kahraba* "close an electric circuit" all describe instantaneous agentive events. In fact, even some mental events are agentive, such as *ʔixtaar* "choose". For example, if a magician asks John to choose a playing card (in his head), John can think about it for a while, but choosing the card is instantaneous. As mentioned earlier, agentivity is not a privative feature since durative atelic events can be agentive (e.g., running) or non-agentive (e.g., dreaming and bleeding), durative telic events can be agentive (e.g., building a house) or non-agentive (e.g., growing old), and the same applies for achievements. In fact, some states can be considered agentive such as standing still and being on the phone (Binnick 1991). Since all types of eventualities can be described as agentive, agentivity cannot be used to distinguish aspectual classes. Therefore, there is no motivation for positing a language-specific aspectual class of agentive statives.

It is often noted that many Egyptian Arabic verbs are ambiguous between a stative and an achievement sense, as they can be used to describe potentially recurrent states as well as the inchoative instantaneous events that bring these states about, as is the case with the English verbs *remember, realize,* and *recognize* (El-Tonsi 1982, Mitchell & El-Hassan 1994, Eisele 1999, Brustad 2000). However, there is no agreement as to how to decide whether a verb is ambiguous or not because these verbs denote non-agentive event descriptions with no internal structure; hence, they pass the tests for statives as well as achievements. What makes it even more difficult to distinguish non-agentive achievements from statives in Egyptian Arabic is that inchoative achievements allow durative adverbials as in (34).

(34) en-nuur raaħ noṣ saaʕa w-ragaʕ
the-light went off half hour and-returned
"The lights went off for half an hour and came back on."

Events such as the teacher's entering a classroom, the lights' going off, and the disappearance of a mirage are instantaneous, and the verbs that describe these events have no readings that describe durative eventualities. However, they co-occur with durative adverbials. These adverbials do not describe the punctual events as durative. Rather, they are semantically licensed as predicates of the resultant states that these inchoative events necessarily entail. For example, it is the state of the lights being off that lasted for half an hour. The fact that inchoative achievements license durative predicates blurs the distinction between the statives and achievements. Another complication for distinguishing inchoative achievements from statives is that many inchoative achievements that describe mental and emotional changes of state are not acceptable with *in X time* adverbials just like statives, as in (35a) and (35b).

(35) a. #el-fikra ṭelʕet fi dimaaɣ-i fi ʕašar daʔaayeʔ
the-idea came up in head-my in ten minutes
"The idea occurred to me in ten minutes."
b. #ʔana ʔitfagaʕt men ek-kalb fi ʕašar daʔaayeʔ
I got scared from the-dog in ten minutes
"I got scared of the dog in ten minutes."

The main motivation for positing sub-classes of achievements is that sentences with active participles derived from inchoative achievements do not pattern uniformly with regard to temporal adverbials. Some of these participles allow punctual adverbials, such as *mistanni* "wait$_{(AP)}$" in (36a), while others do not, such as *naasi* "forget$_{(AP)}$" in (36b). Moreover, some active participles derived from achievements allow *in X time* adverbials, as in (36c), while others do not, as in (36d). Finally, some such participles allow durative adverbials, as in (50e), while others do not, as in (36f).

(36) a. ʔana mistannii-k bukra es-saaʕa xamsa
I wait$_{(AP)}$-you tomorrow the-hour five.
"I am waiting for you tomorrow at five o'clock."
b. #ʔana naasi el-maʕaad es-saaʕa xamsa
I forget$_{(AP)}$ the-appointment the-hour five
"I have forgotten the appointment at five o'clock."

c. ʔana faahim ħal el-masʔala fi noṣ saaʕa
I understand$_{(AP)}$ solution the-problem in half hour
"I understood the solution of the problem in half an hour."
d. #ʔana ṣaabir fi noṣ saaʕa
I be patient$_{(AP)}$ in half hour
"I become patient in half an hour."
e. ʔaadam naayim li-moddet noṣ saaʕa
Adam fall asleep$_{(AP)}$ for-period half hour
"Adam has slept for half an hour."
f. #ʔaadam misameħ-ni li-moddet noṣ saaʕa
Adam forgive-me$_{(AP)}$ for-period half hour
"Adam has forgiven me for half an hour."

This inconsistency is only apparent. In fact, sentences with active participle predicates derived from inchoative achievements have the same semantics, yet the pragmatic context induces the anomalies associated with temporal adverbials. Therefore, there is no motivation for positing further sub-classes of achievements as discussed below.

The truth conditions of sentences with active participles derived from inchoative achievements involve quantification over three eventuality variables: the onset instantaneous event, the target state denoted by the participle, and the resultant state that starts to hold as a necessary outcome of the completion of the onset. Temporal adverbials can be predicated of any of the three eventuality arguments. The active participle *naayim* "fall asleep$_{(AP)}$" is a case in point as demonstrated by the following example: Adam is a patient in a hospital where a nurse gives him some sleeping pills and watches him. The nurse can utter the sentence in (37a) to specify the time between his taking the pill and his falling asleep. The adverbial *fi xamas daʔaayeʔ* "in five minutes" is predicated of the onset event of falling asleep. The nurse can use the sentence in (37b) to report the exact time of his falling asleep. Again, the punctual adverbial is associated with the onset event. Two hours later, the nurse can use the sentence in (37c) to describe the duration of the resultant state of Adam's being asleep. Finally, after he wakes up, the nurse can use the sentence in (37d) to report to him on his sleeping pattern. The adverbial *dilwaʔti* "now" is predicated of the target state of having fallen asleep, and the durative adverbial describes the resultant state of his being asleep, which does not hold at speech time.

(37) a. ʔaadam naayim fi xamas daʔaayeʔ
Adam fall asleep$_{(AP)}$ in five minutes
"Adam is in a state of having fallen asleep in five minutes."
"Adam fell asleep in five minutes."
b. ʔaadam naayim es-saaʕa sabaʕa biẓẓabṭ
Adam fall asleep$_{(AP)}$ the-hour seven exactly
"Adam is in a state of having fallen asleep at seven o'clock exactly."
"Adam fell asleep at seven o'clock exactly."
c. ʔaadam naayim saʕteen liħad dilwaʔti
Adam fall asleep$_{(AP)}$ two hours until now
"Adam is in a state of having fallen asleep for two hours now."
"Adam has been asleep for two hours (now)."
d. ʔinta dilwaʔti naayim talat saʔaat biẓẓabṭ
you now fall asleep$_{(AP)}$ three hours exactly
"You are now in a state of having fallen asleep for three hours exactly."

Although the semantics of participles derived from inchoative achievements license the different types of adverbials exemplified above, many such participles do not co-occur with the full range of possible adverbials because of pragmatic constraints. In fact, the participle *naayim* "fall asleep$_{(AP)}$" is rather unique in that both the onset event and the resultant state are overt kinds of behavior that can be observed and located in time. For example, the participle *naasi* "forget$_{(AP)}$" usually does not co-occur with punctual adverbials such as *es-saaʕa xamsa* "at five o'clock" or *in X time* adverbials. That is because it is difficult to specify an event that leads to forgetting and it is not always possible to specify when forgetting occurs. However, the sentence in (38a) is acceptable if it is part of the interlocutors' shared background knowledge that Mona is forgetful, and the adverbial *fi xamas daʔaayeʔ* "in five minutes" is understood as describing the time between Mona's hearing my name and her forgetting it. Another example is the participle *mirakkiz* "focus$_{(AP)}$", which is usually unacceptable with durative adverbials even though the change entails the beginning of a durative resultant state of being focused. However, in a context where the subject of change is expected not to be able to focus and the duration of being focused is salient, a durative adverbial is acceptable, as in (38b).

(38) a. mona nasya ʔism-i fi xamas daʔaayeʔ
Mona forget$_{(AP)}$ name-my in five minutes
"Mona is in a state of having forgotten my name in five minutes."
"Mona forgot my name in five minutes."
b. el-mariiḍ ṭiliʕ men el-ɣaybuuba w-mirakkiz xamas daʔaayeʔ kamliin
the-patient got out from the-coma and-focus$_{(AP)}$ five minutes complete
"The patient came out of the coma and he is in a state of having become focused for a whole five minutes."
"The patient came out of the coma and focused for a whole five minutes."

Two diagnostics definitively distinguish non-agentive inchoative achievements from statives: (a) the grammaticality of using the active participle, and (b) the use of the *bi-* imperfect to describe states that hold at speech time rather than habitually. On a stative reading the *bi-* imperfect form of an ambiguous verb has a true present reading, and no deverbal active participle can be derived from it due to presupposition failure. On an achievement reading, an ambiguous verb may allow *in X time* adverbials, and a deverbal active participles can be derived from it, but no true-present reading is available for its *bi-* imperfect form. For example, the verb *šaaf* "see/spot" is ambiguous. A deverbal active participle can be derived from this verbs on the achievement reading as in (39a), but not on the stative readings, as in (39b). On a stative reading the *bi-* imperfect forms of these verbs have true-present interpretations, as in (39c), but not on the achievement reading, as indicated by the ungrammaticality of (39d).

(39) a. ʔana šaayif ʕali hinaak
I spot$_{(AP)}$ Ali there
"I am in a state of having spotted Ali over there."
"I see Ali over there."
b. *ʔana šaayif be-ʕeen-i el-yimiin ʔaħsan men eš-šimaal
I see$_{(AP)}$ with-eye-my the-right better than the-left
"I am in a state of having seen with my right eye better than the left one"
"I have seen with my right eye better than with the left one.
c. ʔana ba-šuuf be-ʕeen-i el-yimiin ʔaħsan men eš-šimaal
I imperf.-see with-eye-my the-right better than the-left
"I see with my right eye better than with the left."
d. *ʔana ba-šuuf ʕali hinaak
I imperf.-spot Ali there
"I spot Ali over there (now)."

These two diagnostics demonstrate that in fact there are only a few verbs in Egyptian Arabic that are truly ambiguous between an inchoative achievement reading and a stative one. Ambiguous verbs include those in (40a), and inchoative achievements that have no stative readings include those in (40b).

(40) a.	ʕirif	know/get to know	istaɣrab	wonder/start to wonder
	šaaf	see/spot	iʕtabar	consider/start to consider
	ħabb	love/fall in love	šakk	doubt/start to doubt
	kereh	hate/start to hate	ʔadar	be able to/become able to
	xaaf	fear/get scared	simiʕ	hear/recognize
b.	waħaš	cause s.o. to miss	raḍa	become satisfied
	ʔitšaaʔim	become pessimistic	saraħ	become absent minded
	ʔitfaaʔil	become optimistic	ʔiftakar	remember
	ʔiħtaar	become puzzled	nisi	forget
	ʕaaz	start to want	naam	fall asleep
	ʔiħtaag	start to need	fihim	understand
	ṣabar	become patient	ziʕil	become upset
	ṣiħi	wake up	ħass	start to feel
	ʔistanna	start to wait	saddaʔ	start to believe
	taʕaaṭaf	start to empathize	rakkez	become focused

6. Activities and Pseudo-inchoatives

Activities are verbs that describe durative changes of state with no natural terminal points such as running, swimming and typing. These verbs are specified for the features [+dynamic] and [+durative]; therefore, they have progressive readings, as in (41a), and they occur in embedded circumstantial clauses, as in (41b). The fact that the *bi*-imperfect forms of activity verbs have progressive readings distinguishes them from both statives and achievements.

(41) a. samiir bi-yelʕab koora dilwaʔti
Samir prog.-play soccer now
"Samir is playing soccer now."
b. kallemt mona w-eħna bi-netmašša
talked.1st.s. Mona and-we prog.-stroll
"I talked to Mona while we were strolling."

Since activity verbs are not marked for the feature [+telic], active participles cannot be derived from them. For example, both the sentences in (42a) and (42b) are ungrammatical because a sentence with an active participle predicate is grammatical only if the state denoted by the predicate is preceded by a complete telic onset. Running and bleeding are not telic events; therefore, they cannot be onsets.

(42) a. *ʕali gaari
Ali run$_{(AP)}$
"Ali is in a state of having run."
"Ali has run."
b. *el-mariiḍ naazef
the-patient bleed$_{(AP)}$
"The patient is in a state of having bled."
"The patient has bled."

Because activities are not marked for the feature [+telic] they can acquire telicity via conversational implicature. For example, if it is part of the speakers' shared background knowledge that Ali runs a mile every day, the sentence in (42a) is acceptable on an accomplishment interpretation. The lack of active participles distinguishes activity verbs from those marked for the feature [+telic], viz. achievements and accomplishments.

There are, however, certain cases where active participles are not only grammatically derived from verbs that have been previously classified as activities, but they also have present progressive interpretations. For example, sentences with participle predicates derived from *ʔištaɣal* "run (for a machine)", *šaal* "carry", *taabiʕ* "follow", and *saaʔ* "drive", as in (43a) and (43b) are interpreted as describing progressive events.

(43) a. el-motoor lissa šaɣɣaal
the-engine still run$_{(AP)}$
"The engine is still running."
b. maħmuud šaayil baṭṭiixa
Mahmoud carry$_{(AP)}$ watermelon
"Mahmoud is carrying a watermelon."

The arguments presented below demonstrate that these verbs do not pose a problem for an analysis of participles as complex adjectival forms that denote target states and entail complete preceding onsets. Moreover, I argue that verbs such as *šaal*, *raaʔib*, and *saaʔ*, which are usually glossed as "carry", "watch", and "drive", cannot be grouped in a language-specific sub-class of activities. That is because these verbs do not describe activity events in Egyptian Arabic. Rather, they describe achievements such as an engine's starting up and Mahmoud's lifting a watermelon. In other words, the logical forms of sentences with active participle predicates derived from these verbs include quantification over three eventuality variables: an inceptive onset achievement, a target state, and a resultant event in a fashion similar to that discussed in relation to inchoative achievements and the participles derived from them. These resultant durative atelic events, such as an engine's running, are only entailed to have started at the same moment the target states begin to hold. Whether these resultant events are in progress at speech time or not is only a matter of conversational implicature.

The behavior of the *bi-* imperfect forms of verbs such as *saaʔ* "drive" and *ʔištaɣl* "run" suggests that they are not activity verbs because they have habitual, but no progressive readings, i.e., these verbs do not describe durative events, as in (44a) and (44b).

(44) a. ʕali bi-ysuuʔ bi-surʕ-a
Ali prog./hab.-drive with-speed-fem.
"Ali drives fast."
NOT "Ali is driving fast."
b. el-ʕarabiyya bi-ti-štaɣal kwayyis
the-car prog./hab.-run well
"The car runs well."
NOT "The car is running well."

Another difference between verbs such as *ʔištaɣal* "run" and true activities is that only activities can be used in aspectual serial verb constructions. In these constructions the bare imperfect form of an activity verb co-occurs with an aspectual verb, such as *fiḍil* "remain" or *ʔaʕad* "sit", to emphasize that the durative event described by the second verb is in progress at the reference time of the aspectual verb, as in (45a). The serial verb construction *fiḍilu yaklu* "kept eating" in (45a) describes the activity event of eating as taking place over an interval that starts before and extends through the past reference time of the perfect verb *fiḍilu* "remained". Verbs such as *šaal* "carry" and *saaʔ* "drive" are ungrammatical in these constructions, as exemplified in

(45b), providing further evidence that these verbs do not describe durative eventualities.

(45) a. fiḍil-u y-akl-u liħad ma xallaṣ-u es-samak
remain-3rd.pl. 3rd.m.-eat-pl. until pro finished-3rd.pl. the-fish
"They kept eating until they finished the fish."
b. *maħmuud fiḍil ye-šiil el-baṭṭiixa
Mahmoud remained 3rd.m.s.-carry the-watermelon
"Mahmoud kept carrying the watermelon."

Further evidence in support of the hypothesis that verbs such as *šaal* "carry", *saaʔ* "drive", and *ʔištaɣal* "run" do not describe activity events comes from their behavior when used as complements of *baṭṭal* "stopped" and *badaʔ* "started". The only verbs that can occur in these constructions without inducing habitual readings are those that describe durative events, whether activities, as in (46a), or accomplishments, as in (46b). Verbs such as *ṭaar* "fly", *saaʔ* "drive", *šaal* "carry", and *ʔištaɣal* "run" are not allowed in these constructions as in (47a) and (47b). These sentences are grammatical only if interpreted on habitual readings, i.e., if Nora quits her habit of driving and the car gets fixed and starts running again.

(46) a. el-wilaad baṭṭal-u ye-lʕab-u
the-children stopped-3rd.pl. 3rd.-play-pl.
"The children stopped playing."
b. badaʔ-na ni-bni el-beet
started-1st.pl. 1st.pl.-build the-house
"We started building the house."
c. *nuura baṭṭal-et ti-suuʔ
Nora stopped-3rd.f. 3rd.f.s.-drive
"Nora stopped driving."
d. *el-ʕarabiyya badaʔet te-štaɣal
the-car started 3rd.s.f.-run
"The car started running."

There is sufficient evidence that verbs such as *ʔištaɣal* "run", *šaal* "carry", and *saaʔ* "drive" do not describe durative activity events. This analysis is based on the observations that (a) these verbs have no progressive readings, (b) they are not allowed in aspectual serial verb constructions, and (c) they cannot be used as complements of *baṭṭal* "stopped" and *badaʔ* "start".

Interestingly, the perfect forms of these verbs display properties that are typical of activities as well as the properties of telic events. For example, verbal predicates such as *ʔištaɣal* "run", and *saaʔ* "drive" grammatically license durative adverbials as in (48a), where the adverbial denotes an interval during every sub-interval of which the engine is running. Yet, the same verb allows adverbials that co-occur with achievements such as *fi talata daʔaayiʔ* "in three minutes", as in (48b), where the adverbial denotes the time period that elapsed before the beginning of the running of the engine. True activity verbs do not allow *in X time* adverbials, as in (48c).

(48) a. el-motoor ʔištaɣal li-moddet xamas saʕaat
the-engine ran for-period five hours
"The engine ran for five hours."
b. el-motoor ʔištaɣal fi talat daʔaayiʔ
the-engine ran in three minutes
"The engine ran in three minutes."
c. *ʔaadam ʕaam/raʔaṣ/ʔitkallim fi talata daʔaayiʔ
Adam swam/danced/talked in three minutes
"Adam swam/danced/talked in three minutes."

Analyzing Egyptian Arabic verbs such as *ʔištaɣal* and *šaal* as ambiguous between an activity sense, namely *run* and *carry*, and an achievement sense, namely *start up* and *lift*, fails to explain why the activity sense does not allow progressive interpretations or why it is restricted to the perfect forms. A more viable account is to analyze these verbs as achievements that describe only the starting points of other larger events. Such achievements are necessarily followed by immediate consequent activity events, e.g., an event of an engine's starting up is necessarily followed by the engine's running, even if the consequent events continue for only a few moments. When such verbs are used in their perfect forms, the consequent events are entailed to have started before speech time. However, whether the consequent activity is in progress at speech time or not is only a matter of conversational implicature.

One of the advantages of analyzing Egyptian Arabic verbs such as *šaal* "lift" and *ʔištaɣal* "start up" as achievements, rather than activities or ambiguous predicates, is that such an account explains why they have habitual but no progressive interpretations. Furthermore, this analysis accounts for the fact that the imperfect forms of these verbs do not occur in aspectual serial verb constructions and that they cannot be used as complements of *baṭṭal* "stop" or *badaʔ* "start". That is because the events described by verbs such as *ʔištaγal* "start up" are punctual changes of states while constructions such as the progressive and *start/stop doing* allow only verbs describing durative eventualities. Finally, it accounts for the observation that only the perfect forms of these verbs entail the beginning of the resultant activity events that license durative adverbials. Sentences with participles derived from verbs such as *šaal* "lift" and *ʔištaγal* "start up" are grammatical because the onset events are telic achievements.

Temporal adverbials in sentences with active participles derived from these achievement verbs can be licensed as predicates of the onset instantaneous events, the resultant durative events, and the states denoted by the participles. Therefore, these sentences can have present progressive implicatures only if the addressee assumes that the resultant activity events such as carrying and running are in progress at speech time. In fact, all sentences with active participle predicates derived from these verbs are pragmatically ambiguous between a present perfect implicature and a present progressive one depending on how the resultant events are construed. For example, the adverbial *lissa* in (49) is ambiguous between a *just* sense, where it is predicated of the onset achievements, and a *still* sense, if it is predicated of the resultant durative events.

(49) el-motoor lissa šaγaal
the-engine still/just get started$_{(AP)}$
"The engine is in a state of having gotten started."
"The engine just started."
"The engine is still running."

The arguments presented above demonstrate that 'inceptive' verbs such as *šaal* "lift", *ʔištγal* "start up", and *saaʔ* "start driving" are achievements even though they have always been analyzed as activities. Sentences with participial predicates derived from these verbs license temporal adverbials as predicates of three eventuality variables just like inchoative achievements discussed earlier. They differ only in that 'inceptives' are necessarily followed by activities whereas inchoatives are necessarily followed by states. Examples of true activity verbs include those in (50a), and examples of achievements that entail resultant activities are in (50b).

(50) a.	gara	run	kabar	grow
	hazzar	kid	raʔaṣ	dance
	ħaawel	try	dawwar ʕala	look for
	fakkar	think	sarrax	scream
	ʔigtahad	strive	ɣanna	sing
b.	ħaḍan	embrace	saaʔ	start to drive
	šaal	lift	raaʔib	start to follow
	taabeʕ	start to follow	weleʕ	start to burn
	ʔištaɣal/daar	start up	misik	start to hold

7. **Accomplishments and Translocatives**

Accomplishments are verbs that are marked for the features [+durative], [+telic] and [+dynamic]; therefore they denote descriptions of durative events with inherent end points. The *bi-* imperfect forms of accomplishments have progressive readings, which distinguishes them from statives and achievements. For example, the imperfect forms *yemla* "fill" and *yefaḍḍi* "empty" in (51a) and (51b) describe processes that are in progress at speech time. What distinguishes accomplishments from activities is that participles derived from accomplishments are grammatical, as in (52a), whereas those derived from activities are not, as in (52b).

(51) a. ʕali bi-yemla el-barmiil
Ali prog.-fill the-barrel
"Ali is filling the barrel."
b. ʕali bi-faḍḍi el-barmiil
Ali prog.-empty the-barrel
"Ali is emptying the barrel."
c. ʕali maali el-barmiil
Ali $\text{fill}_{(AP)}$ the-barrel
"Ali is in a state of having filled the barrel."
"Ali has filled the barrel."
d. *ʕali gaari
Ali $\text{run}_{(AP)}$
"Ali is in a state of having run."
"Ali has run."

The verbs termed ‘translocatives’, ‘locationals’, or ‘verbs of motions’ such as *rawwaħ* “go home”, *saafir* “travel”, and *geh* “come” are designated as an independent language-specific class in most aspectual classifications of Egyptian Arabic (Wild 1964, Woidich 1975, El-Bakry 1990, Michell & El-Hassan 1994, Brustad 2000). There are two observations that motivate analyzing these verbs as an independent class. First, unlike ‘resultative’ participles, those derived from ‘translocative’ verbs are ambiguous between a present progressive and a future interpretation, as in (53a). The other observation is that the perfect forms of ‘translocatives’ allow both *in X time* adverbials as well as durative adverbials, as in (53b) and (53c). The arguments presented below demonstrate that there is no motivation for positing a language-specific aspectual class for ‘translocatives’ because these verbs are achievements just like *šaal* “lift” and *ʔištaɣal* “start up” discussed in the previous section.

(53) a. mona gayya el-beet
Mona come$_{(AP)}$ the-house.
“Mona is coming home.”
“Mona will come home.”
b. ʔaadam geh el-beet šwayya w-miši
Adam came the-house a while and-left
“Adam came for a while and left.”
c. ʔaadam geh el-beet fi ʕašar daʔaayeʔ
Adam came the-house in ten minutes
“Adam came home in ten minutes.”

‘Translocatives’ are expected to pattern as accomplishments if they describe telic durative events such as going home or as activities, and acquire telicity via goal arguments. However, ‘transloctives’ do not pattern as either activities or accomplishments because their *bi*-imperfect forms have no progressive readings as in (54a), and they cannot be used in embedded circumstantial clauses, as in (54b). Moreover, the bare imperfect forms of these verbs cannot be grammatically used as complements of the aspectual verbs that co-occur only with verbs describing durative eventualities such as *fiḍil* “remained” and *ʔaʕad* “sat”, as in (55a) and (55b).

(54) a. *ʔaadam lissa bi-yrawwaħ
Adam sill prog.-head home
"Adam is still going home."
"Adam is still on his way home."
b. *ʔaabilta-ha w-heyya bi-truuħ es-suuʔ
met.-her and-she prog.-go the-market
"I met her while she was going to the market."
c. *mona ʔaʕadet tenzel es-suuʔ
Mona sat go down the-market
"Mona kept going to the market."
d. *fiḍil yesaafir liħad ʔaswaan
remained travel until Aswan
"He kept traveling until Aswan."

These examples clearly demonstrate that 'translocatives' do not describe durative events of change of location or being in a location. It is important to note here that not all verbs that describe change of location are 'translocatives'. For example, the verbs *gara* "run", *zaħaf* "crawl" and *ʔeddaħrag* "roll" describe changes in location but they are activities that have progressive readings and they do not have grammatical participles. Therefore, denoting a change of location is not enough to classify a verb as a 'translocative'.

So-called 'translocatives' are in fact achievement predicates that describe only the initial phases of larger events of change of location, and they vary only in the direction of that change. For example, the verb *saafir* "travel" denotes the instantaneous change from a state of being at the source to a state of not being at the source. A sentence with the imperfect predicate *bi-ysaafir* "travel" does not assert or entail that the subject of change reached the destination or even that the subject is in transition towards the destination at speech time. This explains why the imperfect forms of these verbs have habitual, but not true-present or progressive readings. Sentences with the prefect forms of these verbs assert that the subject has moved from the source and entail that the subject started the transition, i.e., they do not assert or entail reaching the destination. Therefore, the truth conditions of sentences with perfect forms of 'translocative' verbs involve quantification over the instantaneous event denoted by the predicate as well as the entailed activity or accomplishment event of moving toward the destination. This explains why these sentences allow *in X time* adverbials as well as durative adverbials. The *in X time* adverbials are predicated of the instantaneous event of leaving the sources, whereas the durative adverbials describe the entailed resultant event.

Sentences with active participle predicates derived from 'translocatives' allow temporal adverbials to be semantically predicated of the onset instantaneous event, the resultant activity of moving from the destination to the source, and the target state of having left the source. For example, the adverbial *fi ʕašar daʔaayeʔ* "in ten minutes" in (56a) describes the time that elapsed before Mona's leaving for the market (e.g., the time it took her to get ready). The adverbial *es-saaʕa xamsa* "at five o'clock" in (56b) locates the instantaneous event of her leaving. Note that this sentence does not entail that Mona is in the market at speech time, or that she is still on her way, as indicated by the fact that denying both propositions does not result in logical contradiction as in (56c) and (56d).

(56) a. mona nazla es-ssuʔ fi ʕašar daʔaayeʔ
Mona go down(AP) the-market in ten minutes
"Mona is in a state of having left for the market in ten minutes."
"Mona left for the market in ten minutes."

b. mona nazla es-ssuʔ es-saaʕa xamsa biẓẓabṭ
Mona go down(AP) the-market the-hour five exactly
"Mona is in a state of having left for the market at five o'clock exactly."
"Mona left for the market at five o'clock exactly."

c. mona nazla es-ssuʔ es-saaʕa xamsa biẓẓabṭ
Mona go down(AP) the-market the-hour five exactly
bass lissa ma-waṣalet-š hinaak liħad dilwaʔti
but still neg-arrived-neg there until now
"Mona is in a state of having left for the market at five o'clock exactly, but she has not arrived there yet."
"Mona left for the market at five o'clock exactly, but she has not arrived there yet."

d. mona nazla es-ssuʔ es-saaʕa xamsa biẓẓabṭ
Mona go down(AP) the-market the-hour five exactly
w-kallemit-ni min hinaak
and-called-me from there
"Mona is in a state of having left for the market at five o'clock exactly, and she called me from there."
"Mona left for the market at five o'clock exactly, and she called me from there."

Finally, many 'translocative' verbs describe agentive events, which explains why they are readily accepted on futurate readings, but all present tense sentences can have futurate readings if the state denoted by the predicate is planned or predicted to hold in the future. Therefore, being accepted on futurate readings is not sufficient to motivate classifying 'translocatives' as a language-specific aspectual class. Besides, 'translocative' verbs cannot have futurate readings if the implicature of planning or prediction is cancelled by adverbials such as *ʕala ɣafla* "unexpectedly", as in (57).

(57) #eḍ-ḍiyuuf gayyiin le-na bukra ʕala ɣafla
the-guests come$_{(AP)}$ to-us tomorrow unexpectedly
"The guests are coming over tomorrow unexpectedly."

The arguments presented above demonstrate that 'translocatives' have the same patterns of licensing temporal adverbials as 'inceptive' verbs such as *šaal* "lift", and *ʔištaɣal* "start up" as well as inchoative achievements such as *fihim* "get to understand" and *itfagaʕ* "get scared". This similarity suggests that these verbs can be grouped together in one aspectual class even though it is not the case that all 'inceptives' or inchoative achievements describe changes of location. However, being 'inceptive' or inchoative is not enough to classify them as an independent language-specific class. That is because accomplishments can also be inchoative and result in durative changes of location or mental and emotional states.

8. Summary and conclusion

The diagnostics developed above indicate that Egyptian Arabic verbs can be classified according to their aspectual properties into four classes: statives, achievements, accomplishments, and activities, with statives further divided into individual-level statives and stage-level statives. Individual-level statives do not have *bi*-imperfect or perfect forms, which distinguishes them from all other classes. The *bi*-imperfect forms of stage-level stative verbs have no present progressive readings; therefore, they do not occur in embedded adjunct circumstantial clauses. The lack of progressive readings distinguishes stative verbs from accomplishments and activities. Moreover, active participles cannot be grammatically derived from stative verbs because of presupposition failure, which further distinguishes them from accomplishments and achievements. The *bi-* imperfect forms of achievement verbs have no true progressive readings, i.e., they do not induce the imperfect paradox, which distinguishes them from accomplishments and activities. Activities differ from accomplishments in that deverbal active participles cannot be derived from activities.

In this paper I have argued that aspectual classification concerns properties of verbs according to the event descriptions in their denotations rather than eventualities in the real world. Such classification is based on the universal privative features [+durative], [+telic], and [+dynamic], as proposed by Olsen (1997). These three features determine the morphological and syntactic behavior of all verbs in Egyptian Arabic. Moreover, it has been demonstrated that the patterns of licensing temporal adverbials in sentences with active participle predicates cannot be used to determine the lexical aspect of the verbs they are derived from. That is because all sentences with participial predicates have present tense semantics, yet they allow present, past and future adverbials. The logical forms of sentences with participial predicates involve existential quantification over the states denoted by the participles, the onset events that bring them about, and the resultant eventualities, if any. Therefore, there is no motivation for the language-specific aspectual classes that have been proposed to accommodate the alleged varied temporal interpretations of sentences with participial predicates such as 'translocatives', 'pseudo-inchoatives' and 'inceptives'.

A cursory look at how the diagnostics developed in this paper apply to other dialects of Arabic suggests that the event descriptions denoted by verbs vary from one dialect to another. From example, the verbs *ṭaar* "take off" and *saaʔ* "start to drive" are achievements in Egyptian Arabic, but they describe durative events in Moroccan and Lebanese Arabic. Moreover, some of these diagnostics are based on the interpretations of the *bi-* imperfect, which encodes the habitual and progressive formal aspects in Egyptian Arabic. The prefix *bi-* in Lebanese Arabic is used with individual-level statives, as it is the prefix *ʕam-* that marks the progressive and habitual aspects in Lebanese. The Egyptian Arabic data used in this paper do not represent all dialects, since many of them have limited use of the active participle, as is the case with Palestinian Arabic. Finally, the observation that individual-level stative verbs do not occur in the perfect indicates that formal and lexical aspect interacts in complex ways, the whole range of which is yet to be explored.

REFERENCES

Al-Tawħiidii, Abu-ħayyaan. [1985]. *Al-'imtaa' wa al-mu'aanasa* [ed. by Mohammad Amin]. Beirut: Manshuuraat Daar Maktabat al-Hayaat.

Bache, Carl. 1995. *The study of Aspect, Tense, and Action*. New York: Peter Lang.

Bertinetto, Pier & Denis Delfitto. 2000. "Aspect vs. Actionality: Why they should be kept apart". *Tense and Aspect in the Languages of Europe* ed. by Östen Dahl, 189-226. New York: Mouton de Gruyter.

Binnick, Robert. 1991. *Time and the verb: A guide to tense and aspect*. New York: Oxford University Press.

Brustad, Kristen. 2000. *The Syntax of Spoken Arabic*. Washington, DC: Georgetown University Press.

Cantarino, Vicente. 1975. *Syntax of Modern Arabic Prose: The simple sentence* Vol. 1. Bloomington, IN: Indiana University Press.

Carlson, Greg. 1977. "A Unified Analysis of the English Bare Plural". *Linguistics and Philosophy* 1:3.413-456.

Cowell, Mark. 1964. A *Reference Grammar of Syrian Arabic*. Washington, DC: Georgetown University Press.

Davidson, David. 1969. "The Individuation of Events". *Essays in Honor of Carl H. Hempel* ed. by Nicolas Rescher, 216-234. Dordrecht: Reidel.

_____. 1967. "The Logical Form of Action Sentences". Reprinted in D. Davidson 2001: *Essays on Actions and Events*. Oxford: Clarendon.

Dowty, David. 1979. *Word Meaning and Montague Grammar*. Dordecht: Reidel.

_____. 1977. "Toward a Semantic Analysis of Verb Aspect and the English Imperfective Progressive". *Linguistics and Philosophy* 1.45-77.

Eisele, John. 1999. *Arabic Verbs in Time: Tense and aspect in Cairene Arabic*. Wiesbaden: Harrassaowitz.

_____. 1988. *The Syntax and Semantics of Tense, Aspect, and Time Reference in Cairene Arabic*. Ph.D. dissertation, University of Chicago.

El-Bakry, Fathia. 1990. *Active Participle in Colloquial Egyptian Arabic: A functional analysis*. Ph.D. dissertation, Georgetown University.

El-Tonsi, Abbas. 1982. *Egyptian Colloquial Arabic: A structure review*. Cairo: American University in Cairo Press.

Fleischman, Suzanne. 1990. *Tense and Narativity from Medieval Performance to Modern Fiction*. Austin: University of Texas Press.

Gadalla, Hassan. 2000. *Comparative Morphology of Standard and Egyptian Arabic*. Munich: Lincom Europa.

Higginbotham, James. 2000. "Events and Event Talk: An introduction". Higginbotham et al. 2000. 49-80.

_____, Fabio Pianesi & Achille Varzi. 2000. *Speaking of Events*. New York: Oxford University Press.

_____. 1985. "On Semantics". *Linguistic Inquiry* 16.547-593.

Jelinek, Eloise. 2002. "Agreement, Clitics, and Focus in Egyptian Arabic". *Themes in Arabic and Hebrew Syntax* ed. by Jamal Ouhalla & Ur Shlonsky, 71-106. London: Kluwer.

_____. 1983. "Person-Subject Marking in AUX in Egyptian Arabic". *Linguistic Categories: Auxiliaries and related puzzles* ed. by Frank Heny & B. Richards, 29-49. Dordrecht: Reidel.

_____. 1981. *On Defining Categories: AUX and predicate in Egyptian Colloquial Arabic*. Ph.D. dissertation, University of Arizona.

Krifka, Manfred. 1998. "Nominal Reference, Temporal Constitution, and Quantification in Event Semantics". *Semantics and contextual expression* ed. by Renate Bartch, Johan van Bentham & Peter van Emde Boas, 75-115. Dordrecht: Foris.

Kenny, Anthony. 1963. *Action, Emotion and Will*. London: Routledge.

Landman, Fred. 2000. *Events and Plurality: The Jerusalem lectures*. Dordrecht: Kluwer.

Lombard, Lawrence. 1986. *Events: A metaphysical study*. Boston: Kegan Paul.

Mitchell, Terence & Shahir El-Hassan. 1994. *Modality, Mood, and Aspect in Spoken Arabic with Special Reference to Egypt and the Levant*. London: Kegan Paul.

Mughazy, Mustafa. 2004. *Subatomic Semantics and the Active Participle in Egyptian Arabic*. Ph.D. dissertation, University of Illinois, Urbana-Champaign.

_____. 2003. "Metalinguistic Negation and Truth-function". *Journal of Pragmatics* 35.1143-1160.

Olsen, Mari. 1997. *A Semantic and Pragmatic Model of Lexical and Grammatical Aspect*. New York: Garland.

Parsons, Terence. 2000. "Underlying Events and Time Travel". *Speaking of Events*. Higginbotham et al. 2000. 81-94.

_____. 1990. *Events in the Semantics of English: A Study of subatomic semantics*. Cambridge: MIT Press.

Qafisheh, Hamdi. 1968. *English Pre-nominal Modifiers and Corresponding Modern StandardArabic Structures: A contrastive analysis*. Ph.D. dissertation, University of Michigan.

Ratib, Salah. 1975. *ya 'ana ya huwwa*. Cairo: Al-Hay'a Al-Miṣriyya li-l-kitaab.

Rothstein, Susan. 2004. *Structuring Events*. Oxford: Blackwell.

Ryle, Gilbert. 1949. *The Concept of Mind*. London: Hutchinson.

Smith, Carlota. 1997. *The Parameter of Aspect*. London: Kluwer.

Sanz, Montserrat. 2000. *Events and Predication: A new approach to syntactic processing in English and Spanish*. Philadelphia: John Benjamins.

Steward, Helen. 1997. *The Ontology of Mind: Events, processes, and states*. Oxford: Clarendon.

Vendler, Zeno. 1967. *Linguistics in Philosophy*. NY: Cornell University Press.

Verkuyl, Henk. 1972. *On the Compositional Natures of the Aspects*. Dodrecht: Reidel.

Verkuyl, Henk. 1993. *A Theory of Aspectuality: The Interaction between temporal and atemporal structure*. Cambridge: Cambridge University Press.

Wager, Janet. 1984. *Complementation in Moroccan Arabic*. Ph.D. dissertation, Massachusetts Institute of Technology.

Wild, Stefan. 1964. "Die Resultative Funktion des Aktiven Patizeps in den Syrisch-Palastinichen Dialekten des Arabischen". *ZDMG* 114.239-254.

Wise, Hilary. 1975. *A Transformational Grammar of Spoken Egyptian Arabic*. Oxford: Blackwell.

Woidich, Manfred. 1975. "Zur Funktion des Aktiven Partizeps im Kairenischen-Arabischen. *ZDMG* 125.273-293.

BUILDING A COMPUTATIONAL LEXICON FOR ARABIC
A CORPUS-BASED APPROACH

Sameh Al-Ansary
University of Alexandria, Egypt

1. Introduction

The linguistic knowledge formulated in existing grammars and dictionaries is unsuitable for language technology tools for two reasons. First, most of it is not corpus-based. Rather it reflects the individual linguist's (lexicographer's) competence based on a collection of data (citations) and no matter how large their collection may be, it is permeated by a bias that cannot be avoided. Second, traditional grammars and dictionaries have been devised for human users. Human users differ substantially from machines. Humans use inductive reasoning and can draw analogies easily. Faculties like these are taken for granted and are reflected in the traditional arrangement and presentation of processed linguistic data. Language technology tools cannot take recourse to common sense. For language technology applications, all knowledge has to be spelled out in the form of rules, lists and probabilities.

This task is sufficiently demanding in itself. In order to carry it out, we have to go back to the sources. The only source for linguistic data is the corpus, the authentic and actual texts in their unannotated representation. However, anyone who has gone to the sources has also experienced the problem that when we start analyzing language as it occurs in a corpus, we gain evidence that renders existing grammars and dictionaries as very unreliable repositories of linguistic knowledge. We discover that our traditional linguistic knowledge gives us a very biased view of language, a view that has its roots in the contingency of over two thousand years of linguistic theorizing. We are so accustomed to this view that we take it for granted. It is true that traditional grammars and dictionaries have helped us, fairly satisfactorily, to overcome the linguistic problems we humans have to deal with. However, they will not suffice for language technology applications.

This is why, however cumbersome and expensive it may be, language has to be described in a way that will be appropriate for Natural Language Processing. In the Council of Europe corpus project of the Multilingual Dictionary Experiment (project leader, John Sinclair, with participants from Croatia, England, Germany, Hungary, Italy and Sweden), it has been demonstrated that monolingual and bilingual dictionaries are of no (or only little) use when it comes to automatically translating a word from one language into another in cases where there is more than one alternative. A close analysis of the problems involved in the translation of nominalizations between German, French, and Hungarian (also corpus-based) has shown that all the descriptions available in traditional dictionaries and grammars are inadequate, incomplete, and ultimately useless (Sinclair 1995). To reduce the cost of building a corpus-based language analysis from scratch, which is indispensable, corpus exploitation tools have to be developed which arrange the hard facts (including statistic-driven devices for context analysis) and which process them (with a great deal of human intervention for the semantic interpretation of data) into algorithmic linguistic knowledge, into rules derived from objective data rather than individual competence. Perhaps this will result in the finding that traditional categories like 'noun', 'verb' and 'adjective' do not, after all, reflect categories useful for NLP.

In this paper we discuss how to build a natural language tool (i.e., a computational lexicon) from a RUNNING CORPUS. The primary aims of this project include:

a) To Present a powerful strategy for detecting entries of an Arabic computational lexicon from authentic data,
b) To build a tool that helps in analyzing a huge corpus of Arabic,
c) To draw broad lines for an Arabic Lexical Database parallel to that of English, CELEX,[1] that can be released over the net for Arabic linguistic research and

[1]http://libwww.essex.ac.uk/Database_Guides/celex.htm.

d) To build a base infrastructure for Arabic NLP applications.

To achieve these objectives, the following sub-aims will be needed:

a) A corpus for MSA (authentic data)
b) A text analysis interface to analyze the Arabic corpus (on word level) formally and objectively
c) A linguistic database management system to examine automatically the analyzed data
d) Formalism to implement the lexicon.

Therefore, this paper discusses the following component/ stages of the proposed Arabic lexicon:

- Text analysis stage
- Linguistic features and lexical categories
- Analyzed corpus/ linguistic database conversion.
- Implementation of the lexicon
- Tested applications and future uses of the built lexicon
- Some primary conclusions and hints for the next stage

2. Text Analysis Stage

A text analysis interface was built to analyze a huge corpus of MSA selected from different genres (politics, art, economy, sports, social news, advertisements, etc.,) collected from different sources: newspapers, magazines, novels, academic writings, etc. The system relies on five main components.

2.1 *Morphological component*

This component performs some morphological tests to extract the stem of the word depending on suffix-prefix compatibility. This component is needed for three reasons: first, to get all possible ways of analyzing or dividing the word in question; second, to help minimize the number of entries in the lexicon consequently the time used in the search; third, to extract root, categorical information (section 2.2 below) and linguistic features (section 2.3 below). The morphological component works in coordination with the interactive component as we will see in section 2.4 below. It is important to note here that this subroutine is called a morphological component not a morphological analyzer, since it sometime fails in getting the correct analysis. However, in this case it learns from the user how to analyze a given word correctly in the future.

2.2 *Categorical component*

Traditionally, Arabic words are classified into three subclasses: nouns, verbs and particles. Verbs are generated from trilateral or quadriliteral radicals. Nouns are classified into derivational and non-derivational nouns. Derivational nouns are those derived from Arabic verbs. They are semantically related to the root and their measures (morphological patterns) for each category are fixed. Non-derivational nouns are nouns that do not have verbs from which they are derived (e.g., رجل *rajul* "man"). Particles form a closed set. Their number is relatively small and their features are well established.

Computationally, the traditional classification of Arabic parts of speech (noun, verb and particle) is not an adequate division that permits detailed information about lexical items inside a lexicon that is intended to be used in NLP applications. For example, although كاتب *ka:tib* "writer" and كتاب *kita:b* "book" can be considered as related to the main category 'noun' and derived from the same root, there is a morphological difference in the surface form—as they describe different entities—that can not be ignored. As entries inside the lexicon should be tagged with respect to detailed information that make NLP tasks easier, the two nouns should be recognized by the analysis interface as belonging to different subclasses of nouns. As we will see later, texts which are analyzed using the interface will be the base upon which the entries of our planned lexicon will be selected.

Therefore, our analysis interface is enriched with a consistent detailed hierarchical description of Arabic main parts of speech. This hierarchical description contains information about the word's main class—to separate it from other classes—and its subclass to differentiate it from other surface forms derived from the same root. Accordingly, nouns were classified into 46 subclasses, such as active participle, passive participle, adjectival noun, adverbial noun, verbal noun, pronoun and common noun, etc.; verbs into 3 classes, (past, present and imperative); and particles into 23 subclasses, such as preposition, additional, resumption, conjunction, conditional, conformational, prohibition, optative and dubious and so on.

2.3 *Linguistic features component*

After the categorical information have been set, we found that sub-classification is not sufficient to describe each word. Words have to be supplied with a set of linguistic features that completes the view of the nature of words inside texts. This will enrich the text with more linguistic features on word level and help in building a good comprehensive lexical database. Processing the database accordingly will absolutely lead to extract the entries needed for building the proposed lexicon together with their features used in the text as follows:

- Verbs are described by using seven linguistic features to show the following characteristics:

Perfection	=perfective or imperfect.
Radicals	=strong or weak.
Augmentation	=augmented or unaugmented.
Transitivity	=intransitive, transitive, ditransitive, tritransitive.
Voice	=active or passive.
Form	=the verb form (I, II, III etc.).
Root type	=triliteral or quadriliteral.

- Nouns are described using the following eight linguistic features:

Derivation	=derivational or primitive
Number	=singular, dual or plural
Gender	=masculine or feminine
Noun end	=strong, semi-strong, *maqṣūr*, *manūṣ* or *mamdūd*
Person	=first, second or third
Root type	=triliteral or quadriliteral
Nominal transitivity	=in case the noun plays the role of the verb inside the sentence

Humanity	=human, non-human or God [2]
Agglutination	=whether the noun appears in isolation or bound to another form.[3]

- Particles are described by using three linguistic features:

Agglutination / Status	=free or bound.
Role	=the grammatical role it plays.
Precedence	=what part of speech the particle precedes
Semantic function	=particle subclass according to its semantic meaning in context

2.4 *Interactive component*

We were careful about minimizing the possibility of committing errors during raw text analysis. The components discussed in (3.1), (3.2) and (3.3) are not advanced in the initial stage of the work, consequently giving the possibility to store analysis errors with texts if the decision were to be taken 100% automatically. In addition, sometime the disambiguation process needs information exceeding the morphological level which is far from the reach of the system in the present stage. Therefore, it was very important to find a compromise between the weak points of the system and minimizing the possibility of storing analysis errors within texts. The best solution considered was to include two other components to be working coordinately with the morphological component: an interactive one and a statistical one. These two components will be eliminated when the rules inside the interface are adequate enough to carry out the task of the analysis automatically. The former concerns making the text analysis interface work in a semi-automatic way, i.e., a confirmation from the user is needed to store the correct analysis with each word in the text. The latter will be dealt with in section 2.5. Consider a traditional example to explain what the interactive component is. Suppose that the word in question is فهم , the system will suggest the following:

[2]'god' feature is derived to describe the humanity status of words like الله *Allah* "God". This word can not be described in terms of humanity as being nonhuman.
[3]This feature is used to describe pronouns.

فهم : Transitive, Active , Verb in past, Perfect, Strong, Unaugmented

If the user did not confirm this analysis, the morphological component would prompt the following:

فهم : Standard verbal noun, Derivational, Singular, Masculine, Strong

If, again, the user did not give confirmation, the morphological component would prompt again:

فـ: Coordinative, Bound, Conjunctive particle, Precedes a pronoun,

+

هم : Pronoun, Plural, Masculine, Third person, Free

The process continues until the system gets an accepted analysis. Most of the times, the component predicts the correct analysis from the first time.

2.5 *Statistical component*

The system stores statistical information about each word and each analysis as it runs. The system updates this type of information every time a word is accepted. This information will be useful in the following ways:

- In case the interface is developed to take the decision about the correct analysis without the intervention of the user: in this case, if it finds multiple analysis of the word without any clue of supporting one of these analyses, the statistical information will be the base upon which the preferred decision will be made, i.e., the higher the frequency of a given analysis, the more likely it will be output.
- To collect statistics of actual usage of the vocabulary, categories and linguistic features as a whole.

2.6 *Implementation of the analysis interface*

The text analysis interface is implemented using Visual Basic 6.00. Figure 1 (below) is a snap shot of its main screen showing how the raw text is analyzed. If we concentrate on one of the analyzed words inside the text, the diagram in Figure 2 (below) can be sketched to represent the flow of information stored with each word. The diagram states that the word القاهرة *alqa:hira* "Cairo" has the main class 'Noun' and subclass 'Proper noun of Place'. It is transformed from an active participle (its morphological surface form is *fa:ʕil*), its root is قهر *qhr* and its lemma is القاهرة. In addition, this word can be described inside the text, using six linguistic features describing its derivational state, number, gender, person, word ending and humanity status. After the text has been analyzed, we obtained an analyzed text as illustrated in Figure 3 (below).

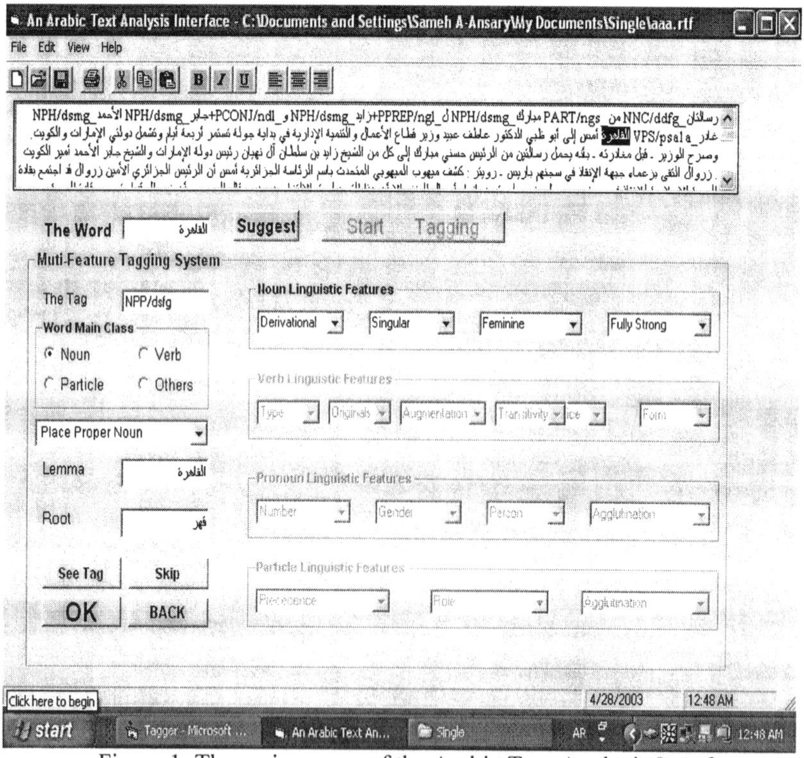

Figure 1. The main screen of the Arabic Text Analysis Interface.

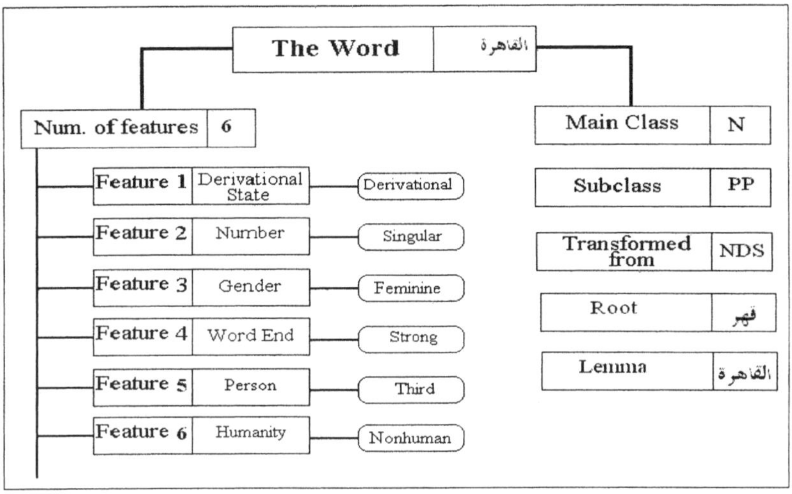

Figure 2. Example of the flow of information stored with each word

رسالتان_NNC/ddfg من_PPREP/ngs مبارك_NPH/dsmg ل_PPREP/ngl+زايد_
NPH/dsmg و_PCONJ/ndl+جابر_NPH/dsmg الأحمد_NPH/dsmg غادر_VPS/psa1a
القاهرة_NPP/dsfg أمس_NAT/ssxg إلى_PPREP/ngs أبوظبي_NPP/sxfn ل_PART/nrl
+دكتور_NOP/ssmg عاطف_NPH/dsmg عبيد_NPH/dsmg وزير_NNP/ssmg قطاع_
NNC/dsmg ل_PART/nrl+أعمال_NIS/dbmg و_PCONJ/pdl+ل_PART/nrl+تنمية_
NIS/dsfg ال_PART/nrl+إدارية_NW/dsfg في_PPREP/ngs بداية_NIS/dsfg جولة_
NNC/dsfg تستمر_VPR/pza1a أربعة_NE/ssfg أيام_NT/sbmg و_PCONJ/vdl+تشمل_
VPR/psu1a دولتي_NNC/sdfg الإمارات_NPP/drfg و_PCONJ/pdl+الكويت_NPP/ssfg. و_
PRES/vrl+صرح_VPS/psu1a ل_PART/nrl+وزير_NNP/ssmg - قبل_NAT/sxxx
مغادرت_NIS/dsfg+ه_NRN/sm3l - ب_PREP/pgl+أن_PCONF/nks+ه_NRG/sm3l
يحمل_VPR/psu1a رسالتين_NNC/ddfg من_PPREP/ngs ال_PART/nrl+رئيس_
NNP/dsmg حسني_NPH/dsmn مبارك_NPH/dsmg إلى_PPREP/ngs كل_NZ/sxmg من_
PPREP/ngs ل_PART/nrl+شيخ_NNP/dsmg زايد_NPH/dsmg بن_NNC/dsmg سلطان_
NNC/ssmg ل_NNC/ssmg نهيان_NPH/ssmg رئيس_NNP/dsmg دولة_NNC/ssfg
الإمارات_NPP/drfg و_PCONJ/ndl+ل_PART/nrl+شيخ_NNP/dsmg جابر_NPH/dsmg
الأحمد_NPH/dsmg أمير_NPH/dsmg الكويت_NPP/ssfg . زروال_NPH/ssmg التقى_
VPS/pda1a ب_PPREP/ngl+زعماء_NNP/dbmg جبهة_NNC/dsfg ال_PART/nrl+إنقاذ_
NIS/dsmg في_PPREP/ngs سجن_NNC/dsmg+هم_NRG/pm3l - رويتر_NPP/ssmg :

Figure 3. Example of an analyzed text.

A linguistic database management system is needed to examine and browse analyzed texts. However, such a system does not exist. Thus we had to build it.

3. **Analyzed Text / Linguistic Database Conversion**

It is evident from Figure 3 that texts in their analyzed format can not be studied manually. Therefore, the analyzed corpus is converted into a searchable relational linguistic database using the Arabic Analyzed Text Browser (AATB), a hand-built interface programmed in visual basic 6.00. The interface is capable of storing all information about all details obtained from the analysis interface including word subclass, word structure, linguistic features, etc. Using the AATB, one can get information including the following:

- Frequency of word tags
- Tag sequences (this can be considered as a kind of context examination)
- Tag collocations
- Different words that have the same tag
- Different tags of the same word
- Browse words according to their assigned linguistic features
- Representation of morphological structure of words in terms of tree diagrams.

Figures 4-5 below are snap shots of AATB's opening screen and an example of an interrogative query. The interrogative query examines 44 contexts in which common nouns (NNC) can occur.

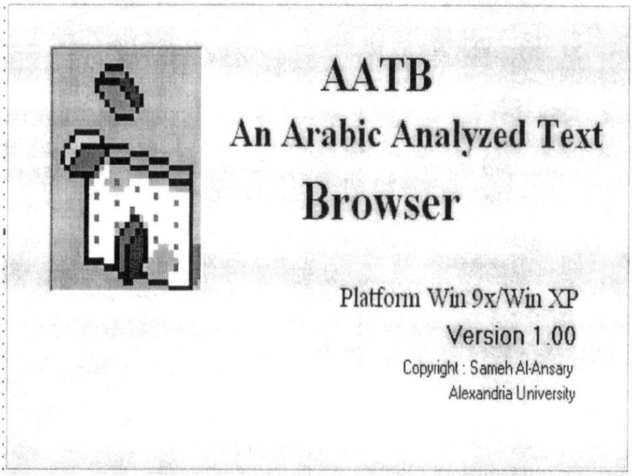

Figure 4. The opening screen of the Arabic Analyzed Text

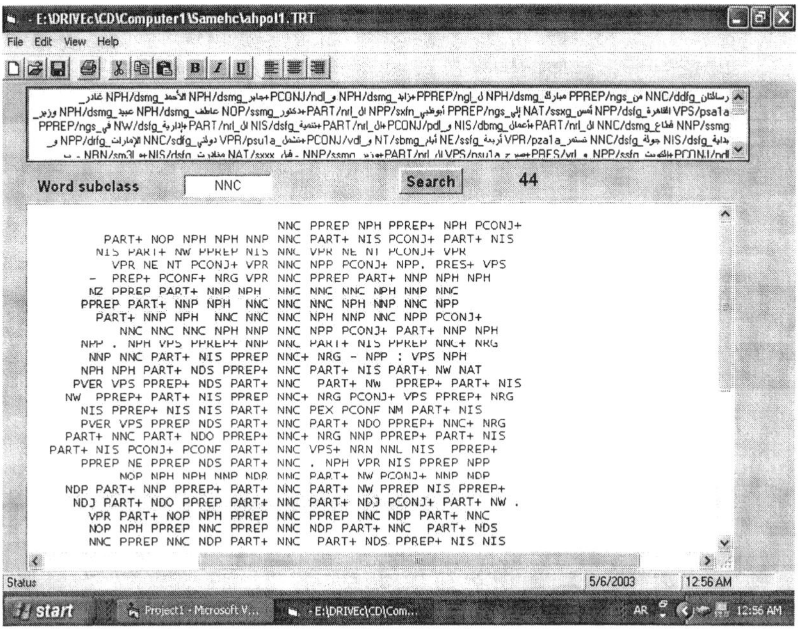

Figure 5. Example of an interrogative query using AATB.

The AATB is also capable of exporting its data files to be examined under other systems that have more statistical capabilities; e.g., MS Excel. Figure 6 illustrates an example of the whole database that can be examined statistically under MS-Excel. (Any other statistical package can be used.)

J	I	H	G	F	E	D	C	B	A	
Root	Lemma	F6	F5	F4	F3	F2	F1	Subclass	Word	1
رسل	رسالة	x	0	g	f	d	d	NNC	رسالتان	2
NONE	من	x	0	0	s	g	n	PPREP	من	3
برك	مبارك	x	0	g	m	s	d	NPH	مبارك	4
NONE	ل	x	0	0	l	g	n	PPREP	ل	5
زيد	زايد	x	0	g	m	s	d	NPH	زايد	6
NONE	و	x	0	0	l	d	n	PCONJ	و	7
جبر	جابر	x	0	g	m	s	d	NPH	جابر	8
حمد	الأحمد	x	0	g	m	s	d	NPH	الأحمد	9
PUN	PUN	PUN	PUN	PUN	PUN	PUN	PUN	FULLSTOI	.	10
غدر	غادر	III	a	1	a	s	p	VPS	غادر	11
قهر	القاهرة	x	0	g	f	s	d	NPP	القاهرة	12
مسي	أمس	x	0	g	x	s	s	NAT	أمس	13
NONE	إلى	x	0	0	s	g	n	PPREP	إلى	14
NONE	أبوظبي	x	0	n	f	x	s	NPP	أبوظبي	15
NONE	الدكتور	x	0	g	m	s	s	NOP	الدكتور	16
عطف	عاطف	x	0	g	m	s	d	NPH	عاطف	17
عبد	عبيد	x	0	g	m	s	d	NPH	عبيد	18
وزر	وزير	x	0	g	m	s	s	NNP	وزير	19

Figure 6. Examining the AATB output using MS-Excel.

Finally, AATB can extract lexical entries according to the required formalism. Now we are ready to move to the next point.

4. Implementing the Lexicon

The Affix Grammar over Finite Lattices (AGFL) formalism has been chosen for the implementation. Therefore, our proposed lexicon can be used with any corpus analysis software or any grammar written in AGFL.[4]

4.1 *What is Affix Grammar over Finite Lattices (AGFL)?*

AGFL is a grammar workbench developed in Nijmegen University, the Netherlands. The AGFL formalism consists of a collection of software systems for Natural Language Processing and grammar development. The grammar workbench enables the user to edit

[4]For more details, see Akkerman et al. (1988).

grammars, to perform a consistency checks on a grammar, to compute gra-mmar properties and to assist in performing grammar transformations and to generate examples. Affix Grammar over a Finite Lattices is a simple form of two-level grammars admitting quite efficient implementations. The first level consists of context-free syntax rules, rewriting nonterminals to terminals or to other nonterminals; e.g., SENTENCE: SUBJECT, VERB. The second level is a level where affix domains are defined by rewriting affix-nonterminals; e.g., number: PLURAL, SINGULAR. AGFL has proved adequacy in describing a number of natural languages including:

- English (Oostdijk 1984)
- Spanish (Hallebeek 1990, 1992; del Rio 2002)
- Modern Standard Arabic (Ditters 1986, 1988, 1992, 2000, 2001; Al-Ansary 2001a, 2001b, 2002a, 2002b)
- German (Aarts & Meijs 1984).[5]

4.2 *Types of AGFL rules used in the implementation*

To implement a lexicon in AGFL format we must deal with two types of rules:

a) **Affix rules:** For defining terminal and non-terminal affixes that describe each lexical item inside the lexicon; this constitutes the definition file (*.def). According to AGFL, the following notations should be followed in writing affix rules:

- affix names are written in lower case
- affix values are written in upper case
- multiple values are separated by a semicolon
- a double colon represents the rewrite symbol
- a period ends each rule.

- **Affix rules for the verbal entries:**

- vsubclass : : VPR; VPS; VIM.
- type : : PERFECTIVE; IMPERFECTIVE; NASEKH.

[5]For further details, see Koster (1991, 1996a, 1996b, http://www.cs.kun.nl/agfl/).

- radicals : : vstrong; weak.
  vstrong : : FULLY; EMPHATIC; MAHMOUZ.
  weak : : MITHAL; HOLLOW; DEFICIENT; lafi:f.
  lafif : : 2&3;1&3.
- augmentation : : AUG; UNAUG.
- voice : : ACTIVE; PASSIVE.
- verb form : : I; II; III; IV; V; VI; VII; VIII; IX; X; XI; XII; XIII; XIV.
- vroot : : TRILITERAL; QUADRILITERAL.
- transitivity : : trans; INTRAS.
  trans : : MONOTRANS; DITRANS; TRITRANS.

- **Affix rules for nominal entries:**

- nsubclass : : NPH; NPRO; NPGOD; NIA; NIS; NOP; NNC; NNP; NE; NPP; NT; NDS; NDS; NIM; NDP; NF; NDJ; NDR; ND; NU; NQTM; NQTUM; NDO; NDE; NNL; NW; NM; NCONF.
- nroot : : TRILITERAL; TETRALITERAL; NEMPTY.
- derivation : : DERIVATIONAL; PRIMITIVE.
- ntransitivity : : NINTRANS;NMONO; NDITRANS; EMPTY.
- agglutination : : BOUND; FREE.
- nounend : : STRONG; SEMI-STRONG; MAQṢŪR; MANQŪṢ; MAMDŪD; UNAPP.
- gender : : FEM; MASC; BOTH.
- number : : SING; DUAL; plu.
  plu : : BPLU; RPLU.
- person : : FIRST; SECOND; THIRD.
- humanity : : HUMAN; NONHUMAN; GOD.

- **Affix rules for the particle entries:**

- grammatical role : : COODINATIVE; JUSSIVE; CAUSATIVE; GENITIVE; NASEKH; INDICATIVE; NONE.
- precedence : : NOUN ; VERB ; PARTICLE.
- semantic function : : RESUMPTION; INDEFINITE; CONDITIONAL; OPTATIVE; CONFIRMATIONAL; PROHIBITION; NEGATION; VERIFICATION; VOCATION; EXCEPTION; ANSWERING; INTERROGATIVE; CONJUNCTION; IMPERATIVE; DEFINITENESS;

FUTURE; EXCLAMATION; REASONAL; SIMILE; DUBIOUS.

- status : : FREE; BOUND

b) **Lexical rules:** For storing lexical entries together with their affix terminal values. This constitutes the lexicon itself (*.lex). According to AGFL, the following notations should be followed in writing lexical rules:

- a colon represents the rewrite symbol (:)
- alternatives are separated by a semicolon (;)
- a period ends each rule (.)
- lexical terminals are enclosed between double quotes(" ").

The following are examples of lexical rules (lexical entries):

VERB (vsubclass, vroot, type, radicals, augmentation, form, transitivity, voice):

VERB (VPS, TRI, PERFECTIVE, FULLY, AUG, III, INTRANS|MONO, ACTIVE): "غادر ".
VERB(VPS, TRI,PERFECTIVE, HOLLOW, UNAUG, III, INTRANS|MONO, ACTIVE): "قال ".

NOUN (nsubclass, nroot, number, gender, person, nounend, ntransitivity, humanity)

NOUN(NPRO, NEMPTY, SING, BOTH, FIRST, UNAPP, EMPTY, HUMAN):"أنا ".
NOUN(NPRO, NEMPTY, SING, FEM, THIRD, UNAPP, EMPTY, Humanity)[6]: " هي ".
NOUN(NNC, TRILITERAL, SING, MASC, THIRD, STRONG, NEMPTY,HUMAN): "ولد " ، "شاب " ، "بطل "، "انسان ".
NOUN(NNC, TRILITERAL, SINGMASC, THIRD, STRONG, NEMPTY, NONHUMAN): "بيت " ، "سطح " ، "قطاع ".
NOUN(NIS, TRILITERAL, SING, MASC, THIRD, STRONG, NDITRANS,

[6]'Humanity' is non-terminal in this rule because"هي" can be used with human and nonhuman. Thus terminal value will be taken according to the use of "هي" in the context.

NONHUMAN): "تقديم" ، "اعتبار".

PARTICLE (semantic function, grammatical role, status, precedence):

PARTICLE(LOCATIVE, GENITIVE, FREE, NOUN): " في " ، "على ".
PARTICLE (NEGATIVE, NASEKH, FREE, NOUN): "لعل " ، "ليت".
PARTICLE (INTERROGATIVE, NONE, BOUND, NOUN|VERB): "أ ".

5. **Testing the Lexicon**

Al-Ansary (2001a, 2001b, 2002a, 2002b) wrote a two-level grammar in terms of alternating functions and categories levels to account for NP structure types in spoken and written MSA in which a preliminary version of this lexicon was used. With the current version of the lexicon, it was possible to enhance our earlier grammar to eliminate undesired parses. In addition we started to shift our description to deal with sentence level.[7] Due to space limitations here, it was not possible to demonstrate all successful application trials that are based on the current version of the lexicon.[8] Therefore, in this paper, testing the lexicon is limited to improving parsing algorithms. Below, we can see a tree diagram[9] of a complicated NP structure.

أسباب جميع عمليات الإرهاب والعنف والقتل ومحاولة السيطرة على المجتمع البريء لتقويض أركانه والاستيلاء على الحكم

ʔasba:bu gami:ʕi ʕamaliyya:ti ʔal-ʔirha:bi walʕunfi walqatli wamuħa:walati lsayṭarati ʕala lmugtamaʕi lbari:ʔi litaqwi:ḍi ʔarka:nihi walisti:la:ʔi ʕala lħukm
"The reasons of all terrorist operations, violence, killing and attempt to control the innocent society to destroy its pillars and confiscate the authority."

NP(NHEAD
(NOUN
(NNC(أسباب))),
POD

[7]A preliminary two-level grammar that accounts for sentence level in MSA is forthcoming.
[8]A paper dealing with tools for Arabic corpus analysis and which focuses on using the lexicon in morphological decomposition of words, tagging and corpus look up is forthcoming.
[9]Because of the complicated graphic view of the tree diagram that could not be drawn in the page space, the tree diagram is presented in the vertical format given.

```
(NP
  (NHEAD
    (NOUN
      (NQTM(جميع))),
   POD
    (NP
      (NHEAD
        (NOUN
          (NNC(عمليات))),
       POD
        (COORDINATED NPs
          (NP
            (PREDET
              (ARTICLE(الـ)),
             NHEAD
              (NOUN
                (NIS(إرهاب))))),
          COORD
            (PCONJ(و)),
          NP
           (PREDET
              (ARTICLE(الـ)),
           NHEAD
             (NOUN
               (NNC(عنف)))),
          COORD
            (PCONJ(و)),
           NP
            (PREDET
               (ARTICLE(الـ)),
             NHEAD
              (NOUN
                 (NIS( قتل)))),
          COORD
            (PCONJ(و)),
          NP
            (NHEAD
              (NOUN
                (NIS (محاولة))),
             POD
              (NP
                (PREDET
                   (ARTICLE (الـ)),
```

```
            NHEAD
              (NOUN
                 (NIS(سيطرة))),
            PPOM
              (PP
                (PHEADER
                   (PREP(على)),
                 PCOMPLEMENT(
                   NP
                     (PREDET
                        (ARTICLE(الـ)),
                      NHEAD
                        (NOUN
                           (NNC(مجتمع),
                     ADJPOM
                       (ADJP
                          (PREDET
                             (ARTICLE(الـ)),
                           ADJHEAD
                             (NDJ(بريء)))))))))))),
     PPOM
       (PHEADER
          (PREP(لـ)),
        PCOMPLEMENT(
          COORDINATED NPs
            (NP
              (NHEAD
                 (NOUN
                    (NIS(تقويض))),
               POD
                 (NP
                    (NHEAD
                       (NOUN
                          (NNC(أركان))),
                     POD
                       (NP
                          (NHEAD
                             (NOUN
                                (NPRO (ـهـ-)))))))),
             COORD
               (PCONJ(و)),
             NP
               (PREDET
```

```
      (ARTICLE(ال)),
    NHEAD
      (NOUN
        (NIS(استيلاء))),
    PPOM
      (PHEADER
        (PREP(على)),
      PCOMPLEMENT(
        NP
          (PREDET
            (ARTICLE(ال)),
          NHEAD
            (NOUN
              (NIS(حكم))))))))))))))))))).
```

6. Areas of Near-future Refinements

Near future enhancements are planned to go in two directions. The first direction concerns adding some affix values to account for complement types of transitive verbs (cf. Schnefeld 2001, Zaring et al. 1996, Geest & Jaspers 1989). The following are some examples:

DC-H:	Direct complement with non-human
DC+H:	Direct complement with human
ICP:	One complement with a preposition
IC2P:	Two complements with a preposition
IC-H:	Indirect complement with non-human
IC+H:	Indirect complement with a human.

The second direction concerns preparing the lexicon to be used in semantic analysis of corpora (Pustejovsky 1993). This will add some affix values including, for example:

- Making reference to semantic relations between lexical entries
- Adding semantic features that help in word sense disambiguation
- Adding features that help in detecting semantic irrelevancy to the root.

7. Conclusion

In this paper we discussed a corpus-based approach by which a computational lexicon for MSA can be built. This approach depends on analyzing a set of authentic data and building the tools required for the analysis tasks, then extracting lexical entries in the required formalism. This lexicon is contemporary, since it is based on a corpus. It is also possible to enrich this lexicon with statistical information that the analysis interface collects as it runs on more texts. This gives our lexicon an advantage that is missing in traditional lexicons.

The initial proposed lexicon, however small (1500 entries), has proved adequate with respect to the limited application in which the lexicon has been tested; e.g., tagging, lemmatization, morphological decomposition of words, and parsing. We believe that after the planned enhancements have been applied, it will be possible to use the lexicon in a wide range of high quality Arabic NLP applications.

REFERENCES

Aarts, Jan & Williem Meijs. 1984. *Corpus Linguistics: Recent developments in the use of computer corpora in English language research.* Amsterdam: Rodopi.

Al-Ansary, Sameh. 2002a. "An Affix Grammar for a Comparative Corpus-based Study on Spoken and written NPs in MSA". Paper presented at the 2nd AGFL Workshop, Nijmegen University, The Netherlands.

_____. 2002b. A *Comparative Corpus-based Study of Spoken and Written Modern Standard Arabic.* Ph.D. dissertation, Alexandria University.

_____. 2001a. "NP–Structure Types in Spoken and Written Modern Standard Arabic (MSA) Corpora: A formal based approach". Paper presented at the 15th ALS Annual Symposium on Arabic Linguistics, 2-3 March 2001, Salt Lake City, Utah, the United States.

_____. 2001b. "A Formalization Tool for Comparing Syntax Structures in Written and Spoken MSA Corpora". *Proceedings of the ACL Arabic Natural Processing Workshop*, 103-110. Toulouse, France.

Akkerman, Eric, Hetty Zutphen Voogt-Van & Willem. Meijs. 1988. *A Computerized Lexicon for Word-level Tagging: ASCOT report no 2.* Amsterdam: Rodopi.Commission of the European. *CELEX. Offical Legal Database of the European Communities.* [London]: Context Ltd. Commission of the European Communities.

Ditters, Everhard. 2001. "Distinct(ive) Sentence Functions in Descriptive Arabic Linguistics". Paper presented in the 15th ALS Annual Symposium on Arabic Linguistics, 2-3 March 2001, Salt Lake City, Utah, the United States.

_____. 2000. "Basic Structures of Modern Standard Arabic Syntax in Terms of Function and Categories". *Proceedings of the International Conference on Artificial and Computational Intelligence for Decision Control and*

Automation in Engineering and Industrial Applications, 83-88. Monastir, Tunisia.

_____. 1992. *A Formal Approach to Arabic Syntax: The noun phrase and verb phrase*. Ph.D. dissertation, Nijmegen University.

_____. 1988. "A Formal Grammar for Automatic Syntactic Analysis and other Applications". *Proceedings of the Regional Conference on Informatics and Arabization* Vol. 1:128-145. Tunisia: IRSIT.

_____. 1986. "An Extended Affix Grammar for the Noun Phrase in Modern Standard Arabic". *Corpus linguistics II: New studies in the analysis and exploitation of computer corpora* ed. by Jan Arts & Williem Meijs, 47-77. Amsterdam: Radopi.

Geest, Wim De & Dany Jaspers. 1989. *Sentential Complementation and the Lexicon: Studies in honour of Wim de Geest*. Dordrecht: Foris.

De Rio, Maria Paula Santalla. 2002. "A Formal Grammar of Spanish for Phrase-Level Analysis Applied to Information Retrieval, Lalia, 14, Series Maior". University of Santiago de Compostela, Santiago de Compostela. [Available at http://www.usc.es/spubl]

Hallebeek, Jan. 1992. *A Formal Approach to Spanish Syntax*. Amsterdam: Radopi.

_____. 1990. *Een Grammatica voor Automatische Analyse van het Spaans*. Ph.D. dissertation, University of Nijmegen.

Koster, Cornelis H. A. 1996a. "The Family of Affix Grammars". *Proceedings of the First AGFL Workshop*, 5-16. Nijmegen, the Netherlands: Computing Science Institute, University of Nijmegen.

_____. 1996b. "Developments in AGFL". *Proceedings of the first AGFL Workshop*, 45-58. Nijmegen, the Netherlands: Computing Science Institute, University of Nijmegen.

_____. 1991. "Affix Grammars for Natural Languages: Attribute grammars, applications and systems". *Attribute Grammars, Applications and Systems, International Summer School SAGA*, Prague, Czechoslovakia, June 1991. *Lecture Notes in Computer Science*, volume 545. Berlin: Springer-Verlag.

Oostdijk, Nelleke. 1984. "An Extended Affix Grammar for the English Noun Phrase". Aarts & Meijs 1984. 95-122.

Pustejovsky, James. 1993. *Semantics and the Lexicon*. Dordrecht: Kluwer.

Schnefeld, Doris. 2001. *Where Lexicon and Syntax Meet*. Berlin: Mouton.

Sinclair, John & J. Ball. 1995. *Text Typology (External Criteria)*. Draft Version, Electronic Document on the Pisa EAGLES ftp server, Birmingham.

Zaring, Laurie Ann & Johan Rooryck. 1996. *Phrase Structure and the Lexicon*. Dordrecht: Kluwer.

POLITICAL TRANSITION, LINGUISTIC SHIFT
HOW A POLITICAL COMMUNIQUÉ (*BAYAAN*) HAS COME TO BE WHAT IT IS*

Naima Boussofara-Omar
The University of Kansas

1. Introduction

Text regulations and language regimentation are rich sites for investigating how choice of linguistic codes and selection of nearly every aspect of language—from its phonological features, to lexical items, to grammatical structures, to stylistic levels—for a final linguistic product are often determined by language ideology. Institutions of power (e.g., government, media, legal systems, and educational institutions) play a significant role in producing and reproducing language ideologies (Bourdieu 1991; Errington 2000; Philips 2000; Mertz 1998; Spitulnik 1998, 1999; Haeri 1997, 2003) which are variously and complexly imbricated in discourses of power. Politicians use language as the site at which they legitimate their power and rationalize their representations of political and social order, whether overtly, e.g., through language policies and language planning, and/or covertly, e.g.,

*This essay was in part supported by funding from the University of Kansas (NFRG, Big XII fellowship) and the American Institute for Maghreb Studies. I am particularly grateful to the participants of the XVIII Arabic Linguistics Symposium and the colloquy of the Linguistics Department at the University of Kansas (May 2004) for their questions and helpful comments. I warmly thank Mushira Eid and Dil Parkinson for their generous assistance and useful commentaries. I would like to also thank Keith Walters for starting me on the path of sociolinguistics and Haeri for being a source of inspiration for my project on language and ideology in Arabic-speaking communities.

through linguistic choices and linguistic practices in speech-making. But, as Spitulnik rightfully observes:

> "It is only recently…that scholars have focused their gaze below the level of the overall ideological function and effect of institutions to look more closely at how *specific practices* within institutions give value to different languages and to different ways of using language." (1998:165)

It is only very recently that a probing gaze—cursory as it may be since it is at its early stages—has been lowered to consider form-ideology dialectic within institutions of power in Arabic-speaking communities (e.g., Haeri 2003). This essay aims at contributing to the on-going discussion of the linkages between language ideologies, and speakers' language valuation (Spitulnik1998), linguistic practices and ways of using language in institutions of power with a special focus on political speeches in diglossic and bilingual Tunisia.

Political speeches are critical sites of ideology and form at work. They are delivered to the public to carry the voice of authority of the government but they are carefully crafted linguistically to be heard as the voice of the collectivity, truth, reason, and promises for a better future. They are elaborately composed, carefully revised and edited, and minutely proofread. Rarely, if ever, does an audience have access to the original draft of a presidential public political speech or any other text, for that matter. Such drafts (or pre-texts) are not intended to be shared with the public. The behind-the-scene manipulations, modifications, and changes—brought to a text—are assumed to be invisible. What gets to be shared is always a final linguistic product which "is not the *mere* result of any one individual's effort nor the mere result of any one set of institutions, ideologies or contexts", as Haeri (2003:57) points out. Rarely, if ever, do we have access to the original text or manuscript of a presidential speech with corrections scribbled in red. This essay is an analysis of such a document. It analyzes the changes brought to the original handwritten draft of the first presidential speech (see appendix 1 and appendix 2) that Ben Ali,[1] the current president of

[1]Ben Ali was appointed Secretary of State in the Ministry of Interior in 1984. On October 25, 1985, he was promoted to become the minister of National Security. On April 28, 1986, he became the Minister of Domestic Affairs. Nearly a year later

Tunisia, delivered November 7, 1987 to announce the end of President Bourguiba's thirty-year rule (1956-1987), and to declare the beginning of a New Era that Ben Ali and the Tunisians will inaugurate together "in an atmosphere of trust, safety and security" (November 7, 1987 Communiqué).[2] Specifically, the dialectic relation between form and ideology are explored through an analysis of HOW [the] text [of the Communiqué] has come to be what it is" (Haeri 2003:56), i.e., in terms of the socio-political conditions of its production and in terms of its linguistic forms.

The paths of where to look for how the text of the Communiqué has come to be what it is are, in a way, drawn through the visibility of its manipulations (i.e., inclusions, exclusions, and changes scribbled in red in the original draft). But the visibility of the changes by no means entails transparency of the conditions of the text production or embodies the meanings of those changes. Neither does it make room for an interpretation of a linear correspondence between linguistic forms and socio-political context of the production of the text on the one hand or between linguistic choices, language valuation, linguistic forms and linguistic ideology, on the other. This essay simply argues that the analysis of such traces provides significant paths to conceptualize the ways such links are formed, knowing that "language

---

=(May 16, 1987), Bourguiba appointed him Prime Minister. Bourguiba, who had always kept the military away from the government, brought him in to crack down on the Islamists. On November 7, 1987, Ben Ali made the bold move to depose Bourguiba (1956-1987) and put an end to a dying regime.

[2]It is important to note here that the original handwritten draft of the final version of the *bayaan*, Communiqué, was respectively published in 1992 in a book entitled *aθ-θawra al-haadiʔa* (*The Peaceful Revolution*) and in 1995 in *Ben ali wa aṭ-ṭareeq ʔila at-taʕaddudiyya* (*Ben Ali and the Road to Pluralism*). In the first book, the draft was published along with three other official documents: first a copy of a medical report (ironically composed in French) signed by seven medical doctors, at 6:00 a.m., proclaiming the president to be incapable of fulfilling his duties and hence legally entitling Ben Ali to step into Bourguiba's shoes to become the second president of independent Tunisia, second a copy of three annotations ("observations" *mulaaħaẓaat* according to the official version) that relate to the changes brought to the manuscript, the time of its recording and the typing of the final text, and third a copy of the 'cleaned up' final version. The "observations" indicate that the Communiqué was 'amended' at 4:30 a.m., recorded at 5:45 a.m. and broadcast on the national radio at 6:30 a.m. These documents serve as symbols of the etiquette of the New Era and its new rhetoric of visibility, accessibility, transparency and truth.

ideologies and processes of language valuation are never just about language" and that "[l]anguage ideologies are, among other things, about the construction and legitimation of power" (Spitulnik 1998:164). The analysis of the changes will first examine the socio-political context of the production of the Communiqué through an examination of the linguistic shift that accompanied the political transition from the OLD to the NEW political era. Second, it will describe and discuss the ideological significance of the linguistic modifications introduced to the text of the Communiqué. Such analysis will shed light on the complex intersection between linguistic choices, language valuation, linguistic forms, linguistic ideology, and the socio-political context of the production of a text.

This analysis of the Communiqué draws on the studies of scholars who worked on language and its symbolic power and language ideologies in institutions of power (e.g., Bourdieu 1991; Errington 2000; Philips 2000; Mertz 1998; Spitulnik 1998, 1999; Haeri 2003). Drawing particularly on Spitulnik's (1998:164) concept of language valuation and evaluation "as processes through which different social values and referents come to be associated with languages, forms of speaking, and styles of speaking", this essay will examine how the valuation of Classical Arabic/Modern Standard Arabic (which is subsumed under the term *fuṣħaa)* as the symbol of a homogeneous and united nation (i.e., a group of people that has the same language, the same rich history, culture and religion) implicitly naturalizes its association with valued inherent attributes (e.g., purity, beauty, eloquence, truthfulness, clarity) which, in turn, index authority and power of the code itself as well as of its speakers. I will examine how such a process naturalizes the same cluster of features as attributes of its users, that is how a language emblematizes a people and indexes specific attributes that they derive from the language. Drawing heavily on Haeri's (2003) recent work on the relationship between language, text regulations and sites of ideology, this essay takes the argument further to demonstrate that constructs of prestige, power and authority of a linguistic code do not accrue transparently and automatically to the privileged social group that uses it. Through the description and analysis of the changes brought to the Communiqué, this essay demonstrates how *fuṣħaa* pragmatically demands the translation of its ideologization as the variety of *faṣaaħa (*eloquence) and purity into serving its repertoire of correctness (morphological, syntactic, lexical, and stylistic) and pragmatic appropriateness. Professional and non-professional *fuṣħaa* users need to learn "to serve" (Haeri 2003) its authority. Through a detailed examination of the institution of "correction" as a site of mediation of ideology and the role of "correctors" (i.e., professionals) as agents of mediation processes, Haeri (2003) shows how the ideologization of Classical Arabic is produced and reproduced institutionally in printed texts, in Egypt. Like professional correctors, non-professional correctors are equally conscious of correction as an institution and of *fuṣħaa* as a language of authority, as it will become clear through the analysis of changes introduced to the text of the Communiqué.

2. Political Transition, Linguistic Shift: From bilingual and diglossic discourse to a monolingual discourse

The dialectic relation between linguistic choices and linguistic ideologies in political speeches becomes especially pertinent and worth investigating in multilingual communities (e.g., simultaneously diglossic and bilingual communities) where the choice of a particular language or variety is never "value-free" (Spitulnik 1998:164). The processes through which languages or varieties come to be associated with certain values tend to be rationalized and naturalized when they conflate with political interests and contribute to the construction of political aura and the legitimation of power. The valuation of a linguistic code as an index of a distinct group of people, as an emblem of power and legitimacy, or as an attribute of the linguistic code itself (e.g., inherent linguistic beauty, power, and clarity) is an ideological construct that tends to naturalize the relation between the code and what it indexes, symbolizes or emblematizes. The processes of language valuation are accomplished with various degrees of implicitness and explicitness. In this section, I focus on the implicit process of language valuation through the examination of the choice of *fuṣħaa* as the sole variety of the new official political speeches. Specifically, this essay explores the significance of the linguistic shift that accompanied the political transition that took place in Tunisia in 1987.

On November 7, 1987, Tunisians woke at 6:30 a.m. to the national anthem and some verses from the Qur'an as usual, but unlike the other mornings, the ritual was disrupted. Bourguiba's daily morning program "From the directives of the president" *min tawjeehaat ar-raʔiis* was preempted. The Tunisian national radio station broadcast a Communiqué (Bayaan) in which Zine El Abidine Ben Ali, Bourguiba's newly appointed Prime Minister (October 2, 1987), solemnly addressed the nation to first declare, "In the Name of Allah, Most Gracious, Most Merciful", that President Bourguiba was severely incapacitated by old age and grave sickness; second, to proclaim his self-investiture as the new President and Commander in Chief of the Tunisian Armed Forces with "the Blessings and Grace of Allah", and third, to announce the beginning of a "new era" *ʕahd jadeed* (see text of the Communiqué, Appendix 2).

One of the symbolic indications of the political change was the linguistic shift that Ben Ali made in his first Communiqué and in his subsequent public political speeches. While Bourguiba used a constellation of linguistic codes—Classical Arabic, Modern Standard Arabic, Tunisian Arabic, and French, Ben Ali chose to reclaim *fuṣħaa* as the only official variety of Arabic to use in public political speeches. The linguistic shift is far more than a mere substitution of a bilingual and diglossic discourse for a monolingual text. From my point of view, the shift plays a significant role in legitimizing the political coup, imagining and constructing the new social and political order of the New Era, and establishing the new tone of the new régime. Privileging *fuṣħaa* over the more accessible and less focused (Walters 2003:80) variety of Arabic (i.e., Tunisian Arabic) perpetuates the rhetoric of the political discourse that *fuṣħaa* is the national language. And as such it is construed as available to all when, in fact, it is still inaccessible to a considerable number of Tunisians.

The high reverence for *fuṣħaa*, its perfection, its purity of speech, and eloquence (*faṣaaħa*), remains as widely prevalent nowadays as it was in pre-Islamic era. *Fuṣħaa* is "a language that embodies authority and bestows authority on those who know it" (Haeri 1997:796). Its indexical sense blurs the line between the reverence that educated and uneducated speakers alike have for *fuṣħaa* and the reverence they would have for the aura of the office and for the person who will occupy that office. There is an indexical transfer of the values accrued to *fuṣħaa* to its users. Under Ben Ali's regime, *fuṣħaa* is emblematic of an intellectual character. It is "ideologized as distinctive and implicating a distinctive kind of people" (Woolard 1998:18). In the New Era, Tunisians who understand *fuṣħaa* are acknowledged as a people who have greater intellectual maturity than they were credited by the former regime. The identification of a language with a people once again demonstrates that "[l]anguage ideologies and processes of language valuation are never just about language…[They] are, among other things, about the construction and legitimation of power" (Spitulnik 1998:164). The linguistic practice of the new regime is a process to naturalize and rationalize not only the inherent positive attributes of *fuṣħaa* but also of its users. *Fuṣħaa* is viewed as emblematic of *waʕy* "awareness", *nuḍž* "intellectual maturity" of a people capable of "participating constructively" (*al-mušaaraka al-bannaʔa*) in "running their affairs", (*fii-taṣriifi šuʔuunihi*), and participating fully in building a democratic country and a modern nation. The new speaker's formal tone and serious voice emphasized that the "children"—that Bourguiba claimed as his for three decades (i.e., the Tunisians)—had grown to "adulthood" and gained "intellectual maturity", and as such they should be treated accordingly and addressed appropriately. The linguistic code that credits their intellectual maturity and personal worth is *fuṣħaa* since it is ideologically valued more highly than the dialect (Tunisian Arabic). It is the variety of the educated. To the nationalist ideology of language is superposed the image of a people of great intellectual and personal worth. Ben Ali's promise to restore the dignity to the country and its people is embodied in the new linguistic practice and symbolized by the use of the 'appropriate' variety of the Arabic language (*fuṣħaa*) to address a people who 'have come of age'. The very same Tunisians, who Bourguiba used to address, affectionately at times and conde-scendingly at others, as his children (*banaatii l-fuḍhlayaat abnaaʔi l-afaaḍhil* "my good daughters and my good sons") became under Ben Ali's regime *abnaaʔ tuunisi-na l-ʕaziiza* "the children of our dear Tunisia".

The representation of the new social world, as envisioned by Ben Ali, is evidently couched in a different linguistic ideology and enacted in a different linguistic practice, undoubtedly, dissimilar to Bourguiba's. Ben Ali's call to rally the same masses around him is expressed in a variety of Arabic that is inseparable from ceremonial etiquettes, solemnity, formality (Irvine 1984), and institutional authority and power (Bourdieu 1991) in which he wants his public persona and his presidency to be shrouded. The exclusive and rigorous use of *fuṣħaa* as the only legitimate language in the Communiqué and in the subsequent public political speeches is, in a way, an effort to "erase" (Irvine & Gal 2000:59) Bourguiba's three-decade rule and linguistic legacy of violations in presidential political speeches and to re-establish the linguistic hierarchy. Ben Ali's ideological representations of the linguistic situation is enacted in his effort to "tidy up" (Irvine & Gal 2000:59) a complex sociolinguistic situation in Tunisia first by erasing Bourguiba's diglossic switching (i.e., the switching between *fuṣħaa* and Tunisian Arabic) and code switching (i.e., the switching between Arabic and French) from public political discourse, second by redrawing the boundaries of the linguistic map, hence re-establishing the linguistic hierarchy (and restoring dignity to presidential public political speeches), and third by re-appropriating Classical Arabic as the emblem of the state, and the New Era. Historical and political discontinuity is achieved through "erasure", a tactful semiotic process of linguistic differentiation that Irvine and Gal (2000:38) define as "the process in which ideology, in simplifying the sociolinguistic field, renders some persons or activities (or sociolinguistic phenomena) invisible". While the economic, social, and political chaos, in which the Tunisians were held captive in the 80s under Bourguiba's regime, is overtly rejected in the text of the Communiqué, the linguistic transgressions are covertly erased through the linguistic shift, more precisely through Ben Ali's choice to reclaim the variety of rationality, clarity, correctness, and order as the only linguistic code of public political speeches.

Reclaiming *fuṣħaa* as the only variety of public political speeches not only makes the other linguistic codes and practices invisible but also the speaker who promoted their 'inappropriate' and 'incorrect' use in public political speeches. The new speaker's linguistic practice and ideology bring afore some kind of linguistic essentialism that "implicitly or explicitly convey the impression that domains of usage for either variety [or language] never change, touch, or merge" (Haeri 2000:66). *Fuṣħaa* is brought back as the homogeneous, standardized, and unifying national language. Such a perspective ignores and devalues the intricately imbricated linguistic repertoires that are available to and strategically used by the Tunisians. But, as Irvine and Gal (2000:76) aptly state, "homogeneous language is as much imagined as is community". In a diglossic, bilingual, and an increasingly trilingual situation with the "seeping spread" of English (Walters 1998:14)[3] in the social and linguistic fabric of Tunisia, code boundaries that appear to be distinct at a formal linguistic level or are rendered to be distinct through official linguistic practices are not experienced or even functionally operationalized as such in contexts of use by 'real' users. The attribution of sedimented traits to linguistic codes (e.g., superiority, purity, formality, and correctness of *fuṣħaa*, or inferiority, simplicity, informality, and incorrectness of daarija) neglects terrains of fluidity that exist between and across those codes. It also downplays the dynamic ways in which speakers—as individuals or as communities—negotiate their boundaries and experience their appropriation as symbolic indices of their various social roles and multiple identities. In a symbolic and indexical sense, Ben Ali's rigorous use of *fuṣħaa*, as the exclusive variety of public political speeches, stands as an antithetical linguistic choice (and linguistic ideology) to Bourguiba's. Spitulnik (1998:166) reminds us that "there is an indexical component to the use of a language or a variety, which extends beyond the indexing of a social group associated with the code: the code chosen indexes the code not chosen". Even though, the dialect is implicitly silenced in the official political discourse and devalued for the nation, it is highly valued by individual speakers because it indexes an aspect of their identity that *fuṣħaa* does not: their Tunisian-ness.

2.1 *Authority of fuṣħaa*

Ben Ali chose to speak to the Tunisians across the airwaves in *fuṣħaa*. But the choice to use *fuṣħaa* comes with a price because as

---

[3]A cursory glance at major historical linguistic events that have shaped the linguistic situation in Tunisia, would point to its 'arabization', then 'frenchification', and finally what Walters (1998:14) mockingly called "Anglicization", a phenomenon that he carefully distinguishes from the French government's efforst to "systematic[ally] frenchify the country during the colonial period". Whether Tunisia is being "anglified", whether the "seeping spread" of English may give rise to a local variety of English in Tunisia, whether English will continue to creep into the Tunisians' linguistic practices, or, more importantly, whether there will be shifts in the fates of Arabic, French, and English are some of the increasing complex issues of the debate on the linguistic situation within the circles of the Tunisian intellectuals.

Haeri (2003:69) aptly points out: "Like the use of other written languages, the use of Classical Arabic is a performance that is cleaned up and rehearsed backstage by a host of figures". The 'clean-up' is usually invisible. It is the first time, in the history of Tunisia, that the behind-the-scene changes of a public political speech or any other text for that matter have been accessible and visible to the reader; thus exposing the regulations and regimentation of the use of linguistic codes through the visible manipulations of the text. The interventions changed some words, shuffled the order of some others, altered the structure of some phrases and sentences, and corrected some grammatical mistakes and spelling errors. The visible process of the manipulations capture the new discursive authority and linguistic ideology in the making, as it will become clear throughout the essay.

Just like any other text in *fuṣħaa*, a presidential speech is subjected to correctors' scrutiny and approval. It does not escape the authority of *fuṣħaa* that is ironically and paradoxically bolstered through state institutions (e.g., parliament, and educational institutions). A presidential speech in *fuṣħaa* escapes presidential decrees or parliamentary bills because the authority of *fuṣħaa* overrides other sources of power and authority. Its authority is unquestionable. *Fuṣħaa* derives its authority from various sources. It is partly due to its intrinsic linguistic properties (e.g., its complex grammatical rules, the density of its vocabulary), and partly from its religious, historical, and cultural roots. It is the language of the Qur'an, religious duties and rituals of all Muslims as well as the carrier of a vast literary heritage that remains the pride of each Arab. *Fuṣħaa* is also construed as the variety of formality, hence authority, with regard to what Rubin (1968 cited in Irvine 1984:212) characterizes as "limitations on the kinds of linguistic behaviors that are acceptable and on the amount of allowed variation conceived as deviation from a norm". Such traits constrain individual users to a high degree of conformity because it subjects them to strict judgments of correctness, as illustrated in the modifications introduced to excerpts (1) through (4). In (1a), the phrase *ħaqqa qadrihaa* is substituted for one word *makaanataha* in excerpt (1b). In excerpt (2a), the lexical item *manzila* is substituted for *makaana* in (2b). In excerpt (3b), *laa siyyamaa* replaces *ʔaxuṣṣu bi ð-ðikri min-haa* in (3a), and finally in excerpt (4a) the phrase *maʕa baʕḍinaa baʕḍ* is substituted for one word *maʕan* in (4b). The replacements in the four excerpts are presumably judged 'more' or 'better' *fuṣħaa* obeying norms of exactitude, accuracy and, most importantly, economy in *fuṣħaa*.

(1) a. Initial version (see Appendix 1:219)
yuuli al-muʔassasaat ħaqqa qadri-haa
"It gives organizations their [adequate] status/leverage"
b. Final version (see also Appendix 2:223)
yuuli al-muʔassasaat makaanata-haa
"It gives organizations their [adequate] status/leverage"
(2) a. Initial version (see Appendix 1:221)
al-manzila
"The status"
b. Final version (see also Appendix 2:223)
al-makaana
"The status"
(3) a. Initial version (see Appendix 1:221)
ʔaxuṣṣu bi -ð-ðikri min-haa
"I make special mention of them"
b. Final version (see also Appendix 2:223)
laa siyyamaa
"Especially"
(4) a. Initial version (see Appendix 1:221)
maʕa baʕḍ inaa baʕḍ
"With one another"
b. Final version (see also Appendix 2:223)
maʕan
"Together"

Any 'inappropriate' or 'incorrect' use of *fuṣħaa* may strip the authority away from the user. *Fuṣħaa* dictates its own criteria of exactitude, accuracy, and correctness. It disallows any departures from its grammatical rules and stylistic nuances. Even what looks like an 'insignificant' spelling mistake, in the Communiqué, is caught and corrected, as illustrated in (5a) and (5b). In fact, the instance involves a set of complex grammatical rules of *fuṣħaa* on *rasm al-hamza*, orthography of al-hamza, in *fuṣħaa*.

(5)* a. Initial version (see Appendix 1:219)
البنّائة
"constructive"

b. Revised version (see also Appendix 2:223)
البنّاءة
"constructive"

Proficiency to speak in *fuṣħaa*, as prescribed by early Arab grammarians, philologists, or Arabists in Arabic departments in Arab universities, is rarely attained if ever attainable without monitoring one's speech. In extemporaneous speech for example, in cases where Tunisians cannot maintain the 'perfect' *fuṣħaa*, they produce some fudged forms that are between *fuṣħaa* and the dialect (Boussofara-Omar 1999, 2003). The complex grammatical rules as well as the subtle stylistic variations of *fuṣħaa* escape non-experts as well as the experts who dismiss variations of *fuṣħaa* or "fuṣħiyyaat" as Baccouche (1990) calls them. The correctors of the Communiqué, who are neither Arabists, nor linguists or 'professional correctors' were no exception. An error in the choice of a lexical word visibly escaped their scrutiny at the first stage, i.e., in the handwritten draft (Appendix 1), but it was clearly caught during the typing since it was replaced with the target word in the final typed version of the Communiqué (Appendix 2). In the initial draft, the use of the erroneous verbal noun *al-ʔiṭṭilaaʕ* in the phrase *al-ʔiṭṭilaaʕ bi-mahaammihi* (assuming his duties) instead of the target word *al-ʔiḍṭilaaʕ* and target phrase *al-ʔiḍṭilaaʕ bi-mahaammihi* (assuming his duties) is an instance of an error of lexical selection. Had the mis-accessed verbal noun *al-ʔiṭṭilaaʕ* not been corrected, in the final stage, it would have resulted in a subcategorization rule error, because the verb *ʔiṭṭalaʕa* subcategorizes for the preposition *ʕala* and not *bi-* as used in the initial draft. Such an error is 'unpardonable' in the purists' view since they judge print and spoken language against the same normative paradigms.

The practice of correction of the Communiqué embodies and captures the purist doctrine of linguistic correctness in the Arabic intellectual tradition (Suleiman 2003). Such tradition used and continues to promote the prescriptive normative paradigm by censoring any deviation from the norm and promoting correctness in language. And it is in the context of censuring any linguistic flaw or deviation, even the slightest, from the prescribed correct forms of the language of eloquence and perfection that *fuṣħaa* texts are 'revised'. No *fuṣħaa* text, whether it is produced to be read silently or aloud, may escape scrutiny, revision, or correction, even a president's speech. Furthermore, linguistic proficiency and pragmatic competency in *fuṣħaa* are expected from a president. Hence, Ben Ali's initial draft of the speech was carefully scrutinized, dissected, and corrected. What is interesting to note here, however, is that the 'corrections', 'revisions' and 'changes' are presented as 'amendments' *tanqiiħaat*, by the officials, even though some of them are corrections of unambiguously grammatical mistakes, lexical and spelling errors as respectively illustrated in excerpts (6a) through (8a). Each excerpt is corrected in the original draft as demonstrated respectively in (6b) through (8b)

(6) a. Initial version (Appendix 1:219)
la majaala **ʔila** riʔaasa mada l-ħayaat wa la **ʔila** xilaafa ʕaaliyya
no room to presidency DEF-life and no to succession automatic
"There is no room for presidency for life and no room for automatic succession"
b. Revised version (see also Appendix 2:223)
la majaala **li**-riʔaasa mada l-ħayaat wa la **li**xilaafa ʔaaliyya
no way to-presidency the-life and no to-succession automatic
"[There is] no room for presidency for life and no room for automatic succession"
(7) a. Initial version (Appendix 1:217)
ʔaṣbaħa ʕaajizan tamaaman ʕ**ala** ʔiṭṭilaaʕ bi-mahaammi-hi
He became incapable totally on assuming with-duties-his
ka-raʔiisin l-il-jumhuriyya
as-president to-the-republic
"He became totally incapacitated to perform his duties as the president of the republic"
b. Initial version (see also Appendix 2:217)
ʔaṣbaħa ʕaajiz tamaaman ʕ**ani** al-ʔiṭṭilaaʕ bi-mahaammi riʔaasat l-jumhuriyya
"He became totally incapacitated to perform the duties of the presidency of the republic"
(8) a. Initial version (Appendix 1:217)
al-ʔiṭṭilaaʕ bi-mahaammihi
examining with-duties-his
b. Revised version (see also Appendix 2:222)
al-ʔiḍṭilaaʕi bi-mahaammi-hi
assuming with-duties-his

In examples (6a) and (7a), two subcategorization rules were 'violated'. In (6a), note the incorrect use of the preposition *ʔila* "to" in *la majaala ʔila* "no room to" in the initial version. The same error is repeated twice in the same excerpt. In example (7a), note the incorrect use of the preposition *ʕala* "on". The verb *ʕajaza* subcategorizes for the preposition *ʕan* and not *ʕala*. None of these errors would have affected the meaning or would have been perceived as errors in oral speech but a *fuṣħaa* text has to be perfect. Besides, the Communiqué was going to become a historical document, i.e., a written text that the president, his advisors, cabinet members, ministers, government officials, religious leaders, TV anchors, media reporters, to name but a few, quote profusely and cite frequently.

Further incorrect uses of *fuṣħaa* involve stylistic errors whose subtleties are noticeable only to a handful of experts in *fuṣħaa*, yet they do not escape the necessary touches of the non-professional correctors to perfect the text. Consider example (9). In (9a), the sentence in the initial draft is a 'calque' phrase from French as illustrated in the translation in (9b).

(9) a. Initial version (Appendix 1:219)
muraajaʕa ʔaṣbaħat al-yawm mutaʔakkida
revision has become today necessary
"A revision [of the constitution] that has, today, become necessary"
b. French calque version
muraajaʕa ʔaṣbaħat al-yawm mutaʔakkida
révision devenue aujourdhui, nécessaire
"Une révision (de la constitution) devenue, aujourd'hui, nécessaire"

In the revised version in (9c), the participle *mutaʔakkida* was changed into a verb form *taʔakkadat* following the verb pattern *tafaʕʕala*. The use of a verb form is preferred to the use of a verb and a participle in accordance with the principle of economy and focus in a verbal sentence in *fuṣħaa*. This instance is, in a way, similar to examples (1a) through (4a) discussed earlier with regard to the economy principle.

(9) c. Revised version (see also Appendix 2:223)
muraajaʕa taʔakkadat al-yawm
revision has become necessary today
"A revision that has, now, become necessary"

The last category of changes pertains to the strategic use of what Errington (1985) calls "pragmatically salient" alternates. The suggested changes are presumably construed as alternates that better mediate the dialectic relationship between the politics of form (or what I call the politics of *fuṣħaa*) and the politics of function (or the politics of message). The proposed alternates are believed to be crucial linguistic mediators that first translate better the discursive authority of the New Era—which, in 1987, was a faceless unfamiliar voice transmitted across the airwaves, second naturalize the new voice of authority, and third rationalize its acceptance. The changes, which visibly embody discursive authority in the making, consist in either replacing some words which are intuitively judged to sound 'more *fuṣħaa*' than the words used in the original draft or shuffling word order to subtly correct the focal point of the message.

3. 'How to Do Things with Words': When words are changed

The presidential accoutrement to legitimize Ben Ali's first encounter with the Tunisian people was absent. There were no visible microphones, no visible cameras, no visible lights, no journalists, no photographers, no visible dignitaries gathered around, and especially no "direct communication" or "close contact" (*ʔittiṣaal mubaašir*) with the audience which was Bourguiba's slogan for a thirty-year strategy and stratagem to rally his "sons and daughters" for *farħat al-ħayaat* "the joy of life" (i.e., the pursuit of happiness). Ben Ali's choice of the physical separation has symbolically defined the to-be-accepted political discourse of the New Era and embodied the linguistic code chosen (i.e., *fuṣħaa*) to index the intended boundaries of participation and involvement of the Tunisians in "running their affairs" (*taṣriifi šuʔuunihi*). But, more importantly, it has accorded primacy to words. Because Ben Ali's words were going to mark the passage from the Old to the New Era, and because they were going to create belief in the legitimacy and authority of an unfamiliar voice (rather than a face), and an unknown speaker, they had to be carefully selected. But "words alone cannot create this belief", Bourdieu (1991:170) argues. In the case of Arabic, I believe, words in *fuṣħaa* magically create this belief because with the correct and appropriate use of *fuṣħaa* accrues a voice of authority and "[t]he only authority that is unquestioned belongs to the language", as Haeri (2003:69) puts it. One may wonder, however:

In light of the changes introduced, whose voice is being heard in the delivery of the Communiqué besides the voice of authority of *fuṣħaa*?

4. **Whose Voice is it, Anyway? A voice in the making**

The political arena is the site of competition for individuals to become representatives of groups, to be endowed with the power to act on behalf of and to speak in the name of those groups. The passage to become the legitimate voice of a people (as their president for example) is sanctioned and institutionalized by an act, a ritual, or a performance; each of which makes the passage known and recognized by the public. While the investiture accords privileges and even authorizes some linguistic transgressions (clearly unauthorized in the case of *fuṣħaa*), it imposes the learning of the "linguistic habitus"[4] (Bourdieu 1991) of the institution. Besides using correct *fuṣħaa*, Ben Ali, the then Prime Minister, has to acquire the voice of *fuṣħaa* and the linguistic habitus of the presidential voice which, ultimately, consists of a complex host of other voices and linguistic habituses, e.g., the voice of the people, the voice of the government, the voice of the party, and the voice of the fellow citizen, to name but a few.

An interesting aspect to explore, in this section, to demonstrate a presidential voice and linguistic habitus in the making, are the changes brought to the 'incorrect' and/or 'inappropriate' use of the verbal inflections of first person singular versus first person plural pronouns in the present tense *ʔa-* versus *na-* as in *ʔu-ħaafiẓu* (I preserve) versus *nu-ħaafiẓu* (we preserve) and the possessives *-ii* versus *-naa* (my/our) as in *masʔuuliyyaatii* (my responsibilities) and *masʔuuliyyaatinaa* (our responsibilities). Manifestly, the corrections suggest lack of familiarity and inability to navigate between and across the "'I'-ness" and "'we'-ness" constructs to borrow Silverstein's (2000:115) words. The

[4]In his introduction to Bourdieu's book *Language and Symbolic Power*, Thompson (1991:12) summarizes Bourdieu's definition of habitus as "a set of dispositions which incline agents to act and react in certain ways. The dispositions generate practices, perceptions and attitudes which are 'regular' without being consciously coordinated or governed by any 'rule'". Linguistic habitus does not refer only to ways of speaking or choice of words and expressions but ways of being as well. It refers to a practical sense *sens pratique* of actions and inclinations that are ingrained in the body. It is a way of being that is translated and reflected into ways of speaking and using language à propos.

boundaries between the individual and collectively shared spaces (between the soon-to-be president and his soon-to-be people, *šaʕb*) are being mapped in front of our eyes through the changes. The tone of the new authoritative voice of the speaker and the contours of the people's voice (as a newly "imagined community" in the post-Bourguiba era) are being redrawn through the corrections scribbled in red in the draft.

It is rather risky for a self-proclaimed successor, even though he presents himself as the legitimate successor and savior, to ignore the strong bond between the 'old' leader and his people. The Tunisians are not ready to think of Bourguiba, the 'father', in the past tense. They had to be reminded that the 'leader' was too old, now, to "fulfill his duties as the president of the republic" and that the deposition of the incapacitated leader was "the national duty" *al-waajib al-waṭaniy* of each Tunisian, as it were. The use of the inclusive 'we' in "we have loved him and we have respected him" (excerpt [10]), although ambiguous, makes the Tunisians emotionally involved and renders Bourguiba's incapacity to lead a "collective truth" (Bourdieu 1991:212) and his deposition a collective duty as illustrated in excerpts (10)-(11).

(10) Initial and final versions (see Appendices 1-2:217, 222)
wa laakinna l-waajiba al-waṭaniyy yafriḍu ʕalay-**naa** al-yawm
and but the-duty the-national imposes upon-us today
ṭuuli šayxuuxati-**hi** wa ʔistifħaali maraḍi-**hi**
length old age-his and gravity sickness-his
"His senility and grave sickness"

(11) Initial and final versions (see Appendices 1-2:217-218, 222)
"But the national duty compels **us** today, given his old age and grave sickness that **we** declare that he has become totally incapacitated to assume his responsibilities as the President of the Republic and a medical report, signed by…has confirmed this"

The absence of a possessive in "but the national duty" and the use of the inclusive first person plural pronoun as an object in "upon us" contrast significantly with the use of the third person singular possessive in such utterances as "his old age", "his sickness", and "his duties as the president", as illustrated in excerpt (10). The use of "his" in the utterance "his duties" and the direct reference to Bourguiba through the use of "the president" in the phrase "as the president of the republic" were a faux pas. The misstep imbues the utterances with a personal tone which contradicts the message of collective truth, and collective duty or rather "impersonal duty" (Nietzsche 1968 cited in Bourdieu 1991:210) that the prelude of the Communiqué wants to communicate to the Tunisians. The faux pas was corrected through the deletion of "his" in the phrase "his duties", the use of a construct state *ʔiḍaafa* in *mahaammi raʔiis al-jumhuuriyya* where the word *raʔiis* is indefinite, and the use of the impersonal word "presidency" (i.e., referring to the office) instead of the personal word "president" (i.e., referring to the person who occupies the office) as illustrated in the revised excerpt (12b). In the revised version, the *fuṣħaa* utterance is heard not as the opinion or voice of the Prime Minister but rather as the "unimpeachable voice of the collectivity" (to borrow Gal's words 1998:323)

(12) a. Initial version (see Appendix 1:217)
wa laakinna l-waajiba al-waṭaniyy yafriḍu ʕalay-**naa** al-yawm
and but the-duty the-national imposes on-us today
ʔamaama ṭuuli šayxuuxati-**hi** wa ʔistifħaali maraḍi-**hi**
in front of length old age-his and gravity sickness-his
ʔan nuʕlina ʔanna- hu ʔaṣbaħa ʕaajizan ʕala al-ʔiṭṭilaaʕ
that we declare that-he became incapacitated on the-assuming
bi-mahaammi-**hi** ka-raʔiis li-l-jumhuuriyya
with-responsibilities-his as-president to-the-republic
"But the national duty compels us today, given his old age and the gravity of his sickness, to declare that he became incapacitated to fulfill his duties as the president of the republic"

b. Revised version (see also Appendix 2:222)
wa laakinna l-waajiba al-waṭaniyy yafriḍu ʕalay-**naa** al-yawm
and but the-duty the-national imposes on-us today
ʔamaama ṭuuli šayxuuxati-**hi** wa ʔistifħaali maraḍi-**hi**
length old age-his and gravity sickness-his
ʔan nuʕlina ʔanna- hu ʔaṣbaħa ʕaajizan ʕan al-ʔiḍṭilaaʕi
that we declare that-he became incapacitated on the-assuming
bi-mahaammi riʔaasat al-jumhuuriyya
with-responsibilities presidency the-republic
"But the national duty compels us today, given his old age and the gravity of his sickness, to declare that he became incapacitated to fulfill the duties of the presidency (of) the republic"

Bourguiba's deposition, as was mentioned earlier, is presented as a collective decision, hence the use of the first person plural in *ʔan nuʕlina…*"that we declare…" But whose voice does the collective "we" carry? Is it the voice of the Prime Minister, the government, the Tunisians, the panel of the seven medical doctors who were convened on the eve of November 7 to proclaim the head of state to be incapable of fulfilling his duties or Article 57 of the constitution that legally entitles a prime minister to proclaim his presidency in such a situation? The 'correct' use of the ambiguously inclusive 'we' and 'us', in excerpt (11), clashes significantly with the 'incorrect' use of the first person inflection in *ʔatawalla* "I take command" as illustrated in the initial and revised versions in (13a) and (13b) respectively.

(13) a. Initial version (see Appendix 1:218)

ʔa-tawallaa	riʔaasat	al-jumhuuriyya
1 SG IMP-take command	presidency	the-republic

"**I** will take command…the presidency of the republic"

b. Revised version (see also Appendix 2:223)

na-tawallaa	riʔaasat	al-jumhuuriyya
1 PL IMP-take command	presidency	the-republic

"**We** will take command … the presidency of the republic"

The incorrect use of first person singular inflected to the verb *ʔa-tawalla* "I take command" is rendered starkly visible because it contrasts sharply with the 'correct' use of six markers of ambiguously collective first person plural, in the prelude. In announcing a self-proclaimed presidency, the speaker's use of the inflection marker of first person singular (*ʔa-tawalla*) constructs power as personalized (reminiscent of Bourguiba's regime) and clashes with the message of Bourguiba's deposition as a collective undertaking. In the initial version of the draft, the use of first person singular in "I take command" (that Ben Ali utters to proclaim his presidency) brings afresh the cult of personality of the previous regime. In other words, it re-echoes the rhetorical practices, the symbolic images of the previous regime and the daily televised rituals of the deposed president (e.g., his cabinet meetings, his inaugurations, his daily swimming exercises, his trips, his month-long birthday parties) of which the Tunisians were tired and from which Ben Ali wanted to distance himself and his regime through the linguistic shift, as I explained earlier. But shifting linguistic codes does not automatically erase the rhetoric and practices of the previous regime. Neither does the authority of *fuṣħaa* accrue automatically to its speakers when they use it inaccurately and inappropriately. The corrections seem to suggest the speaker's lack of realization that political power and authority accrue to the president through the use of the presidential first person plural *naħnu* "we". They also seem to suggest lack of awareness (or recognition) that the use of the ambiguously inclusive "we" is crucial to establish what Bourdieu terms "symbolic power" which is "misrecognized" as power (because it is "invisible", Bourdieu argues) and hence it is "recognized" as legitimate. What is interesting, however, is that "symbolic power requires, as a condition of its success, that those subjected to it believe in the legitimacy of power and the legitimacy of those who wield it". The subtle changes of the "I" into a "we", in the utterances discussed in this section, are crucial to presumably establish "a kind of ACTIVE COMPLICITY on the part of those subjected to [this authoritarian "we"]" (Thompson 1991:23).

The changes seem to bring rhythmic interweaving between individual and collective spaces on one hand and coherent linguistic patterns between collective and individual voices. The flow established between the collective and the individual voices after the changes is evidenced in the fluid flow between the inclusive, exclusive, and ambivalent use of the pronoun 'we' in the 'cleaned-up' version (see Appendix 2). The flow between those voices reinforces the voice of authority of the new speaker. What is ironic, however, is that it is not the LANGUAGE of authority (i.e., *fuṣħaa*) that enabled the new speaker to invest himself as the new president and enact presidential authority. French, the colonial language that the six Tunisian medical doctors used in their medical report,[5] has played a major role, if not the major role, in deposing the leader who fought against French occupation. Although *fuṣħaa* is reclaimed as the language of authority and national identity, as was explained earlier, it is evident that it still has to

[5]The medical report, attached to the Communiqué, was the only document composed in French. It is ironic that French—the language of 'Belles Lettres' that Bourguiba cherished, advocated, used eloquently in his public speeches, and defended as the language of progress, advancement, and modernization—decided his fate by declaring him incapacitated to continue a three-decade rule.

compete for its niche in the increasingly complex web of languages in contact, of dramatic social changes, and of dynamic linguistic practices in Tunisia as well as the rest of the Arab world. Silencing other linguistic codes in a bilingual and diglossic speech community, through a linguistic shift in official public speeches, does not automatically erase them or devalue their use. Tunisian Arabic (which has increasingly gained domains that were inaccessible, e.g., television, radio, and newspapers to a lesser extent) and French, because of the "seeping spread of English" (Walters 1998), have reinvented themselves to remain legitimate, viable, and apparently more appealing linguistic codes than *fuṣħaa*, especially among younger generations of educated Tunisians who have no qualms using both linguistic resources in formal and informal speech. Advocates and users of *fuṣħaa* have not succeeded in ushering it to new domains of use. Many of these domains remain inaccessible to *fuṣħaa* despite the government's claim and efforts to diversify its "spheres of activity" (Bakhtin 1986 [1981]). Medical prescriptions, diagnoses, or medical reports (e.g., Bourguiba's doctors medical report) are never written or explained to patients in *fuṣħaa*. They are written in French and explained to the patients either in Tunisian Arabic or a mix of French and Tunisian Arabic. French remains the language of science, technology, and medicine, despite the government's conspicuous efforts to claim the success of its arabization policy in education. *Fuṣħaa*, the variety of Arabic that Bourguiba's successor reclaimed and appropriated as THE language of the state, remains the variety that is canonically associated with writing and with the prescriptive tradition associated with it. Such tradition continues to rationalize its correctness, purity, perfection, even inimitability *ʔiʕjaaz*, and authority. Its users cannot question its authority. This authority becomes an imminent threat to the user because, first, as was argued earlier, any incorrect or faulty use of *fuṣħaa* takes authority away from its user, especially when the text is a presidential official speech. Second, the belief and "expectation [...] that the president of the country must know the language very well" (Haeri 2003:69) must be upheld even when the corrections expose the process as a public clean-up performance and hence override other forms of authority or render them invisible (e.g., the authority of a soon-to-be president).

5. **Conclusion**

In my exploration of the question of "how a [political Communiqué] has come to be what it is", I have demonstrated that the answer involves far more than its formal analysis as a linguistic production, because, following Spitulnik (1998:163), "[t]he analysis of language ideology in institutions of power is not just a matter of locating WHERE ideologies are produced but also HOW they are produced" (emphasis in the original). The process of how linguistic choices and valuations are made and how language ideologies are produced and reproduced in political speeches is as important as the sites where they are produced. Taking the politics of *fuṣħaa* in political speech-making in Tunisia as an example, I have demonstrated that the linguistic shift that accompanied the political transition in 1987 is highly symbolic—ideologically—but rather costly in the case of the linguistic choice, i.e., the choice of *fuṣħaa*. Anyone who uses *fuṣħaa*, even a soon-to-be president, has to obey its authority by subjecting their linguistic production to scrutiny and thorough examination to ensure the 'correct' use of its linguistic forms and the appropriate use of its pragmatics. Authority will not accrue to *fuṣħaa* users unless they obey its linguistic rules and pragmatic appropriateness.

Appendix 1

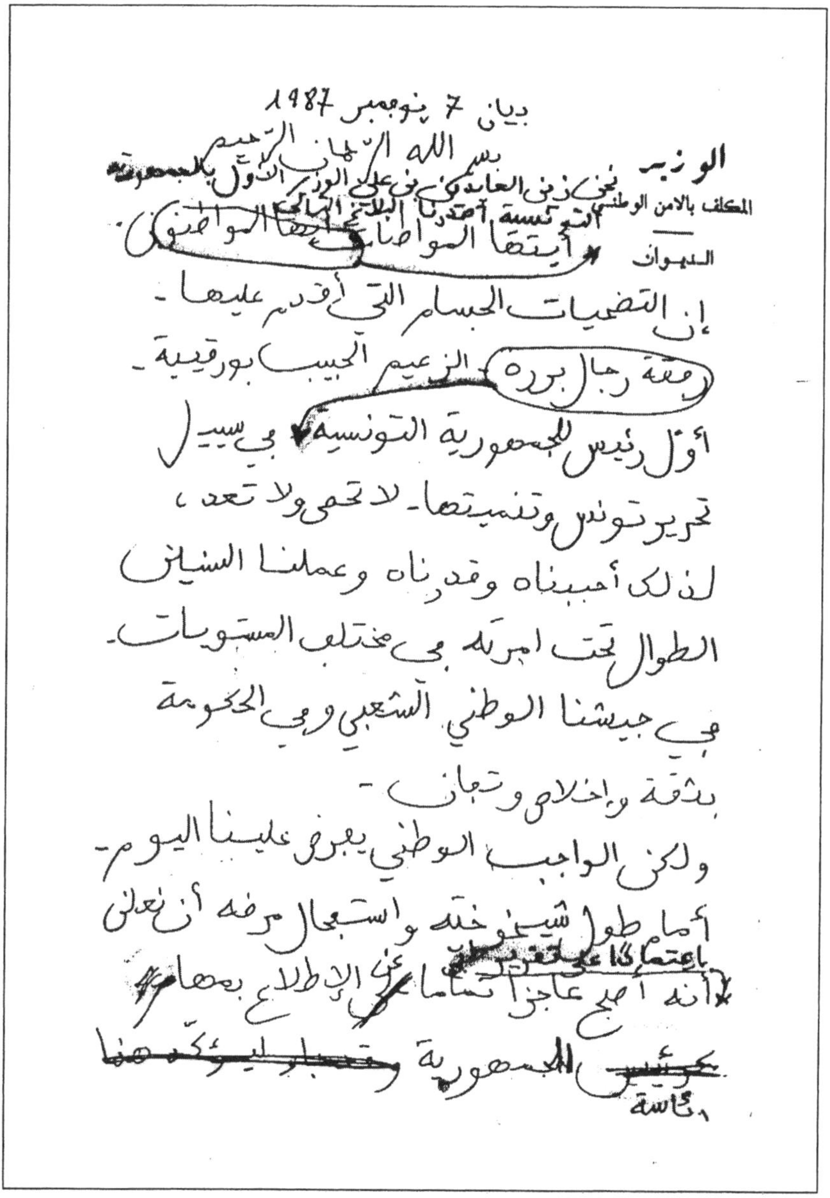

بيان 7 نوفمبر 1987

بسم الله الرحمن الرحيم

الوزير نحن زين العابدين بن علي الوزير الأول بالجمهورية

المكلف بالامن الوطني التونسية أصدرنا البلاغ التالي

أيتها المواطنات أيها المواطنون

الديوان

إن التضحيات الجسام التي أقدم عليها

الزعيم الحبيب بورقيبة رفقة رجال بررة

أول رئيس للجمهورية التونسية في سبيل

تحرير تونس وتنميتها لا تحصى ولا تعد،

لذلك أحببناه وقدرناه وعملنا السنين

الطوال تحت امرته في مختلف المستويات.

في جيشنا الوطني الشعبي وفي الحكومة

بثقة وإخلاص وتفان.

ولكن الواجب الوطني يفرض علينا اليوم.

أمام طول شيخوخته واستفحال مرضه أن نعلن

باعتمادا على تقرير طبي

أنه أصبح عاجزا تماما عن الاضطلاع بمهام

رئيس الجمهورية وتحمل أعبائها

محاسة

الوزير
المكلف بالامن الوطني

الديوان

~~تقرير طبي أطباء~~ ....

وبناء على ذلك وعملا بالفصل 57 من
الدستور تولى بعون الله
وتوفيقه رئاسة الجمهورية والقيادة
العليا لقواتنا المسلحة.
وسنعتمد في مباشرة مسؤولياتنا
في جو من الثقة والأمن والاطمئنان
على كل أبناء تونسنا العزيزة، ولا مكان
للحقد والبغضاء والكراهية.
إن استقلال بلادنا وسلامة ترابنا ومناعة
وطننا وتقدم شعبنا هي مسؤولية كل
~~تونسي بدون تمييز~~ التونسيين

الوزير

المكلف بالامن الوطني

الديوان

وحب الوطن والذود عنه والرفع

من شأنه واجب مقدس على كل مواطن

أيها المواطنون أيتها المواطنات

إن شعبنا بلغ من الوعي والنضج ما يسمح

لكل أبنائه وبناته بالمشاركة البناءة

في تصريف شؤونه، في ظل نظام جمهوري

يولي المؤسسات ~~حرمتها~~ مكانتها ويوفر

أسباب الديمقراطية المسؤولة، وعلى

أساس سيادة الشعب كما نص عليها

الدستور الذي يحتاج إلى مراجعة ~~أكيدة~~ تأكدت

اليوم ~~متأكدة~~، ولا مجال ~~اليوم~~ في عصرنا

لرئاسة مدى الحياة ولا لخلافة آلية

لا دخل فيها للشعب.

الوزير
المكلف بالامن الوطني

الديوان

إن شعبنا جدير بحياة سياسية
متطورة ~~متفتحة~~ ومنظمة، تعتمد بحق
تعددية الأحزاب السياسية
والتنظيمات الشعبية.
وإننا سنعرض قريبا مشروع قانون
للأحزاب ومشروع قانون للصحافة
يوفران مساهمة أوسع بنظام ومسؤولية
في بناء تونس ودعم استقلالها،
وسنحرص على إعطاء القانون حرمته، ولا
مجال للظلم والقهر كما سنحرص على إعطاء الدولة
هيبتها، ولا مكان للفوضى والتسيب
ولا سبيل لاستغلال النفوذ أو التساهل
في أموال المجموعة ومكاسبها.

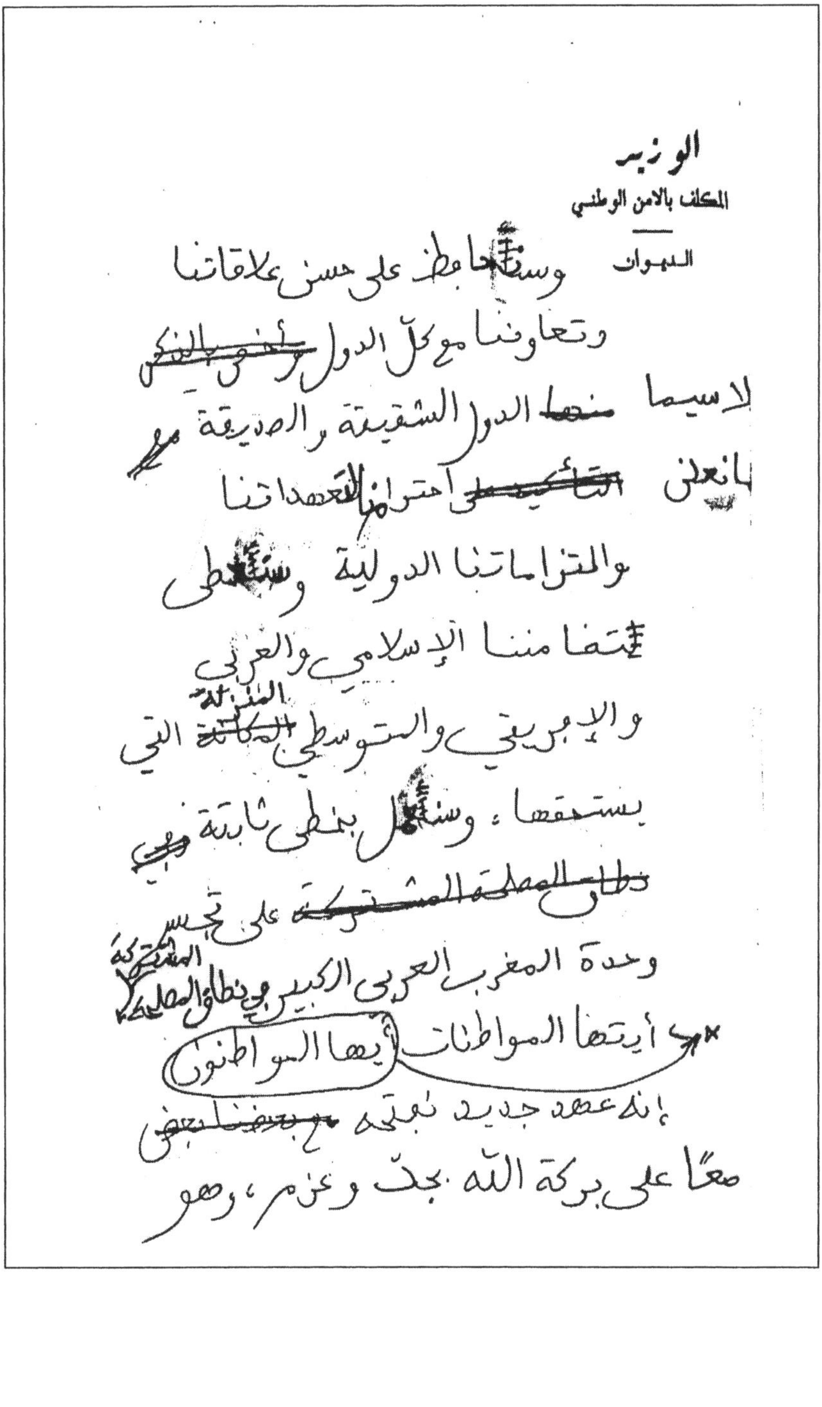

الوزير
المكلف بالأمن الوطني
الديوان

وسنحافظ على حسن علاقاتنا
وتعاوننا مع كل الدول بغض النظر
لا سيما منها الدول الشقيقة والصديقة مع
ما نعلن التأكيد على احترامنا لتعهداتنا
والتزاماتنا الدولية وسنعطي
تضامننا الإسلامي والعربي
والإفريقي والمتوسطي المكانة المنزلة التي
يستحقها وسنعمل بخطى ثابتة في
نطاق المصلحة المشتركة على تجسيم
وحدة المغرب العربي الكبير في نطاق المصلحة المشتركة
أيتها المواطنات أيها المواطنون
إنه عهد جديد نفتحه مع بعضنا بعض
معًا على بركة الله بجد وعزم، وهو

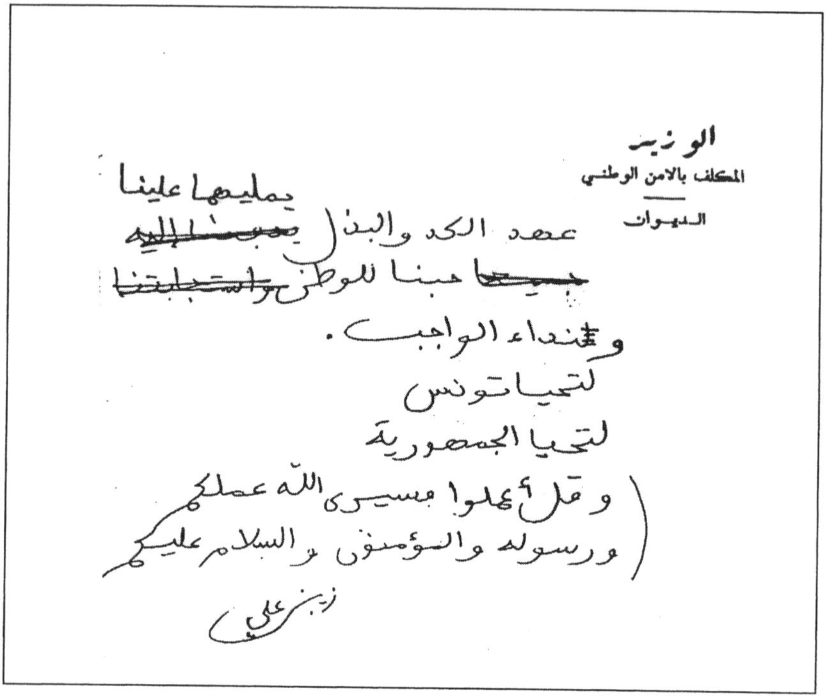

الوزير
المكلف بالامن الوطني
الديوان

يمليها علينا
عهد الكد والبذل ~~يحبب اليه~~
~~حبا~~ حبنا للوطن ~~واستجابتنا~~
ونداء الواجب.
لتحيا تونس
لتحيا الجمهورية
وقل اعملوا فسيرى الله عملكم
ورسوله والمؤمنون والسلام عليكم
زين علي

Appendix 2

بيان ٧ نوفمبر

بسم الله الرحمان الرّحيم

أيها المواطنون ، أيتها المواطنات

نحن زين العابدين بن علي الوزير الأوّل

بالجمهوريّة التونسيّة أصدرنا البلاغ التالي:

إنّ التضحيّات الجسام التي أقدم عليها الزعيم الحبيب بورقيبة أول رئيس للجمهوريّة التونسيّة رفقة رجال بررة في سبيل تحرير تونس وتنميّتها لا تحصى ولا تعدّ لذلك أحببناه وقدّرناه وعملنا السّنين الطوال تحت أمرته في مختلف المستويات في جيشنا الوطني الشعبي وفي الحكومة بثقة وإخلاص وتفان ولكن الواجب الوطني يفرض علينا اليوم أمام طول شيخوخته واستفحال مرضه أن نعلن اعتمادا على تقرير طبّي أنه أصبح عاجزا تماما عن الإضطلاع بمهام رئاسة الجمهوريّة .

وبناء على ذلك وعملا بالفصل ٥٧ من الدّستورنتولّى بعون الله وتوفيقه رئاسة الجمهوريّةوالقيادة العليا لقوّاتنا المسلّحة وسنعتمد في مباشرة مسؤولياتنا ، في جوّ من الثقة والأمن والإطمئنان على كل أبناء تونسنا العزيزة ، فلا مكان للحقد والبغضاء والكراهيّة. إنّ استقلال بلادنا وسلامة ترابنا ومناعة وطننا وتقدّم شعبنا هي مسؤوليّة كلّ التونسيّين وحبّ الوطن والذّود عنه والرفع من شأنه واجب مقدّس على كلّ مواطن .

أيها المواطنون ، أيتها المواطنات

إنّ شعبنا بلغ من الوعي والنضج ما يسمح لكل أبنائه وفئاته بالمشاركة البنّاءة في تصريف شؤونه في ظل نظام جمهوري يولي المؤسّسات مكانتها ويوفّر أسباب الدّيمقراطيّة المسؤولة وعلى أساس سيادة الشعب كما نصّ عليها الدستور الذي يحتاج إلى مراجعة تأكّدت اليوم فلا مجال في عصرنا إلى رئاسة مدى الحياة ولا لخلافة آلية لا دخل فيها للشعب ، فشعبنا جدير بحياة سياسية متطوّرة ومنظمة تعتمد بحقّ تعدّدية الأحزاب السّياسيّة والتنظيمات الشعبيّة.

وإنّنا سنعرض قريبا مشروع قانون للأحزاب ومشروع قانون للصحافة يوفّران مساهمة أوسع، بنظام ومسؤوليّة، في بناء تونس ودعم استقلالها.

وسنحرص على إعطاء القانون حرمته ، فلا مجال للظلم والقهر ، كما سنحرص على إعطاء الدّولة هيبتها فلا مكان للفوضى والتسيّب ولاسبيل لاستغلال النفوذ أو التساهل في اموال المجموعة ومكاسبها .

وسنحافظ على حسن علاقتنا وتعاوننا مع كلّالدّول ، لاسيما الدّول الشقيقة والصّديقة كما نعلن احترامنا لتعهّداتنا والتزاماتنا الدوليّة .

وسنعطي تضامننا الاسلامي والعربي والإفريقي والمتوسّطي المنزلة التي يستحقّها .

وسنعمل بخطى ثابتة على تجسيم وحدة المغرب العربي الكبير في نطاق المصلحة المشتركة .

أيها المواطنون ، أيتها المواطنات

إنّه عهد جديد نفتحه معا على بركة الله ، بجدّ،وعزم ، وهو عهد الكدّ والبذل يمليهما علينا حبّنا للوطن ونداء الواجب .

لتحيا تونس – لتحيا الجمهوريّة

وقل اعملوا فسيرى الله عملكم ورسوله و المؤمنون. صدق الله العظيم .

ـ والسّلام عليكم ورحمة الله وبركاته ـ

Source:http://www.bibliotheque.nat.tn/Doc-Re/decl7/index11.htm

REFERENCES

Baccouche,Taieb.1990. "Hal Al-fuṣħaa wa Al-daarija Luɤataani". *Al-Majalla Al-Tunusiyya li-l-ʕuluum al-ʔijtimaaʕiyya* 100.80-95. Tunis: CERES.

Bakhtin, Mikhail. 1986 [1981]. *The Dialogic Imagination: Four essays by M.M. Bakhtin* ed. by M. Holquist. Austin: University of Texas Press.

Ben Abdallah, Abdelkrim. 1992. *7 November: Al-Thawra Al-Haadi'a*. Tunis: Ben Abdallah Press.

Boussofara-Omar, Naïma. 2003. "Revisiting Arabic Diglossic Switching in Light of the MLF and its Sub-models". *Bilingualism* 6.33-46.

_____. 1999. *Arabic Diglossic Switching in Tunisia: An application of Myers-Scotton's MLF model*. Ph. D. dissertation, University of Texas at Austin.

Bourdieu, Pierre. 1991. *Language and Symbolic Power* ed. by John B. Thompson. Cambridge, MA: Harvard University Press.

Chaabane, Sadok. 1995. *Ben Ali and the Road to Pluralism*. Tunis: CERES.

Errington, Joseph J. 2000. "Indonesian('s) Authority". Kroskrity 2000. 271-284.

_____. 1985. "On the Nature of the Sociolinguistic Sign: Describing the Javanese speech levels". *Semiotic Mediation* ed. by Elizabeth Mertz & Richard J. Parmentier, 287-310. Orlando: Academic Press.

Gal, Susan. 1998. "Multiplicity and Contention among Language Ideologies". Shieffelin et al. 1998. 317-331.

Haeri, Niloofar. 2003. *Sacred Language, Ordinary People*. New York: Macmillan

_____. 2000. "Form and Ideology: Arabic sociolinguistics and beyond". *Annual Reviews Anthropology* 29.61-87.

_____. 1997. "The Reproduction of Symbolic Capital: Language, state, and class in Egypt. *Current Anthropology* 38:5.795-816.

Irvine, T. Judith. 1984. "Formality and Informality in Communicative Events". *Language in Use: Readings in sociolinguistics* ed. by John Baugh & Joel Sherzer, 211-228. Irvine, NJ: Prentice Hall.

Irvine, Judith & Susan Gal. 2000. "Language Ideology and Linguistic Differentiation". Kroskrity 2000. 35-83.

Kroskrity, Paul. 2000. *Regimes of Language: Polities and identities*. Santa Fe, NM: School of American Research Press.

Mertz, Elizabeth. 1998. "Linguistic Ideology and Praxis in U.S. Law School Classrooms". Schieffelin et al. 1998. 149-162.

Philips, Susan. 2000. "Constructing a Tongon Nation-State Through Language Ideology in the Courtroom". Kroskrity 2000. 229-257.

Shieffelin, Bambi, Woolard, Kathryn & Paul Kroskrity. 1998. *Language Ideologies: Practice and theory*. Oxford: Oxford University Press.

Silverstein, Michael. 2000. "Whorfianism and the Linguistic Imagination of Nationality". Kroskrity 2000. 85-138.

Spitulnik, Debra. 1999. "The Language of the City: Town Bemba as urban hybridity". *Journal of Linguistic Anthropology* 8:1.30-59.

_____. 1998. "Mediating Unity and Diversity: The production of language ideologies in Zambian broadcasting". Shieffelin et al. 1998. 163-188.

Suleiman, Yasir. 2003. *The Arabic Language and National Identity: A study in ideology*. Washington, DC: Georgetown University Press.

Walters, Keith. 2003. "Fergie's Prescience: The changing nature of diglossia in Tunisia". *International Journal of the Sociology of Language* 163.77-109.

_____. 1998. "'New Year Happy': Some sociolinguistic observations on the way to the 'anglicization' of North Africa". *English in North Africa* ed. by Mohamed Jabeur, Adal Manai & Mongi Bahloul, 33-63. Tunis: Imprimerie El Habbib/ Tunisian Society for Anglo-Saxon Studies.

Woolard, Kathryn. 1998. "Introduction: Language ideology as a field of inquiry". Shieffelin et al. 1998. 3-47.

AGREEMENT ALTERNATIONS
HOW OPTIONAL PATTERNS OF AGREEMENT ARISE

Heidi Lorimor
University of Illinois, Urbana-Champaign

1. Introduction

Semantic agreement effects are interesting because they provide evidence for the influence of semantic meaning on the expressed morphology. This most often occurs when a plural marker is expressed on a verb, even though the syntactic head noun is singular, or when the default agreement pattern would otherwise specify that the verb should be singular. Semantic agreement effects arise in Arabic, and one environment in which they have been attested is when plural verb agreement is expressed, even though the default agreement would be feminine singular (Belnap 1999).

One possible extension of the scope of semantic agreement is to the phenomenon of first conjunct agreement, which does exhibit an agreement alternation: the verb is able to agree either with just the first conjunct or to take both conjuncts as its grammatical subjects and to agree with both. What's more, there does seem to be a semantic component to first conjunct agreement. When the verb agrees with both conjuncts, Number Sensitive Items (NSIs) that require plural subjects are more often permitted, and with first conjunct agreement, the ungrammaticality of these NSIs demonstrates that the verb is in an agreement relationship with a singular subject.

A series of recent experiments in psycholinguistics have explored semantic agreement effects, showing a cross-linguistic pattern for speakers to sometimes produce a plural verb that "disagrees" with its singular grammatical subject, depending on the subject's notional (or semantic) plurality. These results have demonstrated that varying the notional plurality of a subject can affect agreement patterns, which may override the grammatical number of the head noun, and a renegade plural marker, generated by the subject's notional plurality, may intervene and mark the verb as plural, thus strengthening the case for semantic agreement effects.

Standard Arabic and its dialectal varieties provide a unique venue of investigation for semantic agreement effects due to their postverbal agreement patterns. Proposals for where one might find semantic agreement are these: with singular and plural agreement with inanimate plurals (Belnap 1999) and for postverbal conjoined subjects (Munn 1999). Belnap has shown that the postverbal agreement patterns in Cairene Arabic show robust semantic agreement effects, and Munn makes an attempt to attribute the difference between first conjunct agreement and postverbal agreement with both conjuncts to these same semantic effects. Belnap's proposal to account for a continuum of agreement types is consistent with the psycholinguistic work showing patterns of notional agreement. However, the alternation between first conjunct agreement and full agreement with both postverbal conjuncts is better captured with a syntactic analysis, in which these constructions are interpreted as involving the coordination of IPs and NPs, respectively (Aoun et al. 1994, 1999).

This paper will consider where semantic agreement effects in Arabic do arise and will discuss the data from Arabic first conjunct agreement to show how these postverbal agreement alternations are not consistent with the patterns that are explained by a psycholinguistic model of notional agreement (Bock et al. MS).

2. Semantic Agreement Effects

Semantic agreement effects are demonstrably present in both English and in the varieties of Arabic when there is a cooccurrence of singular and plural agreement with the same subject NP and in the same syntactic configuration. Semantic plural agreement appears when a plural marker is generated by the notional plurality of the subject, which marks the verb as plural when the syntactic structure and grammatical number of the subject would otherwise suggest that the verb should be singular.

2.1 *Semantic agreement effects in Cairene Arabic*

In Cairene Arabic when verbs have plural subjects, the verbs either agree with their plural subjects, or they take the feminine singular form. Corbett (2000) characterizes the full (plural) agreement pattern as semantic agreement and the feminine singular agreement as syntactic agreement. This analysis is supported by the distribution of agreement patterns that were collected by Belnap (1999). The highest rate of plural verb agreement is with human sound plurals, followed by human broken plurals. Next on the continuum come plural animal subjects, which induce plural agreement on the verb with about thirty percent of the utterances. Inanimate subjects least often cause plural agreement with the verbs, with the sound plurals ranking slightly higher than broken plural inanimates.

Table 1. Agreement with plural noun phrases in Cairene Arabic

head noun	**Example**	**Plural agreement %**	**N**
human sound plurals	*banaat* "girls"	94	34
human broken plurals	*ʔawlaad* "boys, children"	90	140
animal broken plurals	*ʔaraanib* "rabbits"	35	20
inanimate sound plurals	*ḥagaat* "things"	4	144
inanimate broken plurals	*biyuut* "houses"	3	191

(Belnap 1999:174; examples of plurals are from Belnap 1993.)

Belnap (1999) attributed these differences in the rates of plural agreement to differences in notional (or semantic) plurality. He correlates animacy, agency, and distributivity with semantic plurality, which are some of the most important semantic agreement factors in the psycholinguistic literature (Vigliocco & Hartsuiker 2002). Therefore, this distribution of agreement data provides evidence that there is a tendency in one of the Arabic dialects to use plural verbs more often when subjects are notionally plural – a semantic agreement effect.

2.2 *Semantic agreement effects in English*

Since much of the research into semantic agreement has been done in English, it is fitting to outline some English semantic agreement effects in order to further explore the causes of semantic agreement effects in order to understand where these effects would be expected to surface cross-linguistically.

While most speakers of American English use a singular verb to agree with most collective nouns, sometimes plural verbs surface after notionally plural (although still syntactically singular) collective nouns (Bock et al. 2004a). These lexically singular nouns that are susceptible to plural interpretation are what den Dikken (2001) terms "pluringulars", although these collective nouns do not become plural themselves, even if they have a plural semantic interpretation, as is demonstrated by the ungrammaticality of the plural determiner in (1c). (Data are from den Dikken 2001.)

(1) a. The committee has decided
b. The committee HAVE decided
c. *These committee have decided

This notional plurality is able to affect even formal speech and writing as is illustrated by the following examples. Den Dikken cites Richard Nixon as a "pluringularist" who has been quoted as saying, "In this period of our history, the educated class *are* decadent", where 'class' is construed as a plurality and therefore induces plural verb agreement. Other such pluringulars in English are 'couple', 'crew', and 'group', which can agree with a singular verb when they denote a unit, but which agree with a plural verb when individuality is emphasized.

(2) a. And this fall the couple EXPECTS its first child.
b. A Florida court ruled against a Pennsylvania couple who CONTEND May's 10-year-old daughter is actually their child. (Reid 1991:272)

(3) a. Each week "Pirate TV"'s scruffy crew, supposedly transmitting from a barge off Manhattan, TAKE aim at the deadliest forms of airwave pollution.
b. *The* crew of the Calypso INVADES dry land to liberate the fish in pet stores. (Reid 1991: 273 – *a* and *b* taken from the same article by Harry Waters in *Newsweek*).

(4) One group of faculty members TEACHES a great deal, and is paid very little; the other group TEACH very little, but are paid considerably more. (Reid 1991: 230 – from a paper by Robert Davis in the *Journal of Mathematical Behavior*)

What is particularly intriguing is that, although these pluringulars can invoke plural verb agreement, they will only allow singular adjectives and demonstratives inside the DP (1c), which means that, within the DP, they remain syntactically singular. They are also unable to take quantifiers that quantify over plurals (e.g., *many*), although they do enter into an agreement relationship with a plural verb, which demonstrates that this is an instance of semantic plural agreement.

Both the Cairene Arabic agreement continuum and the English collective nouns show semantic agreement effects when they are marked as plural verbs which would otherwise be expected to surface as singulars. Based on these observations, we might also expect postverbal conjoined subjects in Arabic to be potential loci of semantic agreement effects, since in Standard Arabic the verb has the option of agreeing with just one or with both conjuncts. At first glance, the postverbal agreement patterns of conjoined subjects do seem to follow the patterns of notional agreement. However, conjoined subjects do not behave as conventional subject head nouns, as will be explored in the next section.

2.3 *Conjunctions as potential showcases of semantic agreement effects*

Conjunctions are problematic syntactic elements, especially in terms of determining the agreement controller with conjoined subjects. Corbett (2000) describes conjoined subject noun phrases as exhibiting behaviors varying from true coordination to adjunction in which one of the elements is irrelevant to agreement. In a wide range of languages, when two noun phrases are conjoined, there is the option of the verb agreeing with just one of them, which can be either first or last conjunct agreement, depending on the position of the verb relative to the subject. However, even with conjuncts, sometimes agreement does not occur either with the coordinated noun phrase as a whole or with the local noun. Instead, the conjunction can be perceived as a single unit, despite its surface plurality. Certain plural conjunctions in English, such as *bacon and eggs* agree with singular verbs because they are construed as a single unit (Humphreys & Bock in press). This construction is particularly interesting because the local noun *eggs* is plural, so it cannot be argued that the agreement is just with the local noun. Also, *bacon and eggs* is not interpreted as an adjunction construction (see Munn 1999), since the phrase does not refer to bacon that has a flavor/hint of eggs. Instead, it is a full-fledged conjunction, in which bacon and eggs are both equally important parts of the whole breakfast. Conjunctions are troublesome because there is no single, identifiable subject noun, and while they most often agree with plural verbs in English, corpus counts (such as Lorimor 2004) are demonstrating the wide range of agreement patterns found with conjoined subjects. Three instances in which singular agreement would be most likely found are as follows: what appears to be conjoined NPs might actually be conjoined clauses with a gapped verb, the conjoined subject might actually be adjunction, or the conjoined subject might be a name that refers to a singular element.

3. Agreement in Standard Arabic

To understand how semantic effects could be realized in conjunctions, it is important to understand the alternations in agreement that occur due to the subject's position relative to the verb.

3.1 *Full and partial agreement in Standard Arabic*

In Standard Arabic, full agreement only occurs when the subject precedes the verb, and partial agreement (only gender, not number) occurs when the subject follows the verb. These data from Standard Arabic were provided by Aoun et al. (1994).

(5) a. naama l-ʔawlaad-u. (SA)
slept.3ms the-children-nom
"The children slept."
b. ʔal-ʔawlaad-u naamuu.
the-children-nom slept.3mp
"The children slept."
c. *naamuu l-ʔawlaad-u.
slept.3mp the-children-nom
d. *ʔal-ʔawlaad-u naama.
the-children-nom slept.3ms

3.2 *First Conjunct Agreement in Standard Arabic*

Preverbal conjoined subjects exhibit full agreement with the verb, while postverbal conjoined subjects show only gender agreement on the verb. When the conjoined subjects occur post-verbally, the verb may agree in gender with the first conjunct, as in (6b), but the verb can optionally agree with both conjuncts as well. This induces masculine agreement on the verb (6a), which is what we would expect if the verb were to agree with both conjuncts. The contrast between first conjunct agreement in Standard Arabic and full agreement is shown in these (SA) data from Aoun et al. 1994

(6) a. qaraʔa ʕumar wa ʕaliyaa/l-qiṣṣa (V-msc.sg. NP-fem.sg. NP-masc.sg.)
read.3ms Omar and Alia the-story Agreement with both conjuncts
"Omar and Alia read the story."
b. qaraʔat ʕaliyaa / wa ʔumar l-qiṣṣa (V-fem.sg. NP-fem.sg. NP-masc.sg)
read.3fs Alia and Omar the-story First conjunct agreement
"Alia and Omar read the story."

There are two competing explanations for this alternation between first conjunct agreement and agreement with both conjuncts. Munn (1999) attributed the difference between these agreement patterns to semantic plurality. His analysis involves first conjunct agreement being the default agreement pattern for Standard Arabic and for the dialects, and he attributes agreement with both conjuncts as due to the presence of a null (plural) pronominal. This null pronominal is generated by the notional plurality of the conjoined subject, so when the verb agrees with both conjuncts rather than with just the first conjunct, this is due to semantic agreement effects.

Aoun et al. (1999) responded to Munn's analysis by arguing that the null plural pronominal approach does not sufficiently account for the data. Instead, they propose an analysis that relies on the difference between clausal conjunction and the conjunction of NPs, and they support their clausal analysis of first conjunct agreement with data from collectives and Number Sensitive Items.

To evaluate these competing approaches to first conjunct agreement, we need to look at the nature of agreement processes themselves and what actually happens when semantic agreement occurs.

4. Accounting for Syntactic and Semantic Agreement

4.1 *Syntactic models of agreement*

Agreement, especially subject-verb agreement, has been traditionally classified as a strictly syntactic phenomenon. Within the Principles and Parameters framework, this typically occurs in a Spec-

Head or c-command relationship. Syntactically singular subjects agree with syntactically singular verbs, and plural subjects in general agree with plural verbs. The verb therefore enters the derivation unmarked for number, and it generally obtains its number from the subject's number marking. Semantic plural agreement can be explained in such a framework by the introduction of an intervening plural element that was generated by the notional plurality of the subject and that marks the verb as plural, thus overruling the subject's lexical subject-marking properties. In other frameworks such as HPSG and the Minimalist Program, both the subject and the verb enter into the derivation fully specified for number. Agreement involves a checking procedure that ensures the number specifications of the subject and the verb match. Notional agreement would occur when different number specifications were generated on the subject and the verb, and these unmatched items would be produced because the checking procedures failed to flag the error and make the derivation crash.

4.2 *Psycholinguistic models of agreement (See Figure 1)*

Psycholinguists have also formulated models of language production in which agreement occurs during syntactic planning, with no interaction between the semantic, syntactic, and phonological components (Levelt 1989, Bock & Levelt 1994). Within these models, message planning occurs first, and this determines the number of the subject, but subject-verb agreement occurs during the next stage, which is syntactic planning/grammatical encoding. The final stage, phonological encoding, should proceed after all the grammatical encoding has occurred, and therefore, the autonomy of syntax is preserved. However, there seem to be cases in which the notional number and grammatical number clash, and this clash has an effect on agreement. In some cases, this might include a grammatically singular subject with a plural verb, and in other cases, speakers produce plural pronouns referring to grammatically singular antecedents (data from Bock et al. 2004b).

(7) a. The gang on the motorcycles WERE…
    b. The crowd at the Olympic event enjoyed THEMSELVES

Bock et al.'s (MS) explanation for the appearance of plural verbs and pronouns in these positions relies on an introduction of a plural marker, very much in line with Munn's (1999) null pronominal analysis for agreement with both postverbal conjuncts. Bock et al. propose a system of agreement in which the plural marker can be generated either by the subject noun or by the semantics, independent of the noun's number (refer to Appendix 1 for a discussion of Bock et al.'s (MS) model of agreement production). This plural marking is then fed into the system that generates the morphological plural marker on the verb, which illustrates the main departure of Munn's analysis from the Bock et al. model: the plural marker is still not present on the verb in Standard Arabic, even when the verb agrees with both conjuncts. Instead, full agreement (with both conjuncts) is flagged by gender agreement that takes the second conjunct into account, rather than just reflecting the gender of the first conjunct, as is illustrated in (6a) and (6b).

4.3 *Syntactic models that account for semantic influences on number agreement*

In addition to the psycholinguistic models, there have been several recent attempts to account for semantic agreement effects syntactically. These approaches have relied on elements such as null plural pronominals or on notional *phi*-features that are visible to some syntactic elements (the VP), while other elements (determiners or other elements within the DP) remain immune to these notional features and are influenced by the lexical, syntactically relevant agreement features.

4.3.1 *Agreement with a null pronominal (Munn 1999, den Dikken2001)*

Since, for pluringulars, the nouns inside the DP will agree only with singular demonstratives, den Dikken has proposed that there are pronominally headed *committee*-type noun phrases that invoke plural agreement with the verb, the structure of which is shown in (8c). (Data from den Dikken 2001)

(8) a. This committee has/have decided.
 b. *These committee have decided.
 c. $[_{DP1}$ $pro_{[+PLUR]}$ $[_{DP2}$ the $committee_{[-PLUR]}]]$

Therefore, the noun *committee* is still singular within the DP, but the notional plurality of this subject noun phrase has summoned the presence of a null plural pronominal that will become the (covert) head of a new subject noun phrase and that will induce plural agreement on the verb. This is an attractive solution because of the "strength" of pronouns in inducing full agreement, such that they are much more rigorous agreement controllers cross-linguistically than ordinary lexical subjects (den Dikken 2001), and as discussed before, this analysis of attraction might be compatible with the psycholinguistic data, since what is being introduced is an independently generated plural marker.

When the null plural pronominal analysis is extended to Arabic, however, it fails to account for first conjunct agreement. At first, it seems like a plausible option, since in the Standard Arabic VS word order, partial agreement only occurs with lexical noun phrases, but pronouns are consistently required to exhibit full agreement regardless of word order. (Data are from Aoun et al. 1994.)

(9) a. naamuu hum. . (SA)
slept.mp they
"They slept."
b. *naama hum
slept.ms they

The problem with this analysis is that verbs agree with pronouns in number, even when the pronouns surface postverbally. If agreement with both postverbal conjuncts were really an instance of a null plural pronominal heading the noun phrase, then we would expect to see a plural feature on the verb, consistent with the behavior with other pronouns in Arabic. This is not the case with postverbal conjoined subjects in Standard Arabic, which lends support for an analysis that differentiates between the two agreement patterns with postverbal conjoined subjects without invoking the null plural pronominal.

4.3.2 *Mereological features (Sauerland & Elbourne 2002)*

Another attempt to account for notional agreement has come through the specification of semantic features that are only visible to parts of the syntactic derivation. Sauerland and Elbourne account for semantic agreement effects by proposing that there are two number features associated with each NP: *number* and *mereology*. The mereological feature comes from the notional specification of the NP, and it is able to mark the verb, but not a determiner, for plurality. That is how they explain sentences from British English, such as (10). (Data are from Sauerland & Elbourne 2002.)

(10) A northern team are likely to be in the finals.

When the number and the mereological features clash, the number feature marks the determiner, *a*, as singular, and the mereological feature marks the verb as plural. A variant of this analysis might be applicable to the Arabic data, since perhaps this mereological feature would circumvent the problem introduced with the null pronominal analysis: the lack of an overt plural marker on the verb, since there is no a priori reason that a mereological plural feature would have to surface as a morphological plural marker. If verbs are consistently singular when they precede non-pronominal subjects, as is the case in Standard Arabic, then a mereologically plural conjoined noun phrase could induce gender agreement with both conjuncts while still having singular agreement on the verb, which is a desirable result.

This mereological approach, however, is untenable, as has been demonstrated through a comparison of British and American English. The subsets of collective nouns in American and British English that take plural verbs are different, but when tested, both British and American speakers of English have rated nouns such as *group, faculty,* or *team* identically for their notional plurality, even though they tend to agree with plural verbs in British English and singular verbs in American English (Bock et al. 2004a). The ratings demonstrate that, if mereological features are present in both American and British English, then the sets of pluringulars in both varieties of English should be the same, so the difference cannot be that speakers of British English construe *team* as plural, while speakers of American English consider *team* to be a singular entity.

To circumvent this proposal, another explanation could be that mereological features are only active in languages and dialects, while being irrelevant to agreement in others. If this were the case, then we would expect to find no pluringulars in American English, but the examples in (1)-(4) would suggest that this is not the case. Instead, American English does have a set of nouns that behave as pluringulars, so it is not possible to explain the difference between British and American agreement patterns to the activity (or lack thereof) of mereological features that mark notional plurality. The plausibility of such an explanation is suspect, since it would require that speakers of some languages are influenced by notional plurality, while speakers of other languages are immune to such notional agreement effects, especially since they have been widely attested in a variety of languages (Humphreys & Bock 2004).

5. Analysis of First Conjunct Agreement in Arabic

The structure of a sentence is built without reference to the number or gender of the lexical items involved in the sentence. With a postverbal conjoined subject, both nouns could be plural, but it is equally plausible that both nouns be singular or that one be singular and the other plural. The job of the syntax at this stage is to configure the structure that will properly express the relationships between all the items in the sentence. Based on the Bock et al. (2001) model of message production, the message formation stage should contain all the semantic information necessary for the utterance, and this message-level information should be able to specify to the syntax whether it is to build a structure of conjoined clauses or NPs. Lasersohn (1995:12) demonstrates the difference between conjoined clauses (11a) and conjoined NPs (11b) in terms of their semantic representations.

(11) a. John and Mary are asleep.
 b. John and Mary are a happy couple.

While the verb is marked as plural in both instances, in (11a), the meaning of the sentence is that JOHN IS ASLEEP and MARY IS ASLEEP. But the meaning of (11b) is not that JOHN IS A HAPPY COUPLE, AND SO IS MARY. This option of clausal agreement is also available in Arabic, and Aoun et al. (1994, 1999) have demonstrated that, by relying on the properties of clausal agreement, they are able to account for the patterns found in postverbal first conjunct agreement. This is not notional agreement, per se, but it is a case in which the message generates the relevant syntactic structure to properly express the desired meaning.

5.1 *Message formulation and agreement in Arabic*

Aoun et al. (1994) demonstrate that there is a need to account for both syntactic and semantic agreement, since they found that, by introducing Number Sensitive Items (NSIs), such as "both" *b-žuuž* in Moroccan Arabic (MA), "together" *sawa* in Lebanese Arabic (LA) or "each" *l-waħd* (MA), they could induce restrictions on syntactic number agreement and force full agreement. While first conjunct agreement is available in both MA and LA in postverbal conjoined subjects, this cannot co-occur with number sensitive items that require duality or plurality. (Data are from ABS, 1994.)

(12) a. ʕumar w saʕid mšaw b-žuuž l-l-madrasa. (MA)
Omar and Said went.p with-both to-the-school
"Omar and Said went to school together."
b. *mša ʕumar w saʕid b-ZuuZ l-l-madrasa.
went.3ms Omar and Said with-both to-the-school
c. mša ʕumar w saʕid l-l-mdrasa.
went.3ms Omar and Said to-the-school
"Omar and Said went to school."

(13) a. kariim w marwaan raaħo sawa. (LA)
Kareem and Marwaan left.p together
"Kareem and Marwaan left together."
b. *raaħ kariim w marwaan sawa.
left.3ms Kareem and Marwaan together
c. raaħo kariim w marwaan sawa.
left.p Kareem and Marwaan together
"Kareem and Marwaan left together."

For sentences such as (13a) and (13c), Aoun et al.'s (1994) analysis shows how these are analyzable in terms of NP and IP conjunction, respectively. Sentence (13b) is ungrammatical because the conjunction is not between two NPs, but instead between two IPs. Since clauses are conjoined, with a gapped verb in the second clause, the NSI's requirement of having a plural subject is not met. However, when no NSI is present, then the conjunction of two IPs is completely grammatical, as is shown here by (12c). This sentence would be grammatical whether or not Omar and Ali left together, which supports the conjoined IPs, gapping hypothesis of Aoun et al. (1994).

5.2 *The difference between gender agreement and number agreement*

One of the problems with postverbal conjunct agreement is that number and gender behave differently, so that even with plural conjoined subjects, the verb is still marked as singular. As Bahloul and Harbert (1993) noted, there is a striking difference in the behavior of gender and number agreement. While number agreement depends on the relative position of the lexical subject and the verb, gender agreement is always present. (Data are from Bahloul & Harbert 1993.)

(14) a. qadim-a (/*qadim-uu) al-ʔawlaadu. (SA)
came.3ms (came.3mp) the boys.3mp
"The boys came."

b. al-ʔawlaadu qadim-uu (/*qadim-a).
the boys.3mp came.3mp (came.3ms)
"The boys came."

c. qadim-at (/*qadim-ataa) al-bint-aani.
came.3sf (came.3df) the girl(f).3d
"The two girls came."

d. al-bint-aani qadim-ataa (/*qadim-at).
the-girl(f).3d came.3df (came.3sf)
"The two girls came."

The Bock et al. (2001) model for sentence production provides a natural account for the difference in number and gender agreement. While number agreement can be "notional" and inserted into the syntax, gender agreement behaves differently. A plural marker can enter into the derivation via the semantic meaning because there is something about the subject that is notionally plural, even if its lexical specification is as a singular noun. Grammatical gender agreement is not due to the extrinsically gendered nouns involved in the derivation, but it expresses a relationship between the verbs and the nouns themselves, rather than between the verb and the noun's number meaning. This provides a natural explanation for why, regardless of word order, gender agreement is still exhibited on the verb, and this gender/number asymmetry provides even further support for a clausal analysis of first conjunct agreement.

5.2.1 *Gender "concord" - another argument for the clausal analysis of first conjunct agreement*

Gender agreement always occurs in Arabic, regardless of the word order. However, in first conjunct agreement, the verb exhibits only the gender features of the first conjunct, not the second. Sentences (15a) and (15b) illustrate this contrast.

(15) a. qaraʔa ʕaliyaa wa ʕumar / l-qiṣṣa. (V-masc.sg. NP-fem.sg. NP-masc.sg)
read.3ms Alia and Omar the-story (SA)
"Alia and Omar read the story."

b. qaraʔat ʕaliyaa/ wa ʕumar l-qiṣṣa. (V-fem.sg. NP-fem.sg. NP-masc.sg)
read.3fs Alia and Omar the-story (SA)
"Alia and Omar read the story."

(15b) is a case of first conjunct agreement. The verb is singular and agrees in gender with the first noun and not the second. However, gender agreement tends to hold in Arabic regardless of word order. That would lead us to predict that, if both masculine and feminine nouns were present in the agreeing noun phrase, the default agreement should be masculine agreement. However, feminine agreement is still possible. This strongly argues for a clausal analysis of first conjunct agreement, since the local concord relationships in first conjunct agreement are preserved.

6. **Conclusion**

There are semantic agreement effects in Standard Arabic, as well as in the Arabic dialects. These effects are visible when the verb is marked as plural when its plurality is not dictated by the syntax, as Belnap (1999) demonstrated with Cairene Arabic. However, these agreement effects cannot explain the first conjunct agreement phenomenon in Arabic. This, instead, is best analyzed as involving different kinds of conjunction: both NP conjunction and clausal conjunction. This analysis also provides a natural explanation for the behavior of pronouns and for the asymmetry in gender and number agreement. Bock et al.'s (2001, MS) models of sentence production are consistent with these analyses. The message formulation level is able to generate the syntactic structures that properly express the relationships between the elements in the sentence, including either conjoined NPs or clauses. When semantic plurality is present, it is indicated by a plural marker on the verb, and not by the presence of a gender marker that indicates that two nouns are in the subject noun phrase. Therefore, Aoun et al.'s (1994, 1999) clausal analysis of first conjunct agreement is preserved, as notional plurality can only be indicated when the plural element itself is morphologically expressed.

Appendix 1

A Psycholinguistic Model of Agreement Production

The model depicted in Figure 1 gives an account of how agreement is computed and as well as how semantic agreement effects may occur. At the message level, before lexical items are selected or the syntactic structure is assembled, the speaker gives a notional number valuation to the message. This number marking is transmitted both to the lexicon and to the syntax. In the lexicon, appropriate lexical items are chosen, and in the syntax, the structure of the sentence is assembled, and plural specifications are generated (called "marking" here, but this does not refer to morphological markers, just to number specifications). The next stage involves the selection of morphemes to inflect the items chosen from the lexicon and attaching those morphemes to the items within the sentence structure, which is called structural integration.

Semantic agreement effects occur when a plural marking is generated, which is sent to the syntax, although no corresponding plural subject is chosen. The arrows are bidirectional between the syntax and lexicon at both the functional assembly and structural integration stages, which indicates that the plural marker that was generated in the syntax can send a message to the lexicon to request a plural marker for the verb, independent of the number marking on the subject noun. Within this model, agreement is still generally dictated by the number of the head noun in the subject noun phrase, but there are opportunities for notional plurality to intervene and to mark the verb as plural, creating a case of semantic agreement effects.

FIGURE 1. OVERVIEW OF THE COMPONENTS OF NUMBER FORMULATION IN LANGUAGE PRODUCTION (BOCK ET AL. MS)

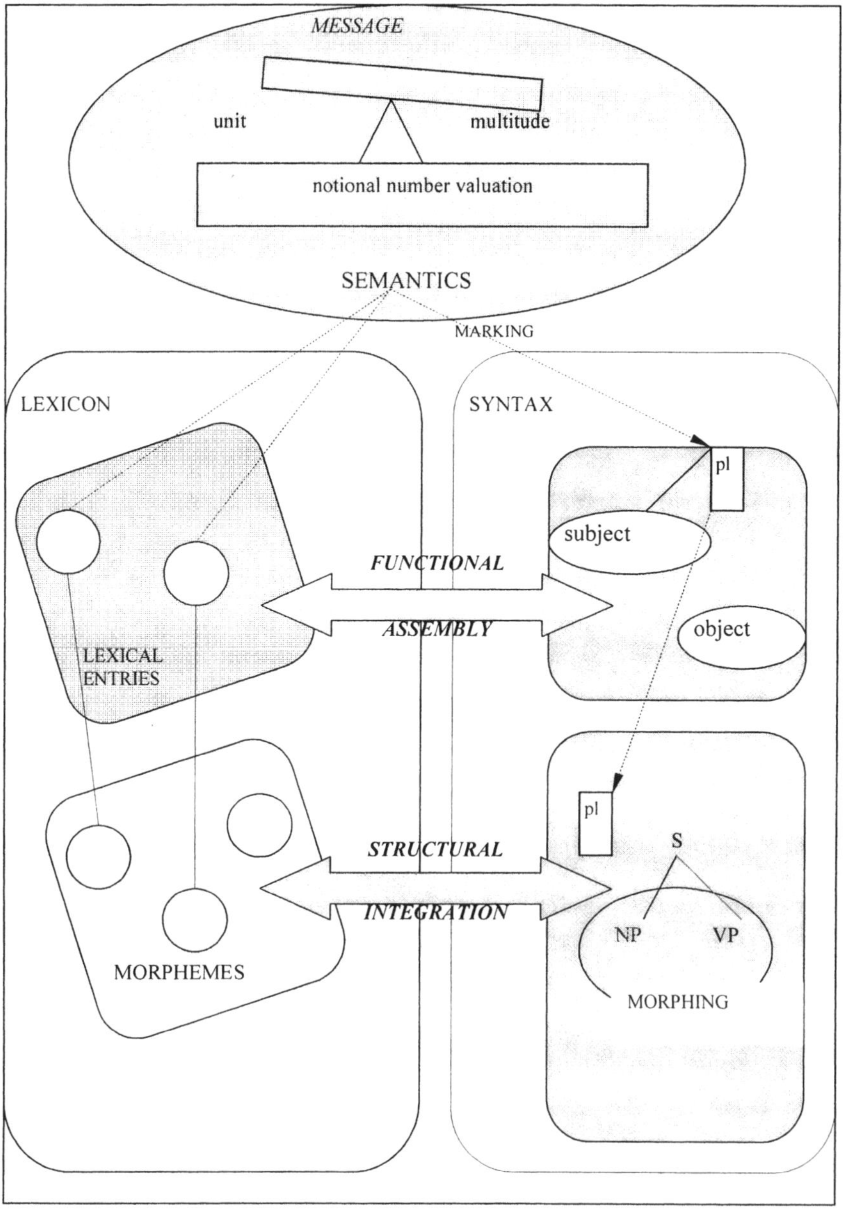

REFERENCES

Aoun, Joseph, Elabbas Benmamoun & Dominique Sportiche. 1999. "Further Remarks on First Conjunct Agreement". *Linguistic Inquiry* 30.669-681.

_____.1994. "Agreement, Word Order, and Conjunction in Some Varieties of Arabic". *Linguistic Inquiry* 25.195-220.

Bahloul, Maher & Wayne Harbert. 1993. "Agreement Asymmetries in Arabic". *Proceedings of the Eleventh West Coast Conference on Formal Linguistics* 15-31. Stanford, CA: CSLI Publications. [Distributed by Cambridge University Press.]

Belnap, R. Kirk. 1993. "The Meaning of Deflected/Strict Agreement Variation in Cairene Arabic". *Perspectives on Arabic Linguistics V* ed. by Mushira Eid & Clive Holes, 97-117. Amsterdam and Philadelphia: John Benjamins.

Bock, Kathryn, Sally Butterfield, Anne Cutler, J. Cooper Cutting, Kathleen M. Eberhard & Karin Humphreys. 2004a. "Whence Anglo-American discord? Collective agreement in British and American English". Manuscript in preparation.

Bock, Kathryn, Kathleen M. Eberhard & J. Cooper Cutting. 2004b. "Producing Number Agreement: How pronouns equal verbs". *Journal of Memory & Language* 51.251-278.

Bock, Kathryn, Kathleen M. Eberhard, J. Cooper Cutting, Antje S. Meyer & Herbert Schriefers. 2001. "Some Attractions of Verb Agreement". *Cognitive Psychology* 43.83-128.

Bock, Kathryn & Willem J. M. Levelt. 1994. "Language Production: Grammatical encoding". *Handbook of Psycholinguistics* ed. by Morton Ann Gernsbacher, 945-984. Dordrecht: Kluwer.

Bock, Kathryn, Kathleen M. Eberhard & J. Cooper Cutting. "Making Syntax of Sense: Number agreement in sentence production". Manuscript.

Corbett, Greville G. 2000. *Number*. Cambridge: Cambridge University Press.

Dikken, Marcel den. 2001. "'Pluringulars', Pronouns and Quirky Agreement". *The Linguistic Review* 18.19-41.

Humphreys, Karin. & Kathryn Bock. (In Press). "Notional Number Agreement in English". *Psychonomic Bulletin & Review.*

Lasersohn, Peter. 1995. *Plurality, Conjunction and Events*. Doredrecht: Kluwer.

Levelt, Willem J.M. 1989. *Speaking: From intention to articulation*. Cambridge, MA: MIT Press.

Lorimor, Heidi. 2004. "Counting Conjunctions: Agreeing with the whole or the sum of its parts". Research in progress.

Munn, Alan. 1999. "First Conjunct Agreement: Against a clausal analysis". *Linguistic Inquiry* 30.643-668.

Reid, Wallis. 1991. *Verb and Noun Number in English: A functional explanation*. London and New York: Longman.

Sauerland, Uli & Paul Elbourne. 2002. "Total Reconstruction, PF Movement, and Derivational Order". *Linguistic Inquiry* 33.283-319.

Vigliocco, Gabriella & Robert J. Hartsuiker. 2002. "The Interplay of Meaning, Sound, and Syntax in Sentence Production". *Psychological Bulletin* 128.442-472.

ACQUISITION OF ARABIC WORD FORMATION
A MULTI-PATH APPROACH [1]

Fatima Badry
American University of Sharjah

1. Introduction

Berko's (1958) pioneering work on the acquisition of English morphological rules demonstrated the productivity of the morphological system and paved the way for subsequent cross linguistic research that documented that, around the ages of two to three, children begin to recognize constituent formal properties and establish relationships between word forms in their lexicon. Later crosslinguistic studies further suggested that structural properties of the input language also influence the type of strategies children develop. Their acquisitional strategies seem to be influenced both by their universal predispositions as well as by the pervasiveness, productivity, transparency, and regularity of the word formation rules in their language. Investigating morphological acquisition of Semitic lang-uages, with their system of consonantal roots and surface patterns combinations in word formation should shed light on such strategies. This study investigates cognitive and typological predispositions employed in the development of lexical derivational processes by Moroccan Arabic speaking children with the objective of providing further insight into the mental organization of Semitic lexicons, the productivity of derivational processes and the psychological status of the root.

[1] I am grateful to comments and suggestions by an anonymous reviewer as well as editorial suggestions by Dr. Mohammad Alhawary, I remain, however, solely responsible for possible errors and unavoidable omissions in this chapter.

2. The Verbal Derivational System in Moroccan Arabic

Semitic lexicons reliance on derivation to form most of their content words makes them of special interest in the study of productivity in derivational morphology. In Moroccan Arabic (MA) as in all other varieties of Arabic,[2] lexicons are based on a system of underlying consonantal roots (usually tri-consonantal, CCC)[3] which are associated with an abstract semantic core. Most content words are formed by combining these roots with specific verbal and nominal patterns (P), themselves associated with specific semantic roles. In Modern Standard Arabic (MSA) which is the variety used in all literacy functions by all Arabic speakers, there are ten productive verbal patterns (PI-X) (Holes 1995) but in most dialects, not all ten are productive although they may all be used with some roots. Seven of the MSA patterns have corresponding MA patterns (see table 1). Pattern 1 (P1) CCeC is generally recognized as the basic pattern and it has several syntactic and semantic functions.[4] P1 verbs can be either transitive or intransitive, and depending on the core meaning of the root, they can convey causative, inchoative or reflexive meanings. Other patterns tend to be more specialized but some may also have more than one semantic function. For example, in MA, the underlying consonantal root *D-X-L*, has the core meaning of "enter", and surfaces in several verbal and nominal patterns such as P1 (basic) *DXeL* "he entered", P2 (causative) *DeXXel*[5] "he brought in", P5 (medio-passive) *tDeXXeL* "he interfered", as well the nominal patterns *məDXeL* "entrance", *məDXuL* "income", *DaXi:L* "intruder", *Da:XeL* "incoming", etc.

[2]There are several dialects of Arabic spoken in the various geographical regions of the Arab world and each referred to by the country in which it is spoken. They are all closely related to the Modern Standard Arabic variety used by all Arab speakers in literate activities.

[3]C is used throughout to represent the consonants in the root template

[4]To distinguis2h between reference to patterns in MSA and those in Moroccan Arabic, Roman numerals are used for MSA and Arabic numbers for Moroccan Arabic.

[5]The transcription adopted here is very broad. MSA short vowels are either dropped or reduced in MA. /e/represents any of the reduced short vowel and in many cases could be transcribed as a schwa.

Table 1: Verbal derivations in MSA and MA

Pattern	MSA	MA	Gloss	Semantic function
PI/P1	CvCvCv* DaXaLa** ŠaRiBa KaBuRa	CCvC DXeL ŠReB KbeR	 "enter" "drink" "grow"	Multiple
PII/P2	CaCCaCa DaXXaLa	CeCCeC DeXXel	 Bring in	Causative
PIII/P3	Ca:CaCa Ṣa:ĦaBa	Ca:CceC Ṣa:ĦeB	 "befriend s.o."	Conative/reciprocal
PIV/P4	ʔaCCaCa ʔaDXaLa	-------	 "bring about"	Causative
PV/P5	taCaCcaCa taDaXxaLa	tCeCceC tDeXxel	 "get (oneself) involved/interfere"	Reflexive/medio-passive
PVI/P6	taCa: CaCa taDa:XaLa	tCaCeC tDaXeL	 "interact"	Reciprocal
PVII/ P7	ʔinCaCaCa ʔinʕaKaSa	-------	 "reflect"	Medio-passive
PVIII/P8	ʔiCtaCaCa ʔiʕtaRaḌa	-------	 "block/obstruct"	Reflexive
PIX/P9	ʔiCCaCca ʔiĦMaRra	CCaC .ĦMaR	 "become red"	Inchoative
PX/P10	ʔistaCCaCa ʔistaʕRaḌa	steCCeC staʕReḌ	"review/ present"	Multiple

* Consonantal roots are represented by capital letters

**Verb citation forms are in 3rd person, masculine, singular.

MA has only one P1 form instead of the three MSA forms because of the phonological process of neutralization of the contrast between the MSA short vowels a-i- u which distinguish the three verbal forms of PI (CaCaCa, CaCuCa & CaCiCa). In addition, MSA passivization of PI verbs by short vowel alternation, CuCiCa for all three forms, is lost in MA due to this neutralization. Together with the elision of the initial glottal stop, these processes have resulted in fewer patterns being productive in MA, in comparison to MSA. Specifically, MSA patterns PIV (causative), PVII (reflexive) and PVIII (passive) are not used productively in MA (Harrell 2004). MA uses only one pattern for each of the above mentioned semantic functions, namely, P2 for causatives and P5 for reflexives, although a variant of P7 is used in some regions of Morocco (Harrell 2004). Moreover, MA uses P2 much more productively since it has lost other MSA causative patterns.[6] Overall, however, the function of the verbal patterns in MA is roughly the same as the corresponding MSA verbal patterns.

This system of semantic core and derived patterns in Arabic and other Semitic languages provides a good area for the study of the interrelation between the universal conceptual and linguistic development, the role of typological biases in acquisition, and presents a promising ground for the investigation of the productivity of word formation devices and directionality of derivation in the acquisition of the Arabic lexicon.

3. Universal and Typological Paths

Slobin's (1973) seminal paper on the role of cognitive prerequisites in language acquisition, set the stage for a whole new perspective in studies of language development. Slobin argued that based on observed regularities in acquisition crosslinguistically, one can conclude that children must possess certain operating principles (OPs)[7] that enable them to develop the grammar of their language. These OPs are strategies based on perceptual and cognitive prerequisites which are universal and which guide grammatical development. Before the child is able to talk about location or causation, for example, he needs to have first developed the prerequisite concepts. Slobin's approach was taken up by many psycholinguists (e.g., Johnston 1985, Peters 1985, Bowerman 1985) and used to explain observed developmental stages in acquisition of typologically diverse languages (De Villiers & De Villiers 1985 for English; Clark 1985 for French; Berman 1985 for Hebrew; Toivainen 1997 and Dasinger 1997 for Finnish, Estonian and Hungarian; Stephany 1997 for Greek; and MacWhinney 1985 for

[6]Moroccan Arabic has word forms based on the MSA patterns not included here but these words seem to be borrowed from MSA and are usually pronounced with an MSA phonology. The increasing interaction between dialectal and MSA forms in educated speech may bring back the obsolete patterns in the dialects and revive their productivity.

[7]I am avoiding the issue of innateness, language specific or general learning strategies here. At this point the focus is on empirical evidence which lends support to the universality of these strategies regardless of whether they are innate or learned through universal capabilities.

Hungarian).[8] Later reformulations of the operating principles approach took into consideration processes that are typologically predominant in the language to be acquired as playing a role in either sharpening and strengthening these universal predispositions (Slobin 1997a) or causing them to wither away when they are not utilized in the particular language being acquired by the child. For instance, Slobin (1997a) suggested an operating principle which he identified as *OP strengthening*. Relying on this OP, the child is guided in his acquisition of the grammatical rules of his language by the following strategy: *Whenever an attempted solution succeeds, apply the same strategies to similar problems.* This strategy is supported by evidence from several morphological domains. Dasinger (1997) reported that children learning Finnish, Hungarian and Estonian were engaged in a type of verbal play that suggests that they are aware of the importance of vocalic length. In addition, from very early on, children are guided by a universal principle that phonetic segments can be moved around systematically. The child KNOWS that linguistic units, probably defined by intonational contours, are in fact combinations of similar phonological elements (either syllabic or segmental units). This initial knowledge leads him to look for consistencies in ways in which these phonological elements are put together thus deriving information about what constitutes a possible word in his language. At more advanced stages of language acquisition, paying attention to phonological combinations leads the child to make predictions about different word classes based on formal structures.

Other OPs, such as those classified by Slobin (1985a) under "entering and tagging information in storage" are likely to be strengthened by the root/pattern combinations of Semitic lexicons. These include the following two OPs which must be very useful for Arabic and Hebrew speakers in discovering productive word formation processes in their language:

> OP (STORAGE): CO-OCCURRENCE. For every segment unit within an extracted speech string, note its co-occurrence with any preceding or following

[8]The five volumes of *The crosslinguistic study of language acquisition* edited by Dan Slobin. (1985, 1992, 1997) are devoted to this approach being applied to studying the acquisition of 28 languages from about 16 families.

unit and store sequences of co-occuring units, maintaining their serial order in the speech string.
OP (STORAGE): UNIT FORMATION. If you discover that two extracted units share a phonologically similar portion, segment and store both the shared portion and the residue as separate units. Try to find meanings for both units.

Similarity, or lack of it, in phonological structure has also been used to explain the ease or difficulty in acquisition of formal paradigms in other languages such as English past tense, and French and Spanish irregular verb conjugations. In a study of errors in irregular past tense forms in English, Bybee & Slobin (1981) found that the subjects tested made generalizations about different classes of irregular verbs based on phonological properties. Data gathered from preschoolers, eight to ten year olds, and adults' production of English irregular verbs, indicated that these forms were memorized and stored in the lexicon. However, speakers seemed to organize irregular verbs according to what the authors called "schemas".[9] According to Bybee and Slobin (1981), "the task of matching a past form with a base form must depend upon both semantic and phonological shape", that is, the child must recognize that "break" and "broke", for example, share the same core meaning and that the difference in form expresses a different tense of the same core meaning. In particular, the identical consonantal structure must be a facilitating factor in this task. The authors arrived at these conclusions analyzing the different percentages of errors of regularization produced by preschoolers relative to the phonological structure of the verb. For example, in verbs with both initial and final consonants or clusters such as "break", "sing", and "bite", regularization ranged between 32% and 55%, whereas in verbs with initial consonant or cluster only such as "blow", "know", and "see", regularization reached 8%. The effects of phonological distance on storage and access of irregular verbs was also observed with adults tested in this study. Similar conclusions were arrived at based on French acquisition data (Clark 1985). In French the irregular verb *prendre* "to take" loses its two final consonants and

[9]A 'schema' is defined as "a statement that describes the phonological properties of a morphological class (in this case past tense). 'Schemas' differ from 'rules' in that they do not relate a base to its derived form but limit their description to the outcome class.

undergoes vocalic changes when it is conjugated. For example, in the present perfect, it has the form *pris* (participial form); in the present tense it has the forms, *prends* (d & s are not pronounced), for the first person singular, *prenons* for the first person plural, etc. Clark found that children commonly created the form *prendu* in an apparent attempt to preserve the consonantal skeleton of the infinitive, in the conjugated forms.

By the end of the 20th century, this strong universal cognitive basis for linguistic development was questioned by some of those same researchers that had championed it earlier (e.g., Slobin 2001, Carey 2001). The ever expanding research on typologically different languages eventually revived the interest in the Whorfian hypothesis which proposed that the type of language being acquired influences the how, when, and what gets acquired. In a remarkable change of perspective, Slobin declared that "children come to formulate experience for linguistic expression in quite different ways depending on the type of language they are learning.... each type of language fosters its own modes of 'thinking for speaking'" (2001:442).

The role of the input and its nature had been recognized earlier by many psycholinguists who had adopted a more interactionist approach and pointed out that the social interactions of the child with his environment were essential and affect the route of acquisition (see for example, Berko-Gleason 2001, Tomasello 1992). These researchers called for both universal and innate predispositions for language and the input received from the environment as shaping the course of language acquisition. Another explanation which attempts to account for the differences found in the way different languages categorize world experiences was proposed by Schlesinger (1979). He suggested that any conceptual domain should be regarded as a continuum rather discrete categories and that different languages lexicalize different points in the continuum while the conceptualization of the domain is universal. English for example, has several words to express the concept of "cutting" depending on what is being cut and how it is cut. One slices bread, shreds paper, dices or chops vegetables, crosses the street, cuts or trims hair, severs relations, and so on.

In Moroccan Arabic, all these activities are referred to with one word *QTeʕ* "cut". This does not mean that English and Moroccan Arabic speakers have different conceptualizations of the act of cutting.

English speakers readily recognize that all the lexical items referred to above label the concept of "cutting".

In summary, various positions in the literature seem to converge towards a more inclusive approach that recognizes that children come to the task of language acquisition with certain universal conceptualization predispositions which are shaped by the social environment and language specific features all impacting the processing and organizing of the linguistic system being acquired.

In Semitic lexical acquisition, the salient, regularly occurring, word formation processes lead the child to develop a typological bias which favors derivation over other word formation processes such as compounding or periphrastic constructions. The application of the OPs, mentioned above, by Arabic and Hebrew speaking children must receive maximum strengthening from their input, which eventually leads them to pattern discovery through horizontal derivation, and root extraction leading to vertical derivation. Based on her investigations of the acquisition of Moroccan Arabic verbal and nominal patterns, Badry (1982, 1983) concluded that when children begin to analyze verbal forms (around age 31/2), their initial strategy appears to be to identify different verbal patterns based on both semantic and formal similarities. For example, the child notices that verbs sharing the semantic component of "cause" also share a similar phonological pattern, namely, CeCceC as in *HeRreS* "break" *WeKke*L "feed", *LeBbeS*[10] "dress someone". These semantic and formal similarities help the child extract the formal causative pattern CeCceC and enable him to perform horizontal derivations from one pattern to another. These conclusions were supported by evidence from children's performance with nonce words. Moroccan children found it difficult to derive verbs from nonce forms while they had no problem deriving novel forms filling lexical gaps from meaningful basic patterns. The errors with nonce forms decreased with age. Older children (7 year olds) were gradually able to use information carried by phonological structure of surface forms to relate various surface forms to an underlying consonantal root. For example the child notices that forms like *LBeS* "wear", *LeBbeS* "dress someone" *meLBu:S* "worn" *La:BeS* "dressed" all have to do with clothing and they all share the same three consonants *LBS*. Noticing

[10]Consonantal roots are represented with capitals.

these similarities serves as a semantic and morpho-phonological bootstrapping that enables him to formulate vertical derivational rules which would generate all sorts of surface patterns from a common consonantal root. Such explanation is also supported by data from Hebrew (Clark & Berman 1984). Also, Berman's analysis of children's lexical innovations in Hebrew revealed that when Hebrew speakers were asked to come up with innovative (non conventional) verb forms from nouns and adjectives, children and adults' performance revealed that they were able to extract consonantal roots and apply the appropriate verbal patterns to coin new verb forms (Berman 1993, 1999). In addition to underlying conceptual principles, Clark (1993) suggested that in acquiring their lexicon, children, from a relatively early age (age 2), are guided by two general assumptions about language, which she identified as the principles of conventionality and contrast. She argued that children must come to the task of acquiring word meanings by assuming that "words contrast in meaning, that established words pre-empt the use of others that would be synonymous with them, that unfamiliar words fill gaps, and that innovations can be coined when needed, again to fill gaps". To be able to do so children "must analyze the structure of familiar words into roots and affixes, and map the meanings onto each one". Such analysis is affected by the two factors of transparency and simplicity (1993:108). A word is transparent if the meaning of its constituents is clear and known to the child; if there is a one to one correspondence between form and meaning. It is simple when its constituents (root and affixes undergo no change in form. The data to be presented below support the hypothesis that, as the child is exposed to more input from the language spoken around him, his general underlying conceptual principles are shaped into structured typological biases which alert him to the more productive rules and salient features of his language.

4. The Study

Acquisition data were collected from forty Moroccan boys and girls between the ages of 3;5 and 9;9 from four grade levels, kindergarten, first, third and fourth grades. The selection of this age range was based on findings from previous work, that revealed that Arabic and Hebrew speaking children begin to use the derivational system productively around age three and that they continue to reorganize their mental lexicon using both vertical (deriving from the root) and horizontal (deriving from other surface patterns) derivations well beyond preschool years. The present study discusses the types of strategies used by children in lexical derivation and attempts to assess the influence of typological biases in lexical innovations and word formation.

5. **Materials and Procedures**

Data to be analyzed were collected by means of two elicitation procedures: story-retelling and the verbal pattern derivation production task.

5.1 *Story re-telling*

A story (see appendix 1) with actions described by a total of 45 surface forms derived from thirty-one roots was used: 28 verbs in the basic pattern (P1), 11 in the causative (P2), three in the reciprocal (P6), and three in the middle-voice (P7). Of the 28 P1 forms, 11 appeared in other derived patterns as well. Each child listened to the researcher tell a picture illustrated story which he/she is expected to recount with the help of the same pictures.[11] The instructions used to introduce the story are as follows:

> ɣædi nʕæwed lək waħəd lqiṣṣa dyal waħəd lweld, smiyyətu karim, u xtu kbər mənnu, smiyyəthæ næbilæ, mʕæ walidihum, melli kayfiqu fəṣbaħ u kaywežždu rashum baš yəmšiw –əl-mdrasa. ɣædi təsmeʕ liyæ məzyæn baš teqder tʕawed hæd lqiṣṣa l-----. u-ɣædi nsežžluha baš tesmeʕ rasek fə-ssežælæ.
> "I am going to tell you a story about a little boy named Karim and his older sister Nabila with their parents as the children are getting ready to go school. Listen carefully because I would like you to retell the story to ___ (name of friend) and we will record it so that you'll have a chance to hear yourself on tape."

The researcher then proceeded to tell the story pointing to the pictures illustrating the activities described. Probing questions such as *aš kæy*

---

[11] I would like to thank E. Pardo for offering me her pictures and Fadia Salfiti for illustrating the story.

diru hnæ? "what are they doing here?" pointing to the pictures, are used to elicit more speech especially from the youngest children.

5.2 *Verbal patterns production*

The verbal task included four out of the six patterns used productively in Moroccan Arabic verbal derivations. These are the basic pattern (P1: CCeC), the causative pattern (P2: CeCCeC), the reciprocal pattern (P6: tCaCeC), and the medio-passive pattern (P7: tCeCCeC). A total of 30 pictures illustrating the actions referred to by the task items were sequentially presented to each child (see appendix 2). The targeted forms were novel forms not conventionally used by adults but possible semantically and formally derivable patterns. The researcher described each picture using a verb in either the basic (P1) or causative (P2) patterns (in all, 24 P1 forms and 6 P2 forms were used), then asked the child a question which required a response containing the same verbal root in another derived pattern. The responses targeted were ten causative (P2), ten reciprocal (P6), and ten medio-passive (P7) patterns. To familiarize children with the task at hand, three additional pictures were used during a practice session immediately preceding testing. Three types of questions were used to elicit the targeted verbal patterns. For causatives, the probe was "What is x doing to y?" For reciprocals it was "What are they doing to each other?" and for passives, the question was "What has happened to x?" For example, the researcher would show a picture of a girl in a bathtub with her mother bathing her and then would say:

> had I bent ka-tʕu:m (P1) "this girl is bathing"
> aš ka-t-di:r-1ha mamaha? "what is her mother doing to her?"
> Targeted response: ka-t-ʕuwwemha (P2) "she is bathing her" (from weak root *ʕwm* "bathe").[12]

Each child was tested in three separate sessions over a period of seven weeks. The linguistic responses of the subjects were audio-recorded and supplemented by field notes when possible.

The lexical items selected for use in the two tasks came from a word list compiled from children's spontaneous speech samples obtained during earlier work (Badry 1982). Additional criteria for

---

[12]Weak roots are roots where one of the consonantal positions is a glide.

selection took into consideration the inclusion of verbs from weak/irregular roots. Specifically, roots with either a glide or a geminate consonant (e.g., *BWS* "kiss" and *ŽRR* "pull") made up roughly one third of all roots used in the present research. The inclusion of irregular roots was motivated by findings from pilot work that showed that most errors occur in the derivation of patterns from irregular roots. Such errors expose the strategies children may be operating with to segment and construct derived patterns.

6. The Results

6.1 *Story re-telling*

Three year-old children showed better attention to and retention of activities that had explicitly stated agents. They remembered scenes with agents better than agentless events. They hardly used any middle voice P7 verb forms and extensively used the causative P2 verb forms in appropriate but non-conventional ways. The causative pattern was used more frequently by the children than in the adult input itself. Their retelling also included a high frequency of the basic pattern which corresponded to its high ratio in the adult story. However, while verbs in the basic pattern outnumbered the causatives by a ratio of almost 3 to 1 in the story as told by the researcher, in the younger children's retelling both patterns were used almost equally, and in few cases the causative patterns even outnumbered basic pattern verbs. By age five both basic and causative patterns were used equally. This is an indication that although children are becoming aware of adult conventional use of the basic P1 to mark multiple semantic roles, explicit marking of agentivity seems to still dominate over conventionality. By seven, the basic P1 is used predominantly showing a progression towards the adult's heavy reliance on P1 as the unmarked pattern in support of Clark's (1993) conventionality principle. Length and verb frequency increased with age as indicated by percentages of each verb pattern presented in Table 2.

Older children's (9 year olds) stories included reciprocal patterns to express predicate relations of reciprocity while reflexive, agentless, and causative notions were expressed either by the appropriate corresponding patterns or by an analytical phrase consisting of P1+ reflexive pronoun for reflexives, a participial form for middle-voice, and a transitive P1 for causation. These preferences for P1 and periphrastic constructions instead of derived specialized patterns correspond to conventional use in adult speech. Overall, in the story retelling task, children at all ages tested used a variety of verbal patterns, but the basic and the causative patterns had the highest frequency among the younger groups (KG and 1st grade). The 7 and 9 year olds used reciprocal, reflexive and middle voice patterns but relied more on the basic patterns to express a variety of semantic relations. The younger children's stories were generally shorter and as a result had fewer verbs.

Table 2: Mean percentages of verb patterns in story re-telling

Pattern	KG	Grade 1	Grade 3	Grade 4	Adult story
P1	33	39	43	45	51
P2	41	38	36	36	19
P5	13	12	12	06	09
P6	05	04	04	06	06
P7	06	07	05	07	15

The roots listed in Table 3 were derived in more than one surface pattern. These derivations tended to increase with age. The majority of the derived patterns among the 3;5 year olds were in the causative (P2) which, sometimes, was used erroneously in place of the conventional basic P1 or middle voice P5. For example, younger children used P2 *HəRRSu* "he broke it" instead of (P5) *tHəRRes* "it broke" and (P2) **ka-tWəKKeL buħdha* "she is feeding by herself" instead of (P1) *ka-t æ:Kul* "she is eating". By grade 3 the basic pattern regains its predominance while all other patterns are also produced.

Table 3: Derived patterns tokens from 7 frequent roots in the story

Root	Core meaning	KG	Grade 1	Grade 3	Grade 4
FYQ	wake up	2	2	2	7
NWD	Get up	--	1	4	--
ʕKL	Eat	1	3	9	9
LBS	Wear	6	8	9	9
ŠRB	Drink	2	1	2	1
ʕWM	Bathe	--	1	1	3
HRS	Break	--	1	--	2

6.2 *Verbal patterns*

Children's responses were grouped as pragmatically correct or incorrect responses. Correct responses included patterns that matched the targeted form in both root and pattern, responses that were in the targeted pattern but from a synonymous root, and responses that were both semantically and formally appropriate but not in the target pattern nor from the input root. For example, instead of the targeted P6 *kæy-tNæTFu* "they are pulling each other's hair" some children responded *kæy-tQæMŠu* "they are fighting". In place of the targeted P2 *XeWweFhæ* "he frightened her" they responded with P1 *XLeʕhæ* "he scared her". Incorrect responses included repetitions, irrelevant responses or no response at all. Also considered incorrect were responses with periphrastic constructions such as *kæt-gul lihæ* "she tells her" + targeted verb in imperative form. For example, *kæt-gul lihæ ʕuMi*: "she tells her bathe" or the verb *DæR* "he did" with a deictic to demonstrate the action, *DæRet- lihæ hækka* "she did this to her".

The analysis of the results from the verbal patterns production task shows that verbal patterns become productive at different stages in linguistic development. By age 3;5, the causative pattern P2 is already stabilized. It is followed by the reciprocal P6 and medio-passive P7 patterns. As Table 4 shows, the use of the reciprocal pattern started out higher than that of medio-passives but its rate of increase was slower compared to the latter which reached 60% by age 9. At the same time, the percentage of reciprocal patterns dropped by 8%.

Table 4: VPPT: Mean percentages of correct pattern responses

	KG	**Grade 1**	**Grade 3**	**Grade 4**
P2 Causative	62%	62%	63%	63%
P6 Reciprocal	22%	35%	65%	57%
P7 Medio- passive	07%	33%	52%	60%

Statistical analysis revealed an overall main effect of age but the rate of increase from one age group to the other varied according to pattern. Unlike causative patterns percentages which remained constant across all age groups, the rate of acceleration in correct reciprocal and medio-passive patterns responses was different, with the biggest jump occurring between ages 5 and 7.

An analysis of variance conducted on the correct pattern categories revealed an overall main effect of age (F (df=3)) = 12.36, p<.00), and pattern (F (df=2 = 16.65, p<.00), as well as a significant interaction of age with pattern (F (df=6) = 4.23, p<.00). To determine where these differences lie, several two-way contrasts of age and patterns were performed. Results indicated that across age groups the difference between causative (P2) and medio-passive (P7) patterns was statistically significant (F (df=1) = 35.05, p<.00). The difference between P2 (causative) and P6 (reciprocal) was also significant (Fdf=1) = 19.22, P<.00). There was no statistically significant difference, however, between P6 and P7.

The same main effects were found when a within subjects analysis was performed on the correct pattern responses obtained from KG (age 3;7) and first grade (age 5;5) children. On the other hand, although similar trends were observed in results from third (age 7;5) and 4th graders (age 9;5) they did not reach statistical significance.

Third and 4th graders substituted the P1 pattern for targeted causative or reciprocal patterns often demonstrating their awareness of conventional use at the expense of the productivity of the system. Their P1 responses were derived either from the same root given in the input or from a different but pragmatically appropriate root. For the targeted medio-passive, they sometimes responded with participial forms, also pragmatically correct in adult speech, to express resultative states For example: for the targeted P6 (reciprocal to describe a picture where 2 children are washing each other, responses included: (P1) *ka-y-ɣəSL-u* "they are washing" rather than the targeted novel form (P6) *ka-y-tɣæSL-u "they are washing each other*".

Other responses were derived from roots different from those in the input. For instance, for the targeted *(P2) ṬiYyeHætu* "she dropped it" some 7 year olds responded in P1 *RMætu* "she threw it".

The P7 medio-passive was replaced with participials. For example for the targeted P7 form *tWeSSX-u* "they got dirty", many children responded with the participial form *mWeSSXi:n* "they are dirty".

The percentage of inappropriate responses was particularly high among KG children. Errors made up 28% of elicited causatives, 70% of elicited reciprocals, and 77% of elicited medio-passives. A large proportion of these were repetitions. At all ages tested, repetitions were relatively higher for targeted reciprocal than either the medio-passive or the causative patterns.[13]

7. **Discussion**

The results support the hypotheses that the Semitic lexicon is organized around an underlying consonantal root, which gains psychological reality for Arabic speaking children around the ages of three to four, and that children use both horizontal and vertical derivational processes productively to generate new words. To claim that the root is a psychological construct in the mental representation of the Arabic speakers' lexicon does not entail that every time a speaker uses a word form, he calls on the root construct to derive his forms. Rather, speakers resort to it whenever they are faced with a new task such as coming up with novel words or dealing with words from weak roots.

The developmental progression found in the Moroccan Arabic study is, by and large, similar to that reported by Berman (1985) for Hebrew speaking children with the exception of the delayed productivity of the middle voice. However, this overuse of the causative pattern at the expense of the middle voice supports Slobin's (1979) notion that children's attention is drawn to more "prototypical transitive events" and as a result they are more likely to pay attention earlier to events with salient agents causing a perceptible change.

Their performance in the story-retelling task revealed that by age 3;5 Moroccan children seemed to understand the semantic and syntactic relations expressed by the verbal patterns used by the researcher in telling the story. Such understanding is evidenced by their retelling it in a way that generally preserved the original meaning although not always the narrator's perspective on the events vis-a-vis agentivity.

Preference for P1 seemed to be situationally conditioned and points to the importance of taking context and the communicative function of language into consideration when assessing the productivity of specific linguistic forms. Clark (1981, 1987, 1988,

[13]It should be noted that most repetitions recorded from the fourth graders came from one subject who produced 33% of all repetitions.

1993) suggested that in acquiring meanings of words, children are guided by the principles of semantic transparency, productivity and conventionality. Although some linguistic word formation devices may be transparent and productive in the system, conventional use may curtail their use in forming new words. In Arabic, the reciprocal pattern is semantically transparent but conventionally not utilized productively by adult speakers as many reciprocal functions are expressed with analytical phrases including P1 and a pronominal form "each other". To assess the extent of the conventional principle, an analysis of variance was conducted. Results indicate a main effect of age (F (df=3) = 3.43, p<.02) which suggests that with age, children tend to rely on more than one means to express the same semantic notions. Older children in particular, more often exploited the use of the P1 option to express several complex meanings such as causatives and reciprocals. In fact, well over one quarter of the appropriate responses for causatives were in the P1 substitution responses. This trend, however, did not reach statistical significance (F (df=2) = 2.31, p<.10).

The earlier acquisition of causative patterns compared to the other patterns tested supports Piaget's (1962) sequence of conceptual development that causation is one of the earlier relational concepts to be mastered by children. MA speaking children's overextension of the causative pattern parallels the phenomenon of late errors in the use of English causative verbs discussed by Bowerman (1979, 1982), Clark and Clark (1977) and (Slobin 1985a). In the story retelling, the three-year-olds analyzed the causative pattern and overextended its use to other contexts where adults would use a basic pattern with a reflexive pronoun, using incorrect forms such as *hadi *ka-t-WeKKeL* (P2) *buħdha* "she is feeding by herself" instead of the adult form: *ka-taKuL* (P1) *buħdha* "she is eating by herself". The use of causative patterns also tended to replace middle voice (P5) forms used in the adult story. For example, some children used *HeRReS* (P2) "he broke", instead of *t-HeRReS* (P5) "it broke", *KeFFeħ* (P2) "he spilled" instead of *tKeFFeħ* (P7) "it got spilled". Interestingly, and in further support of Slobin's view on the saliency of agentive events, some agentless events were simply ignored by the children and not recounted as part of the story retelling.[14] Another factor that could have affected children's choices may have been the use of pictures in the elicitation tasks. The presence of animate agents in some of the pictures may have drawn children's attention to the agents and led them to use more causative patterns even when they were asked by the researcher to focus on the result of an activity. Although children may have productive knowledge of certain linguistic forms, at any given stage of development they may opt not to use forms because they add no communicative value in that particular setting. As Budwig put it "... children exploit particular devices to mark various kinds of perspectives that can be taken on a given scene" (1995:10).

The development of the reciprocal pattern supports Clark's conventionality principle as kicking in at a later age to curb productivity of certain derivations. Summarize Clark's principles here. While reciprocal patterns derivation steadily increased between the ages 3;6 to 7;9, it dropped from 65% among the 7 year olds to 57% among the 9-year-olds. Such progression supports a U shaped curve of development. The productive use of verbal derivational processes led to overgeneralizations explaining children's ability to produce novel verb forms. Some of the targeted verbal patterns were novel forms not normally derived by adults. The older children were beginning to conform to adults' conventional usage where reciprocals are not very frequent and the notion of reciprocity is sometimes expressed by the multifunctional basic pattern (P1). For example, older children responded with (P1) *ka-y-γes-l-u* "they are washing" rather than the novel form (P6) *kay-y-tγa:SL-u* "they are washing each other" when describing a picture eliciting reciprocals where two children are washing each other.

The development of reciprocals also conforms to the order of acquisition of Hebrew patterns proposed by Berman (1980, 1985). Its later acquisition can be explained by the complex semantic relations of simultaneity which it expresses, as the child has to coordinate two perspectives at the same time, namely that the action is performed by two agents which are at the same time affected by, and affecting the action expressed in the reciprocal pattern. This finding is also in line

[14]Slobin (1985) referred to this prototypical event as Manipulative activity scene.

with the reports in the literature about later acquisition of conjunctions expressing simultaneity (Clancy et al. 1976, Clancy 1985, Aksu-Koc & Von Stutterheim 1994). The later emergence of the medio-passive, on the other hand, contradicts the generally observed developmental sequence that children as young as 2:6, learning other languages, begin to talk about agentless events (Slobin 1968, Maratsos & Abramovitch 1975, Savasir & Gee 1982, De Villiers & De Villiers 1985). This unexpected low percentage of medio-passive patterns use may be attributed to pragmatic rather than developmental factors. It may be that for these young children, the use of medio-passive is associated with situations when they want to disclaim personal involvement or responsibility for a particular act.[15] In the experimental situation, however, the actions described by the researcher did not involve the children directly and were about agents which were pictured in the input situation. In fact, the presence of the doer of the action in the pictures is likely to have resulted in a testing situation bias that influenced the results. The pictures used to represent verb pattern contrasts included the agent and the researcher's description contained an active sentence with either a P2 or P1 pattern (generally with a causative meaning) before the child was asked to switch focus to the result in order to describe what has happened to the patient. Many 3 to 4 year olds responded by simply repeating the input sentence as if they were unable to switch focus away from the prototypically transitive event of action-agent-patient (Slobin 1981, 1985a). This strong effect of pictures, prompting children to describe transitive rather than intransitive events was evident in data from both tasks.

Acquisition data[16] from typologically diverse languages such as Hebrew, Hungarian, Polish, Turkish, and Kaluli all support children's early marking of transitivity. In Slobin's terms: "In Basic Child Grammar, the first Scenes to receive grammatical markings are "prototypical", in that they regularly occur as part of frequent and salient activities and perceptions, and thereby become the organizing points for later elaboration of the use of functors" (1985:1175). How transitivity is expressed by the child will of course depend on the

---

[15]In Moroccan adult speech the medio passive is frequent in conversations. It allows the speaker to disclaim responsibility in reporting events without having to commit to knowing who has done it.

[16]See Slobin (1985b) for reports of acquisition of these and other languages.

formal means available in the input language. How productive and transparent the specific linguistic devices used in adult language to express transitivity will determine its appearance and acquisition. For example Semitic acquiring children will have to realize that "verb morphology [has to] be enlisted in order to describe a situation as an intransitive event rather than a transitive action". (Berman 1993:645) The English or French child, on the other hand, needs to see that transitivity is marked syntactically.

7.1 *Errors as evidence of productivity of the derivational system*

Misformed patterns derived from defective roots provide evidence of children's productive use of derivational patterns. These types of errors were particularly predominant in responses obtained from the younger children. Misformed patterns were derived from two weak (defective) but frequent verb forms from the roots *W-K-L* (P1 imperf. *ya- KuL*) "he eats" and *B-W-S* (P1 imperf. y- *BuS*) "he kisses". In both forms the underlying glide does not surface in the basic perfective and imperfective patterns but is required surfaces in the causative and reciprocal patterns. Younger children produced reciprocal forms without the required glide such as **ka-y-tKa:Lu*[17] instead of ka-y-*tWa:KLu* "they are giving each other to eat" or **ka-y-tBa:Su* instead of *ka-y-tBa:WSu* "they are kissing each other". Such errors suggest that although young children are still unable to supply the glide missing in the basic pattern for defective roots, the production of these erroneous roots is evidence that word stems are analyzed rather than rote learned. The reciprocal pattern tCa:CCu is combined with root consonants extracted from the basic pattern with a missing consonant.

7.2 *The root in the adult mental lexicon*

The psychological reality of the root in the mental lexicon of Arabic and Hebrew speakers has been subject to heated debate in the recent literature on Semitic morphology. The traditional approach considers that the consonantal root is an underlying morphological and semantic unit which has psychological reality for Arabic and Hebrew speakers. Recently, however, an alternative approach, the word based

[17]This form corresponds to an existing form with a passive meaning: "They are being eaten." It is unlikely, however, that the child meant to use the passive here.

derivation approach, opposing the root construct to various degrees has been defended by others such as Arad (2001), Bat El (2001), Benmamoun (1999), Larcher (1995), and Ratcliffe (1997), among others. According to this view, morphological rules that operate on non derived nouns are sufficient to also operate on derived words. As a result and for the sake of theoretical simplicity there is no need to postulate the additional level of the root.[18] The root based approach to Semitic morphology has been argued for in Modern linguistics by McCarthy starting with his seminal paper in 1981and defended by him and others. Empirical evidence from different sources provides support for the root as a real construct in the mental lexicon of both Arabic and Hebrew. Such evidence comes from studies of slips of the tongue (Abd-El-Jawad & Abu-Salim 1987, Berg & Abd-El-Jawad 1996), aphasic errors (Prunet et.al. 2000), Arabic hypocoristics (Davis & Zawaydeh 2001, Frisch & Zawaydeh 2001), language evolution, as well as child language (Badry 1982, 2004; Berman 1985, 1999).

7.3 *Slips of the tongue*

Abd-El-Jawad and Abu-Salim (1987) examined slips of the tongue made by Jordanian Arabic speakers and found that errors of metathesis were much more frequent than other types of errors reported in studies of slips of the tongue in other languages. They also found that vowel errors were rare in the Arabic data. According to the authors, "[t]he root morpheme is represented on an autosegmental tier and the vocalic pattern on another tier. The two tiers are then mapped onto a third tier called the prosodic template or the CV tier, which consists primarily of C's and V's and which refers to the canonical syllable pattern of the utterance" (see also McCarthy (1981) for this approach to Arabic Morphology). In a similar study which compared adult speech errors by German, English, and Arabic speakers, Berg and Abd-El-Jawad (1996) found that German and English speakers had more slips of the tongue than their Arabic counterparts that were between word slips.

[18]This is an oversimplified statement of this position. The fascinating debate for or against the root in theoretical linguistics is very complex and beyond the scope of this study which is focused on interpreting empirical evidence to understand how Arabic speakers organize their mental lexicon and use derivation in word formation

The Arabic data also supported the earlier finding that within word slips were much more frequent than between word slips. They concluded that "interacting consonants in Arabic stay closer together than interacting consonants in German (and English)".

7.4 *Aphasics' errors*

In a study of errors of an aphasic Arabic/French bilingual, Prunet, Beland & Idrissi (2000) found that their subject had frequent metathesis in all four Arabic tasks in the study (reading aloud 32.8%; repetition 31.9%; writing to dictation 14.3%; and picture naming 21%). However, in the French corpora, a very small percentage of errors were metathesis errors. The authors further observed that in Arabic only consonantal roots in verbal, nominal and adjectival forms were reversed. Vocalic patterns and consonantal affixes were unchanged. In another aphasic case, a Hebrew speaking aphasic's metathesis was pattern centered (Barkai 1980 reported in Prunet et al. 2000). Prunet et al. dismissed phonological and semantic motivations as possible explanations for these errors and argued that the preponderance of metathesis in Arabic over French in their subject (a proportion of 25 to 1) is due to a different morphological representation of the two mental lexicons. The presence of metathesis at the level of the consonantal root in Arabic and its presence at the level of the pattern in Hebrew, lends support to the notion that the Semitic mental lexicon is organized along separate tiers.

7.5 *Arabic hypocoristics*

Davis and Zawaydeh (2001) present evidence from hypocoristics to support the reality of the triconsonantal root in Arab speakers' mental lexicons. Their analysis revealed that only consonantal roots appear in hypocoristics, which have the template C1aC2 C2 uuC3, regardless of the form of the input name. For example, both *Muhammed* and *Ha:med* have the hypocoristic form *hammu:d*; and *ʔbtisa:m* and *Basma* have *Bassu:m*. The authors considered several explanations but concluded "that hypocoristic formation in Arabic crucially references the consonantal root, distinguishing root consonants from affixal and epenthetic consonants..." (For a different view and discussion of the role of the root in derivation, see Bat-El 2001, Bentin & Frost 2001, and Ratcliffe 2002).

7.6 *Language change*

The phenomenon of 'Semiticization' of borrowed words which undergo root extraction and casting into existing lexical patterns also points to the centrality of the root in underlying representations of the Semitic lexicon. For example, Moroccan Arabic incorporates French words by identifying the 3 or 4 consonants to be used as a root and then each word undergoes normal Arabic derivation processes (see appendix 3). The same process is adopted by other Arabic speakers as the examples (see appendix 4) from the Palestinian dialect, where the contact language is English, show.

8. **Conclusion**

In summary, the developmental sequence of the verbal patterns in Arabic speaking children shows that 3;5 year olds are already able to derive the causative patterns P2 and have began to derive reciprocal patterns followed by the medio-passive pattern. Such sequence of development is in line with the order of acquisition of these notions in children acquiring other languages. It lends further support to the notion that conceptual development is a pacesetter to linguistic development. In addition to universal predispositions, children also use a specific path to derive new word in Arabic. The pervasiveness of root-based derivations in the Arabic lexicon draws their attention to such processes and leads them to rely on root/pattern alternations in their production of novel words to fill lexical gaps. Their errors with defective roots reveal incomplete mastery but productivity of the system. The choice of other roots rather than the input root in cases where older children responded with the targeted pattern but used another root, which was semantically and pragmatically correct for that situation, suggests that older children have two paths leading them to coining new words. They use both vertical as well as horizontal derivations in novel word formation. When the root is regular (3 strong consonants) and the alternations with the vocalic patterns are transparent, it serves as a base for a vertical derivation. When the root is irregular (root containing a glide or glottal stop) a surface pattern serves as a base for a horizontal derivation but the reality of the root construct leads older children and adults to supply a third consonant to fill the gap in the surface form. The reliance on both word based and root based derivation is further supported by data from adult errors. In addition, derived specialized patterns were the preferred choices in word formation, although some children made use of other options besides the use of the synthetic patterns to express the semantic notions of causation, reciprocity, and eventivity. The preference for derivation in word formation at all ages tested, and, in particular, the fact that even the younger children were able to produce patterns which are considered formally complex lends further support to the argument that criteria for measuring formal complexity are language specific and depend on typologically useful strategies. So, while interruption of the phonological elements of a stem may be difficult because such interruptions are infrequent in the input received by a child learning English, this same process is the norm in the Arabic input. Both children and adult speakers of Arabic operate with typological biases that enable them to use the root and pattern combinations in word formation. The errors with defective roots revealed incomplete mastery but productivity of derivational processes in the Arabic lexicon. Slips of the tongues, hypocoristics, aphasics' errors, and assimilation of borrowed words all support the need to postulate a root tier in the mental representation of the Arabic lexicon. Children's discovery of the root is gradual and goes through several stages. Both horizontal and vertical derivations are at work in Semitic word formation. Errors produced by both adults and children reveal that the root is a real mental construct and that the road to lexical derivation is a multi-path one.

Appendix 1

Story

Faq karim fəṣṣbaħ u mšæ ʕənd mama-h. ɣeslæt-lu wež-hu, ʕuwwəmæt-u lebbsæ t-lu ħwayž-u. æmma nabilæ ɣir fiyyeqæt-hæ mama-hæ u hiyæ tədxəl lel-ħemmæ m, u həkkæt snæn-hæ u ʕæmet fəlbanyo, u mən beʕd meštạt šʕer-hæ ərras-hæ u lebsæt ħwayž-hæ. melli kemmlæt duxlæt l-bit lmæklæ u lqæt mama-hæ kat-wekkel karim u tšerrb-u lʕaṣir u hiyæ tgul lmama-hæ: ana kbert u kaneʕref nakul u nešreb ərrasi. ma kanəħtæž ħedd iʕəwwem-ni wa-la illebs-li ħwayž-i. smeʕ-hæ karim u huwæ ihezz lkæs baš išreb buħdu sæʕæ ṭiyyəħ-u. therres lkas u tkeffeħ lʕ æṣṣir. təxleʕ karim u ṭleb mən mamah tsamħ-u. gælet-lu had nnubæ llah isa:meħ wa lakin ma tʕæwedš. melli kemml-u ləfṭur, tʕa:nq-u ləwlidat u tbaws-u mʕæ mama-hum. tšæ:ddu men iddiyat-hum u ddæ-hum baba-hum ləl mədrasa.

When Karim woke up in the morning, he went to his mom. She washed his face, bathed him, and dressed him. As to Nabila, as soon as mom woke her up, she went into the bathroom, brushed her teeth, bathed, then combed her hair by herself and put on her clothes. When she finished, she entered the dining room and found her mom feeding karim and making him drink juice. She said to her mom: I have grown up now and I know how to eat and drink by myself. I don't need anyone to bathe me or dress me. When Karim heard that he picked up the glass to drink by himself but he dropped it. It broke and the juice got spilled. Karim was afraid and asked his mom to forgive him. She told him that she forgave him this time but that he should not do it again. When they finished breakfast, the little kids, hugged each other and kissed their mom. They held each other's hand and their dad took them to school.

Appendix 2

Verbal Patterns task forms

Root	Input Pattern	Target Pattern	Picture used
NʕS	NʕeS (P1)	NeʕʕSat (P2)	Mother putting girl to sleep
LBS	LBeS (P1)	LeBbSat (P2)	Mother dressing girl
ʕWM	ʕa:M (P1)	ʕeWweMat (P2)	Mother bathing girl
QRʔ	QRa (P1)	QeRrat (P2)	Mother teaching boy
MŠṬ	MŠeṬ (P1)	MeŠšeṬat (P2)	Mother combing boy's hair
ṬLʕ	ṬLeʕ (P1)	ṬeLlʕat (P2)	Mother taking girl upstairs
FZG	FZeG (P1)	FeZzGat (P2)	Girl wetting boy
XWF	XaF (P1)	XeWweF (P2)	Dog frightening girl
ṬYĦ	ṬaĦ (P1)	ṬiYyeĦat (P2)	Girl dropping glass
ṬYB	ṬaB (P1)	ṬiYyeBat (P2)	Mother cooking food
RŠŠ	ReŠŠ (P1)	tRa:Ššu (P6)	2 boys spraying each other
NTF	NTeF (P1)	tNa:Tfu (P6)	2 girls pulling each other's hair
ʕNQ	ʕeNneQ (P1)	tʕa:NQu (P6)	2 children hugging each other
ĐRB	ḌReB (P1)	tḌa:RBu (P6)	2 boys hitting each other
ɣSL	ɣSeL (P1)	tɣa:Slu (P6)	2 girls washing each other
XBṬ	XBeṬ (P1)	tXa:BṬu (P6)	2 cars colliding
ŠDD	ŠeDD (P1)	tŠa:DDu (P6)	2 boys holding each other
BWS	BuS (P1)	tBa:WSu (P6)	2 girls kissing each other
ʔKL	WeKkeL (P2)	tWa:KLu (P6)	2 boys feeding each other
SLM	SeLleM (P2)	tSa:LMu (P6)	2 girls greeting each other
ĐRB	ḌreB (P1)	tḌeRBat (P7)	A car hit
RMY	RMa (P1)	teRMat (P7)	A ball thrown
QṬʕ	QṬeʕ (P1)	tQeṬtʕat (P7)	A ribbon cut
ŠRB	ŠReB (P1)	TeŠReB (P7)	Drunk juice (empty glass)
ĦLL	ĦeLL (P1)	tĦeLL (P7)	An opened window
ŽRR	ŽeRR (P1)	tŽeRR (P7)	A boy being pulled
XLʕ	XLeʕ (P1)	tXLeʕ (P7)	A scared girl
XZN	XZeN (P1)	TeXZeN (P7)	A hidden boy
KFĦ	KeFfeĦ (P1)	TKeFfeĦ (P7)	Spilled juice

Appendix 3

Assimilated Words from French into MA

French Loans	P2	P7	Participial	Diminutive	Root
Douche (shower)	DeWweŠ	tDeWweŠ	mDeWweŠ	teDWIŠa	
	gave a shower	got showered	showered	little shower	DWŠ
Place (place)	P1				
	BlaṢa	teBLaṢa	mBLaṢi:	BliYeṢa	BLṢ
	Park	got parked	parked	small place	

Appendix 4

Assimilated words from English into Palestinian Arabic

English loans	P1	P7	Participial	Root
Nervous	NeRFeZ	tNeRFi:Z	mNeRFi:Z	NRFZ
	get angry	became angry	is angry	
Insure	ʔaNŠaR	tʔaNŠar	mʔaNŠi:R	ʔNŠR
	insure	become insured	insured	
	P2			
Save	SeYyeF	-------	mSeYyeF	SYF
	save (files)		Saved	

REFERENCES

Abd-El-Jawad, Hassan & Issam Abu-Salim. 1987. "Slips of the Tongue in Arabic and Their Theoretical Implications". *Language Sciences* 9:2.145-171.

Aksu-Koc, Ayhan & Christiane Von Stutterheim. 1994. "Temporal Relations in Narrative: Simultaneity". *Relating events in Narrative: A Crosslinguistic Developmental Study* ed. by R. Berman & D. Slobin, 515-538. Hillsdale, NJ: Lawrence Erlbaum.

Arad, Maya. 2001."The Stuff Roots are Made of: On verbal/nominal asymmetry in Hebrew". Paper presented at the conference on the syntax and semantics of Semitic languages. University of Southern California. May 3-6, 2001

Badry, Fatima. 2004. *Acquiring the Arabic Lexicon: Evidence of productive strategies and pedagogical implications*. Bethesda, MD: Academica Press.

_____. 1983. *Acquisition of Lexical Derivational Rules in Moroccan Arabic: Implications for the development of Standard Arabic as a second language through literacy*. Ph.D. dissertation, University of California, Berkeley.

_____. 1982. "The Centrality of the Root in Semitic Lexical Derivation". *Papers & Reports on Child Language Development*, 9-15. Stanford University.

Bat-El, Outi. 2001. "In Search for the Roots of the C-Root: The essence of Semitic morphology". Handout. U. Workshop on Root and Template Morphology. May 6, 2001. University of Southern California, Los Angeles.

Benmamoun, Elabbas.1999. "Arabic Morphology: The central role of the imperfective". *Lingua* 108.175-201.

Bentin, Shlomo & Frost Ram. 2001. "Linguistic Theory and Psychological Reality: A reply to Boudelaa & Marslen-Wilson". *Cognition* 81.113-118.

Berg, Thomas & Hassan Abd-El-jawad. 1996. "The Unfolding of Suprasegmental Representations: A crosslinguistic perspective". *Journal of Linguistics* 32. 291-324.

Berko-Gleason, Jean. 2001. *The Development of Language*. 5th edition. Boston: Allyn Beacon.

Berko, Jean. 1958. "The Child's Learning of Morphology". *Word* 14.15-177.

Berman, Ruth A. 1999. "Children's Innovative Verbs versus Nouns: Structured elicitations and spontaneous coinages". *Methods in Studying Language Production* ed. by Lise Menn & Nan Bernstein Ratner, 69-93. Mahwah, NJ: Lawrence Erlbaum.

_____. 1993. "Marking of Verb Transitivity by Hebrew-speaking Children". *Journal of Child Language* 20:3.641-669.

_____. 1985. "The Acquisition of Hebrew". Slobin 1985b. 255-371.

_____. 1980. "Child Language as Evidence for Grammatical Description: Preschoolers construal of transitivity in the verb system of Hebrew". *Linguistics* 18.677-701.

Bowerman, Melissa. 1985. "What Shapes Children's Grammars?" Slobin 1985c. 1257-1319.

_____. 1982. "Starting to Talk Worse: Clues to language acquisition from children's late speech errors". *U-Shaped Behavioral Growth* ed. by S. Strauss, 101-145. New York: Academic Press.

Budwig, Nancy. 1995. *A Developmental-functional Approach to Child Language*. Mahwah, NJ: Lawrence Erlbaum.

Bybee, Joan & Dan I. Slobin. 1981. "Rules and Schemas in the Development and Use of the English Past Tense". *Language* 58.265-289.

Carey, Susan. 2001. "Whorf versus Continuity Theorists: Bringing data to bear on the debate". *Language, Culture & Cognition 3* ed. by Melissa Bowerman & Stephen Levinson, 185-214. Cambridge: Cambridge University Press.

Clancy, Patricia. 1985. "The Acquisition of Japanese". Slobin 1985b. 373-524.

Clancy, Patricia, T. Jacobson & Marilyn Silva. 1976. "The acquisition of conjunction: A cross sectional study". *Papers & Reports on Child Language Development*. Stanford University. 12.71-80.

Clark, Eve. 1993. *The Lexicon in Acquisition.* Cambridge: Cambridge University Press

_____. 1988. "On the Logic of Contrast". *Journal of Child Language* 15.317-335.

_____. 1987. "The Principle of Contrast: A constraint on language acquisition". *Mechanisms of Language Acquisition* ed. by Brian MacWhinney, 2-33. Hillsdale, NJ: Lawrence Erlbaum..

_____. 1985. "Acquisition of Romance with Special Reference to French". Slobin 1985b. 687-782.

_____. 1981. "Lexical Innovations: How children learn to create new words". *The Child's Construction of Language* ed. by Deutsch Werner, 299-328. London: Academic Press.

_____ & Ruth Berman. 1984. "Structure and Use in the Acquisition of Word-Formation". *Language* 60.542-590

Clark, Herbert & Eve Clark. 1977. *Psychology and language: An introduction to psycholinguistics.* NY: Harcourt Brace Jovanovich.

Dasinger, Lisa. 1997. "Issues in the Acquisition of Estonian, Finnish and Hungarian: A crosslinguistic comparison". Slobin 1997b. 1-86.

Davis, Stuart & Bushra A. Zawaydeh. 2001. "Arabic Hypocoristics and the Status of the Consonantal Root". *Linguistic Inquiry* 32.512-520.

De Villiers, Jill G. & Peter A. De Villiers. 1985. "The Acquisition of English". Slobin 1985b. 27-139.

Frisch, Stephan. & Bushra A Zawaydeh. 2001. "The Psychological Reality of OCP-place in Arabic". *Language* 77.91-106.

Harrell, Richard S. 2004. *A Short Reference Grammar of Moroccan Arabic: Georgetown classics in Arabic language and linguistics.* Washington, DC: Georgetown University Press.

Holes, Clive. 1995. *Modern Arabic: Structures, functions and variations.* London: Longman.

Johnston, Judith. R. 1985. "Cognitive Prerequisites: The evidence from children learning English". Slobin 1985c. 961-1004.

Larcher, Pierre. 1995. "Où il est montré qu'en arabe classique la racine n'a pas de sens et qu'il n'y a pas de sens à dériver d'elle". *Arabica* XLII.292-314.

MacWhinney, Brian. 1985. "Hungarian Language Acquisition as an Exemplification of a General Model of Grammatical Development". Slobin 1985c. 1069-1155

Maratsos, Michael & Rona Abramovitch. 1975. "How Children Understand Full, Truncated and Anomalous Passives". *Journal of Verbal Learning and Verbal Behavior* 14.145-157.

McCarthy, John J. 1981. "A Prosodic Theory of Nonconcatenative Morphology". *Linguistic Inquiry* 12.373-418.

Peters, Ann. 1985. "Language Segmentation: Operating principles for the perception and analysis of language". Slobin 1985c. 1029-1067

Piaget, Jean. 1962. "The Stages of the Intellectual Development of the Child". *Bulletin of Menninger Clinic* 26:3.

Prunet, Jean Francois, Renee Beland & Ali Idrissi. 2000. "The Mental Representation of Semitic Words". *Linguistic Inquiry* 31.609-648.

Ratcliffe, Robert R. 2002. "Analogy in Semitic Morphology: Where do new roots and patterns come from?" *Papers in Honor of Robert Hetzron* ed. by Andrej Zaborski. Wiesbaden: Otto Harrasowitz.

_____. 1997. "Prosodic Templates in a Word Based Morphological Analysis of Arabic". *Perspectives on Arabic Lingusitics* X ed. by Mushira Eid & Robert Ratcliffe, 147-171. Amsterdam & Philadelphia: John Benjamins.

Savasir, Iskender & Julie Gee. 1982. "The Functional Equivalents of the Middle Voice in Child Language". *Proceedings of the 8th Anuual Meeting of the Berkeley Linguistic Society*. 607-616. Berkeley, CA: Berkeley Linguistic Society.

Schlesinger, Izchak M. 1979. "Cognitive and Linguistic Structures: The case of the instrumental". *Journal of Linguistics* 15.307-324.

Slobin, Dan I. 2001. "Form-function Relations: How do children find out what they are?" *Language, Culture & Cognition* Vol. 3 ed. by M. Bowerman & S. Levinson, 406-449. Cambridge: Cambridge University Press.

_____. 1997a. "The Universal, the Typological, and the Particular in Acquisition". *The Crosslinguistic Study of Language Acquisition* Vol. 5 ed. by Dan I. Slobin, 1–39. Hillsdale, NJ: Lawrence Erlbaum.

_____. 1997b. *The Crosslinguistic Study of Language Acquisition.* Vol.4.Hillsdale, NJ: Lawrence Erlbaum.

_____. 1992. *The Crosslinguistic Study of Language Acquisition.* Vol.3. Hillsdale, NJ: Lawrence Erlbaum.

_____. 1985a. "Introduction: Why study acquisition crosslinguistically?" Slobin 1985b. 3-24

_____. 1985b. *The Crosslinguistic Study of Language Acquisition* Vol.1. Hillsdale, NJ: Lawrence Erlbaum.

_____. 1985c. *The Crosslinguistic Study of Language Acquisition* Vol.2. Hillsdale, NJ: Lawrence Erlbaum.

_____. 1981. "The Origins of Grammatical Encoding of Events". *The Child's construction of Grammar* ed. by Werner Deutsch, 185-200. London: Academic Press.

_____. 1979. *Psycholinguistics*. Palo Alto, CA: Scott.

_____. 1973. "Cognitive Prerequisites for the Development of Language". *Studies of Child Language Development* ed. by Charles A. Ferguson & Dan I. Slobin, 407-432. New York: Holt.

_____. 1968. "Recall of Full and Truncated Passive Sentences in Connected Discourse". *JVLVB* 7.876-881.

Stephany, Ursula. 1997. "The Acquisition of Greek". Slobin 1997b. 183-333.

Toivainen, Jorma. 1997. "The Acquisition of Finnish". Slobin 1997b. 87-182.

Tomasello, Michael. 1992. "The Social Basis of Language Acquisition". *Social Development* 1.67-87.

L2 ACQUISITION OF ARABIC MORPHOSYNTACTIC FEATURES
TEMPORARY OR PERMANENT IMPAIRMENT?

Mohammad T. Alhawary
The University of Oklahoma

1. Introduction

A number of impairment proposals have recently been posited about the representation of functional categories and functional features in second language acquisition (SLA). One such proposal, the Local Impairment Hypothesis (LIH), claims that features associated with functional heads are permanently impaired (feature strength is 'inert' or unspecified) irrespective of the first language (L1) (Beck 1997, 1998; Eubank et al. 1997, Eubank & Beck 1998). A second proposal, the Failed Functional Features Hypothesis (FFFH), claims that the Interlanguage (IL) system of the second language learner (L2er), specifically that of the functional feature system, is constrained by what is available in L1 and, therefore, permanently impaired depending on the nature of L1 system (Hawkins & Chan 1997; Hawkins 1998, 2001). A third proposal, the Missing Surface Inflection Hypothesis (MSIH), claims that the feature system is temporarily impaired at the morphophonological (surface) level due to complexity in mapping between surface forms and underlying abstract features (Lardiere 1998, 2000; Prévost & White 2000; cf. De Garavito & White 2002). The nature of impairment according to the third proposal depends on the L2 learner figuring out the mapping complexity and spelling it out properly.

All three hypotheses are related to a central issue: Universal Grammar (UG) access and L1 transfer (or more generally the nature of

IL competence). The LIH is silent about early presence or access to functional projection through L1. It assumes that functional projections are attainable in L2 but considers feature strength associated with functional projection permanently 'inert'. That is, permanently impaired. Accordingly, no transfer of (abstract) feature strength from L1 takes place. This proposal is a departure from the stronger claim that assumes UG access is completely impaired (including functional projections) in L2 (e.g., Felix 1984; Clahsen 1988; Meisel 1991, 1997). Under the latter proposal, the L2er is assumed to have access instead to universal cognitive principles or constraints.

The FFFH proposal follows Tsimpli and Smith's (1991) and Smith and Tsimpli's (1995) position that maintains that UG is partially unavailable in L2. Beyond the critical period, the features associated with functional categories (except those already encoded for specific lexical items) become permanently fixed and subsequently inaccessible for modification (or for resetting of parameters).

The MSIH proposal is in line with other UG access proposals such as the (unimpaired) Full Access/Full Transfer model (Schwartz & Sprouse 1994, 1996) which proposes that the L2er has access to UG through L1, that in principle the entirety of L1 system, including functional categories and feature system,[1] is available at the initial stage of L2 and that subsequent restructuring (i.e., parameters, including feature strength, can be reset) depends on availability of positive evidence in the input. When positive evidence for a given structure is obscure or missing altogether from input, then the structure is predicted to become a candidate for fossilization.

2. Predictions and Previous Findings

Each of the forgoing impairment proposals makes specific assumptions and predictions about IL representation and approximation to the target L2 system. Under the LIH proposal, adult L2 competence exhibits a selective deficit (in functional feature system) that distinguishes it from native L1 competence. While functional projections are attainable, functional feature system is not; the feature strength is simply 'inert' in L2. For example, with respect to L2 inflectional knowledge and verb movement, the (abstract) morphosyntactic

[1]This excludes the (surface) phonetic matrices of lexical/morphological items.

features that license or prohibit verb raising are claimed to become impaired during the course of L2 maturation, resulting in grammars that overgenerate (verb raising instances in contexts not required). This position is based on findings of one study (Beck 1998) conducted on English speaking learners of German as an L2. This language pairing is chosen, because English is a non-raising language and German is a verb-raising language. The study consisted of an oral translation task and a sentence matching task to measure response latencies of 48 German L2ers (grouped as "more advanced" and "less advanced") on grammatical and ungrammatical stimuli with respect to adverb placement, such as (1)-(2) below (Beck 1998:327):

(1) Der Vater liest selten die Zeitung
    the father reads seldom the newspaper
(2) *Der Vater dann schreibt ein Lied
    the father then writes a song

According to the main (stronger) prediction of the proposal, however, L2ers at any stage of acquisition will not differentiate between raised and unraised verbs. The main finding of the study was that the less advanced subjects (Ss) were able to differentiate between raised and unraised verbs while the more advanced Ss were not. The findings, specifically those of the more advanced Ss, are interpreted to provide support for the LIH.[2]

The main prediction that follows from this and other studies (e.g., Eubank et al. 1997, Eubank & Beck 1998) is that regardless of the

[2]The operationalization of Beck's Ss as "more advanced" and "less advanced" groups may be problematic. The Ss are grouped following "standard practice at many universities in the US": 1 year of high school German = roughly 1 semester of college German, 2 months of in-country exposure = roughly 1 semester of college German, 1 month of in-country exposure with intensive instruction = roughly 1 semester of college German. However, Beck's Ss may turn out to be rather more intermediate and less intermediate. Accordingly, the proposed analysis does not seem to take into account the U-shape acquisition phenomenon (widely attested in the literature) where Beck's "more advanced" Ss rather seem to have reached the bottom of U where they are at the stage of overgeneralizing the forms (hence they did not show any preference for raised or unraised verbs) as opposed to her "less advanced" Ss who were able to differentiate between raised and unraised verbs.

nature of L1 and L2 systems (i.e., whether or not they exhibit similar inflectional feature system), a main consequence of the LIH is that the L2ers "incorporate an impairment" to (inflectional) feature strength, resulting in the appearance of optional head movement in main clauses.

According to the FFFH, UG is partially inaccessible in L2 acquisition. Specifically, following Tsimpli and Roussou (1991) and Smith and Tsimpli (1995), Hawkins and Chan (1997) assume that functional features (associated with functional categories C, AGR, D) which determine parametric differences between languages become inaccessible to modification beyond the critical period and, depending on the nature of L1, this may result in a (permanent) divergence from native speaker representation of L1 if the L2 functional feature system (or parameter setting) is different from that of L1.[3] Hawkins and Chan (1997) investigated the grammaticality judgment on English restrictive relative clause by Chinese and French speakers learning English as an L2. This particular pairing (Chinese and French = L1 and English = L2) is chosen, since English and French restrictive relative clause constructions involve *wh*-operator movement in overt syntax, but Chinese counterpart constructions do not. The study consisted of seven groups of subjects: 3 experimental Chinese groups at different age and proficiency levels and 3 control (for reliability and validity of test instrument) groups of native French speakers comparable in age and proficiency levels to the Chinese groups and an additional control group of English speakers. It was found that with increasing proficiency of L2, the L1 Chinese learners of L2 English became progressively more accurate in their intuitions about English predicative CP morphology and [CP...gap] in simple restrictive relative clause constructions, but at the same time their accuracy and ability to correct Subjacency violations declined. According to Hawkins and Chan, this suggests that the Chinese subjects' mental representation of the construction in question appear not to involve *wh*-operator movement. On the other hand, the results of L1 French learners of L2

[3]Tsimpli and Smith (1991) and Smith and Tsimpli (1995) investigated the linguistic knowledge of Christopher, a cognitively impaired L2 learner whose linguistic ability was still intact, in fact, even extraordinary with his ability to translate into English no fewer than 16 languages. Christopher's case is cited as (neurolinguistic) evidence for modularity (i.e., the dissociation between a linguistic competence module and a general cognitive one) and IL variation.

English showed that their accuracy and ability to correct Subjacency violations increased with proficiency. In the latter case, the L2ers may be able to map the functional features of their L1 entries onto new L2 (surface) morphophonological material, but they will not be able to have FULL access to functional features.[4]

More recently, Hawkins (2001) concludes that where L1 does not exhibit functional feature specifications similar to those of L2, it is possible that certain parameter values associated with functional categories are "difficult" or "impossible" to acquire while others seem to be perfectly acquirable. These conclusions are based on findings from an unpublished study (Hawkins 1998a) of 20 advanced English speakers learning French as an L2. The study produced mixed evidence: while the L2ers were able to acquire the appropriate Noun-Adjective word order in French (i.e., they acquired the strong inflection feature that licenses N raising), the same L2ers (at the advanced level) continued to have difficulty in establishing a parameterized gender feature as evidenced in their error rates of supplying the appropriate gender of the definite and indefinite articles agreeing with the following noun. Hawkins (2001) does not speculate on this explanation further and leaves it as an open question.

The predictions that follow from the FFFH proposal is that L2ers whose L1 exhibits different functional feature specifications from those of L2 will not fully acquire the same representation as native speakers of the L2. Accordingly, this explains the observation that many L2ers never fully attain L1 competence as native speakers do despite length of exposure to L2.[5] Another prediction that follows from FFFH, although it does not seem to follow from an a priori explanation (since the assumption is that functional features associated with functional categories which determine parametric differences between languages become inaccessible to modification beyond the critical period) is that L2ers, whose L1 system exhibits similar functional feature specifi-

[4]This means that this impairment proposal is only partially in agreement with the Full Access/Full Transfer model (Schwartz & Sprouse 1994, 1996).

[5]By extension, according to this proposal, functional categories not present in L1 will not be acquired in L2. That is, functional categories will also be impaired, not just functional features associated with functional categories. This would probably compound further the problem of L2 acquisition.

cations as those of the L2, will approximate quite closely to the L2 system as exposure to L2 increases.

Unlike the LIH and the FFFH, the MSIH (Prévost & White 2000) attributes no such serious impairment to the IL system of the L2er in the domain of functional categories. Rather, the variable (or optional) use of inflectional morphology, found during the course of L2 development (reported in the old morpheme order studies of the 1970s; e.g., Dulay & Burt 1974, Bailey et al. 1974) and sometimes even at the end-state of L2 grammar, is a consequence of a "superficial" problem. The problem is simply that of mapping (surface) morphological onto (abstract) underlying features, following proposals such as Lardiere's (1998, 2000).[6] Prévost and White (2000) investigated longitudinal data from four adults: two Arabic Speakers learning French as an L2, one Spanish Speaker Learning German as an L2 and one Portuguese speaker learning German as an L2. The findings show that finite verb forms largely occur in finite (raised) positions and do not occur in non-finite contexts (e.g., after a preposition or a negator or with another verb in the same clause) while non-finite forms occur in both finite and non-finite positions. Prévost and White suggest that where non-finite forms occur in non-finite contexts, they do so correctly and where they occur in finite contexts, they are used as finite default forms thus explaining the missing of the surface forms position (i.e., the L2ers are aware of agreement but are not accessing the appropriate surface forms and instead is using a certain form as a default). Similarly, verbal agreement in L2 French and L2 German subject clitics was found to be largely accurate (more so in the L2 French than the L2 German) and that non-finite forms are used as default finite rather than instances of incorrect agreement. Prévost and White conclude that their data disconfirm LIH which would otherwise predict greater variability and lack of any systematic (finite) use in the data and confirm their MSIH in that their L2ers were able to reset the feature strength to [+strong]. Errors result due to mapping problems between surface forms and abstract features and that even when an acquired form is specified for

[6]Other proposals in line with Prévost and White's position, that similarly suggest a production/performance problem (in identifying the proper surface morphological realizations of functional features) include: Epstein et al. (1996), Grondon and White (1996), Haznedar and Schwartz (1997) and Lardiere and Schwartz (1997).

the appropriate features (before Spell Out), it may become temporarily blocked or irretrievable from the lexicon, due perhaps to communication pressure or processing demands.

De Garavito and White (2002) re-examined the same assumptions of the MSIH on L2 Spanish DPs. They reported on their investigation of production data from 42 adult speakers of French (a [+ gender] language) learning Spanish (a [+ gender] language) as an L2. The data were examined for noun-adjective word order and gender agreement on determiners and adjectives. The results were then compared with those reported by Hawkins (1998b) on 30 advanced English (a [- gender] language) speakers learning French as an L2.[7] De Garavito and White's Ss belonged to two levels: 30 low proficiency and 12 low intermediate. The findings revealed that the L2ers used N-A rather than A-N order consistently. The L2 order that they were able to adjust to from early on is the same in their L1. Agreement use on determiners was similarly consistent but less so with indefinite than definite determiners. However, agreement use on adjective contexts (in both attributive and predicative) was significantly less accurate and there was no significant difference between the two groups. A comparison between errors in natural gender with those in grammatical gender reveal that the subjects were significantly less accurate on natural gender than on grammatical gender with respect to the performance of the low proficiency learners. The findings also show variability with respect to the use of feminine or masculine agreement as the default agreement on adjectives with the masculine form occurring more often than the feminine. De Garavito and White interpret their findings as disconfirming the LIH (which would otherwise predict variability in N-A order and gender agreement on determiners) but in support of the MSIH. Following Lardiere (1998,

[7]Unfortunately, due to the unavailability of Hawkins study (1998b) in print, it was not possible to verify his data and conclusions independently from De Garavito and White (2002). According to them, the results which Hawkins reported in his study (1998b) are as follows: (a) consistent use of N-A order as evidenced by the low number of errors (4/156), (b) consistent use of gender agreement on determiners with errors being significantly higher in indefinite contexts, and (c) no results are reported on gender agreement on adjectives. The results of Hawkins (1998b) seem to be identical to those of Hawkins (1998a) discussed earlier. It is not clear whether or not both refer to the same study, since Hawkins (2001) discusses results of 20 participants and De Garavito and White (2002) include results of 30 participants.

2000), they suggest that presence or absence of gender in L1 appears to be irrelevant and that the gender agreement problem is rather due to mapping underlying abstract features to appropriately inflected surface forms, since the generalization of the endings {-0} and {-a} as masculine and feminine gender markers, respectively, is a misleading one and insufficient to account for many cases. They suggest that L2ers resort to a default gender marking when they are uncertain of the proper morphological realization in certain cases.

Acknowledging the limitations that their Ss may not be really advanced, De Garavito and White cited White et al. study (2001), which included advanced L2ers of Spanish (of L1 English and L1 French backgrounds) and which examined the scoring of the Ss on a comprehension task involving gender and number features. The findings showed that despite presence of performance differences (attributed to L1) at lower stages of L2 development, advanced L2ers adjusted well to the L2 system and their performance did not differ significantly from that of L1 native speakers.

De Garavito and White (2002) additionally reported on a study (Parodi et al. 1997) that investigated the acquisition of German nominals by adult (immigrant) speakers of Romance (which is a [+strong] feature language with Noun-Adjective order), Korean and Turkish (which are [-strong] feature languages with adjective-noun order). The target forms examined in the production data included presence/absence of determiners, plural marking and noun-adjective word order. Among the most significant findings was that raising of nouns over adjectives did not occur in the IL systems of the Korean and Turkish speakers (coinciding with the German Adjective-Noun order) whereas such raising did occur in the IL systems of the Romance speakers with ratios ranging from 0% to 37.5% of all DPs. De Garavito and White (2002) point out, following Schwartz (1998), that such results are incompatible with the LIH, since accordingly the data of all the L2ers examined should exhibit variable adjective placement regardless of the L1 language backgrounds.[8]

The prediction that follows from the MSIH proposal (Prévost & White 2000, De Garavito & White 2002) is that, contrary to the predictions of the LIH and FFFH, no impairment within MSIH is

[8]Note this, in essence, is evidence for role of L1 transfer.

attributed to functional categories and functional features at an abstract level. The prediction is that verbal morphology can be acquired and feature strength can be reset and, as a consequence, exhibits a systematic use though not completely error free, due to difficulty mapping surface forms to abstract features arising from communication pressure or processing demands. Accordingly, this sets L1 and L2 acquisition apart where (normal) native L1 speakers always acquired the appropriate features and use them always consistently accurately. The implied prediction here is that the problem of the presence of some inconsistencies cannot be attributed to presence or absence of certain features in L1.

To summarize the predictions of the three proposals discussed above, LIH proposes that L2ers (even at later stages of acquisition) "incorporate an impairment" to feature strength and therefore it predicts appearance of optional head movement and (by extension) variable use of surface inflections. FFFH proposes that functional features which determine parametric differences between languages become inaccess-ible to modification in L2 and, therefore, predicts that L2ers whose L1 exhibits different functional feature specifications from those of L2 will not fully acquire the same representation as native speakers of the L2 do. Another FFFH prediction is that L2ers whose L1 system exhibit similar functional feature specifications as those of the L2 will (as proficiency in L2 increases) approximate quite closely to the L2 system although, as suggested above, there is no a priori explanation as to how this prediction follows from the premise itself which states that functional features become inaccessible to modification in L2. MSIH proposes that L2 competence suffers from no serious impairment and that variable use of head movement and inflectional morphology is due to a production problem of mapping (surface) morphological forms onto (abstract) underlying features. MSIH predicts therefore that in principle functional categories and features are attainable in L2 and that presence or absence of features in L1 is irrelevant in L2 development.

In the sections immediately below, we report on a study conducted with the aim to examine claims made by the three positions discussed above. The study examined feature agreement properties of DPs and INFL in the IL systems of Arabic L2ers with two different typological constellations (L1 English and L1 French learning Arabic as an L2) and at three distinct and comparable levels of L2 proficiency. The advantage of including L2ers at different levels of development is to test these predictions more rigorously and overcoming the limitations of other studies, such as those of De Garavito and White (2002). Additionally, as can be seen from the review of previous findings, previous studies mostly focused on syntactic phenomena with some notable exceptions mentioned above (see also Alhawary 1999, 2002).

3. **Methods**

3.1 *Participants*

Fifty-three Arabic L2ers, belonging to two different native language backgrounds, American English and French, were invited to participate in the study in their own home institutions. Participants, males and females, were grouped according to their placement by their home institution and according to length of exposure to Arabic as part of their academic programs. Table 1 summarizes the details of the participants. The figure to the left of the plus sign indicates additional required sessions. The L1 English participants were required to attend at least one hour weekly of lab (for 1st year) and conversation sessions (2nd and 3rd year). With respect to L1 French participants, they were required to attend a session on Arabic structure and grammar in French, for 1st and 2nd Year, and in Arabic, for 3rd Year. The length of this session is in fact 1.5 hours, but since the session for 1st and 2nd years was conducted totally in French and the lecturer was doing almost all the talking, it is decide here to consider this session equivalent to half the length of the period of a normal language classroom. This would help account for length of exposure better across groups.

The crucial point here is that the participants were selected, because they had little or no exposure to Arabic prior to joining their academic institutions (in France and the US) and who are not heritage speakers who would speak Arabic occasionally or often at home. In particular, first year students of both language groups had zero exposure and had made no trips to Arabic-speaking countries. A few participants from both language groups at other levels had traveled to Arabic-speaking countries but did not stay there for a significant period of time. One student (French L1, Year 3) stayed in Egypt one year. Her performance in the study, however, was about average among her group

Table 1. The participants of the study

Groups English L1	Length of Exposure	Credit Hours Enrolled in	M/F	Ages Range	Ages Means
Group1 (n=9)	Year 1	5 +1	4/5	18-21	19.22
Group2 (n=9)	Year 2	4+1	5/4	20-29	22.22
Group3 (n=9)	Year 3	3+1	6/3	22-34	29.11
French L1					
Group1 (n=9)	Year 1	6+.75	5/4	18-32	21.33
Group2 (n=9)	Year 2	6+.75	1/8	21-36	26.22
Group3 (n=8)	Year 3	6+1.5	3/5	23-28	25.75

M/F= Total Males/Total Females

Participants of both L1 language groups received formal instruction in Arabic with focus on all grammatical forms from early on. The L1 English group used mainly *Elementary Modern Standard Arabic* (Abboud et al. 1983) and *Intermediate Modern Standard Arabic* (Abboud et al. 1997) and the L1 French group mainly used *Manuel d'Arabe Moderne* vols. I-II (Deheuvels 2002, 2003).

3.2 *Target forms*

3.2.1 *Morphosyntactic features of Arabic DPs*

The focus of the present study with respect to the morphosyntactic properties of Arabic DPs in the IL systems of the participants is on the features gender (feminine and masculine) and number (singular). Sentences (3)-(4) below are examples of agreement features examined.

(3) a. radʒul-u-n qaṣiir-u-n
man.**Sg.Msc**-Nom-Indef short.**Sg.Msc**-Nom-Indef
"a short man"

b. ʔal-radʒul-u ʔal-qaṣiir-u
Def-man.**Sg.Msc**-Nom Def-short.**Sg.Msc**-Nom
"the short man"

c. radʒul qaṣiir
Indef.man.**Sg.Msc** Indef.short.**Sg.Msc**
"a short man"

d. ʔal-radʒul ʔal-qaṣiir
Def-man.**Sg.Msc** Def-short.**Sg.Msc**
"the short man"

(4) a. marʔ-**at**-u-n [9] qaṣiir-**at**-u-n
person-**Sg.Fem**-Nom-Indef short-**Sg.Fem**-Nom-Indef
"a short woman"

b. ʔal-marʔ-**at**-u ʔal-qaṣiir-**at**-u
Def-person-**Sg.Fem**-Nom Def-short-**Sg.Fem**-Nom
"the short woman"

c. marʔ-**a** qaṣiir-**a**
Indef.person-**Sg.Fem** Indef.short-**Sg.Fem**
"a short woman"

d. ʔal-marʔ-**a** ʔal-qaṣiir-**a**
Def-person-**Sg.Fem** Def-short-**Sg.Fem**
"the short woman"

The sentences above include examples containing the nominative case, (3a-b)-(4a-b), and do not include the accusative {-an} or the genitive {-in} none of which is the focus of the present study. All the examples above show agreement between the head noun and the attributive adjective in gender and number: singular masculine as in (3) and singular feminine as in (4). Singular masculine in Arabic is realized as a zero morpheme {-0}; that is, it is the same as the base (stem) form. Singular feminine, however, is marked often with a gender suffix {-a} as in sentence (4c) or {-at} when case ending is realized following it as in sentences (4a) and (4b) irrespective of definiteness. DPs of the type consisting of a noun and an attribute adjective display noun-adjective (NA) gender agreement with markings realized on both words in the vast majority of cases.[10] Both cases can be distinguished from the

[9]Given the presentation of this noun in input, it is unlikely that the participants stored the suffix and the base form separately as suggested by the gloss—contrary perhaps to derived forms such as *ṭaalib* "male student" vs. *ṭaalib-a* "female students".

[10]This is true of the vast majority of cases in Arabic. There are certain nouns that do not display the gender suffix, such as *ṭariiq* "road", *sabiil* "path" *suuq* "market", *xamr* "wine", etc., that are treated equally as either masculine or feminine in Classical Arabic and almost exclusively as masculine in Modern Standard Arabic so that such forms are not problematic. There are certain other forms that do not exhibit the gender suffix but are treated as feminine, such as *nafs* "self", *ħarb*

phonological clue in word final position and in NA singular feminine agreement. In particular, there is a rhyming effect to signal the agreement. Other less frequent but similar singular feminine gender suffixes include {-ā} and {-āʔ} as in (5)-(8) below are attached on certain lexical items:

(5)	a. qalam-u-n pen.**Sg.Msc**-Nom-Indef "another pen"	ʔaaxar-u Indef.another.**Sg.Msc**-Nom
	b. qalam Indef.pen.**Sg.Msc** "another pen"	ʔaaxar Indef.another.**Sg.Msc**
(6)	a. sayyaar-**at**-u-n car-**Sg.Fem**-Nom-Indef "another car"	ʔuxr-**aa** Indef.another-**Sg.Fem**.Nom(0)
	b. sayyaar-**a** Indef.car-**Sg.Fem** "another car"	ʔuxr-**aa** Indef.another-**Sg.Fem**
(7)	a. qamiiṣ-u-n shirt.**Sg.Masc**-Nom-Indef "a blue shirt"	ʔazraq-u Indef.blue.**Sg.Masc**-Nom
	b. qamiiṣ Indef.shirt.**Sg.Masc** "a blue shirt"	ʔazraq Indef.blue.**Sg.Masc**
(8)	a. sayyaar-**at**-u-n car-**Sg.Fem**-Nom-Indef "a blue car"	zarq-**aaʔ**-u Indef.blue-**Sg.Fem**-Nom
	b. sayyaar-**a** Indef.car-**Sg.Fem** "a blue car"	zarq-**aaʔ** Indef.blue-**Sg.Fem**

="war", *ʔarḍ* "earth", *šams* "sun", etc., that are treated as feminine, but such forms are not problematic to the productivity of the rule, since they constitute a very small subset of crypto-feminine forms (see Ṣaydaawii 1999:297). It is also worth noting here a rule which students usually learn at intermediate or more advance levels, where the feminine gender suffix {-a} can be added to derived active participial forms for emphasis for both male and female referents; e.g., *raħħaala* "widely traveled/constant traveler", *nassaaba* "very knowledgeable genealogist", *ʕallaama* "very knowledgeable scholar", etc. Since affixing this suffix is rule-based and not likely to occur in input in beginning stages, it is not likely to contribute to obscurity of input with respect to singular gender agreement.

As sentences (5)-(8) show, case endings are realized differently than case endings in sentences (3)-(4) which suggests that adjectives in (5)-(8) are special forms so is their treatment of gender agreement. Gender (color) agreement of the type in (7)-(8) is not investigated in the study, since the participants (especially those in the earliest level of exposure, Year 1) may not know the rule for gender agreement on adjectives of color.

The assumption of the structural derivation of Arabic NA-agreement is similar to the position adopted in Alhawary (2002). There, since Arabic nouns and adjectives exhibit rich feature agreement, the feature for gender (and number) in Arabic is assumed to be set to [+strong]. An AGRP can be assumed to project inside Arabic DPs where the noun and adjective raise overtly to Spec and AGRA respectively, in order for the feature gender agreement (and other features) to be checked and the structure to be derived.[11]

With respect to English and French, the L1 language backgrounds of the participants, while nouns and adjectives in French carry strong agreement features, including gender, their English counterparts do not. In other words, we assume that feature strength in French is set to [+strong] like Arabic but unlike English whose feature strength is set to [-strong]. Hence, nouns in English do not raise, whereas nouns in French must raise overtly (in Syntax) over adjectives to NUM for feature checking. However, although nouns do not raise over adjectives in English, it has been proposed that in English there are a few "intrinsically" plural attributive adjectives, such as *numerous* and *various*. Following a Minimalist analysis, such an adjective is assumed to occupy a specifier position within a functional projection FP with an empty functional head and that number agreement is checked via feature percolation (after) of the plural number of the noun up to F position (to satisfy a spec-head relation) where it is checked against the number feature of the adjective (see Radford 1997, Cinque 1994).

[11]Note that whether one argues for an AGR or a NUM projection inside Arabic DPs is not the contention, since adopting either assumption is sufficient for the premise here. French is assumed to project a NUM projection located between D and NP and is set to the feature strength [+strong] quite like Arabic whose feature strength is set to [+strong] but unlike English whose feature strength is set to [-strong]. For specific analyses of French DPs, see Bernstein (1993) and Hawkins (2001).

However, the feature gender, which is itself a ϕ-feature involving syntactic feature checking mechanism within Minimalist framework (Chomsky 1993, 1995), is altogether absent in English (see Namai 2000).

According to the above explanation of agreement features involving DPs, the two following pairings (9)-(10) are found:

(9) American English participants who are speakers of a [-gender] and [-strong] L1, learning a [+gender] and [+strong] L2
(10) French participants who are speakers of a [+gender] and [+strong] L1, learning a [+gender] and [+ strong] L2.

The LIH hypothesis would predict problems with NA-agreement as well as word order in DPs for both the L1 English group and the French L1 group regardless of length of exposure whereas the FFFH would predict for the L1 English group alone to have problems with both forms and to continue to do so regardless of length of exposure. The MSIH hypothesis, on the other hand, would predict that both the English and the French group would adjust or not adjust to the target form (depending on whether or not the target form exhibits complex form function relationship) equally. In other words, no significant difference in performance would be predicted between the two groups.

3.2.2 *Morphosyntactic features of Arabic IPs*

The focus here is specifically on the INFL properties of gender (feminine and masculine) and number (singular) agreement between the subject and the verb. The types of singular masculine and singular feminine agreement reported here include preverbal and postverbal agreement in the perfective and the imperfective as illustrated in sentences (11)-(14) below:

(11) a. ʔal-ṭaalib(-u) **yu**-saafir(-u)[12]
Def-student.**Sg.Masc**(-Nom) **3rd.Sg.Masc**-travels(-Indicative)
"The male student travels/ is traveling."

b. **yu**-saafir(-u) ʔal-ṭaalib(-u)
3rd.Sg.Masc-travel(-Indicative) Def-student.**Sg.Masc**(-Nom)
"The male student travels/is traveling."

[12]The parentheses indicate that mood was not a target feature of the study. Similarly, definiteness was not a target structure.

(12) a. ʔal-ṭaalib(-u) saafara
Def-student.**Sg.Masc**(-Nom) traveled. **3rd.Sg.Masc**
"The male student traveled."

b. saafara ʔal-ṭaalib(-u)
traveled.**3rd.Sg.Masc** Def-student.**Sg.Masc(**-Nom)
"The male student traveled."

(13) a. ʔal-ṭaalib-**at**-u **tu**-saafir(-u)
Def-student-**Sg.Fem**-Nom **3rd.Sg.Fem**-travel(-Indicative)
"The female student travels/is traveling."

b. ʔal-ṭaalib-**a** **tu**-saafir
Def-student-**Sg.Fem** **3rd.Sg.Fem**-travel
"The female student travels/is traveling."

c. **tu**-saafir(-u) ʔal-ṭaalib-**at**-u
3rd.Sg.Fem-travel(-Indicative) Def-student-**Sg.Fem**-Nom
"The female student travels/is traveling."

d. **tu**-saafir ʔal-ṭaalib-**a**
3rd.Sg.Fem-travel Def-student-**Sg.Fem**
"The female student travels/is traveling."

(14) a. ʔal-ṭaalib-**at**-u saafara-**t**
Def-student-**Sg.Fem**-Nom traveled-**3rd.Sg.Fem**
"The female student traveled."

b. ʔal-ṭaalib-**a** saafara-**t**
Def-student-**Sg.Fem** traveled-**3rd.Sg.Fem**
"The female student traveled."

c. saafara-**t** ʔal-ṭaalib-**at**-u
traveled-**3rd.Sg.Fem** Def-student-**Sg.Fem**-Nom
"The female student traveled."

d. saafara-**t** ʔal-ṭaalib-**a**
traveled-**3rd.Sg.Fem** Def-student-**Sg.Fem**
"The female student traveled."

As stated above case endings (nominative, accusative and genitive) on nouns and adjectives are not the focus of the present study. Similarly, mood markings (indicative, subjunctive and jussive) on verbs are not reported on here. Case and mood markings are displayed to show the full contexts of S-V agreement reported on here. What is crucial here is that singular masculine and singular feminine gender agreement between the subject NP and the verb holds the same for both SVO and VSO word order.

Since subjects and verbs in Arabic carry rich agreement features (considering the full paradigm of subject-verb agreement), we can assume that Arabic verbal agreement is [+strong] (see also Radford 1997). Accordingly, both elements must raise overtly from their originating positions within VP to have the agreement features of gender, number and person checked and the structure to be derived. One can assume perhaps an AGRP projection above VP, following Bolotin (1995) and Alhawary (2002), where the NP subject and the verb raise to [Spec, AGRP] and AGR positions, respectively.[13]

French and English, the L1s of the participants of the present study, contrast in their subject-verb agreement in relation to Arabic. While French displays rich verbal agreement, including gender (considering the overall verbal agreement paradigm in French), English lacks the ϕ-feature gender altogether (see Namai 2000) and exhibits poor (number and person) verbal agreement with feature agreement being restricted to {-s} for third person singular and {-0} elsewhere. Thus, French verbal agreement is assumed to be [+strong] where verb-raising to I (assuming an INFL projection over VP for French) takes place (overtly) in the syntax. English verbal agreement, due to the impoverished nature of English morphological agreement system, is assumed to be [-strong]. Radford (1997) suggests that raising in English does take place (covertly) via feature percolation (or attraction) of 3rd.Sg.Nom from V to I where the feature can be checked against that of the subject to satisfy a specifier-head relation (see also Alhawary 2002).

According to the above explanation of agreement features involving subject verb agreement, the pairings (15)-(16) are found:

(15) American English participants who are speakers of a [-gender] and [-strong] L1, learning a [+gender] and [+strong] L2

(16) French participants who are speakers of a [+gender][14] and [+strong] L1, learning a [+gender] and [+ strong] L2.

[13]For the purpose of the present study, assuming simply an INFL projection is equally sufficient.

[14]Verbal agreement involving gender in French should be considered SOMEWHAT strong; i.e., not exactly on a par with that in Arabic, since (subject-verb) gender agreement in French is not exhibited with the same degree of uniformity, involving mainly past participial forms within compound verb tenses, passive voice and pronominal verbs.

Not unlike the predictions with respect to performance on Arabic DPs, the LIH hypothesis would predict problems with SV agreement for both the L1 English group and the L1 French group regardless of length of exposure whereas the FFFH hypothesis would predict the problems for the L1 English alone to continue despite increased proficiency. The MSIH, on the other hand, would predict that both the English and the French group would adjust or not adjust to the target form (depending on whether or not the target form exhibits a complex form-function relationship) equally. In other words, no significant difference in performance will be predicted between the two groups.

To conclude this section, the two types of mophosyntactic agreement features within Arabic DPs and IPs are selected to be examined in the IL systems of L1 English and L1 French learners of Arabic as an L2. Examining two types rather than one allows for the predictions claimed by the three hypotheses, the LIH, the FFFH and MSIH, to provide ample evidence for testing the predictions. As for choosing singular masculine and singular feminine alone in both types, this allows for conducting additionally appropriate comparisons across the two types of morphosyntactic features examined.

3.3 *Data collection and coding*

Data collection aimed at eliciting semi spontaneous production data from the L1 English and L1 French participants of the target forms discussed above. Elicitation tasks included picture description, picture differences and picture sequencing. The tasks were controlled for familiarity through random arrangement of items and inclusion of distracter items so that participants would not know what the elicitor was after. All items were used consistently with all participants and in the same arrangement of the tasks. Elicitation sessions (one per participant, 30-45 minutes) were tape recorded.

The data were then transcribed and coded. Certain items were not coded. These included hesitations and self-corrections except the last attempt. However, certain other tokens *were* coded. These include color adjectives in productive contexts even though they are not quite target-like (TL) utterances (see example 13 in the Section immediately below). Color adjectives are not otherwise coded, as stated above, since they have a specific rule and early beginning learners may not know this rule and therefore coding such tokens may contribute falsely to low agreement ratios.

It is to be noted additionally that in coding subject-verb agreement tokens, agreement was determined by considering the verbal form and whether it is inflected properly, not by identifying first the subject then the verb it agrees with. This is significant, since the verb may agree with a discourse referent subject and the L2er participants may be mindlessly producing the wrong subject, especially when the subjects used are the pronouns *hiya* "she" and *huwa* "he" which are close in their pronunciation (see also Poeppel & Wexler 1993, Prévost & White 2000; Cf. Meisel 1991). Additionally with respect to noun-adjective agreement in DPs, it was decided to collapse agreement involving predicative ideas with attributive adjectives, since agreement for attributive adjectives applies the same to predicative adjectives, assuming similarly an AGRP projection for predicative adjective agreement. The decision is due to two main reasons. First, due to controlling for familiarity factor, the elicitation did not force the participants to produce noun-adjective agreement involving attributive adjectives instances alone. Hence, inclusion of adjectives in predicative contexts has the added advantage of compensating for unproduced or incomplete tokens which the participants could not complete for lack of knowing or recalling some adjective words. Second, since definiteness is not reported on here and the difference between predicative and attributive adjectives has mainly to do with definiteness (the former having to be in the indefinite), this decision should not be problematic.

3.4 *Results*

3.4.1 *Gender and number agreement markings on nouns and adjectives*

As explained above, the results of noun-adjective (attributive) agreement in DPs involving singular masculine and singular feminine also include adjectives in predicative (clausal) contexts of the same agreement features; hence NA/P-agreement (henceforth). The ratios of singular masculine agreement were found to be high across and within the L1 English and L1 French groups. All groups had above 84% of correct agreement in obligatory and productive contexts over all number of obligatory contexts as shown in Figure 1. The French Group 1 had a higher agreement ratio (at 94%), but the ratios are comparable for both groups 2-3, with both L1 English and L1 French groups being above 90% for Group3.

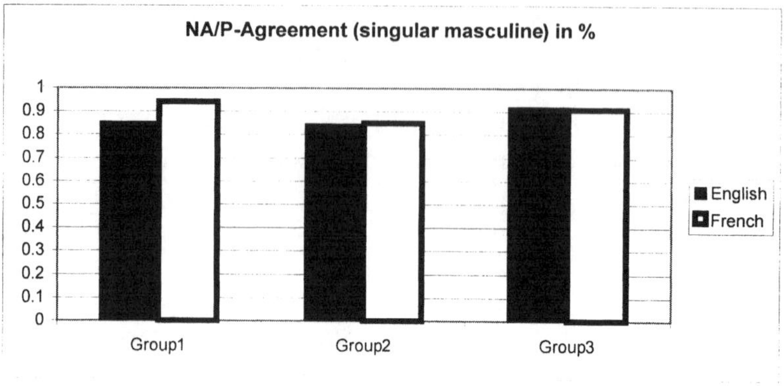

Figure1. Group1=Year1; Group2=Year2; Group3=Year3.

With respect to error ratios across and within all the groups, no statistically significant difference was found. Table 2 displays the total number of errors and total number of correct singular masculine agreement. One can also notice here that the error ratios are the lowest in the Group 3 of both native language background groups.

Table 2. Error ratios: NA/P-Agreement (singular masculine)

English L1	Total Errors/Correct	French L1	Total Errors/Correct
Group1(n=9)	22/127 (.17 %)	Group1(n=9)	7/112 (.06 %)
Group2(n=9)	29/158 (.18 %)	Group2(n=9)	24/136 (.18 %)
Group3(n=9)	16/179 (.09 %)	Group3(n=8)	12/121 (.10 %)

When it comes to NA/P-singular feminine agreement, a totally different pattern emerges. Two main differences and similarities can be observed (see also Figure 2). The L1 French groups, on the one hand, had higher agreement ratios than their English counterparts at all three levels (81%, 79%, and 93%, respectively). Groups 1-2 had somewhat similar agreement ratios whereas the third group had even a higher ratio (well above 90%). On the other hand, the English Groups 1-2 showed identical performance at the lowest end of 60% agreement ratio (at 61 %). However, Group 3 had a much higher agreement ratio than Groups 1-2, coming close to 80 % agreement rate (at 78%).

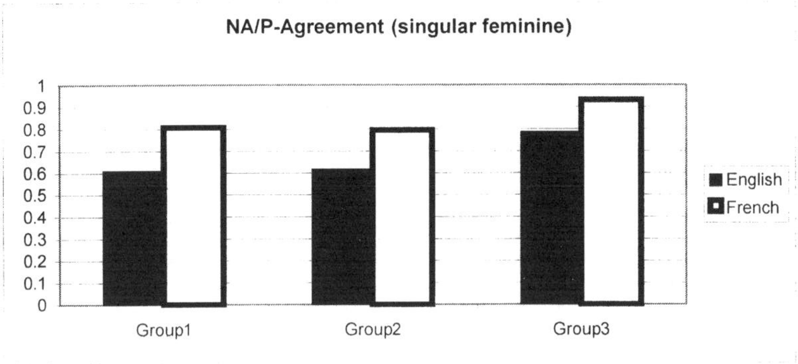

Figure2. Group1=Year1; Group2=Year2; Group3=Year3.

Upon examining the error ratios, a similar difference across the two native language background groups is revealed. Table 3 summarizes the total number of errors and the ratios (calculated here by dividing the total number of errors over the total number of correct agreement tokens).

Table 3. Error ratios: NA/P-Agreement (singular feminine)

English L1	Total Errors/Correct	French L1	Total Errors/Correct
Group1(n=9)	53/82 (.65 %)	Group1(n=9)	28/116 (.24 %)
Group2(n=9)	80/127 (.63 %)	Group2(n=9)	34/131 (.26 %)
Group3(n=9)	40/145 (.28 %)	Group3(n=8)	10/138 (.07 %)

A two-way MANOVA test revealed a significant difference between the English and the French groups: $F(1,47) = 6.410$, $p<.016$.[15] The test did not show a significant interaction effect for proficiency or an interaction effect between L1 background and proficiency. One similarity between the two L1 backgrounds, evident in Table 3, is that

[15]The MANOVA test included both masculine and feminine error ratios. The test revealed a significant difference between the English and French speakers only with respect to singular feminine. In other words, errors involving singular masculine mismatches were not found to be a contributing factor to group difference.

that the error ratios in Group 3 of each of the two native language backgrounds, like those for singular masculine agreement, are lower than those of Groups 1-2.

To investigate whether or not grammatical vs. natural gender contributed to the singular masculine and feminine agreement mismatches across the two L1 background groups, the number of errors was tallied accordingly. Table 4 summarizes the results of the total errors and ratios of all groups. A two-way MANOVA test indicated a significant effect for L1 backgrounds with respect to grammatical gender ($F(1,47) = 11.425$, $p<.002$), a near significant effect for L1 with respect to natural gender ($F(1,47) = 5.232$, $p = .027$) and a proficiency effect for grammatical gender ($F(2, 47) = 6.841$, $p<.003$). It revealed no significant proficiency effect for natural gender and no significant interaction effect between L1 and proficiency. This is corroborated by results of two additional separate one-way MANOVA tests run independently within each native language background groups. While a one-way MANOVA run on gender error ratios of L1 French groups indicated no difference within groups between grammatical and natural gender errors, the same test run on gender error ratios of L1 English groups did indicate a significant difference ($F(2,24) = 4.859$, $p<.018$), suggesting that the L1 English participants, Group 2, were more likely to have problems with grammatical gender than natural gender in comparison to their L1 French counterparts. In other words, grammatical gender for the L1 French participants posed no particular problem to them while it did to the L1 English participants (for the middle group).

Table 4. Error ratios of natural and grammatical gender

Arabic L2 (English L1)	Natural Gender Errors/Correct	Grammatical Gender Errors/Correct
Group1(n=9)	41/126 (.33 %)	34/83 (.41 %)
Group2(n=9)	43/183 (.23 %)	65/102 (.64 %)
Group3(n=9)	28/164 (.17 %)	28/160 (.18 %)
ArabicL2 (French L1)		
Group1(n=9)	22/141 (.16 %)	13/87 (.15 %)
Group2(n=9)	29/158 (.18 %)	29/109 (.27 %)
Group3(n=8)	8/145 (.06 %)	14/114 (.12 %)

It is also worthy to compare the overall NA agreement instances in productive contexts between the two L1 background groups. Table 5 displays all the productive tokens in all groups.

Table 5. Total of NA-Agreement tokens in productive contexts:

English L1	Total Fem.	Total Masc.	French L1	Total Fem.	Total Masc.
Group1(n=9)	0	0	Group1(n=9)	8	1
Group2(n=9)	2	0	Group2(n=9)	7	0
Group3(n=9)	1	0	Group3(n=8)	0	0

Examples of productive use of singular feminine are (17)-(21) below:

(17) **IL**: sayyaar-**a** ʔaḥmar-**a**
car-**Sg.Fem** red.**Masc-Sg.Fem**
TL: sayyaar-**a** ħamr-**aaʔ**
car- **Sg.Fem** red-**Sg.Fem**
"a red car"
(L1 French: Group 1)

(18) **IL**: ʔal-bin-**t** ʔakbar-**at** min ʔal-walad
Def-child-**Sg.Fem** bigger-**Sg.Fem** from Def-boy
TL: ʔal-bin-**t** ʔakbar min ʔal-walad
Def-child-**Sg.Fem** bigger from Def-boy
"The girl is bigger than the boy."
(L1 French: Group 2)

(19) **IL**: huwa fii ɣurf-in ṣaɣiir-in
he in room.**Sg.Masc**-Gen. small.**Sg.Masc**-Gen
TL: huwa fii ɣurf-**at**-in ṣaɣiir-**at**-in
he in room-**Sg.Fem**-Gen. small-**Sg.Fem**-Gen
"He is in a small room."

(20) **IL**: ʔimraʔ-**a** ʔawwal-**a**
person-**Sg.Fem** first-**Sg.Fem**
TL: ʔal-ʔimraʔ-**a** ʔal-ʔuul-**aa**
Def-person-**Sg.Fem** Def-first-**Sg.Fem**
"the first woman"
(L1 English: Group2)

(21) **IL**: sayyaar-**a** ʔaṣɣar-**a**
car-**Sg.Fem** smaller-**Sg.Fem**
TL: sayyaar-**a** ʔaṣɣar
car- **Sg.Fem** smaller
"a small car"
(L1 English: Group 3)

As (17)-(21) show, productive use is similar across and within all groups. What is significant however is that the total number of productive tokens produced by the L1 French groups is more than five times higher than that of the L1 English groups.

3.4.2 *Noun-adjective word order*

Errors involving noun-adjective placement found are extremely low across and within groups. Table 6 summarizes the results of all correct and incorrect noun-adjective placement in all groups, suggesting a high degree of accuracy and adjustment of all the L2ers to Arabic noun-adjective word order from early on.

Table 6. Noun-Adjective word order:

Arabic L2 (English L1)	Noun-Adjective word order	*Adjective-Noun word order
Group1(n=9)	280	4 (.014 %)
Group2(n=9)	389	4 (.010 %)
Group3(n=9)	380	0 (0 %)
ArabicL2 (French L1)		
Group1(n=9)	259	4 (.015 %)
Group2(n=9)	311	14(.045 %)**
Group3(n=8)	280	1 (.003 %)

** Out of the total 14 reversed tokens one learner alone exhibited 9 tokens.

Examples of incorrect noun-adjective placement are illustrated in (22)-(26) below:

(22) **IL**: *waaħid bin-**t**
one.**Sg.Masc** child-**Sg.Fem**
"one girl"
(L1 English: Group 1)

(23) **IL**: *ʔal-kabiir-**a** sayyaar-**a**
Def.big-**Sg.Fem** car-**Sg.Fem**
"a big car"
(L1 English: Group 2)

(24) **IL**: *kabiir-u-n sayyaar-**at**-u-n
big.**Sg.Masc**-Nom-Indef car-**Sg.Fem**-Nom-Indef
"a big car"
(L1 French: Group 1)

(25) **IL**: *θaaniy-**a** ʔimraʔ-**a**
second-**Sg.Fem** person-**Sg.Fem**
"another woman"
(L1 French: Group 1)

(26) **IL**: * kabiir-**a** sayyaar-**a**
big-**Sg.Fem** car-**Sg.Fem**
"a big car"
(L1 French: Group 2)

Sentences (22) and (23) display incorrect noun-adjective placement as well as incorrect gender agreement. However, there are a few tokens exhibiting both types of mismatches. The majority of such tokens display incorrect noun-adjective displacement alone.

3.4.3 *Gender and number agreement markings of verbal agreement*

Here, too, the L1 French groups somewhat outperformed their L1 English counterparts in producing the appropriate verbal agreement markings for singular feminine and singular masculine as they did in producing noun-adjective agreement markings (for singular feminine and singular masculine). However, both L1 English and L1 French, especially the former, had higher agreement ratios. Figure 3 shows that all L1 French groups 1-3 had correct agreement ratios for singular masculine well above 90 % (97%, 96%, and 98%, respectively). The L1 English Groups 1-2 had correct agreement ratios of well above 80% (88% and 86%, respectively) and Group 3 had an agreement ratio of well above the 90% (93%, to be precise). Figure 4 shows some oscillation in the performance of the L1 English groups 1-3 with Group 1 having the highest correct verbal agreement ratios for singular feminine (94%, 67% and 86%, respectively). The L1 French groups 1-3 had correct gradually increasing agreement ratios of 75%, 86%, and 93% respectively.

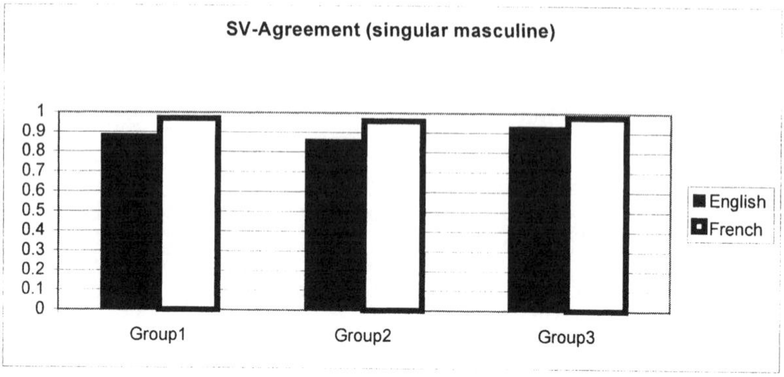

Figure3. Group1=Year1; Group2=Year2; Group3=Year3.

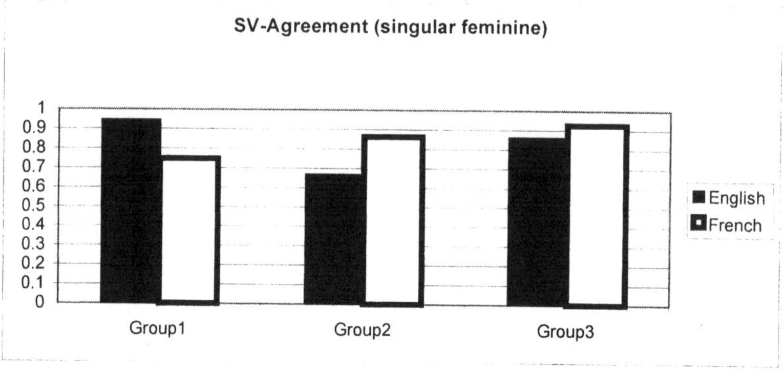

Figure 4. Group1=Year1; Group2=Year2; Group3=Year3.

When the incorrect verbal agreement ratios for singular feminine and singular masculine are considered, we find, among other things, that the oscillation found in the L1 English Group 1, having lower agreement ratios in singular masculine than singular feminine, has a corresponding oscillation in the L1 French Group 1 in the opposite direction; i.e., having lower agreement ratios in singular feminine than singular masculine. Table 7 displays the total number of errors and error ratios for all groups.

Table 7. Error ratios: SV-Feminine & SV-Masculine Agreement

Arabic L2 (English L1)	SV-Feminine Total errors/Correct	SV-Masculine Total errors/Correct
Group1(n=9)	27/135 (.20 %)	22/168 (.13 %)
Group2(n=9)	78/158 (.49 %)	49/298 (.16 %)
Group3(n=9)	34/212 (.16 %)	28/381 (.07 %)
ArabicL2 (French L1)		
Group1(n=9)	46/135 (.34 %)	7/224 (.03 %)
Group2(n=9)	32/204 (.16 %)	13/293 (.04 %)
Group3(n=8)	16/201 (.08 %)	7/335 (.02 %)

A series of MANOVA tests revealed no significant difference across groups and within groups. In other words, neither singular masculine verbal agreement nor singular feminine was found to contribute to group difference, neither between groups (i.e., L1 English vs. L1 French) nor within groups (i.e., within groups of each native language backgrounds).

One final observation is worth reporting here. Subject-verb agreement errors in the singular masculine were all due to use of singular feminine forms. However, subject-verb agreement errors in singular feminine were due to use of singular masculine forms and also, to a much lesser extent, due to use of other gender and person markings, mostly 1st person singular suffix {-tu}. The latter occurs in Groups 1-2 of both the L1 English (3 and 19 of the total of all errors in Groups 1-2, respectively) and the L1 French (4 and 1 of the total of all errors in Groups 1-2, respectively). Examples of subject-verb agreement are given in (27)-(28).

(27) **IL**: *ʔimraʔ-**a** ðahaba
person-**Sg.Fem** went.**3rd.Sg.Masc**
TL: [ʔal]-ʔimraʔ-**a** ðahab-**at**
[Def]-person-**Sg.Fem** went-**3rd.Sg.Fem**
"The woman went."
(L1 English: Group 1)

(28) **IL**: *hiya ðahab-**tu**
she went-**1st.Sg**

TL: hiya ðahab-**at**
she went-**3rd.Sg.Fem**
"She went."
(L1 English: Group 2)

The total number of errors illustrated in (28), as stated above, is a lot less than the number of errors illustrated in (27) (Cf. Table 7).

With respect to noun-adjective agreement, the situation is quite similar although errors in noun-adjective agreement are all due to use of the opposite (singular masculine or singular feminine) gender marking in either case. In other words, all noun-adjective agreement errors are due to either over-generation of the feminine suffix (in singular masculine agreement errors) or to under-generation of the feminine suffix (in singular feminine agreement errors). This may well be expected, since there are only two forms for singular gender agreement in Arabic with the base form being, by default, the masculine form.

The above observation is significant, since if all noun-adjective agreement and almost all subject-verb agreement errors were due to the same phenomenon, we can arrive at the following generalization: choosing either form (singular feminine or singular masculine) is a fifty-fifty chance. Therefore, one way of examining whether or not either of the two forms was used as a default form can be simply checked if an L2er had a ratio in one agreement type error much higher than 50% and much lower than 50% in the other; a 50 % (or close) ratio of correct or incorrect use may have resulted from random hits. Considering this observation and taking into account those few errors resulting from generating a different verbal agreement suffix (for subject-verb agreement), we can identify the specific L2ers in the two native language background groups, who used a certain form as a default agreement form or who just resorted to random production of forms. Tables 8-9 (below) display those L2ers and the default or random forms which they used.

Accordingly, we can speculate that as many as six L2ers (who had the ratios above 90%) used the masculine often as a default for both. One L2er, D (for SV agreement), may have been resorting to mere random hits 20% vs. 49%) while two others, M and N, may have been resorting to random hits but in addition may have been using singular feminine sometimes as a default form.

Table 8. Default/Random use of masculine and feminine NA/P-Agreement

(English L1)	Feminine Ratios of Correct use	Masculine Ratios of Correct use
H:Group1	.22%	.96%
J: Group1	.29 %	.93 %
C:Group1	.41%	.95%
M:Group1	.60%	.37%
T: Group2	.17%	.73%
D:Group2	.32%	.95%
N:Group2	.67%	.48%
(French L1)		
G: Group1	.42 %	1.0 %

Letters (H, J, C, etc.) refer to the individual L2ers in their respective groups.

Table 9. Default/Random use of masculine and feminine SV-Agreement

(English L1)	Feminine Ratios of Correct use	Masculine Ratios of Correct use
C:Group1	.45%	.74%
D:Group2	.20%	.49%
Ga: Group2	.40 %	.98 %
(French L1)		
G: Group1	.17 %	.91 %
K: Group1	.40 %	.94 %

Letters (C, D, Ga, etc.) refer to the individual L2ers in their respective groups.

More significantly, however, there are two noticeable differences in Tables 8-9. First, the number of the L2ers (across the two native language background groups) who exhibited disparity in their correct ratios between singular masculine and singular feminine is greater in noun-adjective agreement than in subject-verb agreement: 7 in the L1 English groups (specifically groups 1-2) and 1 in the L1 French groups (specifically group 1) as opposed to 3 in the L1 English groups (specifically groups 1-2) and 2 in the L1 French groups (specifically group 1). Second, the number of L1 English individuals in both tables is greater than that of the L1 French, more so in noun-adjective agreement. The emerging pattern is use of the masculine form in noun-adjective agreement as the default form by L1 English participants, resulting in under-generation of the feminine ending.

4. **Discussion and Conclusion**

The clearest finding of the study is related to noun-adjective placement within Arabic DPs. It is quite evident that the participants of the study were able to acquire the strong inflection feature that licenses N raising, hence the almost 100% correct ratios for noun-adjective placement across both groups (i.e., L1 English and L1 French) and within groups (i.e., within the three groups grouped according to length of exposure to Arabic). This finding is problematic for the LIH which would otherwise predict greater variability (or optionality) in noun-adjective order in all groups. The finding is similarly problematic for the FFFH, since the L1 English participants were able to reset feature strength to [+strong] for their L2 Arabic although their L1 does not share the same feature specification. Although Hawkins (2001) acknowledges that it is possible that certain values associated with functional categories can be acquired in L2 (but others cannot), this does not follow from an a priori explanation as to why this is so and no explanation is provided. We can safely conclude, therefore, that the findings seem to confirm the MSIH which attributes no serious impairment and predicts the ability of the L2ers to acquire functional categories and functional features including the ability to reset feature strength.

As for noun-adjective agreement markings (involving adjectives in both attributive and predicative contexts), the findings show that the L1 French participants significantly outperformed their L1 English counterparts in both singular masculine and singular feminine agreement and in almost all groups. Correct use is found to generally increase with length of exposure in both native language background groups. The conclusion drawn here is that L1 English participants seem to have problems with singular feminine agreement, since they made more significant errors in singular feminine (by under-generating the feminine agreement suffix) than they did in singular masculine.

With respect to verbal agreement markings, the findings revealed that the L1 French participants performed somewhat better than their L1 English participants in both singular masculine and singular feminine. Correct use here too was found to generally increase with length of exposure in both native language background groups. However, the L1 English participants were not found to have any specific problem with singular feminine (verbal) agreement as opposed to singular masculine (verbal) agreement. The difference in agreement errors was not found to be statistically significant. In other words, the same L2ers did not have a significant problem (in relation to the L1 French participants) with singular feminine marking for verbal agreement while they did for nominal agreement.

According to LIH, agreement features are assumed to be permanently impaired (or 'inert') in L2 regardless of the status of L1. Although 'syntactic' subject-verb agreement is excluded within LIH (Beck 1998) as a locus of potential impairment, noun-adjective agreement is not. Therefore, in order for LIH to be confirmed, the performance of the participants would have to exhibit greater variability in agreement inflection on nouns and adjectives in the IL systems of both the American and French participants—a prediction not borne out by the findings of the present study. Certainly, noun-adjective agreement in the IL systems of the L1 French participants shows highly consistent correct rule application and is overall anything but variable (see Figures 1-2).[16]

As for the FFFH, the findings confirm one prediction but disconfirm another. The findings confirm the prediction that L2ers whose L1 systems exhibit similar functional feature specifications as those of the L2 will approximate quite closely to the L2 system as exposure to L2 increases. This is evident in the performance of the L1 French L2ers who outperformed their English counterparts in almost all groups and in both forms (nominal and verbal agreement markings), although as mentioned above this prediction does not seem to follow from an a priori explanation, since the assumption is that functional features associated with functional categories which determine

[16]The pattern of the French group in Figure 1 does not contradict this conclusion. Somewhat variable performance seems to be taking place within Group 2 where the participants seem to be have more agreement errors than Groups 1 and 3—an observation not quite dissimilar from the U-shape acquisition tendency where the L2ers first start out by producing mostly TL forms, then they go down through a stage of overgeneralizing the forms and then their performance rises as they produce mostly TL forms again.

parametric differences between languages become inaccessible to modification beyond the critical period. The findings disconfirm the FFFH prediction that L2ers faced with a different feature specification in L2 will not achieve a performance level similar to that of the native speakers. There is nothing to suggest that impairment is permanent in this case, since the L1 English participants continued to show improvement with increased exposure in both forms. In fact, some of them even attained 100% correct rule application as evident in Figure 4 which displays the performance of Group 3 of both L1 English L1 French participants for both singular feminine NA-agreement and singular feminine SV-agreement. As Figure 4 shows, at least one L1 English participant had 100% correct ratio in singular feminine NA-agreement and as many as three had 100% correct ratio in singular feminine SV-agreement (as opposed to 3 and 2, respectively in the French group). Moreover, Participant Number 1 had 100% correct ratios in both forms (so did the L1 French counterpart #1). This observation suggests that even full attainment in both groups is possible.

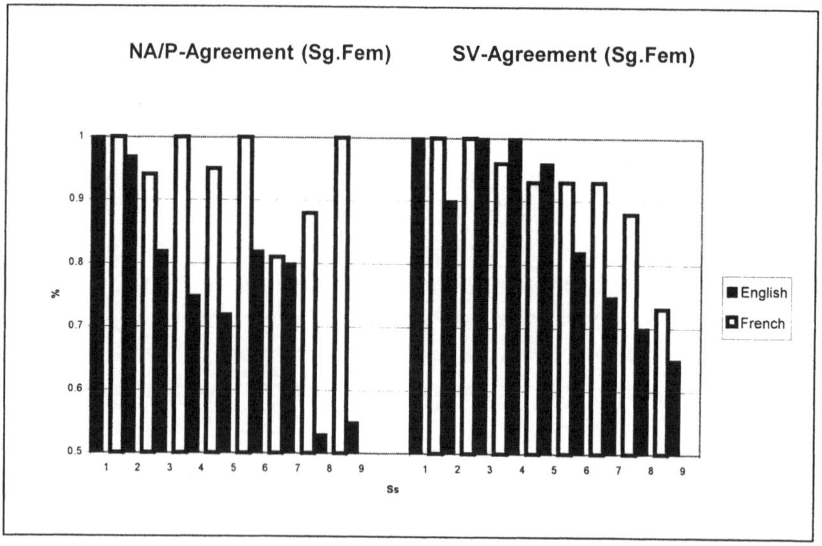

Figure 5

As for MSIH, the conclusions here are only partially in support of the predictions. According to MSIH: 1) temporary impairment is due to a problem of mapping underlying abstract features onto surface forms due to complexity of form- function relationship and communication demands and 2) absence or presence of feature infection, in this case gender, from L1 is irrelevant. While the mapping problem may indeed be a factor in L2 development, especially with the assumption of non-impairment or unimpaired access of UG through L1, the findings suggest that absence or presence of a feature in L1, contrary to MSIH, does contribute to group difference.[17] In the case of the Arabic target forms and in absence of any complexity of mapping gender agreement feature onto surface forms, the L1 [-Gender] English participants still tended to have a problem producing gender agreement (mainly singular feminine in noun adjective agreement) while L1 [+Gender] French participants did not. This is quite possible in light of the following explanation. As De Garavito and White (2002) acknowledge, since the generalization of the endings {-0} and {-a} as masculine and feminine gender markers respectively, is misleading (in Spanish) and insufficient to account for many other obscure cases. For example, there are few feminine nouns that end with {–o} ending, numerous and common masculine nouns that end with {–a} and many (invariant) adjectives that lack overt gender agreement. Following Harris (1991), De Garavito and White consider these endings as word markers rather than gender markers. These observations suggest that the input relating to gender agreement in Spanish DPs which De Garavito and White's subjects received is in fact obscure. Under the Full Transfer/Full Access model (Schwartz & Sprouse 1994, 1996), in the event input is obscure, problems of gender agreement are predicted to occur.

By contrast, the participants of the present study (both the L1 English and the L1 French at three distinct and somewhat comparable proficiency levels) received a clearer, more transparent input where the gender agreement is to a large extent regular (in Modern Standard Arabic). In the vast majority of cases, noun-adjective agreement for

[17]This is not to deny that complexity of form function relationship and communication demands are not contributing factors in L2, but relying on such factors alone does not provide satisfactory explanation to the findings of the present study.

singular feminine is achieved by attaching the suffix {-a} in word final (salient) position on both nouns and adjectives, resulting in a rhyming effect that can serve as a phonological clue to the Arabic L2er. For singular masculine, agreement is realized as zero {-0}, the stem form being the default masculine form. As stated above, there is a statistically significant difference in errors between the L1 French and the L1 English with respect to singular feminine agreement (see also Figure 2). Accordingly, under the Full Transfer/Full Access model (Schwartz & Sprouse 1994, 1996), problems of gender agreement may result due to influence or transfer from L1.

Thus, the Full Transfer/Full Access model can offer somewhat satisfactory account for the data of the present study as well as those of De Garavito and White (2002). Additionally, while close approximation and attainment of L2 is possible, hence the continued improvement of both L1 English and L1 French participants with increased proficiency. The interpretation of the results accordingly allows for a relevant role for L1 transfer: that presence or absence of gender in L1 is likely to cause a temporary impairment in L2 acquisition.

The question is then, if in fact absence of gender feature in nominals (mainly singular feminine in noun-adjective agreement) contributed to the difference in performance between the L1 English and L1 French groups, how is it then that there is no statistically significant difference between the two native language background groups with respect to singular feminine agreement in subject verb agreement? This issue is doubly significant, since results from Alhawary (2002), conducted longitudinally on nine American English speakers learning Arabic as an L2, showed a similar tendency where at least four of the nine the participants tended to have less problems with subject-verb agreement than they did noun-adjective agreement.

In Alhawary (2002), it was maintained that the difference in performance may be due to role of L1 transfer; in particular, to feature checking mechanism. Since noun-adjective agreement can be argued, together with subject-verb agreement, to involve raising via feature percolation (with adjectives that are inherently plural, such as numerous, various, etc.), then it must be due to 'frequency'. This position was not sufficiently elucidated there. The mechanism of raising via feature percolation in English is probably not involved every time a DP is derived; rather it is invoked only when a DP involves a very few "intrinsically" plural adjectives, such as *numerous* and *various* (Radford 1997). With respect to verbal agreement, on the other hand, feature checking mechanism is invoked every time an IP involves a lexical verb.

However, this still does not offer a satisfactory explanation with respect to the role of gender feature in L1. Recall gender, as a formal ϕ-feature participating in syntactic feature checking, is absent in English with respect to both target forms, as discussed above. The position adopted here is that L1 English speakers, rather than their L1 French counterparts, are more likely to have problems with nominal gender agreement (singular feminine and singular masculine) due to absence of the gender feature in the former's L1. However, in addition, there seems to be a semantic role in the mechanism of assigning gender agreement in the Interlanguage systems of the L1 English L2ers. Although English does not exhibit syntactic gender agreement, it does seem to exhibit semantic or natural gender via pronouns, reflexives and other constructions (see Namai 2000). Recall a statistically significant difference in the error rates between GRAMMATICAL and NATURAL gender agreement for the English L1 participants was found, suggesting that natural and grammatical gender agreement were not equally problematic. The L1 English participants were probably relying on a semantic/conceptual checking mechanism of some kind and were able to assign the proper gender agreement marking more so for tokens which where naturally gendered than for tokens which were purely GRAMMATICALLY gendered.[18] On the other hand, the L1 French participants had at their disposal both syntactic gender feature (as an abstract ϕ-feature) and semantic gender which made for them nominal agreement involving gender less problematic. The role of having an abstract gender feature in L1, in particular, is probably that each time a nominal agreement structure is derived, the L2er is prompted to check for the feature gender agreement irrespective of the type of gender involved, natural or grammatical.

[18]De Garavito and White (2002) reported the opposite finding, as their Ss had more problems with natural gender than they did with grammatical gender.

Performance of the L1 English and L1 French participants with respect to verbal agreement involving gender can also be accordingly explained. On the one hand, assuming English does exhibit semantic gender, though not syntactic, the L1 English participants were probably resorting to a semantic gender agreement checking mechanism where verbs are distinctly marked (in input) for the naturally gendered 'he' or 'she' subjects and, therefore, they were able to assign the proper gender marking in verbal agreement more often than they did in nominal agreement. In addition, assuming that since a syntactic checking mechanism (for the features person and number) is invoked every time an IP involves a lexical verb, the English L2ers, would be aided sooner (than in nominal constructions) to reset syntactic parameter for gender feature checking in verbal agreement. On the other hand, the L1 French participants have syntactic gender agreement (i.e., a formal ϕ-feature) and semantic agreement. However, the fact that the absence of gender feature for 3rd person (in non-compound verb forms) in French may have contributed for not having all instances of verbal agreement properly checked for the features gender. Hence, this may also partly explain the absence of a significant difference in the error rates of gender (singular and masculine) subject-verb agreement in the L1 English and L1 French participants.

Whatever the case may be (obviously more research needs to be conducted to examine the exact role of each of the two interacting mechanisms--syntactic and semantic--of gender assignment in L2), the findings of Alhawary (2002), based on longitudinal data, corroborate the present findings (based on cross-sectional data) with respect to the role of L1 transfer not acknowledged in MSIH; i.e., presence or absence of features in L1 is in fact relevant in L2 acquisition. However, like MSIH, there is no evidence in the present study to suggest permanent impairment.

Finally, as to the question of the discrepancy in performance relating to feature strength (word order being accurate) as opposed to the realization of the feature gender, it may be due to the notion that word order is much more salient than an inflectional feature (see Corder 1978, Slobin 1973). Within a minimalist explanation, however, it may be the case as De Garavito and White (2002) suggested that morphological realization of gender causes greater problems than syntactic consequence of feature strength (raising for the feature to be checked). Since raising occurs prior to feature checking and, due somehow to reasons speculated on above, realization of inflection did not occur at the phonological level at Spell Out—hence the derivation was produced (even without the surface inflections realized) and did not crash.

ACKNOWLEDGMENT

I thank all the students who participated in the study. My sincere thanks also go to all those who helped in the study, especially Peter Abboud, Aman Attieh, Jean Tardy, Abdelghani Benali and Georgine Ayoub for their help in recruiting the participants of the study, without whose help this study would not have been possible. The study was supported by grants from the School of International and Area Studies, University of Oklahoma.

REFERENCES

Abboud, Peter, Zaki N. Abdel-Malek, Najm A. Bezirgan, Wallace M. Erwin, Mounah A. Khouri, Ernest N. McCarus, Raji M. Rammuny & George N. Saad. 1983. *Elementary Modern Standard Arabic* Vol.1. Cambridge: Cambridge University Press.

Abboud, Peter, Aman Attieh, Ernest N. McCarus & Raji M. Rammuny. 1997. *Intermediate Modern Standard Arabic*. Ann Arbor, MI: Center for Middle Eastern & North African Studies, University of Michigan.

Alhawary, Mohammad T. 2002. "Role of L1 Transfer in L2 Acquisition of Inflectional Morphology". *Perspectives on Arabic Linguistics XIII-XIV* ed. by Dilworth Parkinson & Elabbas Benmamoun, 219-248. Amsterdam & Philadelphia: John Benjamins.

_____. 1999. *Testing Processability and Effectiveness of Computer-assisted Language Instruction: A longitudinal study of Arabic as a second/foreign language*. Ph.D. dissertation, Georgetown University.

Bailey, Carolyn Madden & Steven Krashen. 1974. "Is There a Natural Sequence in Adult Second Language Learning?" *Language Learning* 24.235-243.

Beck, Maria-Luise. 1998. "L2 Acquisition and Obligatory Head Movement: English speaking learners of German and the local impairment hypothesis". *Studies in Second Language Acquisition* 20.311-348.

_____. 1997. "Regular Verbs, Part Tense, and Frequency: Tracking down one potential source of NS/NNS syntactic competence differences". *Second Language Research* 13.93-115.

Bernstein, Judith. 1993. *Topics in the Syntax of Nominal Structure across Romance*. Ph. D. dissertation, CUNY.

Bolotin, Naomi. 1995. "Arabic and Parametric VSO Agreement". *Perspectives on Arabic Linguistics VII* ed. by Mushira Eid, 7-27. Amsterdam & Philadelphia: John Benjamins.

Chomsky, Noam. 1995. "Categories and Transformations". *The Minimalist Program*, 219-394. Cambridge, MA: MIT Press.

_____. 1993. "A Minimalist Program for Linguistic Theory". *The View from Building 20* ed. by Ken Hale & Samuel J. Keyser, 1-52. Cambridge, MA: MIT Press.

Cinque, Guglielmo. 1994. "On the Evidence for Partial N-movement in the Romance DP". *Paths towards Universal Grammar: Studies in honor of Richard S. Kayne* ed. by Guglielmo Cinque, Jan Koster, Jean-Yves Pollock, Luigi Rizzi & Raffaella Zanuttini, 85-110. Washington, DC: Georgetown University Press.

Clahsen, Harald. 1988. "Parameterized Grammatical Theory and Language Acquisition: A study of the acquisition of verb placement and inflection by children and adults". *Linguistic Theory in Second Language Acquisition* ed. by Suzanne Flynn & Wayne O'Neil, 47-75. Dordrecht: Kluwer Academic Publishers.

Corder, S. Pit. 1978. "Simple Codes and the Source of the Second Language Learner's Initial Heuristic Hypothesis". *Studies in Second Language Acquisition* 1:1.1-10.

De Garavito, Joyce Bruhn & Lydia White. 2002. "The Second Language Acquisition of Spanish DPs: The status of grammatical features". *The Acquisition of Spanish Morphosyntax* ed. by Ana Teresa Pérez-Leroux & Juana Munoz Liceras, 153-178. Dordrecht: Kluwer Academic Publishers.

Deheuvels, Luc-Willy. 2003. *Manuel d'Arabe Moderne* Vols.1, 2nd Edition. Paris, France: Asiathèque.

_____. 2002. *Manuel d'Arabe Moderne* Vols.2, 2nd Edition. Paris, France: Asiathèque.

Dulay, Heidi & Marina Burt. 1974. "Natural Sequences in Child Second Language Acquisition". *Language Learning* 24.37-53.

Epstein, Samuel, Suzanne Flynn & Gita Martohardjono. 1996. "Second Language Acquisition: Theoretical and experimental issues in contemporary research". *Brain and Behavioral Sciences* 19:4.677-758.

Eubank, Lynn & Maria-Luise Beck. 1998. "OI-Like Effects in Adult L2 Acquisition". *Proceedings of the 22nd Annual Boston University Conference in Language Development Vol. 1* ed. by Annabel Greenhill, Mary Hughes, Heather Littlefield & Hugh Walsh, 189-200. Somerville, MA: Cascadilla Press.

Eubank, Lynn, Janine Bischof, April Huffstutler, Patricia Leek & Clint West. 1997. "'Tom Eats Slowly Cooked Eggs': Thematic verb raising in L2 knowledge". *Language Acquisition* 6:3.171-199.

Eubank, Lynn & Sabina Grace. 1996. "Where's the Mature Language? Where's the Native Language?" *Proceedings of the 20th Annual Boston University Conference on Language Development Vol. 1* ed. by Andy Stringfellow, Dalia Cahana-Amitay, Elizabeth Hughes & Andrea Zukowski, 189-200. Somerville, MA: Cascadilla Press.

Felix, Sascha W. 1984. "Maturational Aspects of Universal Grammar". *Interlanguage* ed. by Alan Davies, Clive Criper & Anthony Howatt, 133-161. Edinburgh: Edinburgh University Press.

Grondon, Nathalie & Lydia White. 1996. "Functional Categories in Child L2 Acquisition of French". *Language Acquisition* 5.1-34.
Harris, James. 1991. "The Exponence of Gender in Spanish". *Linguistics Inquiry* 22.27-62.
Haznedar, Belma & Bonnie D. Schwartz. 1997. "Are There Optional Infinitives in Child L2 Acquisition"? *Proceedings of the 21st Annual Boston University Conference on Language Development Vol. 1* ed. by Elizabeth Hughes, Mary Hughes & Annabel Greenhill, 257-268. Somerville, MA: Cascadilla Press.
Hawkins, Roger. 2001. *Second Language Syntax*. Malden, MA: Blackwell.
_____. 1998a. "Explaining the Difficulties of Gender Attribution for Speakers of English". Paper presented at the European Second Language Association, Paris, September 1998.
_____. 1998b. "The Inaccessibility of Formal Features of Functional Categories in Second Language Acquisition". Paper presented at the Pacific Second Language Research Forum, Tokyo, March 1998.
_____ & Yuet-Hung Chan. 1997. "The Partial Availability of Universal Grammar in Second Language Acquisition: The 'failed functional features hypothesis'". *Second Language Research* 13:3.187-226.
Lardiere, Donna. 2000. "Mapping Features to Forms in Second Language Acquisition". *Second Language Acquisition and Linguistic Theory* ed. by John Archibald, 102-129. Oxford: Blackwell.
_____. 1998. "Case and Tense in the 'Fossilized' Steady State". *Second Language Research* 14:1.1-26.
Meisel, Jurgen M. 1997. "The Acquisition of the Syntax of Negation in French and German: Contrasting first and second language development". *Second Language Research* 13.227-263.
_____. 1991. "Principles of Universal Grammar and Strategies of Language Use: On some similarities and differences between first and second language acquisition". *Point – Counterpoint: Universal grammar in the second language* ed. by Lynn Eubank, 231-271. Amsterdam & Philadelphia: John Benjamins.
Namai, Kenichi. 2000. "Gender Features in English". *Linguistics* 38:4.771-779.
Parodi, Teresa, Bonnie D. Schwartz & Harald Clahsen. 1997. "On the L2 Acquisition of the Morphosyntax of German Nominals". Essex Research Reports in Linguistics 15.1-43.
Prévost, Philippe & Lydia White. 2000. "Missing Surface Inflection or Impairment in Second Language Acquisition? Evidence from tense and agreement". *Second Language Research* 16:2.103-133.
Poeppel, David & Kenneth Wexler. 1993. "The Full Competence Hypothesis of Clause Structure in Early German". *Language* 69.1-33.
Radford, Andrew. 1997. *Syntactic Theory and the Structure of English: A minimalist approach*. Cambridge: Cambridge University Press.
Şaydaawii, Yuusuf. 1999. *Al-Kafaaf* Vol. 1. Damascus, Syria: Daar Al-Fikr.
Schwartz, Bonnie D. 1998. "The Second Language Instinct". *Lingua* 106.133-160.
_____ & Rex A. Sprouse. 1996. "L2 Cognitive States and the Full Transfer/Full Access Model". *Second Language Research* 12.40-72.
_____. 1994. "Word Order and Nominative Case in Nonnative Language Acquisition: A longitudinal study of (L1 Turkish) German interlanguage". *Language Acquisition Studies in Generative Grammar* ed. by Teun Hoekstra & Bonnie D. Schwartz, 317-368. Amsterdam & Philadelphia: John Benjamins.

Slobin, Dan I. 1973. "Cognitive Prerequisites for the Development of Grammar". *Studies of Child Language Development* ed. by Charles A. Ferguson & Dan I. Slobin, 175-208. New York: Holt.

Smith, Neil & Ianthi-Maria Tsimpli. 1995. *The Mind of a Savant*. Oxford: Blackwell.

Tsimpli, Ianthi-Maria & & Neil Smith. 1991. "Second Language Learning: Evidence from a polyglot savant". *University College London Working Papers in Linguistics* 3.171-184.

Tsimpli, Ianthi-Maria & Anna Roussou. 1991. "Parameter-resetting in L2?". *UCL Working Papers in Linguistics* 3.149-170.

White, Lydia, Elana Valenzuela, Martyna Kozlowska-Macgregor, Ingrid Leung & Hela Ben Ayed. 2001. "The Status of Abstract Features in Interlanguage Grammars: Gender and number in L2 Spanish". *Proceedings of the 25th Annual Boston University Conference on Language Development Vol. 2* ed. by Anna H.-J. Do, Laura Domínguez & Aimee Johansen, 792-802. Somerville, MA: Cascadilla Press.

INDEX OF SUBJECTS

CURRENT ISSUES IN LINGUISTIC THEORY

E. F. K. Koerner, Editor
Zentrum für Allgemeine Sprachwissenschaft, Typologie
und Universalienforschung, Berlin
efk.koerner@rz.hu-berlin.de

Current Issues in Linguistic Theory (CILT) is a theory-oriented series which welcomes contributions from scholars who have significant proposals to make towards the advancement of our understanding of language, its structure, functioning and development. CILT has been established in order to provide a forum for the presentation and discussion of linguistic opinions of scholars who do not necessarily accept the prevailing mode of thought in linguistic science. It offers an outlet for meaningful contributions to the current linguistic debate, and furnishes the diversity of opinion which a healthy discipline must have. A complete list of titles in this series can be found on the publishers website, **www.benjamins.com**

225 **SHAHIN, Kimary N.:** Postvelar Harmony. 2003. viii, 344 pp.
226 **LEVIN, Saul:** Semitic and Indo-European. Volume II: Comparative morphology, syntax and phonetics. 2002. xviii, 592 pp.
227 **FAVA, Elisabetta (ed.):** Clinical Linguistics. Theory and applications in speech pathology and therapy. 2002. xxiv, 353 pp.
228 **NEVIN, Bruce E. (ed.):** The Legacy of Zellig Harris. Language and information into the 21st century. Volume 1: Philosophy of science, syntax and semantics. 2002. xxxvi, 323 pp.
229 **NEVIN, Bruce E. and Stephen B. JOHNSON (eds.):** The Legacy of Zellig Harris. Language and information into the 21st century. Volume 2: Mathematics and computability of language. 2002. xx, 312 pp.
230 **PARKINSON, Dilworth B. and Elabbas BENMAMOUN (eds.):** Perspectives on Arabic Linguistics. Papers from the Annual Symposium on Arabic Linguistics. Volume XIII-XIV: Stanford, 1999 and Berkeley, California 2000. 2002. xiv, 250 pp.
231 **CRAVENS, Thomas D.:** Comparative Historical Dialectology. Italo-Romance clues to Ibero-Romance sound change. 2002. xii, 163 pp.
232 **BEYSSADE, Claire, Reineke BOK-BENNEMA, Frank DRIJKONINGEN and Paola MONACHESI (eds.):** Romance Languages and Linguistic Theory 2000. Selected papers from 'Going Romance' 2000, Utrecht, 30 November–2 December. 2002. viii, 354 pp.
233 **WEIJER, Jeroen van de, Vincent J. van HEUVEN and Harry van der HULST (eds.):** The Phonological Spectrum. Volume I: Segmental structure. 2003. x, 308 pp.
234 **WEIJER, Jeroen van de, Vincent J. van HEUVEN and Harry van der HULST (eds.):** The Phonological Spectrum. Volume II: Suprasegmental structure. 2003. x, 264 pp.
235 **LINN, Andrew R. and Nicola McLELLAND (eds.):** Standardization. Studies from the Germanic languages. 2002. xii, 258 pp.
236 **SIMON-VANDENBERGEN, Anne-Marie, Miriam TAVERNIERS and Louise J. RAVELLI (eds.):** Grammatical Metaphor. Views from systemic functional linguistics. 2003. vi, 453 pp.
237 **BLAKE, Barry J. and Kate BURRIDGE (eds.):** Historical Linguistics 2001. Selected papers from the 15th International Conference on Historical Linguistics, Melbourne, 13–17 August 2001. Editorial Assistant: Jo Taylor. 2003. x, 444 pp.
238 **NÚÑEZ-CEDEÑO, Rafael, Luis LÓPEZ and Richard CAMERON (eds.):** A Romance Perspective on Language Knowledge and Use. Selected papers from the 31st Linguistic Symposium on Romance Languages (LSRL), Chicago, 19–22 April 2001. 2003. xvi, 386 pp.
239 **ANDERSEN, Henning (ed.):** Language Contacts in Prehistory. Studies in Stratigraphy. Papers from the Workshop on Linguistic Stratigraphy and Prehistory at the Fifteenth International Conference on Historical Linguistics, Melbourne, 17 August 2001. 2003. viii, 292 pp.
240 **JANSE, Mark and Sijmen TOL (eds.):** Language Death and Language Maintenance. Theoretical, practical and descriptive approaches. With the assistance of Vincent Hendriks. 2003. xviii, 244 pp.
241 **LECARME, Jacqueline (ed.):** Research in Afroasiatic Grammar II. Selected papers from the Fifth Conference on Afroasiatic Languages, Paris, 2000. 2003. viii, 550 pp.
242 **SEUREN, Pieter A.M. and Gerard KEMPEN (eds.):** Verb Constructions in German and Dutch. 2003. vi, 316 pp.
243 **CUYCKENS, Hubert, Thomas BERG, René DIRVEN and Klaus-Uwe PANTHER (eds.):** Motivation in Language. Studies in honor of Günter Radden. 2003. xxvi, 403 pp.

244 **PÉREZ-LEROUX, Ana Teresa and Yves ROBERGE (eds.):** Romance Linguistics. Theory and Acquisition. Selected papers from the 32nd Linguistic Symposium on Romance Languages (LSRL), Toronto, April 2002. 2003. viii, 388 pp.

245 **QUER, Josep, Jan SCHROTEN, Mauro SCORRETTI, Petra SLEEMAN and Els VERHEUGD (eds.):** Romance Languages and Linguistic Theory 2001. Selected papers from 'Going Romance', Amsterdam, 6–8 December 2001. 2003. viii, 355 pp.

246 **HOLISKY, Dee Ann and Kevin TUITE (eds.):** Current Trends in Caucasian, East European and Inner Asian Linguistics. Papers in honor of Howard I. Aronson. 2003. xxviii, 426 pp.

247 **PARKINSON, Dilworth B. and Samira FARWANEH (eds.):** Perspectives on Arabic Linguistics XV. Papers from the Fifteenth Annual Symposium on Arabic Linguistics, Salt Lake City 2001. 2003. x, 214 pp.

248 **WEIGAND, Edda (ed.):** Emotion in Dialogic Interaction. Advances in the complex. 2004. xii, 284 pp.

249 **BOWERN, Claire and Harold KOCH (eds.):** Australian Languages. Classification and the comparative method. 2004. xii, 377 pp. (incl. CD-Rom).

250 **JENSEN, John T.:** Principles of Generative Phonology. An introduction. 2004. xii, 324 pp.

251 **KAY, Christian J., Simon HOROBIN and Jeremy J. SMITH (eds.):** New Perspectives on English Historical Linguistics. Selected papers from 12 ICEHL, Glasgow, 21–26 August 2002. Volume I: Syntax and Morphology. 2004. x, 264 pp.

252 **KAY, Christian J., Carole HOUGH and Irené WOTHERSPOON (eds.):** New Perspectives on English Historical Linguistics. Selected papers from 12 ICEHL, Glasgow, 21–26 August 2002. Volume II: Lexis and Transmission. 2004. xii, 273 pp.

253 **CAFFAREL, Alice, J.R. MARTIN and Christian M.I.M. MATTHIESSEN (eds.):** Language Typology. A functional perspective. 2004. xiv, 702 pp.

254 **BALDI, Philip and Pietro U. DINI (eds.):** Studies in Baltic and Indo-European Linguistics. In honor of William R. Schmalstieg. 2004. xlvi, 302 pp.

255 **MEULEN, Alice ter and Werner ABRAHAM (eds.):** The Composition of Meaning. From lexeme to discourse. 2004. vi, 232 pp.

256 **BOK-BENNEMA, Reineke, Bart HOLLEBRANDSE, Brigitte KAMPERS-MANHE and Petra SLEEMAN (eds.):** Romance Languages and Linguistic Theory 2002. Selected papers from 'Going Romance', Groningen, 28–30 November 2002. 2004. viii, 273 pp.

257 **FORTESCUE, Michael, Eva Skafte JENSEN, Jens Erik MOGENSEN and Lene SCHØSLER (eds.):** Historical Linguistics 2003. Selected papers from the 16th International Conference on Historical Linguistics, Copenhagen, 11–15 August 2003. 2005. x, 312 pp.

258 **AUGER, Julie, J. Clancy CLEMENTS and Barbara VANCE (eds.):** Contemporary Approaches to Romance Linguistics. Selected Papers from the 33rd Linguistic Symposium on Romance Languages (LSRL), Bloomington, Indiana, April 2003. With the assistance of Rachel T. Anderson. 2004. viii, 404 pp.

259 **CARR, Philip, Jacques DURAND and Colin J. EWEN (eds.):** Headhood, Elements, Specification and Contrastivity. Phonological papers in honour of John Anderson. 2005. xxviii, 405 pp.

260 **NICOLOV, Nicolas, Kalina BONTCHEVA, Galia ANGELOVA and Ruslan MITKOV (eds.):** Recent Advances in Natural Language Processing III. Selected papers from RANLP 2003. 2004. xii, 402 pp.

261 **KAY, Christian J. and Jeremy J. SMITH (eds.):** Categorization in the History of English. 2004. viii, 268 pp.

262 **VAJDA, Edward J. (ed.):** Languages and Prehistory of Central Siberia. 2004. x, 275 pp.

263 **BRANCO, António, Tony McENERY and Ruslan MITKOV (eds.):** Anaphora Processing. Linguistic, cognitive and computational modelling. 2005. x, 449 pp.

264 **DRESSLER, Wolfgang U., Dieter KASTOVSKY, Oskar E. PFEIFFER and Franz RAINER (eds.):** Morphology and its demarcations. Selected papers from the 11th Morphology meeting, Vienna, February 2004. With the assistance of Francesco Gardani and Markus A. Pöchtrager. xiv, 309 pp. + index. *Expected July 2005*

265 **CORNIPS, Leonie and Karen P. CORRIGAN (eds.):** Syntax and Variation. Reconciling the Biological and the Social. vi, 298 pp. + index. *Expected July 2005*

266 **BOUDELAA, Sami (ed.):** Perspectives on Arabic Linguistics XVI. Papers from the sixteenth annual symposium on Arabic linguistics, Cambridge, March 2002. ca. 250 pp. *Expected October 2005*

267 **ALHAWARY, Mohammad T. and Elabbas BENMAMOUN (eds.):** Perspectives on Arabic Linguistics XVII–XVIII. Papers from the seventeenth and eighteenth annual symposia on Arabic linguistics. Volume XVII–XVIII: Alexandria, 2003 and Norman, Oklahoma 2004. 2005. xvi, 313 pp.